THE WILKES EXPEDITION

MEMOIRS OF THE

AMERICAN PHILOSOPHICAL SOCIETY

Held at Philadelphia
For Promoting Useful Knowledge
Volume 73

FIG. 1. Charles Wilkes, Commander of the Expedition. Portrait painted by Thomas Sully. *Narrative of the United States Exploring Expedition* **1:** frontispiece.

THE WILKES EXPEDITION

The First United States Exploring Expedition
(1838-1842)

DAVID B. TYLER

Professor of History
Wagner College

THE AMERICAN PHILOSOPHICAL SOCIETY
INDEPENDENCE SQUARE • PHILADELPHIA

1968

To
ELIZABETH SLOAN TYLER

PREFACE

Rear Admiral Charles Wilkes narrated the history of the first United States Exploring Expedition, which he commanded, in five thick volumes. These were published at government expense along with sixteen volumes embodying the Expedition's scientific achievements. Congress authorized only one hundred copies of each volume, intending them for distribution among foreign nations as evidence of the accomplishments of the young American republic and as comparable to the scientific publications of the older countries of Europe. Wilkes secured the copyright for his *Narrative* and arranged for the printing of several editions subsequent to the initial one of 1844. The New York Public Library published, in 1942, an excellent bibliography of source materials connected with the Expedition which was prepared by Daniel C. Haskell. It might appear that another history of the Expedition would be superfluous and some explanation seems to be called for.

It is evident that an official narrative written by the Expedition's commander could not tell the whole story. His purpose was to inform the American public about little-known parts of the world and to present the work of the Expedition in as favorable a light as possible. That unfavorable developments were glossed over becomes abundantly clear to anyone who reads the officers' and scientists' journals or Wilkes' "Autobiography." All were required to keep journals as part of the performance of their duties and these documents provide unusually abundant source materials.

In addition to having a general interest in maritime affairs the author of this history has a particular interest in the Wilkes Expedition stemming from his wartime experience as a less than "ninety-day wonder" in the Navy. This made him aware of the many problems that resulted when the necessarily rapid expansion of the armed forces swept into their maw many persons who did not easily become as one with the professionals. It was interesting to have a close look at this early naval expedition which hitched several "scientifics" in tandem with the "regulars." The untold part of the story has to do with the clash of personalities between the hard-driving commander and many under his command who started out with great enthusiasm but ended up separated from him by an unbridgeable gulf.

The very real accomplishments of the Expedition are deserving of recognition today when there is such universal interest in scientific progress and especially because of the concentrated attention given to Antarctica, beginning with the Geophysical Year 1958.

Most of the journals are available in Washington but several had to be tracked down elsewhere, a task made possible by a Guggenheim Fellowship. Some have been lost to sight—possibly reposing forgotten in attic trunks, but more probably, destroyed accidentally or on purpose. As might be expected, they vary considerably in value. Some are so brief as to be little more than copies of a ship's log. While Wilkes issued instructions that personal matters should be excluded, the line between personal and impersonal was difficult to draw and was disregarded by some, including the commander. At least one officer kept a private journal in addition to his official one. The requirement that they be handed in for the commander's perusal meant that opinions were expressed with caution or that, as erasures indicate, second-thoughts often prevailed. Since the journals are such an important source of information, the most literary-minded among the personnel tend to stand out more than those who could not be bothered or whose journals have been lost. Wilkes evidently wrote in great haste and his writing is such a scrawl that some words are undecipherable. The Squadron had no Melville, so the largely illiterate seamen tell little about themselves with the exception of a few, such as Charles Erskine who was able to write a chronicle that found a publisher.

Wilkes' *Narrative* has been used throughout for chronology, for factual background, and for the spelling of names of persons and places. References to the *Narrative* have been footnoted only when there are direct quotations or references to important matters, especially if not mentioned elsewhere.

Since this was, for the most part, a cruise of young men in their twenties, a word should be said as to the subsequent careers of some of them. Wilkes at the age of forty was young to be given command of a squadron. He retired with the rank of Rear Admiral in 1866, eleven years before his death. Hudson died in 1862 having attained the rank of Captain. Ringgold became the leader of an expedition to the North Pacific and retired with the rank of Rear Admiral. Reynolds became Acting Secretary of the Navy in 1873-1874 and, together with Craven and Emmons, reached the rank of Rear Admiral. Case, Knox, Colvocoresses, and Walker all became Captains. Alden was the only one to retire with the rank of Commodore. Dr. Palmer was Surgeon General of the Navy in 1872-1873. De Haven led a search for Franklin in the Arctic in 1850-1851 which so impaired his health that he had to retire while still a Lieutenant in 1852, three years before his death. Whittle and Eld were victims of yellow fever in 1850 and Budd and Couthouy died in action during the Civil War. That war ended the naval careers of Harrison, Hartstene, Lewis, Maury, North, Pinkney, and Sinclair, all of whom joined the Confederate forces. The most notable member of the Scientific Corps was James Dana who became an outstanding authority in the field of geology. Hale and Pickering achieved recognition for their work in philology and ethnography, respectively.

This history has not turned out to be as compact and uncomplicated as first appeared probable. It has left this latter-day historian with the conviction that the United States Exploring Expedition achieved great things and deserves whatever belated notice and appreciation this recital might conceivably produce.

Any researcher working on a subject with many ramifications becomes indebted to innumerable archivists and librarians for their helpfulness and understanding. I shall not attempt to list them by name but would like to express, in particular, my thanks for the assistance rendered by Archibald Hanna in charge of the Western Americana section of the Yale University Library, by Herbert Anstaett, librarian at Franklin and Marshall College, and by Elbert L. Huber formerly of the Navy Department section of the National Archives. I am indebted to Mr. and Mrs. John H. K. Shannahan for the use of William Reynolds' correspondence and to Miss Maria T. Dana for information about her father. The following persons aided me in a variety of ways: Herbert S. Bailey, Jr., Marion V. Brewington, Harold B. Corwin, Charles E. Cunningham, William N. Fenton, Leo Hershowitz, Dr. Donald S. Marshall, W. Patrick Strauss, and Walter M. Whitehill. Various descendents of Charles Wilkes have indicated interest and rendered help, especially Mrs. Paul Runyan and Mrs. Joseph Hull, Jr. The latter, unfortunately, has not lived long enough to read this acknowledgment. Other descendents of Admiral Wilkes who have lent encouragement are Erwin Rankin, Dr. Fred B. Rogers, Commander Charles Denby-Wilkes (deceased), and Dr. John D. Wilkes. My greatest indebtedness is to my wife, Betty, who has helped materially by doing research and spiritually by encouragement and by astute criticism during the several years that rumination, writing, and rewriting have taken place.

D. B. T.

CONTENTS

xiii

ILLUSTRATIONS

page

THE WILKES EXPEDITION

I
Cheers and Sneers

O N AN EVENING in October, 1837, the playbill of a New York
theater announced that a group of naval officers, members
of a squadron preparing for the first United States maritime
exploring expedition, would be present. Upon their arrival
the acting was suspended and "the House rung with plaudits
loud and long." They were cheered again during the "Interlude" and the words "Honor," "Glory," and "all that kind of
thing" rang out followed by a noisy uproar from their friends
in the Pit. One of their number, Lieutenant James Glynn, said
that he felt a little foolish

to receive all these evidences of approbation before we had performed anything to entitle us to distinction. It was gratifying, however, to witness so much interest in the Expedition, by the public,
even yet. We certainly are the Lions of the day; but popular opinion is notoriously fickle, and it may be the fashion to sneer at us
in a month.[1]

Popular opinion did change before August 18, 1838, when
the Expedition finally "shoved off." By that time Lieutenant
Glynn was not one of its members, the *Consort* which he commanded was not one of the vessels, and the port of departure
was not New York. Public interest had been dampened by a
succession of delays and by a change of command which met
with widespread disapproval in naval circles since it went to
a young, comparatively inexperienced lieutenant named
Charles Wilkes.

Although the charting of Pacific waters would be of immediate benefit only to whalers and traders, this was the first time
the Government had sent out a maritime exploring expedition and the romantic view of that vast area beyond the Rocky

---

[1] Glynn to Emmons, Oct. 21, 1837, Emmons Papers, Western Americana, Yale
University Library.

Mountains, coupled with the expectation of important discoveries and additions to scientific knowledge, caught the
imagination of the public.

These objectives had to be accomplished with vessels
under sail. A generation used to jet propulsion cannot easily
visualize what it means to be entirely dependent upon the
wind. Howling gales and tempestuous seas had to be weath-
ered, and long-lasting dead calms endured. Even a moderate
headwind could be troublesome. While under way, the crews
of sailing ships were always busy and even the off-duty watch
was subject to being called out at any moment when "all
hands" were needed. Climbing to the topmast and crawling
out on spars were hazardous undertakings in a high wind and
rough sea, and, in a sudden squall, sail had to be taken in
quickly before it split or spars cracked. Successful seamanship
called for quick decisions, as well as stamina. Speed was not
controlled by means of a throttle, but only by taking in or
letting out sail and by pointing the vessel into or before the
wind. A full-rigged ship had some twenty-odd sails and it took
a good deal of experience to know which to use under changing
circumstances. A sailing vessel was doomed to catastrophe if
caught in a strong wind off a "lee" shore without room to
"claw off." Unchartered shoals and unexpected currents presented less spectacular but equally hazardous dangers. Everything, of course, depended upon the willingness and ability
of the crew to carry out orders and upon the officer in command giving the right orders at the right time.

This expedition lasted three years and ten months. It was
a peacetime but not a pleasure cruise. In addition to the usual
shipboard hardships and dangers, the participants encountered
some unusual ones in Antarctic waters, in their contacts with
hostile natives, and in connection with the never-ending strain
and stress that characterizes survey and scientific work. Many
became ill from exposure and some did not survive the cruise.

After the tumultuous period of the French Revolutionary
and Napoleonic Wars, interest in voyages of discovery was re-
awakened. The purposes of exploration were mainly commercial but scientific and benevolent aims were included. In
those days of sail the main trade routes followed the paths of
the trade winds but fishermen had to wander away from favor-

able winds in search of the feeding grounds of their quarry and this led them into equatorial areas of heat and no wind and into Arctic and Antarctic areas of ice and too much wind. Those in the "skinning business," the sealers, were among the first to poke into the inhospitable waters south of Cape Horn and into the South Pacific. By the 1820's the whalers, also, were "doubling the Cape" for the Atlantic fisheries were becoming less profitable. Migrating whales were most abundant in the unchartered and dangerous waters of the north and South Pacific. Soon news began to filter home of whalers being wrecked or, what was worse, no news came leaving ship-owners and seamen's families with the horrible thought that the crews had been swallowed up by the sea, by hungry canni-bals, or even, as could happen, by the whales themselves.[2] This condition was indicated by the fact that insurance rates for the Pacific were double those for the Atlantic.[3]

To commercial interests was added concern for the advancement of knowledge and for national prestige. Citizens of the youthful United States of America wanted to see their country on a par with the Great Powers in this regard. The published results of exploratory voyages gave lustre to the names of the Englishmen Cook, Vancouver, and Ross; to those of the Frenchmen Bougainville, La Perouse, and D'Urville; and to the Russians Kotzebue and Krustenstern. There were no equally famous Americans except Captain Nathaniel Palmer, a sealer, who accidentally discovered the peninsula south of Cape Horn in 1821. Captain Edmund Fanning, a China trader and sealer of long experience, had persuaded President Madison to sponsor a voyage of discovery, only to have the War of 1812 interfere. With the discovery of the Palmer Peninsula he renewed his petition to the Government.[4] Another petitioner was John C. Symmes who wanted an ex-pedition sent to the polar regions to substantiate his theory

---

[2] William A. Fairburn, *Merchant Sail* (6 v., Center Lovell, Maine, 1955) **2**: pp. 993–1045; Edmund Fanning, *Voyages and Discoveries in the South Seas* (Salem Mass., 1924) ; Eduard A. Stackpole, *The Sea-Hunters* (Philadelphia, Pa., 1953) and A. Starbuck, *History of the American Whale-Fishery* (Waltham, Mass., 1878). Fairburn, **2**: p. 1945, says sealing became unprofitable in the southern Atlantic grounds as early as 1825.

[3] *Register of Debates in Congress*, 20 Cong., 1 Sess., p. 2731.

[4] Fanning, pp. 166–167.

that the world consisted of concentric spheres with openings at the poles into which vessels could sail with safety. No one had, as yet, gone far enough to disprove his theory.[5]

Public interest in the South Sea Islanders was heightened by accounts of voyagers which seemed to support the romantic view of the "noble savage" living in a state of nature, unspoiled and uncorrupted by civilization. However, their contacts with the natives were usually fleeting and missionaries tended to throw cold water on the concept of a Pacific Paradise for, as they saw the native, he was depraved and in need of salvation. Thus the unexplored areas of the Arctic, Antarctic, and South Pacific were a source of curiosity and of concern.[6]

President John Quincy Adams showed his concern when he told Congress in 1825 that the United States should assume her station among civilized nations by contributing her share "of mind, of labor, and of expense to the improvement of those parts of knowledge which lie beyond the reach of individual acquisition, and particularly to geographical and astronomical science." He thought it unworthy of a "great and generous nation" to give a second thought to the cost. "One hundred expeditions of circumnavigation like those of Cook and La Perouse would not burden the exchequer of the nations fitting them out so much as the ways and means of defraying a single campaign of war."[7]

The House of Representatives responded by passing a Resolution in May, 1828, requesting the President to send out "one of our small public vessels," but failed to support it with an appropriation.[8] A "public" vessel could only be a naval vessel and Secretary of the Navy S. L. Southard designated the sloop-of-war *Peacock* for the purpose and proposed that another ship be sent along with her, as was customary on voyages of discovery.[9] This was a time when Congress was very

---

[5] E. F. Madden, "Symmes and his Theory," *Harpers New Monthly Mag.* **65** (1882) : pp. 740–742.

[6] W. P. Strauss' typescript Thesis entitled "Early American Interest and Activity in Polynesia 1783–1842" (Columbia University, 1958) gives a good account of the exploration, trade, and literature of this area at this time.

[7] J. D. Richardson, *Messages and Papers of the Presidents* (Washington, D.C. 1903) **2**: p. 312.

[8] *House Journal*, 20 Cong., 1 Sess., p. 774.

[9] J. N. Reynolds, *Pacific and Indian Oceans* (New York, 1841), pp. 28, 189.

niggardly in voting funds for the Navy, making appropriations only for repairs for existing vessels. As a result, the Board of Commissioners used accumulated repair funds to build anew ships to which they gave the names of the old dismembered ones. The *Peacock* was such a vessel.[10]

In preparation for the intended voyage, Secretary Southard employed a young man named Jeremiah N. Reynolds to visit seaport towns and collect information as to what areas were most in need of exploration. Reynolds, an Ohio lawyer, first attracted attention by giving lectures on the "Symmes Theory" of openings at the poles, but by this time was merely advocating polar exploration as an aid to commerce.[11] Southard sent him to New London, Stonington, Newport, New Bedford, Edgartown, and Nantucket, where he consulted captains, logs, journals, and charts. Reynolds reported that about two hundred vessels averaging 275 tons were engaged in hunting whales and seals; that larger ones were beginning to be used since the voyages were becoming longer; that the annual "take" was eight thousand whales with an additional two thousand wounded; and that the whale fisheries were mostly in areas with no charts other than those which geographers marked "with a sweeping hand, to fill up the mighty space of which the world is as yet ignorant." He listed a number of "discoveries" reported by various navigators and not to be found on any charts.[12]

The Government made no further move at this time but Captain Fanning sent the brigs *Seraph* and *Annawan* to search out new sailing grounds in the South Pacific. He included Reynolds in their complement along with two scientists, Dr. John F. Watson of Philadelphia and James Eights, a naturalist from Albany.[13] Reynolds returned in 1834 on the frigate *Potomac*, having joined her at Valparaiso in the capacity of Secretary to Captain Downes, her commander. His published story of the frigate's cruise gained him something of a reputa-

---

[10] Howard I. Chapelle, *The History of the American Sailing Navy* (New York, 1949), pp. 356–357.
[11] Southard to Reynolds, 30 June, 1828, National Archives, Navy Department, General Letter Book, 16: [Reynolds] *Remarks in Review of Symmes Theory* (Washington, 1827).
[12] *House Report* #94, 23 Cong., 2 Sess., pp. 1, 3–4, 13–37.
[13] Fanning, p. 169.

tion as a voyager and historian as he resumed his lobbying activity in Washington.[14]

Another petitioner was Passed Midshipman Matthew F. Maury, just returned from a year's cruise in the Pacific on the *Vincennes* under Captain J. H. Aulick. Maury, as Sailing Master, found many places on the West Coast mislocated on charts and noticed especially that surveys of the mouth of the Columbia River were "lamentably imperfect."[15]

By way of the Royal Geographical Society of London came the news that in 1831-1832 Captain Biscoe had discovered black peaks above the snows of Antarctica. From the French Government came eleven handsomely printed and illustrated volumes which were entitled *Voyage de la Corvette l'Astrolabe* and which related the scientific achievements of D'Urville in the South Pacific during the years 1826-1829. The English survey ship *Beagle* entered Pacific waters in 1831 and took along a young scientist named Charles Darwin whose *Journal* was published in 1839.

Time was pressing if the United States was not to lag far behind European countries in the matter of exploration. A domestic development of importance, at this time, was the existence of a Treasury surplus. Southard, now a Senator, proposed that a bill calling for an expenditure of $150,000 be made an amendment to the annual appropriations for the Navy and it was passed in that form on May 14, 1836. It authorized the President to use additional means in the control of the Navy Department up to $150,000 and thus made available for exploring purposes the equivalent of $300,000.[16]

---

14 Reynolds' story "Mocha Dick or the White Whale of the Pacific published in *Knickerbocker Magazine* (1839) may have been one of Melville's sources for "Moby Dick."

15 *House Report* #94, 23 Cong., 2 Sess., pp. 39–41.

16 *Cong. Globe*, 24 Cong., 1 Sess., p. 445.

II

Disorganization and Delay

IT HAPPENED that Captain Thomas ap Catesby Jones, recently returned from a tour of the Pacific, called upon Secretary of the Navy Dickerson just at this time. He sought command of the Pacific Squadron but it had already been assigned and he was told that he was needed to advise in the matter of the Exploring Expedition. At President Jackson's suggestion he was offered that command and accepted it on June 29, 1836.[1]

Captain Jones envisioned a large-scale operation. For flagship he requested the newly rebuilt *Macedonian,* a frigate which had been captured from the British during the War of 1812. He wanted the squadron to include two brigs and two schooners to be built expressly for the Expedition with extra strength provided by additional beams and knees, thicker planks, and high quarterdecks. Jones also requested the right to select the commanders of these vessels and they, in turn, to have a voice in the selection of their subordinates. These were unusual requests. Exploring squadrons of foreign powers usually consisted of two medium-sized vessels, but Jones wanted the frigate to overawe the natives and to provide room for the scientists and the brigs and schooners for operation by pairs and to provide for possible losses. Moreover, it was not customary for squadron commanders to designate subordinates independently of the Navy Department, but he argued that it was essential on a long cruise such as this.[2]

President Jackson, about to leave Washington, sent Dickerson a hurried note expressing a "lively interest' in the Expedition and requesting that ample means be furnished, as provided by Congress, and that prompt measures be taken to prepare for its early departure. He also suggested that it would be proper for Mr. Reynolds to accompany it, which "the public expect." Reynolds thought he was to be made the Expedition's

---

[1] *House Doc.* #147, 25 Cong., 2 Sess., p. 6. Jones had fought heroically at the Battle of New Orleans and received a shoulder wound from which he never fully recovered.

[2] Jones to Dickerson, June 30 and July 2, 1836, U.S. Exploring Expedition Letters 1, Navy Dept., Nat'l Archives (hereafter cited as Ex.Ex. Letters).

Secretary but Jackson instructed Dickerson to make him the
Commanding Officer's Secretary with the duty of collecting,
condensing, and transmitting to the Secretary of the Navy the
scientists' reports.[3] Reynolds refused to accept that position and
engaged in a prolonged and acrimonious newspaper exchange
with Dickerson making it certain that he would not go in any
capacity. The scientists were relieved to know that he would
not be supervising their work and interpreting their reports.[4]

This was one of a series of organizational clashes caused
by temperamental differences, jealousies, and honest differences of opinion. A basic cause of the trouble was the low
estate of the Navy. This being a time of comparative peace,
naval officers had few opportunities to distinguish themselves
and Congress was reluctant to spend money on ships. It was
generally believed that any future war involving the United
States would be a defensive one, during which the army and
coast defense would protect our shores while privateers harassed enemy commerce; hence, an extensive and expensive
Navy was not needed and money appropriated only for the
repair of existing vessels produced no new openings for naval
personnel.

Congressional disinterest was reflected in the indifferent
educational requirements for naval officers. There was no
training school, such as the Army had established at West Point
as early as 1802. Midshipmen were appointed at the age of from
fourteen to seventeen and then placed on ships where they
were supposed to learn by observation and where there might
be a schoolteacher or a chaplain to teach them mathematics
or languages. As soon as they were able to pass an examination
on navigation and seamanship they were given the rank of
Passed Midshipman and a boost in annual pay from $400 to
$750. After years of experience at sea and on shore duty they
could expect to be promoted to the rank of Lieutenant, then
to Commander, and, eventually, to Captain. These elevations
depended upon their record, seniority, and, frequently, upon

---

[3] Jackson to Secretary of the Navy, July 9, 1836, Ex.Ex. Letters 1; Dickerson to
Reynolds, Sept. 9, 1836, General Letter Book 22, Navy Dept., Nat'l Archives.
[4] Reynolds, *Pacific and Indian Oceans*, pp. 310–451, 505–507, 514–515; *New York
Times* July–Sept., 1837, and *New York Courier & Enquirer* Dec., 1837–Jan.,
1838. Reynolds signed himself "Citizen" and Dickerson signed himself "A
Friend to the Navy."

"pull." The rank of Commodore was honorary and that of Admiral was not added until 1862. Since there were more officers than were needed for the vessels and posts available, many of them took long leaves of absence and some found employment in the merchant marine. The dates of entering the Service and of commissioning usually determined precedence in securing commands.

In the 1830's a reform movement was on foot, Southard, as Chairman of the Senate's Naval Affairs Committee, introduced a bill calling for the establishment of a training school and the introduction of the rank of Admiral. Many old-line officers, including Captain Jones, opposed the bill which was defeated and this was a reason why some of the younger officers were reluctant to go on the Expedition under his command.[5]

Among the advocates of reform was Lieutenant Alexander Slidell,[6] member of a socially prominent New York family, who had acquired a reputation as a writer by publishing a book about Spain and by writing a description of Columbus' routes across the Atlantic, which was appended to Washington Irving's *Life* of that famous explorer.[7] Slidell wanted to write the Expedition's history and to command one of its brigs, but Jones objected to him, saying that science and the public good might be sacrificed "by placing the Rudder of the Expedition in the hands of one whose prominent merit, is that of wielding the pen."[8]

Lieutenant Charles Wilkes' name became coupled with Slidell's when Dickerson proposed that he be given command of one of the brigs. Like Slidell he came from a socially prominent, well-to-do New York family. At seventeen he had gone to sea despite his widower father's attempt to discourage him.

---

[5] In the matter of naval reform see: [Alexander Slidell] "Special Message to the President of the United States," *American Quarterly Review* (June, 1836), pp. 467–501; Anonymous, "Naval Education," *The Naval Magazine* (May, 1836) pp. 213–218; C. O. Paullin, "Beginnings of U.S. Naval Academy," *U.S. Naval Institute Proceedings* (Feb., 1924), pp. 173–194.

[6] Changed his name to Alexander Slidell Mackenzie in 1838 and captained the *Sumers* at the time of the "mutiny" in 1842.

[7] P. M. Irving, *Life and Letters of Washington Irving* (3 v., New York, 1883) 2: *pp.* 47, 133.

[8] Slidell to Dickerson, May 20, 1836, Ex.Ex. Letters 1; *Jones to Dickerson*, Nov. 7 and Dec. 15, 1836, *House Doc.* #147, 25 Cong., 2 Sess., pp. 167–168 and 204–205; *Army & Navy Chronicle* Dec. 15, 1836.

After acquiring a Midshipman's warrant he had been sent to the Mediterranean and then to the Pacific. During his second cruise he was given emergency command of a merchant vessel at Valparaiso and brought her back safely to Boston. After promotion to Lieutenant in 1826, he married Jane Renwick, who also came from a prominent New York family. Wilkes' bent was towards mathematics and navigation, and he worked with Hassler on coastal survey, gaining the reputation of being the best qualified surveyor in the Navy. He was made Superintendent of the Depot of Charts and Instruments[9] at Washington and, as such, supplied a list of instruments to be taken on the Expedition. Since many of them could only be obtained abroad, he was sent to England, France, and Germany for their procurement and was still there when Dickerson suggested his name. Jones objected to him and Slidell as "gentlemen of high attainments of a peculiar nature" but inferior as commanders to many of the one hundred and two lieutenants who stood above them on the Navy Register. He looked upon Wilkes as one to be put in charge of the instruments and at the head of the surveying party, but "it must be manifest to every one that he cannot be thought of as a commander, or for any other performance of regular naval duty."[10]

While abroad Wilkes made the acquaintance of leading scientists and astronomers who assisted him in every way possible. They assumed, as did he, that he would be a member of the Expedition.[11] Returning in January, 1837, Wilkes learned for the first time of his involvement in the controversy between Captain Jones and Dickerson. The Secretary tried to persuade him to join the Expedition in a civilian capacity, but he declined because of concern for his reputation as a naval officer. He told Dickerson that surveying required close coordination between the Commander and his officers and that he thought Jones' insistence upon rank would deprive him of the assistance of many qualified junior officers and that the Captain's physical disabilities would keep him from participating actively in the duty. Wilkes considered it a mistake to use a frigate

---

9 This Depot was established in 1830 and Wilkes became its Superintendent in 1833.
10 Jones to Secretary of the Navy, Aug. 22, 1836, Ex.Ex. Letters 1.
11 Wilkes to his wife, Nov. 15 and 17, 1836, Wilkes Papers; Wilkes to Dickerson, Sept. 13, 1836, Ex.Ex. Letters 1.

because she would have to come close to shore in shoal waters and, if wrecked, would break up the whole squadron. Furthermore

I should consider myself as possessed of no small degree of hardihood, in undertaking such important duties, where rank has been, and is made the first requisite, and be blind indeed (after the course of military education I have gone through) not to be aware of the impediments, that military etiquette, and formalities, might throw in the way of scientific duties, and thus render abortive all the exertions that might be made to produce accurate results . . . on such an enterprize unanimity of purpose, cordiality of feeling and confidence, ought to exist in its fullest extent among all, and especially between the Commander, and those engaged under him. . . .[12]

Abandoning all idea of any connection with the Expedition Wilkes busied himself making astronomical observations in company with his brother-in-law, Professor James Renwick, at New York and then took command of the brig *Porpoise* on a survey of the Georges Shoal off New England.

By March, 1837, the appropriation which had seemed adequate a year before was all used up and the Exploring Expedition was not ready to start. In addition to the expense of the specially built brigs and schooners a number of items were ordered without careful consideration of their necessity or cost.[13]

Secretary Dickerson took upon himself the selection of the scientific corps and began, auspiciously, by inviting several learned societies to suggest names and matters to be investigated.[14] The American Philosophical Society responded by preparing an extensive outline of scientific needs and the Naval Lyceum and the East India Marine Society of Salem went to considerable trouble to report on the matter.[15] There was no

---

12 Wilkes to Dickerson, Mar. 18, 1837, Ex.Ex. Letters 2.

13 Jones to Secretary of the Navy, Aug. 24, 1836, Ex.Ex. Letters 1; Jones and Dickerson to members of the Board of Commissioners, *House Doc.* #147, pp. 43–44, 230, 247–248, 253–254, 263–264, 288–289.

14 In August, 1836, Dickerson wrote to the American Philosophical Society (Philadelphia), the East India Marine Society (Salem), the U.S. Naval Lyceum (Brooklyn), the Geological Society (New Haven), the Academy of Natural Sciences (Philadelphia), and the Lyceum of Natural History (New York).

15 A copy of the report of the American Philosophical Society is in *House Doc.* #147 and another copy together with the report of the U.S. Naval Lyceum is among the Wilkes Papers.

lack of candidates, including leading scientists such as Asa
Gray, Walter R. Johnson, and Reynall Coates. Altogether
sixteen to eighteen scientists and artists were appointed, but as
the days passed and the Expedition appeared to be making
no progress towards departure, these professional men became
increasingly concerned. Most of them were teachers or had
connections with institutions which employed them by the year
and, having given up their positions in expectation of departure in the near future, found they were not to receive any
salary until finally summoned to duty.[16]

Among the aspirants for the position of historian was
Nathaniel Hawthorne, who got his friend Senator Pearce to
speak for him.[17] Walter Colton, a popular and able chaplain,
was another. Like Reynolds, Colton had written the narrative
of a voyage of a man-of-war. He was favored by Dickerson and
on friendly terms with Captain Jones until he asked for either
double pay or to be relieved of the chaplain's duties. Jones
then expressed a preference for Chaplain Elliott who was
recommended by Senator Butler and had no literary aspira-
tions, but Dickerson proceeded to appoint Colton Chaplain
with the added duty of Historiographer.[18]

On top of these personnel problems came the realization
that the brigs and schooners, constructed according to Jones'
recommendations, were inadequate. Tried out on a coastal
cruise they were unable to "claw off" a lee shore, a serious
defect in vessels intended for Arctic and unchartered waters.
Jones insisted they were seaworthy, but was not supported by
his subordinates, some of whom resigned their commands. A
Board of Inquiry, summoned by Dickerson to consider a reduction in the size of the Expedition, merely recommended a
few alterations.[19]

---

16 Jones' correspondence with the scientists is in *House Doc.* #147, pp. 10–11,
   109–110, 113–114, 213–214.
17 Robert Cantwell, *Nathaniel Hawthorne* (New York, 1948), pp. 200–201 and
   note, 463.
18 Colton to Dickerson, Aug. 5 and Jones to Secretary of the Navy, Aug. 25, 1837,
   Ex.Ex. Letters 3.
19 Tattnall, Jones, Warrington, and Board of Inquiry to Dickerson June–Nov.
   1837, *House Doc.* #147, pp. 322–323, 374–376, 487, 492, 575–576; Fanning
   claimed that the "proper" vessels for an Antarctic expedition were such as
   the late Henry Eckford had built for him—proof against spreading apart or
   being compressed inward by "clamp-framing decks and chain-bracing frame"

These bickerings and consequent delays made it difficult to retain the officers and men who had already signed up. Since this was a voluntary service, men could not simply be assigned to it and, because of the delay, it became necessary to get them to sign anew for a three-year period. Several refused, in spite of the added incentive of a three-months' bonus.

On September 19, 1837, twelve of the scientists were summoned to the Brooklyn Navy Yard where the Squadron was assembled to receive them and to take on heating apparatus and stores. Although confusion reigned, the officers enjoyed the cheers of the audience when they went to the theater. But the disordered mass of things and the bewildered personnel were more than Captain Jones could surmount. His quarrel with the Secretary reached a crescendo when the latter designated Lieutenant Matthew F. Maury as the Expedition's Astronomer and Lieutenant James Glynn, who already commanded the *Consort*, as its Geographer and Hydrographer, both men to receive $1,000 extra pay. Dickerson could hardly wait for the Expedition to depart and, combating a nervous headache with doses of snuff, worked on Instructions which he dispatched to Captain Jones on November 8.[20]

But Jones was not ready to go and complained bitterly that his objections to giving double duty to Colton and Glynn were disregarded. His health was affected and he became confined to bed. He wrote Dickerson that there were "an infinite number of good and sufficient reasons why I sought to withdraw from the expedition, which my present ill health will not allow me even to ennumerate . . ."[21]

Colton sent the Secretary a discouraging picture of what was taking place. He said he managed to keep busy cataloguing books and scientific instruments but was becoming convinced that the Expedition could not get to sea under its present organization: "it is filled with intrigue, and rife with discord . . . There is I believe but one sentiment among the Officers generally and that is that a *reorganization* and *reduction* are *indispensible* . . ."[22]

---

with rudder well guarded and unshipable, Fanning to Dickerson, Aug. 31, 1836, *House Doc.* #147, pp. 52–53.
20 Jones to Dickerson, Nov. 6, 1837, Ex.Ex. Letters 3.
21 Jones to Dickerson, Nov. 14 and 21, 1837, Ex.Ex. Letters 3.
22 Colton to Dickerson, Nov. 25, 1837, Ex.Ex. Letters 3.

Dickerson reminded Jones that he had originally requested the appointment of Colton and Glynn and that, although the scientists' pay exceeded that of a Lieutenant, their
employment was temporary and they had no prospect of promotion or of pensions in case of accident. If he resigned now,
no commander would willingly take over, having had no part
in the selection of the vessels or officers, and this would result
in the total dissolution of the present plan for the Expedition.[23]

In reply Jones requested to be relieved of the duty as
soon as the public interest would permit and, upon the recommendation of the Fleet Surgeon, returned to his home in Virginia on December 4.[24] Two days later Dickerson relieved him
from the command believing, as he confided to his diary, that
the Expedition under Jones' command would have been a
total failure. "I do not believe that for a year past he has intended to go out on this expedition. His failure however will
make infinite confusion, as no one will take the command
in such vessels as he has had constructed, or such arrangements
as he has made."[25]

---

[23] Dickerson to Jones, Nov. 27, 1837, *House Doc.* #147, pp. 578–580. A lieutenant's salary was $1,500 or $1,800 if commanding a vessel and the scientists
were paid $2,500 plus a ration a day.
[24] Jones to Dickerson, Nov. 30 and Dec. 2, Ex.Ex. Letters 3.
[25] Dickerson Papers, Historical Society of New Jersey.

III

Shake Up

THE DAY after Secretary Dickerson relieved Captain Jones of the command the House passed a Resolution asking for the papers relating to the causes for the Expedition's delay.[1] This disturbed President Van Buren, Jackson's successor, and added to Dickerson's nervous headache as he spent most of January, 1838, preparing a report in answer to the Resolution.[2]

As foreseen, it was not easy to find an officer willing to take command. By February 7, when Dickerson's report was presented to the House, Captains W. B. Shubrick, Lawrence Kearney, and Matthew C. Perry had, in turn, refused the offer. Captains Shubrick and Kearney refused because they thought the expedition, as organized, could not carry out its purposes, and Captain Perry refused because as commander of the Navy's first steam warship, the *Fulton*, he was engrossed in the problems connected with integrating engineering officers and men with sail-minded ones.[3] In later years he was to lead the famous expedition to Japan.

Dickerson, busy with his report and unwell, was happy to have the President transfer the task of organizing the Expedition to Joel Poinsett, Secretary of War.[4] Poinsett had had contacts with the Navy in connection with the Seminole War, but a more important qualification was his abiding interest in scientific exploration. At his suggestion Dickerson ordered Master Commandant Francis H. Gregory to take the command.

Gregory requested and was refused promotion to Captain. After two weeks consideration he asked to be relieved of the duty, giving family considerations as his reason. Gregory also said he felt he was being discriminated against since he was

---

[1] *Cong. Globe*, 25 Cong., 2 Sess., 6, p. 16.
[2] Diary entries for Feb. 1, 5, and 7, 1838, Dickerson Papers.
[3] Perry to Dickerson, Jan. 23, 1838, Ex.Ex. Letters 4.
[4] Dickerson wanted to resign but Van Buren was having difficulty finding anyone to take his place. Both Washington Irving and Judge Sutherland refused the appointment.

ordered to take the command whereas the others had had it offered to them to accept or refuse.[5]

During an interview with Lieutenant Maury, who had been designated Astronomer and Hydrographer in place of Lieutenant Glynn, Poinsett asked him what officers he would recommend to command the Expedition, without regard to rank. In a letter to a friend Maury recalled that

I afterwards had reason to suppose that he expected me to name myself and intended to put me in command of it, as really I was the most important personage in it—Hydrographer and Astronomer. But I asked myself, what right have I to draw distinctions among brother officers? So I gave him a list of the officers belonging to the expedition; myself, the youngest lieutenant in the navy, at the bottom of the list. He froze up in disgust . . . and gave Wilkes the command, and so I was the gainer, for I preserved mine integrity.[6]

Poinsett also sounded out Captain Joseph Smith, who had assisted Jones in certain matters of supply and was well acquainted with the Expedition. At Poinsett's suggestion Smith conferred with the Navy Commissioners as to the officers best qualified to command the Squadron's vessels. They agreed upon the names of Lieutenants A. B. Pinkham, C. Wilkes, and G. S. Blake. Captain Smith said he would not decide positively on accepting the command until he learned whether these officers would "willingly and cheerfully embark in and cooperate with me."[7]

Poinsett advised Dickerson to order Wilkes to Washington immediately. He said that, although Lieutenant Maury and his officers were well acquainted with the use of the instruments theoretically, "You are aware of the great importance of having them well acquainted with their practical application."[8] The summons reached Lieutenant Wilkes as he was about to begin a survey of the Savannah River, having just completed that of the St. Georges Shoal. Leaving Lieutenant Overton Carr, his assistant, in command of the brig

[5] Gregory to Poinsett, Feb. 13, 22, and 26, 1838; Poinsett to Gregory, Feb. 19, 1838. Poinsett Papers 10.
[6] H. Hawthorne, *Matthew Fontaine Maury* (New York, 1943), pp. 60–61.
[7] Smith to Poinsett, March 1, 1838, Poinsett Papers 10.
[8] Poinsett to Dickerson, March 1, 1838, Ex.Ex. Letters 4.

Porpoise, he took the mail stage for Charleston, en route to Washington. Upon his arrival, Dickerson introduced him to Poinsett and Captain Smith, the Expedition's prospective commander. He was reluctant to have anything to do with the Expedition and didn't know until later that the Captain had made his participation a condition of accepting the command. Wilkes' principal objection was that all the professors and artists would make the naval officers mere "hewers of wood and drawers of water" with no chance to demonstrate their particular abilities.[9]

Poinsett consulted James Renwick, a professor at Columbia College and Wilkes' brother-in-law, who said that he would rejoice if Wilkes could, with honor, avoid going on the Expedition but that he would go if given command of one of the Squadron's vessels and put in charge of the scientific departments for which he was qualified. That meant "Astronomy, Geodesy, Hydrography, the measure of the Pendulum, and Magnetism, in fact of all the departments for which he had provided instruments." He was lavish in his praise of his brother-in-law's abilities saying that

his Hydrographical & Geodetic skill is manifest in the surveys of Narragansett Bay and Georges Bank. In Astronomy his service at the observatory at Washington has made him among the first observers living. I have observed with him, with Labine, and with Hassler, and I rank him before either of them. In magnetism he was at first my pupil, but he now goes far beyond his teacher.

Renwick added that Wilkes had already made some observations and calculations that were important enough to be published, including a full set of experiments on the pendulum and the magnetic apparatus in London and in New York. This included the determination of the latitude of Columbia Col-

---

9 Wilkes' Autobiography in manuscript, 4: pp. 809–845, Library of Congress; Raphael Semmes expressed similar ideas in a letter to Emmons, Feb. 21, 1838, Emmons Letters, Western Americana, Yale University. Semmes advocated a small squadron officered by young men, Jones' organization having begun "in vanity and ended in smoke!" He particularly disliked the large participation of civilians with "High Admiral Reynolds" in the lead, resembling the army of Xerxes, a "caravan of fidlers, idlers, etc." He advised Emmons to write his own books when he returned "otherwise these scientific gentlemen will be sure to figure, in the histories at least, as the principal personages."

lege with greater accuracy than that of any point in the Western Hemisphere.[10]

When in later years Wilkes wrote his autobiography, he recalled how, in his interviews with Poinsett, he declined to have anything to do with the Expedition but outlined his ideas as to how it should be reorganized.

I felt myself fully master of the subject in all its details, as I had made it a kind of hobby for the few years before, my whole programme was laid open to him, and he complimented me on the clear and forcible views I entertained .& appeared to have new light thrown upon it, and asked me if I thought it all could be carried out—I promptly answered I had not the slightest doubt of it, I left him and said I have no more to say on this subject, and begged I might be set free to return to my command.[11]

Many thought he had declined to serve under Captain Smith because he wanted the command for himself, "but my whole course of conduct was entirely at variance with this, I never thought of such a thing, I was too young an officer to aspire to it."[12] However, his wife Jane told him she thought the command would be offered to him if Captain Smith refused. Summoned again to meet with Poinsett they went over his proposal once more and

after a short interval he turned suddenly round to me and said he was authorized by the President to offer me the Command of the Expedition, I may say I was to use a nautical expression "almost taken aback" and did not answer, why do you hesitate? Are you afraid to undertake it, no Sir, but there are very many reasons that crowd upon me, why I should not accept it. I did not feel any apprehension about being able to perform the duties myself as its Commander. . . .

To his suggestion that it should first be offered to older officers ahead of him on the Register, Poinsett replied that there were none who were qualified to command such an expedition. Urged to accept or decline, he replied that he would

10 Renwick to Poinsett, March 18, 1838, Poinsett Papers 10.
11 Autobiography 4: pp. 846–847.
12 Ibid., pp. 849–851; Smith's correspondence with Poinsett, March 22–23, 1838, Poinsett Papers 10. Smith thought Blake's refusal to go under his command was due to collusion with Wilkes. Nevertheless, he encouraged Wilkes to take the command and this caused him to be severely criticized by his fellow officers. Smith to Wilkes, June 4, 1838, Wilkes Papers, Kansas Historical Society.

accept if his views were carried out and the organization of the Squadron left entirely in his hands, and said he would require a statement to the effect that he had used no influence to secure the command. "I broke off the conversation and told him I could not talk any more that evening about it. I was not fearful of the responsibility or the duties but I felt it was so entirely unexpected I would have to have time to think the matter over." Returning home he and Jane had "a good cry together and then talked the matter all over. She had felt relieved that the suspense had ended and fully joined in feeling that I had acted a high and honorable part and felt sure . . . I should succeed and establish a name which both she and our children would glory in."[13]

Well aware of the probable reaction of his fellow officers he decided to be very circumspect and have no confidant other than his wife. Meeting Poinsett and Commodore Charles Morris the next day he made known his determination to accept no interference. When the Commodore asked him to write a memorandum setting forth his plans he ostentatiously pushed pen and ink away saying that he was not yet prepared to do so. Morris had further reason to be annoyed when, later, he requested Wilkes to come and see him, presumably to give him advice, the Lieutenant warned the Commodore at the beginning of the interview that he was keeping a detailed diary of every day's happenings and Morris, as a result, had nothing to say. Wilkes felt secure in the support of the Secretary and of Poinsett.[14] However, Dickerson was unwell and distracted by personal financial difficulties growing out of the depression of 1837 and informed the President that he would not remain in office after June 30. Poinsett, too, became ill, so ill in fact that for a time he was not expected to live.[15]

The public was fast losing its enthusiasm for what one newspaper referred to as the "Deplorable Expedition."[16] Twenty-four of its officers requested other assignments[17] and

---

13 Autobiography 4: pp. 853, 855–858.
14 *Ibid.*, pp. 872–874.
15 Dickerson Diary, March 2, April 3–4, 1838.
16 *The Long Island Star*, Jan. 25, 1838. Editorial comment was: "Alas, for Yankee decision, and Yankee enterprize, in this our day of nervelessness in high places."
17 *House Doc.* #147, p. 11. Four changed their minds and rejoined the Expedition. They were Dr. Palmer and Lieutenants Pinkney, Hudson, and Claiborne.

immediately after Captain Jones granted the equivalent of three-months' pay as a bounty for reenlistment about 150 sailors deserted.

Wilkes was not disturbed by public disinterest, feeling that it left him freer from interference. The Board of Navy Commissioners had already decided that the frigate *Macedonian* should be replaced by the sloops-of-war *Peacock* and *Vincennes,* the former a completely rebuilt vessel and the latter a veteran of several cruises. His request that the survey brig *Porpoise* be added to the Squadron was acceded to and most of her crew, with whom he had worked, came with her. The unsatisfactory brigs *Consort* and *Pioneer* were detached along with the schooner *Active* and in their place two New York pilot boats of recent construction, the *New Jersey* (120 tons) and *Independence* (90 tons), were purchased. Their masts and sails were shortened, their copper extended, and their names changed to *Sea Gull* and *Flying Fish,* respectively. The store ship *Relief* was retained in the Squadron which now consisted of six instead of five vessels. The reduction in total tonnage, however, made it necessary to reduce the size of the Scientific Corps and the amount of apparatus intended for its use.[18]

For second in command Wilkes chose Lieutenant William L. Hudson, a close friend who came from Brooklyn, had a good reputation for seamanship, and had been one of the original volunteers for the Expedition. He refused at first because his date of commissioning was ahead of Wilkes' but was persuaded to change his mind after the publication of a General Order (June 22, 1838) which stated that the Expedition "is considered to be entirely divested of all military character" and that it would carry armament only for defense against savage attack and, should war occur before its return, its peaceful pursuits would be respected by all belligerents.[19]

Third place was offered to another friend, Lieutenant George Blake, who refused and would not be dissuaded.[20] This

---

18 Autobiography **4**: pp. 858–859.
19 Charles Wilkes, *Narrative of the United States Exploring Expedition* (5 v., Phila., 1844) **1**: append. I–IV, pp. 351–354 (hereafter cited as *Narrative*).
20 Blake to Wilkes, Wilkes Papers, Kan. Hist. Soc. Blake refused to go except as second in command, believing that only Wilkes and the commander of the *Peacock* would be given promotion in rank.

Fig. 2. Captain William L. Hudson, second in command of the Expedition. From
drawing by A. T. Agate. *Narrative* 2: frontispiece.

position and command of the *Porpoise* was accepted by Lieutenant Cadwalader Ringgold who, in Wilkes' opinion, had "a
very high character, both as an officer and gentleman and had
received a good education and would soon fit himself for the
duties we were to be engaged upon." Ringgold came from a
wealthy Maryland family and at thirty-six was four years
younger than Wilkes and had had one year less in the Navy.
Neither Ringgold nor Hudson had had surveying experience.
     Command of the store ship *Relief* was left in the hands of
Lieutenant A. K. Long, even though Wilkes had some doubts

as to his ability. The pilot boats were put under the command
of Passed Midshipmen James W. E. Reid and Samuel R.
Knox in whose seamanship Wilkes had confidence, particularly
the latter who was the son of a Boston pilot and an experienced
sailor.

It was agreed that, with the aid of the naval officers,
Wilkes should undertake the departments of Physics, Surveying, Astronomy, and Nautical Science, and that the number
of scientists, artists, taxidermists, and assistants should be reduced to seven. It was also agreed that all the appointees should
be kept on pay until after the Squadron had sailed, the selected
seven to be told to hold themselves in readiness and ordered
to join the Squadron at the last possible minute. There was
the immediate problem of selecting essential materials from
among the barrels and boxes assembled at the Brooklyn Navy
Yard.

As foreseen, Wilkes' appointment met with serious opposition from officers ranking ahead of him. Commodore
Chauncey, President of the Board of Navy Commissioners,
and Captain Beverley Kennon complained to President Van
Buren and Commodore Elliott made a special trip from the
Great Lakes to ask for the command. Lieutenant C. K. Stribling pressed his claim based on an earlier commissioning date
than Wilkes.[21]

Obstacles were thrown in the way of the Expedition.
The Navy Commissioners refused to permit the substitution
of water casks, useful as buoys in case of emergency, for iron
water tanks, Poinsett was ill and Wilkes appealed directly to
the President. Van Buren responded with an order but it did
not make the Commissioners more cooperative. Work on the
Peacock at Norfolk was done grudgingly and inadequately.[22]

Opposition also appeared in Congress during debate upon

---

[21] Autobiography 4: pp. 859–863, 877; Stribling and Kennon to Van Buren, April
3 and 19, 1838, respectively, Ex.Ex. Letters 4; P. V. Daniel to Van Buren, May
23, 1838, Van Buren Papers 32. Judge Daniel said there was great excitement
and discontent among the officers at Norfolk, the immediate cause being Wilkes'
appointment but extending to misgovernment in the Navy. The discontented
had "multitudes of listeners and bablers as idle as themselves" who spread the
discontents "with such exaggeration and embellishments, as ignorance or malice
may suggest."
[22] Autobiography 4: pp. 875–876, 880; Wilkes to Poinsett, April 29, 1838, Poinsett
Papers 10.

naval appropriations. It was suggested that the Squadron might better be used for coastal survey and commerce protection in the Atlantic and some congressmen wanted to end the matter by eliminating the funds for its support.[23] Dickerson's "small cartload" of documents relating to the Expedition's delay was finally delivered to the House on April 18, and two days later he made the official announcement of Wilkes' appointment to command the "South Sea Surveying and Exploring Expedition."[24]

While he was at the Observatory in Washington rating the chronometers, the Secretary sent Wilkes a round-robin letter signed by fifty-seven petty officers and seamen of the *Macedonian* protesting against being transferred to vessels commanded by junior officers. He suspected that it was instigated by the officers but made light of it to Dickerson. However, he hastened to Norfolk where he boarded the *Macedonian* and mustered her crew. Singling out the signers of the petition Wilkes made them toe up to a line on the deck and read to them the Articles they had signed and his orders. He then told them that he intended to toe the mark himself and to see to it that they followed suit. Saying that he would not take those unfit for the duty, he proceeded to inspect the crew and to place aside those who appeared to be physically unfit. He then granted the remaining ones two days liberty and ten dollars pay along with the admonition that any who overstayed their liberty would be left behind. This had the desired effect; only one man overstayed his leave.[25] On this initial confrontation with the officers and men of the Expedition, Wilkes made a good impression. They saw before them a man slight of build, with brown hair and a ruddy complexion, and an abrupt manner reflecting a sensitive nature and a great store of nervous energy and determination.[26]

As the time for departure approached, the hostility in naval circles showed no sign of abatement. Wilkes and Hudson went to Norfolk on July 5 to take official command of the

23 *Cong. Globe*, 25 Cong., 2 Sess., 6, pp. 273, 280, 301.
24 Dickerson Diary, April 18, 1838; Dickerson to Wilkes, April 20, 1838, Western Americana, Yale University. The decision to appoint Wilkes had been made and become known a month before the official announcement.
25 Autobiography 4: pp. 863–866.
26 H. M. Lyman, *Hawaiian Yesterdays* (Chicago, 1906), p. 52.

Vincennes and *Peacock*. Commodore Warrington told them that the vessels were ready for sea but, as Hudson recorded in his journal, the

usual formalities of giving over the vessels to their commanders was omited—and we were left without further prelude to go on board our ships—ascertain as well as we could what state they were in—and get away from the Yard without the presence, or aid, of any of its officers who treated the whole affair with the utmost indifference. . . .

Sails were "bent," furniture taken on board, etc., and, in the evening, the two vessels dropped down to the Fort and the next day the First Lieutenants chose crews from the men on the *Macedonian*. Hudson could get no information about the *Peacock* other than what he found out for himself.

I could cast my eye nowhere around the ship without being most forcibly struck with the miserable manner in which she had been fitted out—but felt perfectly satisfied from the indications around me that it was not only useless at this stage of affairs to complain —but a paramount duty to get away from the Yard and its influences as soon as possible. . . .[27]

The Squadron enjoyed a moment of exhilaration on July 26, when the President came to Norfolk. He was accompanied by his sons, Poinsett, and the new Secretary of the Navy James K. Paulding, but not one of the Navy Commissioners among other officials. The vessels were decorated with flags, the yards manned, and guns fired. About sixty persons sat down to luncheon and drank toasts to the Expedition's success.[28] This was the moment for the announcement of the promotion of Wilkes and Hudson to the rank of acting Captain. To their chagrin it was not forthcoming. Wilkes had made it very plain that he considered such appointments essential and counted on Poinsett to act in the matter, having gained the impression during their first talks that he would do so.[29] In later years he laid Poinsett's failure to carry out what he considered a

---

[27] William L. Hudson Journal 1: pp. 1–3.

[28] *Ibid.*, p. 4; Autobiography 4: p. 886; Washington *Daily National Intelligencer*, July 24, 27, 30, 1838.

[29] Wilkes to Poinsett, July 19, 1838 and to Paulding, no date, giving ten reasons why he and Hudson should be given appointments as acting commanders, Ex.Ex. Letters 4.

promise to his illness and consequent inability to stand up to the Navy Commissioners.[30]

He expected little from Paulding who had just taken over Dickerson's duties as Secretary. Before taking office on July 2, he had been Navy Agent in New York and before that, from 1815 to 1823, Secretary to the Navy Board. Wilkes had asked Paulding to grant the rank of Acting Lieutenant to twelve of the Squadron's Passed Midshipmen and he had signed the appointments and laid them before the President without hesitation, being under the impression that it had already been agreed upon. He also agreed in writing that all officers doing scientific duty should have additional pay equal to that granted to officers doing coast survey work.[31] Poinsett was at White Sulphur Springs at the time and let Paulding know, too late, that he was opposed to all "acting" appointments. When Captain Smith had proposed them he had supposed it was customary, but had come to feel that such irregular proceedings were bad for the Service. He had told Wilkes that he disapproved but, as he said to Paulding,

I agree however with Lt. Wilkes that if the system is to be continued he & Lt. Hudson ought not to be made exceptions as there are as good if not better reasons for extending the privilege to them than to many others—I would suggest that this would afford a good opportunity to decide on the subject & to promulgate your decision.

Paulding's reasons for not extending the privilege to Wilkes and Hudson can only be surmised. In his reply to Poinsett he said he was most anxious to see "this infernal Expedition" on its way, and that he was beginning to taste the sweets of power "as you may see by some of the Newspapers. Would that Fate when it predestined me to be a great man, had given me a skin like a Rhinocerous . . ."[32] He was referring to the uproar caused by an editorial in the Washington *Globe* of August 1. That paper was considered the Adminis-

---

[30] Autobiography 4: p. 892.

[31] Wilkes to Paulding, July 11, 1838, Ex.Ex. Letters 4. On the back of this document is written in pencil, "Comply with the several requests of Lt. Wilkes." The Passed Midshipmen given the rank of acting lieutenant were: Carr, Walker, Johnson, Hartstene, Alden, Case, Emmons, Perry, Underwood, and Dale.

[32] Poinsett correspondence with Paulding Aug. 10, 15, 1838, Poinsett Papers 10.

tration's mouthpiece since its owner, Francis Blair, was a strong supporter of Jackson and Van Buren. The editorial said, in part:

We are assured, and believe, that there is [in the Navy] a total want of that esprit du corps without which there can be nothing high or ennobling in the profession of arms. Instead of the generous avarice of glory which should inspire every true sailor, it is said that a mean and pitiful jealousy, equally degrading to the man and the profession, pervades all classes of officers; that, instead of cherishing the reputation of every member as a part of their own, and viewing with complacency any favor accorded to merit or services, it is in their habit to contemplate it with the scowl of envy, as an unmerited reward, earned without desert, and conferred without discrimination. A service constituted of such materials, and disorganized by such unworthy principles of discord, can neither merit nor receive the affection and respect of a great and generous nation. It contains within itself the seeds of its life of contempt and insignificance.

The editorial went on to say that, "It is impossible to make heroes of men who adopt the maxims and principles of cobblers and tinkers," men characterized as lazy louts who skulk from work if possible. Opposition newspapers were quick to pick up this reference as an indication of the anti-democratic tendency of the Administration. Navy opinion was scandalized.

The *Globe* did not disclose the name of the author. There can be little doubt that Paulding knew about and probably approved it, if he did not write it. The realization of the political damage it could do if he made his approval too blatant by promoting Wilkes and Hudson may explain why Paulding did nothing in that regard.

Wilkes left Washington and his family, including his newly born daughter, on August 10 and received his Instructions, written, for the most part, by himself,[33] on the thirteenth. The *Vincennes* gave the signal to weigh anchor at 3 P.M. on Saturday the eighteenth. The Squadron got under way with the help of an ebb tide and a light southwest breeze, but the wind died out by 5 P.M. and the vessels were forced to anchor in the Horseshoe. A freshening wind at night enabled them

---

[33] Autobiography 4: p. 889.

to stand down the bay and out past Cape Henry Light by the early morning of the nineteenth. The pilot was dropped by 9 A.M. and the crews mustered for Church two hours later when land was rapidly sinking from view.

Before their departure Wilkes dispatched a letter to Poinsett in which he said:

> I hope you will never feel the mortification that I do at this moment at being left now to grapple with things that the Govt. might have put under my entire control by the one act of giving Mr. Hudson and myself temporary acting appts for this service and which I consider was fully pledged to us.
>
> If my feelings for my country's credit had not outweighed the mortification at being denied, I never would have weighed anchor on this Ship—another time I shall know better—I have one consolation left that everything that we do earn by our exertions will be due entirely to ourselves.
>
> I hope and trust that the Government and country will have no cause to regret the hands in which it has been placed. Nothing will be wanting on my part to serve this expedition of the Nation however much I have myself been disappointed.[34]

Both Wilkes and Hudson had supplied themselves with the uniform of an officer of higher rank in the confident belief that temporary rank would be given them, especially since acting lieutenancies had been granted to the Passed Midshipmen. Wilkes decided that everyone expected the promotions and that, since in fact he was commanding a squadron, he would assume the appropriate rank, that of Captain, and urged Hudson to do the same, saying that he would take responsibility. They agreed, however, to await a more propitious moment to make the change.[35]

---

[34] Wilkes to Poinsett, Aug. 18, 1838, Poinsett Papers **10**.
[35] Autobiography **5**: p. 956.

IV

Shake Down

THE NORFOLK PILOT, having seen the Squadron safely to sea, gave a glowing account of its members' high spirits. He had never seen men "more bent on accomplishing all within their power for the honor and glory of the Navy and of the country, and full of life and zeal."[1]

Just before weighing anchor Wilkes issued General Order No. 1, in which he thanked all hands for their untiring exertions, enabling them to depart on schedule, promised his devotion to their enterprise, and called upon them to strive for harmony and good feeling. He promised impartial justice in the assignment of duties and in making promotions, should any occur.[2] Some considered these vague promises routine,[3] but all were happy to be under way and were aware that this first day at sea was a momentous one in their lives. Most of the officers were young, ambitious, and enthusiastic at the prospect of adventure and admired the energy, scientific reputation, and decisive manner of their commander. Nearly four years were to elapse before the land now sinking below the horizon would be seen again and, for some, it would never again rise to view.

As Church call was sounded on the *Vincennes* the officers gathered on the starboard side of the quarter deck, the men on the larboard, and Chaplain Elliott took his place on a grating placed atop the shot boxes with the flag-draped capstan as his lecturn. The crew listened with close attention as he pointed to the "blue arch of heaven as the ceiling of our temple" and reminded them of their need for an omnipotent God to guide and protect them. On board the *Peacock* Captain Hudson led

---

1 Washington *Daily National Intelligencer*, Aug. 25, 1838 (taken from the *Norfolk Beacon*).

2 *Narrative* 1: append. VIII, pp. 361–362.

3 Eld wrote his father that he felt very little patriotism "flowing in my veins at present." Aug. 17, 1838, Eld Papers.

his crew in prayer and supplication, describing in his Journal
how the men looked

in their neat duck frocks and trousers—blue Jackets and tarpoline
Hats . . . every head uncovered—and the face of the hardy weather-
beaten Tars—assuming an aspect of devotion and eager attention
. . . scarce an eye ball rolled during the service—a stillness reigned
throughout. . . .[4]

On shore apprehensive families watched the vessels disappear from sight. Several unhappy scientists and artists found
themselves "on the beach," out of pocket and their careers
interrupted. The botanist Asa Gray had separated himself
voluntarily, having become tired of delay, but most of them
had given up desirable positions and spent money on equipment. Among them was the naturalist James Eights who had
accompanied Fanning's sealers on a voyage of exploration in
1828-1829. His companion on that voyage, J. N. Reynolds,
who considered himself the originator of the Expedition, was
also left behind and in subsequent weeks employed his pen
in an attempt to blacken Poinsett's reputation as he had previously sought to discredit Dickerson. These former members
of the "scientific corps" importuned Secretary Paulding for
reimbursement and he did what he could, but for the most
part, as he told Dickerson, "I have referred them to Congress,
the Residuary Legatee of all old good for nothing claims."[5]

Two naval personnel detached themselves from the Expedition. One was Lieutenant Matthew F. Maury, who had come
to realize that his interest in astronomy and oceanography too
closely paralleled that of Wilkes.[6] The other was Chaplain
Walter Colton who, having given way to Chaplain Elliott as
regards religious duty, found that Wilkes had no more desire
for an Historian than had Captain Jones.[7]

---

[4] Elliott Journal 1 and Hudson Journal 1, both Aug. 19.

[5] Paulding to Dickerson, Dec. 3, 1838, Dickerson Papers. The other former mem-
bers of the "scientific corps" were: Prof. W. R. Johnson, Reynall Coates, J. R.
Randall, and the artists Raphael Hoyle and Murtrie and two assistants W. M.
Guigan and W. M. Snyder.

[6] Hawthorne, Maury, pp. 60–61. Maury admired Capt. Jones and looked upon
Wilkes as one who had spent most of his naval career on shore and "in Washington, playing politics, and who was utterly unfitted for an expedition like
this one."

[7] Paulding to Colton, Aug. 23, 1838, Naval Archives, Letters to Officers 25; Colton to John O. Sargent, Dec. 22, 1838, Sargent Papers.

One of the first general orders issued to the Squadron required the officers to keep a journal which was to be shown to the commander of their vessel every week. Each day's entry to include the reckoning and recording of noon position, distances, bearings, etc., and remarks upon

all objects of interest however small which may take place during the cruise in the Scientific or any other departments the views of the officers ought to be briefly expressed concerning things that may come under his notice, the very record that nothing has transpired during the day may be of use but it is believed that this will be of rare occurence.

The whole will form a mass of evidence for the use of the government which will tend to illustrate & make clear the transactions and occurrences that may have taken place, also the habits, manners, customs, etc., of the Natives & the positions, descriptions & characters of such places as we may visit . . . with private affairs I have nothing to do, they are & always should be deemed sacred & consequently will form no part of the records.[8]

This order produced a variety of journals. The Midshipmen and some of the other officers tended to copy the ship's log and let it go at that. Some had gaps when nothing was recorded, the scientists omitted or passed over lightly events while at sea and Captain Hudson, for example, did the same for events while at anchor. Although private affairs were usually confined to letters, some persons, Assistant Surgeon Whittle in particular, used their journals as an outlet for their feelings. Passed Midshipman William Reynolds decided to keep a private as well as an official journal, and this allowed him to give free expression to his thoughts and feelings.

The Instructions given Wilkes were patterned after those given to Jones with changes and additions suggested by himself and with Paulding making "some few additions as to conduct and demeanor of the Crew and closing with a paragraph that the successful accomplishment of the duties would entitle us to the thanks and rewards of our country."[9] Wilkes emphasized his expectation of rewards when talking to members of the Expedition, but the wording of the last paragraph was not explicit. It said that since the Expedition was one that

---

8 *Narrative* 1: append. XII, pp. 367–368.
9 Autobiography 5: pp. 954–955.

necessarily attracts the attention of the civilized world, and that
the honour and interests of their country are equally involved in
its results, it was not doubted that the officers will so conduct themselves, as to add to the reputation our navy has so justly acquired
at home and abroad.10

These Instructions were kept under lock and key, not
even shown to Lieutenant Hudson, the second in command.
They began by directing the Squadron to shape its course to
Rio Janeiro

crossing the line between longitude 18° and 22° W., and keeping
within those meridians to about 10° S., with a view to determine
the existence of certain *vigias* or shoals laid down in the charts as
doubtful, and whose position, should they be found to exist, it is
deemed useful to the interests of our commerce to ascertain.11

In the days of sail the best course to Rio was straight
across the Atlantic, taking advantage of the prevailing wester-
lies, and then a southwesterly course using, as far as possible,
the northeast trades. Wilkes decided to break the voyage with
a stop at Madeira. It was soon apparent that the store ship
Relief could not keep up, so she was ordered to take the shorter
route touching at the Cape Verde Islands instead of Madeira.
The other vessels continued in company until separated by
boisterous weather. In spite of some seasickness and homesick-
ness, this first leg was perhaps the pleasantest interval of the
whole four years of the cruise. It was a time when all hands
were becoming acquainted with their ships and with each other.

The crossing was accomplished in twenty-nine days which
was considered good for that time of year. Wilkes was well
pleased with the sailing qualities of the *Vincennes* and with
the ability of the schooners, *Sea Gull* and *Flying Fish,* to keep
up. He knew from experience that the *Porpoise* was a useful
vessel and her captain, Lieutenant-Commandant Ringgold,
had the reputation of being an able sailor. Captain Hudson,
however, was not at all pleased with the condition of the *Peacock*. Shortly after their departure she was found to be leaking
"buckets full" keeping the Store Room, Dispensary, and Berth

10 *Narrative* 1: pp. xxxi.
11 *Ibid.,* pp. xxv.

Deck afloat. The water was run into the hold where it made about an inch an hour.[12]

They arrived at Funchal, the port of Madeira, on the seventeenth of September and within a few hours of each other. The Squadron stayed about a week taking on provisions and making repairs.[13] An observatory was set up on the property of Vice-Consul Burden who opened his house to the officers and scientists. Here, in Hudson's words, "The indefatigable Capt. Wilkes, was our presiding genius—day and night, untiring in his exertions to aid the cause of science—promote the objects of the Expedition—and add to the glory, and honor, of our common country."[14] The scientists and some of the officers took horseback trips into the interior and the naturalists began collecting plant specimens.

After departing on the twenty-fifth the Squadron made the first of a series of sweeps in search of reported rocks and shoals. By forming a line abreast and keeping three miles apart they covered an area eighteen miles wide. On this occasion the weather was clear and they kept a bright lookout. They were sure of their location because they had a good meridian altitude and thirty chronometers whose rates had been checked before leaving the United States and confirmed at Madeira. A cast of lead to 250 fathoms gave no bottom. Under these circumstances they were convinced that the Marias Rocks on Purdy's 1835 chart were nonexistent.[15]

When passing through the equatorial belt, the winds were often baffling or lacking which made sweeping more difficult and tedious. In a fair wind the *Peacock* ranged ahead and had to clew up her lower studding sails and down Royals in order to keep in line abreast. They found nothing at the "overfalls" reported by the brig *Patty* in 1820 or at other reported shoals and concluded that these were illusions caused by cloud shadows, rip tides, schools of fish, or by fields of luminous animalculae. On one occasion a lookout reported breakers and a boat was about to be lowered before this, too,

---

12 Hudson Journal 1, Aug. 20 and Sept. 2.

13 Wilkes Journal 1, Sept. 16–24. The opportunity to stock up on wine was not overlooked, Wilkes himself purchasing five cases.

14 Hudson Journal 1, Sept. 18.

15 *Ibid.* 1, Oct. 1.

was recognized as an illusion. An attempt was made to use a deep-sea, copper sounding apparatus, but it broke after 1,000 fathoms had been reeled out and most of the wire and a copper tube enclosing a thermometer were lost.[16]

Wilkes made his first experiment with the dipping needle, having hung a small swinging table from the beams of his cabin, but found it required more practice and produced only approximate results.[17]

A brief stop was made at Porto Praya, Cape Verde Islands. The *Relief* had not yet arrived, leaving no doubt as to her slowness. Only the *Flying Fish* made a landing, the other vessels standing on and off all night. The voyage from Madeira to Rio took two months, the most tedious part being the equatorial belt where fickle winds and calms slowed their progress. A Saturday night Ward Room ritual was to drink to Sweethearts and Wives, and Sundays were welcomed as days when only essential work was done and Divine Service broke the daily routine. Captain Hudson usually read sermons which might be excellent but seemed interminable on the days when his congregation had to stand uncovered under a hot sun and balance to the ship's motions.[18]

On November 13, the anniversary of a notable "meteoric shower," the scientists and officers were organized into watches and from 2:33 to 4:35 A.M. counted ninety-one shooting stars, a rather disappointing total. It was suspected that some were really the result of the ship's rolling and pitching, for, as the scientist Titian Peale remarked, "sometimes it looks as though the whole firmament was coming down." After crossing the equator they saw what interested them more—the Aurora Australis. They also began to experience strong southwest trade winds and, having passed the area of reported shoals, plunged ahead with all sails set and soon lost contact with one another.[19]

The "shake-down" process involved the relations among officers and men as well as familiarity with the operation of the vessels. The officers were volunteers and presumably united

---

16 *Ibid.* 1, Oct. 11; Emmons Journal 1, Oct. 30; Wilkes Journal 1, Nov. 4.
17 Wilkes Journal 1, Oct. 30.
18 Hudson Journal 1, Oct. 5; Peale Journal 1, Sept. 30, Oct. 4, 7, 14.
19 Hudson Journal 1, Nov. 18; Peale to Patterson, Nov. 13, 1838, Am. Philos. Soc. The *Peacock* averaged eleven knots and for a time did twelve.

in their desire to participate in a cruise of exploration, adventure, and scientific investigation. There were altogether forty-seven commissioned officers and six medical officers. Twenty-one of these had the rank of Lieutenant, including Wilkes, Hudson, Ringgold, and Long, the commanders of the principal vessels. The majority were in their twenties and unmarried, though Lieutenant Underwood and Acting Surgeon Palmer got married shortly before the Expedition sailed. Wilkes' chief reliance for survey work was upon the officers who had been with him on coast survey, i.e., Lieutenants Alden, Carr, and Johnson, Passed Midshipmen Eld, May, and Knox. Certain of the officers had little understanding of survey work, particularly Hudson, Ringgold, Pinkney, and Harrison.

Among those who had joined the Expedition under Captain Jones were some of the lieutenants with early commissioning dates, in particular Craven, Long, Lee, Claiborne, and Pinkney. There was a noticeable distinction between the officers from the North and those from the South. Seven of the latter were to join the Confederate Navy in Civil War times. Among the New Englanders were Emmons from Vermont, Walker from New Hampshire, Eld from Connecticut, and Colvocoresses, who was born in Greece but brought up in Vermont. Notable family names were on the roster, such as O. H. Perry, son of the hero of the War of 1812 of the same name, and W. T. Maury, a relative of Matthew F. Maury. Wilkes' nephew, Wilkes Henry, was a Midshipman member, and Hudson's son, William, was another.

Wilkes at forty was not only young to be given command of a squadron but had had only five or six years of sea duty, less than that of some of the Passed Midshipmen under his command, coast survey work being considered land duty. Realizing that he was looked upon as lacking in knowledge of seamanship and that some expected the Expedition to be a kind of pleasure cruise, since it was declared to be divested of its military character, Wilkes seized every opportunity to demonstrate his seamanship and to emphasize that there would be no relaxation of discipline.[20]

---

[20] Autobiography 5: pp. 936, 947–948. Some naval eyebrows were raised when the "exploring" vessels required New York pilots to conduct them from New York to Norfolk, Charles Morris, *The Autobiography of Commodore Charles Morris, U.S. Navy* (Boston, 1880), p. 104.

Shortly before sailing the Navy Department sent out an order forbidding the wearing of whiskers and mustaches. Wilkes published the order reminding the officers to set a good example for the men but they were slow to obey, feeling, no doubt, that on a cruise such as this the order would be relaxed. The matter was resolved amicably when Wilkes invited the morning watch to have breakfast with him and Lieutenant Johnson, a handsome young Virginian and one of the most popular officers, shaved for the occasion setting an example which the others followed.[21]

To emphasize their unity of purpose Wilkes promulgated a set of regulations to prepare both officers and men for transferral from one vessel to another. No one need wait for an invitation to mess or sleep on board any vessel of the Squadron as occasion required. At each principal stopping point he shifted the officers about.[22]

As might be imagined, the *Vincennes* was a "taut" ship. When commanding the *Porpoise* on survey duty, Wilkes had dined with the officers in the Ward Room, but now, to avoid the development of a "Captain's party" and in his assumption of the dignity of a squadron commander, he dined alone in his cabin. He occasionally invited individual officers and scientists to dine with him, seeking by this means to come to know them but, at the same time, he besought the reputation of a martinette, believing it necessary to emphasize his authority and induce obedience.[23]

If the *Vincennes'* crew had any doubts as to what to expect they were given an indication on September 12 when all hands were mustered on deck to observe the punishment of Seaman Henry Batcheler for sleeping while on lookout. He was given a dozen strokes with the cat, the maximum punishment according to naval regulations.

Two days later they were reminded of the perils of their profession when another sailor, George Porter, fell from the main top-gallant yard while loosening sail. The buntline encircled his neck and he swung to and fro until men aloft were able to bring him into the top and then down to the

---

21 Autobiography 5: pp. 969–971.
22 *Ibid.*, p. 947.
23 *Ibid.*, pp. 939, 951–952.

deck. It was thought he could not survive, but the rope had
been around his jaw and head so that it choked him until his
face was black but didn't break his neck. He came to shortly
and was sufficiently recovered to ask for grog, the drum having
rolled just before his fall.[24] Porter survived this experience
only to die of fever three years later when the cruise was near-
ing its end.

Another part of the "shake-down" process was the inte-
gration of civilians and sailors. Wilkes always considered the
scientists' activities secondary to his survey and meteorological
work and was supported in this by his Instructions, which
stated that the primary object of the Expedition was "the promotion of the great interests of commerce and navigation,"
but that he was to use every occasion, not incompatible with
those objects, "to extend the bounds of science, and promote
the acquisition of knowledge." During the early part of the
cruise the "scientifics," as the sailors called them, had not much
to do and were looked upon as passengers. The officers thought
of them as ranking below themselves irrespective of age or
knowledge. Their landlubberliness was emphasized when one
of them appeared on deck with an umbrella. The Officers of
the Deck were under order to alter course and maneuver so as
to facilitate the capture of aquatic specimens for their inspection and their collection, and the classification of plant life
began at Madeira. The officers' scientific duties included hourly
readings of the temperature of the air at masthead and on
deck and of the water on and below the surface. In calms
and light winds boats were lowered to determine, by means
of an apparatus made of casks and cables, the direction and
force of surface and subsurface currents.

Realizing that the scientists did not consider him an
authority in their respective fields of knowledge, Wilkes tried
to direct them by suggestion rather than command. To make
them feel at home they were ordered to assume the undress
uniform of a lieutenant and to mess with the lieutenants in
the Ward Room. However, having no rank they were subject,
as one of them expressed it, to the usual etiquette of a man-of-
war without any of the privileges, and required to obey the

---

24 William Reynolds Journal 1, Sept. 15.

orders of the officers, many of whom were younger than themselves.[25]

The daily examination of animalculae scooped up from the water provided a welcome diversion during many monotonous days at sea. Occasionally they had the opportunity to examine the contents of a shark's belly. On the *Vincennes* the microscopic examination of the contents of the nets was done by Charles Pickering and drawings made by Joseph Drayton. The sailors gathered around to watch the operation and it amused the Commander to hear "scientific names bandied about between Jack and his shipmates." On the *Peacock* this work was done by James D. Dana who by October had found and described seventy-five distinct species of minute crustacea, mostly cyclops, all of which he thought might be new discoveries. It was no chore for Dana; in later years he recalled this daily activity as one of his happiest memories of the cruise.[26]

Dana was the only scientist with any previous naval experience, having been a schoolmaster on a man-of-war during a Mediterranean cruise. He was described as a slender and active young gentleman of twenty-five who was "completely absorbed in accumulating information."[27] Dana was a protégé of Professor Silliman of Yale whose daughter he married soon after returning from the cruise. Although geology was his principal concern, he also interested himself in crustacea and would have included meteorology but found that any interference with that department was not welcomed by the Commander.[28] He became increasingly skeptical of the officers' interest in science, noting, for example, that in taking the temperature at the masthead they were unmindful of the fact that the thermometer was half of the time in the sun and half in the shade. Passed Midshipman Eld was an exception, making very accurate observations. Wilkes, too, was exceptional in

---

25 Autobiography 5: pp. 957–959; *Narrative* 1: p. xxix; Emmons Journal 1, Aug. 31.

26 Hudson Journal 1, Oct. 9–10; D. C. Gilman *The Life of James Dwight Dana* (New York & London, 1899) and typescript account by Miss Maria T. Dana from her Father's letters; Reynolds to Lydia, Aug. 30, 1883, Reynolds Letters.

27 Lyman, *Hawaiian Yesterdays*, p. 50.

28 Dana to Redfield, 1843, Yale University Library.

his determined pursuit of scientific knowledge and, at this
stage of the cruise, Dana thought him "a far more agreeable
man than was expected."[29]

FIG. 3. James Dwight Dana, Scientist. Miniature painted in 1843 when he was 30.
Daniel C. Gilman, *The Life of James Dwight Dana* (N.Y. & London,
Harper & Bros., 1899).

The naturalist Charles Pickering, M.D., was another very
energetic scientist. He was thirty-three, a Harvard graduate,
and known as a man "of very exact observation and measured
words." His particular interest was in tracing the migration of
races as indicated by the uses and names of plants. The diversity
of his interests and the extensiveness of his knowledge became
evident at Madeira where he "led the van on all occasions."[30]

29 Jessie Poesch, *Titian Ramsey Peale* (Philadelphia, 1961), p. 67 from Eld Papers,
    Aug. 17, 1838.
30 William D. Brackenridge Journal 1, Sept. 16.

Pickering welcomed that glimpse of European vegetation before they proceeded to other quarters of the globe.[31]

The conchologist, Joseph P. Couthouy, was equally enthusiastic but less knowledgeable. He didn't know much about
plants but was helpful because of his "keen eye and unabated
zeal." A man of thirty and the father of two children, Couthouy
was more a man of action than a scholar. He had been captain
of a merchant ship and was included in the corps because no
other conchologist was available and because he had made a
favorable impression upon President Jackson when he said he
was so anxious to take part in the Expedition that he would
go as a sailor before the mast if necessary.

The horticulturalist, William D. Brackenridge, was also
a practical man rather than a scholar. He was a Scot who had
come to America only the year before and had been employed
by Robert Buist, a Philadelphia nurseryman. He was twenty-
eight and his inclusion was due to Poinsett's urging that someone with his experience was needed to care for and ship back
live specimens of plant life.

The oldest in the corps was the artist Joseph Drayton, a
middle-aged widower with two grown sons. His knowledge
and experience as an engraver proved to be particularly valuable when the results of the Expedition were put into print.

The youngest member was Horatio C. Hale, who gradu-
ated from Harvard with distinction in 1837 and had already
written a scientific paper on the subject of Indian languages.
Wilkes was inclined to think a philologist unnecessary but
had been won over by Hale's unassuming manner and enthusiasm.

With Dana and Hale on the *Peacock* was the naturalist
Titian Peale, a son of the well-known artist Charles Willson
Peale. At thirty-eight he was the second oldest civilian and
only two years younger than Wilkes. He had been a member
of Major Long's Expedition up the Missouri River and had
also gone on expeditions to Florida and to South America.
A field naturalist rather than a desk scholar he soon demonstrated his sharp-shooting ability in bringing down bird specimens. Struck by the beauty and stupendousness of the scenery

---

[31] Charles Pickering Journal 1, Sept. 17, 19.

at Madeira, Peale made use of the camera lucida to portray the spectacular mountain notch known as the "Curral." In the days before Daguerre this apparatus was used to reflect landscapes and objects upon a piece of paper making it possible to sketch them fairly accurately.

Peale was the only scientist to get ashore at Porto Praya, Cape Verde Island, where he found some interesting bird and butterfly specimens. However, they spoiled before he could finish making notes and drawings of them, the hatches being covered because of a heavy shower and the skins rapidly de-

FIG. 4. Titian R. Peale, Scientist. Inscription on the back of this portrait reads, "T. R. Peale—by himself with a little help from his brother Rembrandt." Courtesy of American Museum of Natural History.

composing in the eighty-degree heat. His dark and wet gun-deck cabin was not a good place to make drawings or prepare specimens; naval etiquette prevented his use of the spar deck and the only really suitable place, the Captain's cabin, was seldom available. It annoyed him to lose his assistant when the corps was reduced in size. He wrote a friend that the scientific corps was like the officers of the Pennsylvania militia who had to be their own bootblacks and washerwomen. He was told that he would find sailors ready and able to do anything whenever their services were required, but he soon found that they had to attend to immediate duties first and were unwilling to have anything more imposed upon them if they could help it.[32]

Two members of the corps were on board the *Relief;* William Rich, who had originally joined as assistant to Asa Gray and was now the Expedition's official botanist, and Alfred T. Agate, an artist.

One of the most difficult things for the landsmen to get used to was the damp, cramped quarters in which they had to carry on their scientific labors. They had to keep their private and departmental stores in cabins measuring six by seven and a half feet. Dana described himself as "snugly stowed away" with just enough room "between the bureau forward and a large box from Chilton's aft, my bunk on one side and my washstand on the other, to stand without touching either of the above-mentioned articles."[33] Peale, in a letter to his daughters, compared the size of his stateroom to their mother's bedstead. In it, he said,

I have a little bed over and under which is packed clothes, furs, guns, Books and boxes without number, all of which have to be tied to keep them from rolling and tumbling about, and kept off the floor as it is sometimes covered with water. I eat with the Lieutenants and Surgeons in the *Ward room* down underneath the surface of the sea, where we have to have candles burning in the day time, the water we drink is kept in barrels and Iron tanks, it is very warm and now smells very bad, but as we do not come

---

[32] Titian R. Peale Journal 1, Sept. 2, 18 and Oct. 5, 7; Peale to Patterson, Nov. 13, 1838, Am. Philos. Soc.
[33] Gilman, *Dana,* p. 96.

on board ship to be comfortable we content ourselves with anything we can get.[34]

The three-months voyage to Rio would seem to have
been long enough for a complete "shake down" but the most
important part was yet to come—the relationship between the
Expedition's members and its Commander. These first days
were exhilerating and hopes were high. Wilkes' ability and
energy were admired and, most especially, his success in getting the Expedition under way after such a long period of
delay and disorganization. But a subtle change was beginning
to take place. Despite the pronouncement that the Expedition was divested of its military character, rank, which meant
power and privilege, was a continuing source of trouble, as
yet only a small cloud on the horizon but foretelling a storm
to come. The failure of the Navy Department to give temporary promotions to Wilkes and Hudson was a prime source of
trouble and Wilkes' assignment of the pilot-boat commands
to passed midshipmen instead of to lieutenants was a secondary
one.

Passed Midshipman Reynolds expressed his exuberant
feelings in his private journal. He came from Lancaster, Pennsylvania, and had never seen a ship before his appointment
as Midshipman but now, at the age of twenty-three, had had
six years experience at sea. He was elated to be given the duty
of Officer of the Deck, not ordinarily entrusted to one of his
low rank. It meant that he held the trumpet, the symbol of
authority, and that he was considered to have such a thorough
knowledge of the ship and her capabilities as to know what
orders to give when a change of wind called for immediate
action. Furthermore, he must perform this duty in such a
manner that the men under his command would have confidence in his ability to meet any situation.[35] His favorite watch
was from four to eight in the morning when the ship's safety
depended entirely upon his eyes and those of the Quartermaster, the lookout, and the wheelman. There was no one to
look to for advice as he scanned the heavens and decided the
correct moment to shorten sail. The dawn was his reward.

---

34 Poesch, *Peale,* p. 67.
35 Reynolds Journal 1: pp. 46–53.

FIG. 5. Assistant Surgeon John S. Whittle. Daguerreotype courtesy of Manuscripts Division, Alderman Library, University of Virginia.

FIG. 6. Lieutenant William Reynolds. Miniature by Brown and photographed by F. Gutekunst of Philadelphia. Courtesy of Mr. and Mrs. John H. K. Shannahan.

I love to see the stars disappearing one by one before the gray light of day dawns, the brightening of the Eastern sky, the masses of gorgeous clouds, the golden speck on the horizon, as the sun first shows himself, which grows gradually into the full & fiery globe, when he is entirely above water. . . .

Reynolds was particularly pleased with the youthfulness of his fellow officers, "None of those 'hard a weather' characters, of whom there are generally more than one aboard one's ship. We are all in the spring time of life, may we live to reach its winter."[36] Tropical nights entranced and bewitched him,

the towering pyramids of canvas, & the multitude of ropes, like bars of ebony, reaching from spar to spar, with all the accuracy of a picture—all human voices are hushed; the eternal moaning of

---

[36] Reynolds to Lydia, Aug. 30 and Sept. 3, 1838.

the masts & the murmuring of the waters, are the only sounds that
break the stillness of the night, unless it be the warning cries of
the lookout, at half hourly intervals, & the solemn tones of the bell
—these coming from the lofty heights, and different portions of
the ship, having almost an unnatural Effect.[37]

At this stage of the cruise Reynolds filled his journal with
lavish praise of the Commander which he later interlined
with comments indicating a complete reversal of opinion. A
reference to Wilkes as a man "of great talent, perhaps genius"
has the interlined comment "great mistake, did not at this
time know him." He recited the Commander's achievements
including his mathematical ability, his knowledge of navigational instruments, and how he became

an excellent astronomer, & well acquainted with the mysteries of
chemistry & the operations of natural Philosophy—[all in the
wrong—all humbug—a little smattering & much boasting on his
part, deceived others besides myself] he has had Eighteen years
of Service in his Profession—during which his peculiar & valuable
qualities have been noted and appreciated—he speaks several
tongues, and has an exquisite skill in coloring and sketching. . . .
In my humble opinion [woefully changed since] Captain Wilkes
is the most proper man who could have been found in the Navy
to conduct this Expedition, and I have every confidence [soon lost
it] that he will accomplish all that is expected, if accidents do not
interfere, of a kind that cannot be avoided. Well, who knows, [who
did know, how things would change?] what will be the termina-
tion of this cruise? May it be a favorable one, say I, for the honour of America, and for the credit of the humble instruments
employed.

But as they approached Rio, nearly a quarter of a year
since leaving Hampton Roads, the still exuberant Reynolds
was looking beyond Rio to Valparaiso, to " 'the Islands' —
Columbia River! New South Wales — Japan! China and a
thousand other places to go to and fro — whew! the cruise will
pass rapidly — I have not had a long or a heavy hour yet."[38]

The *Peacock,* leading the Squadron, arrived at Rio de
Janeiro November 20, the *Vincennes* coming in three days
later, followed shortly by the *Porpoise, Sea Gull,* and *Flying*

---

37 Reynolds Journal 1: pp. 69–70.
38 *Ibid.,* pp. 41–44, 54–55, 73.

Fish, and the *Relief,* last of all, arriving on the twenty-sixth. The store ship had taken one hundred days, which was ten days longer than the passage time for the slowest merchant vessel on record.

As the *Peacock* entered the harbor she found the U.S. Frigate *Independence,* Commodore Nicolson, at anchor. The frigate's band struck up "Hail Columbia," but the *Peacock,* having only a drummer and an indifferent fifer, could not reciprocate and, because of the scientific instruments, couldn't even fire a salute. Lieutenant Perry was hastily dispatched to explain this omission of naval etiquette to both Nicolson and the authorities on shore. It was not an auspicious beginning for relations between a commodore with one vessel on station and a visiting squadron of five vessels commanded by a lieutenant.

The Squadron's stay at Rio became a rather long one. For one thing, the *Peacock* required considerable repairs which were so costly that it was almost decided to send her home. Upon their completion Captain Hudson took that vessel, the *Porpoise,* and the schooners on a practice survey cruise to Cape Frio shoals. Consequently, their crews spent a rather bleak Christmas at sea. Meanwhile, Wilkes set up an observatory on Hospital or Exenos Island and the scientists found rooms ashore and explored the immediate vicinity. Pickering and Brackenridge managed, despite inefficient guides, lack of knowledge of Portuguese, much rainy weather, and uncomfortable hostels, to penetrate inland as far as the Organ Mountains. By the end of their stay at Rio the scientists had collected enough specimens to fill eighty boxes and bundles which were shipped to the Philadelphia Museum in care of Franklin Peale.

Some mail arrived, always a high point on a cruise such as this. Two passed midshipmen had to be sent home because of illness and a sailor was drowned when accidentally hit by an oar. But Rio, with its beautiful harbor, was an attractive place and the foreign colony was hospitable. Mr. Hunter, American Chargé d'Affaires, took a group of officers to an elaborate celebration of the future Emperor Don Pedro II's fourteenth birthday. Long lines of slaves trotting by with bags of coffee or barrels of flour or water on their heads and a glimpse of the interior of a slave ship presented another aspect of life at Rio.

Wilkes took certain disciplinary measures, but this did not appear at the time, as it did to some in retrospect, as revealing his "cloven foot." Finding that some of the officers at the observatory were careless in recording the instruments, he called a meeting and told them in strong language that he would not permit carelessness or ridicule of the efforts of conscientious officers. Those who were dissatisfied would be sent home. His talk was aimed, in particular, at Assistant Surgeon Gilchrist whom he considered talented and well-educated, but also, lazy, a novice in science, and the ringleader of those who ridiculed the work of others.[39] He berated Lieutenants Emmons and Underwood for climbing Sugar Loaf, a very difficult climb and never before accomplished by Americans, without taking along instruments with which to measure its height. This seemed unreasonable to some as did his order to Lieutenant Long to depart as early as December 19, leaving practically no time for giving liberty to the *Relief's* crew. He disapproved of Hudson's familiarity with his officers, fearing that his amiability and kindliness might be misunderstood. The differences in their ideas of discipline was illustrated one day when, upon mounting the *Vincennes'* quarterdeck, the officers touched their caps and vacated the weather side. Hudson remarked that this would never happen on the *Peacock* where the officers felt free to enter his cabin as if it were part of their own accommodations.[40]

It was probably inevitable that relations with Nicolson would be unfriendly. The Commodore sent an invitation to dine on the *Independence* addressed to "Mister" Wilkes—the customary designation for a lieutenant but not for an officer of higher rank. Wilkes refused the invitation and lectured Nicolson on his lack of manners. In reply Nicolson, whose rank was commander ("Commodore" being an honorary title), emphasized the non-military character of the Squadron and

---

39 Autobiography 5: pp. 993, 1009–1011. In his application to join the Expedition Gilchrist asked to be given charge of Botany as an additional duty, saying that he had devoted much attention to that subject, Gilchrist to Wilkes, April 12, 1838, Wilkes Papers, Kan. Hist. Soc.

40 Autobiography 5: pp. 1013, 1021–1022; Emmons Journal 1, Dec. 15.

sent copies of the correspondence to Secretary Paulding with
the explanation that he would have arrested Wilkes for insubordination had he not realized the importance of the duty on
which he was engaged. Paulding approved Nicolson's conduct
and wrote Wilkes that his letter had shown "a tone of feeling
which does not seem to be called for by the occasion."[41]

Their relations were not improved when Nicolson visited
the observatory and was made to take off his sword before
entering the portable house containing the pendulum and
was not permitted to see Wilkes' orders without a written
demand. Nor were they improved when Nicolson, observing
some bread taken from the *Relief* as too full of weevils to eat,
remarked that he would not have condemned it. Wilkes'
answer to that was to order the bread rebaked and delivered
to the *Independence* after the Squadron's departure, a solution which afforded him and Hudson "many a hearty laugh."[42]

A final difficulty with Nicolson resulted from an exchange
of physically unfit seamen for volunteers from the *Independence* which gave the Squadron the dregs from that ship, men
who, according to Wilkes, were "almost the only persons
attached to the vessels on whom it became necessary to inflict punishment."[43] His officers supported him in his controversies with the Commodore who was not particularly popular
among his own men, several of whom would have liked to
change places with members of the Expedition.[44]

The strain and fatigue of these days became too much.
When Wilkes went ashore to take a warm bath his reaction
was such that he fainted, falling into the arms of his servant
and having to be put to bed in a hotel. He regained consciousness but was, for a time, unable to speak, and Gilchrist, the
Squadron's senior doctor, spread the rumor that his condition
was very serious. Having no confidence in Gilchrist, the Commander called in Dr. Fox, one of the younger surgeons, under
whose advice he stayed in bed, fell into a long sleep and, after-

41 *Ibid.*, pp. 1004–1005; Nicolson to Wilkes and Paulding, Jan. 4 and 8, 1839, re-
    spectively, and Wilkes to Nicolson, Jan. 3, 1839, Ex.Ex. Letters 1.
42 Autobiography 5: pp. 1002, 1005–1007; Wilkes correspondence with Nicolson
    Dec. 29, 30, 31, 1838, and Jan. 2, 3, 1839. Ex.Ex. Letters 1.
43 Autobiography 5: p. 1003; *Narrative* 1: p. 88.
44 Johnson to his Grandmother, July 1, 1839, Johnson Papers.

wards, to everyone's surprise, got up and completed his experiments at the observatory. He also took a day off, going in his barge to a nearby beach where he relaxed and returned in the evening refreshed and in a happier state of mind.[45] The Squadron departed on January 6, 1839, headed for Río Negro, en route to Cape Horn.

Preparations were made for what lay ahead. Although it was summer in the southern hemisphere they would soon be entering high latitudes and so the men were issued warm clothing which had been purchased at high prices and proved to be little better than "ordinary Slop" when put into use.[46] In the hope of improving relations between the officers and scientists, Wilkes called a meeting of the latter. He assured them of his desire to assist them in every way possible in their work which was being watched by the whole world and expressed the hope that he would never have to assert his authority in a way unpleasant to himself as well as to them. The meeting ended with a general expression of good feeling[47] which was put to test sooner than expected.

The channel at the entrance to the Río Negro was uncharted and no pilot came out to meet them. The only signs of life were some horsemen riding along the shore. When the schooners attempted to go in they ran aground and, fearing attack from the shore, sent up rockets and burned a blue light which brought fully armed boat crews from the ships. In the morning a landing party found the pilot, an Englishman, who explained that the fog had prevented the recognition of their flag and it had been assumed that they were part of a French squadron blockading Río de la Plata in retaliation for hostile acts by dictator Rosas. Assured now of a friendly reception Ringgold, Lieutenant Perry, Purser Waldron, and Hale proceeded to El Carmen where they called upon the Governor.

During the next three days the officers surveyed the roadstead and bar while the scientists ranged ashore pursuing

---

45 Autobiography 5: pp. 1011–1012, 1016.
46 Hudson Journal 1, Jan. 10, 11, 1839; Peale Journal 1, Jan. 23, 1839. They were issued fishermen's boots, guernsey frocks and drawers, kersey trousers, pea jackets, mackinaw blankets, and buckskin mitts.
47 Hudson Journal 1, Jan. 26.

their various interests. It was a time of misunderstandings both ashore and afloat. Ringgold left orders that there should be no communication with the shore until it was time to depart and this caused Peale to leave the carcass of a deer on shore to spoil and some of the scientists to wait on the beach for most of a day in 87° heat with little food and only brackish water to drink.[48] The officers on survey duty tied up to the *Porpoise* while Ringgold was ashore and indulged in merry-making. They justified their inactivity as due to foggy conditions and receipt of the information that H.M.S. *Beagle* had recently spent two months surveying these same shores. In consequence Lieutenant Craven, the senior officer present, was suspended from duty and Lieutenant Carr made First Lieutenant of the *Vincennes*. Craven was highly esteemed by his fellow officers and the word got around that the Commander's policy was "punish first and enquire afterwards."[49]

Fog and a sudden gale delayed departure for the Cape until February 3. It had become evident that Río Negro was a poor anchorage, that the channel shifted with every storm, and that there was little prospect for trade, the principal export being salt which was sent out by way of Buenos Aires. The unattractiveness of the locality was indicated by the fact that no one attempted to desert.

FIG. 7. Sketch of the five vessels of the Squadron at Orange Bay, Tierra del Fuego. Courtesy of Peabody Museum of Salem, Mass.

---

[48] Peale Journal 1, Jan. 27–28; Pickering Journal 1, Jan. 28.
[49] Autobiography 5: pp. 1028–1029; Emmons Journal 1, Jan. 30; Couthouy, Feb. 2; Reynolds' typescript Critique of the *Narrative*, p. 10 (hereafter cited as Reynolds' Critique).

Changeable winds and fog made it difficult for the Squadron to remain together as it worked its way southward. The schooners went to windward better than the larger vessels and were ordered to make their way independently to Orange Harbor, the best anchorage in Tierra del Fuego according to Captain King's chart. The others managed to stay together, although the *Peacock* usually forged ahead of the *Vincennes* and both found it necessary, at times, to take in sail so that the *Porpoise* could catch up. On this run the Squadron experienced its first wind of gale strength since leaving the United States. The vessels' sailing qualities were, on the whole, pleasing to their captains and crews. It was noticed that the *Peacock* was improved by being relieved of the weight of her war armament and the *Vincennes* behaved well under short sail "rolling extremely deep but very easy" and being what might be called a "dry ship."[50] It was exciting on deck during the day but sleep at night was impossible owing to the tramping and shouting of men, the bleating and grunting of live-stock, the workings of masts and guns, and the howling of the wind and the smashing of the waves. Meals were a torture for fear of broken dishes and lost mouthfuls.[51]

The weather finally moderated and they entered the Straits of Le Maire with studding sails set. To their surprise and joy the weather was delightful during the passage past Cape Horn. The sun was bright and warm, the thermometer at 60°. It was the first rounding of the Horn for most of the men. The Commander described the passage with these words:[52]

We sailed within two miles of this dreaded promontory, and could not but admire its worn and weather-beaten sides, that have so long been invested with all the terrors that can beset sailors. Here we first encountered the long swell of the Pacific, but there was scarcely a ripple on its surface. Although the landscape was covered with snow, the lowest temperature we had yet experienced was 40° Fahrenheit.

A ten-degree difference in temperature between deck and mast-head levels caused curious mirages. At one time two

---

50 Wilkes Journal 1, Feb. 7.
51 Reynolds Journal 1: pp. 91–93.
52 Eld Journal 1, Feb. 15.

mock or false suns appeared along with the real one and, another time, the vessels saw each other in three images, one above the other, the middle one being upside down.[53]

By coincidence they reached Valentine's Bay on Valentine's Day. The Orange Harbor anchorage, twenty-eight miles north of Cape Horn, was reached February 18. The *Relief* was already there, having arrived three weeks earlier.

---

[53] *Narrative* 1: pp. 109–110; Wilkes Journal 1, Feb. 14. At this time Wilkes decréed that Civil Time instead of Naval Time (the day to begin at noon) would be used for the sake of unity in keeping diaries. Another change in routine was the serving of coffee at midnight.

V

First Antarctic Venture

A T ORANGE HARBOR the schooners were taken from Passed
Midshipmen Reid and Knox and given to Lieutenants
Johnson and Walker. The ostensible reasons for this change
were the failure of the schooners to respond to a signal to join
up with the ships before entering the Harbor and the report
of a drinking bout on board the *Flying Fish* after arrival. It
was probably also to give the lieutenants a chance at the commands. One of them, Lieutenant Claiborne, was so put out
not to be included that he asked to be detached from the Expedition.

Wilkes was convinced that there was a cabal, including
particularly the officers with early commissioning dates who
had joined under Jones, and that its members wanted to see
the Expedition fail. He made up his mind to get rid of them
as opportunity offered. Lieutenant Claiborne was to be the
first to go and Lieutenant Samuel P. Lee was to be the second.
The latter had ended a dispute with Captain Hudson by saying that hereafter he would address him as "Mister" instead
of "Captain." Hudson wanted to disregard the incident but
Wilkes told him he should have "cut him down" for his in-
solence. Lee was suspended from duty and transferred to the
Relief for return to the United States at the first opportunity.
Lieutenant Craven had been restored to duty after writing an
apology but was suspected of sympathy for the cabal because
he was a close friend of Lee's.[1]

Preparations were now made for a dash to the south. The
vessels took on board from the store ship ten months' supplies
to insure survival during the winter in case they became frozen
in. The scientists did some exploring and found an abundance
of geese, ducks, snipe, and hawks, and also of wild cranberries
and celery which had a very good taste to their "salt water

---

1 Autobiography 5: pp. 1034–1040. At this time eleven officers were shifted from
one vessel to another.

mouths." This area was not one, as Pickering said, "such as a Botanist would select for the center of his observations," but he found it interesting as a place little changed by the hand of man, discovering the sole specimen of a "domestic" weed in a deserted hut.[2] A few rather shy, unprepossessing-looking and uncivilized-acting natives made their appearance. Despite the cold they wore only a single piece of fur or nothing at all but kept a fire burning on a clay base in the bottom of their crudely built canoes. They could not understand why flags were flown on February 22, but all hands were glad that Washington's Birthday gave them an excuse for "splicing the main brace."

The Expedition's first real voyage of exploration began three days later when the *Porpoise*, with Wilkes on board and the *Sea Gull* in company, started off amidst cheers from the others heading in Weddell's track southeastward of Palmer's Land. Later, on the same day, Captain Hudson departed with the *Peacock* and *Flying Fish*, heading southwestward and hoping to go beyond Captain Cook's "Ne Plus Ultra," the point where he was stopped by the ice barrier in 1774.

The scientific corps remained behind, except Peale who volunteered to go on the *Peacock*. Hudson was glad to have his company even though there might not be many specimens of natural history to record. Lieutenant Craven was left in charge of the *Vincennes* and Lieutenant Carr set up an observatory on shore.

The uncertainties of weather and ice conditions gave the crews a feeling of adventure and their spirits were high. Those who were left behind felt disappointed, but Wilkes promised that there would be another Antarctic cruise and that they would have a chance to accompany it.

For the first few days the *Porpoise* and *Sea Gull* sailed before a "smacking breeze" at a steady eight-knot rate. Upon reaching the vicinity of icebergs they lay-to during the night. They observed albatrosses, gray and black petrel, Cape pigeons, and many whales, some of which spouted close alongside the schooner, their immense backs appearing to be nearly the size of that vessel.

---

2 Pickering Journal 1, Feb. 19 and March 21.

After passing King George Island they approached Mount Hope, near the northern end of Palmer's Land where the sea, studded with ice islands in shades of opal, emerald, and occasionally black along with pure white, made an awesome sight. As they lay-to at night, fog suddenly set in, followed by a heavy snowstorm, and their situation became dangerous as ice formed quickly on the deck and rigging, making it difficult to work the vessels. The men suffered from the inadequate new-issue clothing. With no evidence of open water next to Palmer's Land and the summer season far advanced, Wilkes decided, March 5, to turn back. The *Sea Gull* was ordered to return independently and to stop at Deception Island en route.

On the way back the *Porpoise* had a misadventure when anchored off Good Success Bay where some of her boats were sent in to gun for game and to pick "scurvey grapes" and wild celery. The surf rose while the boat crews were ashore and Lieutenant Dale's boat was unable to get off. On the following day Lieutenant Hartstein was sent in with two boats and a supply of food. One of these capsized in the surf but Lieutenant Hartstein, in the other, was able to rescue its two non-swimmers, while its two swimmers managed to reach the shore in a rather exhausted and benumbed condition. The onshore wind became so strong that further landing efforts had to be abandoned. After mooring a boat containing food near the breakers, the *Porpoise* put out to sea. A whole week passed before the stranded crewmen were finally picked up and, as a result, the *Porpoise* didn't arrive back at Orange Bay until March 30.

Wilkes suspended Lieutenant Dale from duty, feeling that his failure to get his boat off was due to timidity and lack of perseverance. When the Squadron reached Valparaiso a Court of Inquiry was held and decided that Lieutenant Dale had done all that could be expected, under the circumstances, and had taken as good care of his men as was possible during their uncomfortable stay ashore.[3]

The *Sea Gull*, meanwhile, was also having difficulties. On the day she reversed course water was freezing about the decks, the unmanageable jib hung overboard, and the fore-sheets

---

[3] General Courts Martial 51, #884, Naval Archives.

were so covered with ice that they were the size of a sloop-of-war's cable; scarcely a single sheave would traverse. The schooner reached Deception Island, one of the South Shetland Group, on the tenth and remained anchored in Pendulum Cove for a week, the weather being very boisterous. The thousands of penguins on the island entertained the crew while the officers made an unsuccessful search for a self-registering thermometer left there in 1829, this being the reason for going to this island. After sitting out a three-day snowstorm the *Sea Gull* got away but she was "wet, cold, and comfortless" and a diet of "sea stock" made of penguins and pigeon's, caused half the crew to be sick before arriving back at Orange Bay on the twentieth.[4]

When the *Peacock* and *Flying Fish* departed they had to buck a squally wind, frequently of gale strength. The *Peacock,* under short sail and in a heavy sea, had to wear rather than go about by tacking. At the start Captain Hudson assembled his officers and explained to them that their prime objective was to reach and, if possible, better Captain Cook's "Ne Plus Ultra." Wilkes never explained his objectives in this manner and the officers appreciated Hudson's willingness to do so. He had previously agreed with Lieutenant Walker, the new commander of the *Flying Fish,* upon four different rendezvous points but within two days the vessels lost sight of each other and, although the *Peacock* lay-to at their next rendezvous for twelve hours, the schooner was not seen again until March 25, four weeks later.

It was soon evident that the gun deck of the *Peacock* was going to be constantly wet. The gun ports had been so poorly fitted at Norfolk that not even double tarpaulins could keep the water out and it found its way through hawse holes, numerous other openings and, occasionally, down the main hatch. Peale found his cabin on the gun deck untenable and resorted to a vacant space in the Ward Room for sleeping. The crew were all brought up from the gun to the berth deck. The sur-

---

[4] *Narrative* 1: pp. 143–144; Johnson Journal, March 5–22. They learned later that Captain Smiley, a sealer, touched at Deception Island in February 1842 and found the thermometer. Its lowest recorded temperature was 5° below zero.

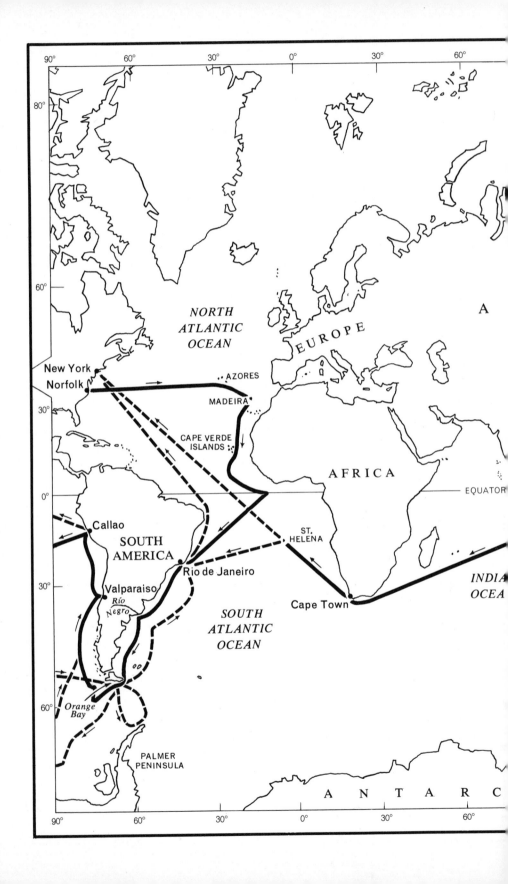

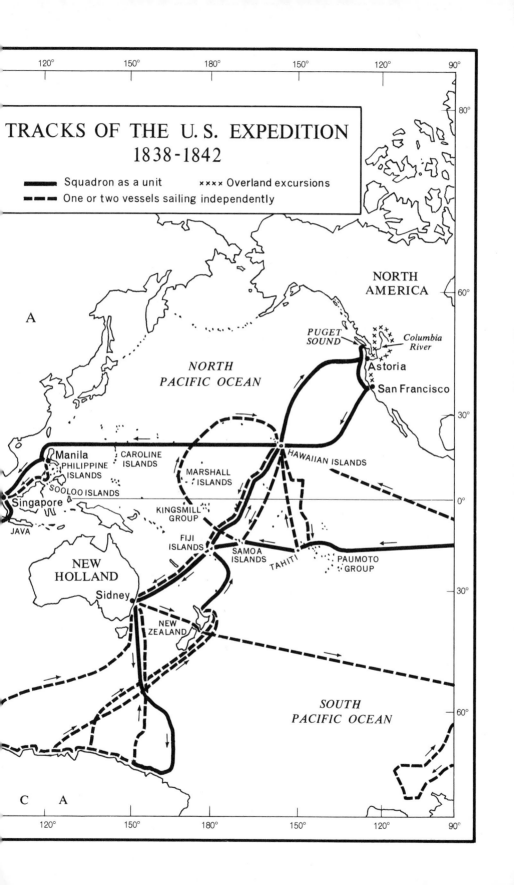

TRACKS OF THE U.S. EXPEDITION
1838-1842

━━━ Squadron as a unit ×××× Overland excursions
╺╸╺╸ One or two vessels sailing independently

NORTH
AMERICA

A

NORTH
PACIFIC OCEAN

PUGET
SOUND
Columbia
River
Astoria
San Francisco

Manila
PHILIPPINE
ISLANDS
CAROLINE
ISLANDS
MARSHALL
ISLANDS
HAWAIIAN ISLANDS
SOOLOO ISLANDS
Singapore
JAVA
KINGSMILL
GROUP
FIJI
ISLANDS
SAMOA
ISLANDS
TAHITI
PAUMOTO
GROUP

NEW
HOLLAND
Sidney
NEW
ZEALAND

SOUTH
PACIFIC OCEAN

C   A

geon expressed surprise at their good health but, before the
cruise was over, many suffered from rheumatism.[5]

The carpenters constructed a crow's nest at the foretop
mast head, providing it with a bench, ports, a hinged door on
top, and covering it with rawhide. But all the dangers involved
in making and taking in sail on Antarctic seas could not be
avoided. This was apparent when William Steward, captain of
the main top, a highly esteemed seaman, fell while reefing the
topsails. His sea boots stuck out of the water and, as the ship
was making little way at the time, they succeeded in throwing
a bowline over his legs and pulling him out; it was too rough
to launch a boat. Steward was in an unconscious state and
had evidently suffered from internal injuries. He lingered for
a day only and was buried at sea.

Rain, hail, squalls, "Scotch Mist," became the daily fare
as the *Peacock* continued in a southwesterly direction. Two
stoves made the half deck space a comparatively dry and warm
place to which the watch could resort when occasion offered.
During the heaviest blows the ship, under short sail, made
little more than steerage-way and her rolling and pitching
chafed holes in the sails. Captain Hudson doggedly conducted
divine services on Sundays with his congregation lying or
squatting on deck and clutching the nearest fixed bulwark.

For those who could appreciate them, there were com-
pensations, such as the beautiful exhibitions of the Aurora
Australis. Finbacked whales, porpoises, and petrel enlivened
the scene. Lying-to at night in a dense fog with no wind, the
only sounds were those of spouting whales, water breaking on
the icebergs, shrieking sea birds, and something like distant
thunder made by bergs breaking apart or turning over.[6]

For several days the *Peacock* made little progress hampered
by intermittent fog and surrounded by icebergs and floe ice.
Then, on the twenty-fifth, the *Flying Fish* was sighted and all
hands were called to man the rigging and give her three cheers.
Captain Walker reported all well except one seaman with a
fractured rib whom they had ingeniously strapped in a "woold-

5 Emmons Journal 1, Mar. 4, Apr. 13; Peale Journal 1, Mar. 6, Apr. 12; Sickles
Journal Mar. 1.
6 Hudson Journal 1, Mar. 5, 15, 17, 20; Peale Journal 1, Mar. 17; Emmons
Journal 1, Mar. 7, 12.

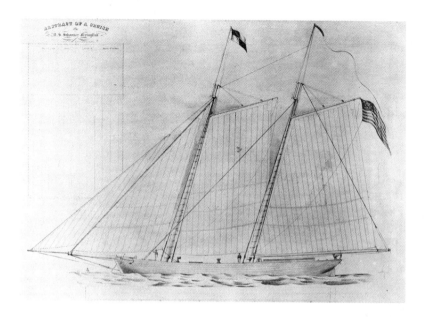

FIG. 8. Drawing of schooner *Flying Fish,* tender to the Exploring Expedition. Courtesy of the Peabody Museum of Salem, Mass.

ing" of canvas and pitch and now transferred to the larger vessel. The schooner had gone almost within a degree of Cook's "Ne Plus Ultra." Her crew had hair-raising tales to tell of their frail craft's encounter with ice, snow, and fog.[7]

Soon after losing contact with the *Peacock* the *Flying Fish* encountered heavy gales which destroyed some of her sails. When lying-to on the night of March 7, the sea swept the decks and crushed the boats, ripped off the companion-slide, washed the larboard binnacle overboard, injured the helmsman and lookout, and half filled the cabin.

Seeing no sign of the *Peacock* at any of the four rendezvous points, the schooner took a southerly course and reached a wall of ice about fifteen to twenty feet high extending as far east and west as the eye could reach. A cast of lead to 100

7 James C. Palmer, *Thulia: a Tale of the Antarctic* (New York, 1843) . This was written in the form of a poem for which Dana composed music. It was reprinted in 1868 entitled, *Antarctic Mariner Song* and included Dr. Palmer's Journal as an appendix.

fathoms found no bottom. Working southeastwardly, the
Flying Fish reached 70° S., and 101° 16' W., on March 22.[8]
On that day, at a moment when Walker had gone below "to
stick his toes in the stove," the lookout called out that the fog
had lifted and that they were surrounded. From the deck it
did look as if icebergs and pack or floating ice were on all
sides. As Dr. Palmer described their situation:

> The vessel was beset with ice, whose pale masses just came
> in sight through the dim haze, like tombs in some vast cemetary;
> and, as the hoar-frost covered the men with its sheet, they looked
> like spectres fit for such a haunt. Morning found them in an amphi-
> theatre of sublime architecture. As the icebergs changed their
> places like a shifting scene, the prospect beyond them seemed to
> reach the Pole. Day came up this boundless plain. The eye ached
> for some limit to a space which the mind could hardly grasp.
> Mountain against mountain blended with a sky whose very white-
> ness was horrible. All things were the same chilling hue. The ves-
> sel looked like a mere snow-bank; every rope was a long icicle; and
> masts hung down like stalactites from a dome of mist; and the
> sails flapped as white a wing as the spotless pigeon above them.
> The stillness was oppressive; but when they spoke, their voices had
> a hollow sound more painful than silence.[9]

Captain Walker, searching for a way out before the vessel
should be carried farther south and held in an icy grip, noticed
some "sutures" where the ice didn't seem to be firm, and tried
the following tactic:

> Having the wind free, I gave her the mainsheet, and manned
> it well, and having got about six knots way on her, kept close to
> the ice, and when at the proper distance, put the helm down,
> hauled the main-sheet forcibly to windward, and let fly the head-
> sheets; this brought her round suddenly, before she had passed
> through sufficient water to deaden her way; the ice cracked, we
> slipped over, or brushed through, and before eight o'clock I had
> got into a tolerably clear sea.[10]

Two days later the schooner was caught again in a similar
situation. Dr. Palmer expressed their feelings:

---

8 Cook's southernmost point was 71°10′ S. Latitude, 106°54′ W. Longitude.
9 Palmer, *Thulia* (appendix) , Mar. 21.
10 *Narrative* 1: append. XXXI, p. 412.

The waves began to be stilled by the large snowflakes that fell unmelted on their surface; and, as the breeze died away into a murmur, a low crepitation, like the clicking of a death-watch, announced that the sea was freezing. Never did fond ear strain for the sign of love, more anxiously than those devoted men listened to each gasp of the wind, whose breath was now their life. The looks of the crew reproached their commander with having doomed them to a lingering death; and many an eye wandered over the helpless vessel, to estimate how long she might last for fuel.[11]

Preparations were made to sheath the bow with wood so as to protect the copper, but the water was freezing too fast to permit any delay, all sail was crowded on and the maneuver that worked so well before was repeated. After a four-hour struggle they regained the open sea, headed north, and, the next day, sighted the *Peacock*.

Because of the shortness of the days and the miserable condition of the *Peacock*, Captain Hudson concluded it was time to turn north. Calling the officers into his cabin, he stated his opinion and asked for theirs. All agreed with him, although some were disappointed not to reach the ice barrier. The crew was then summoned to the quarter-deck and informed of this decision and thanked for its prompt and cheerful obedience to orders.[12] Foggy weather made it difficult for the two vessels to keep together, in spite of burning blue lights and firing guns, therefore, on April 1, Walker was ordered to return to Orange Harbor while the *Peacock* headed for Valparaiso.

While still in icy seas, the *Peacock* had a fire scare. Smoke poured out of the hold, general quarters was drummed, and preparations made to flood the magazine. The smoke was found to issue from a bag of roasted coffee which had been placed there while still hot. Had the vessel burned in that location there was little prospect for the crew's survival in open boats in the midst of rain, snow, and when the noon temperature was 37°.

By April 11, it was possible to open the upper half of the deck ports for the first time since leaving Orange Bay, a period of over two months. Three days later they reached the "Trades" and the gun-deck ports could be left open. The officers shed

11 Palmer, *Thulia*, Mar. 24.
12 Hudson Journal 1, Mar. 25; Eld Journal 1, Mar. 25.

musty overcoats and caps and the men prepared themselves
for the boatswain's order to wear blue jackets and trousers and
black hats.

After the store ship *Relief* arrived at Orange Harbor on
January 30, Captain Long began keeping an hourly register of
the tide, set up a guide light on Burnt Island, and put his
crew to work cutting cords of wood in preparation for the
arrival of the rest of the Squadron. The scientists found the
wet and soggy terrain very uninviting and all enjoyed a measure of leisure as they waited, knowing that things would be
different as soon as the other vessels arrived. Indeed, one of
the first things Wilkes did, upon his arrival, was to reprimand
Long for not being more active. As the other vessels prepared
to depart on their southern excursions, the scientists Hale,
Dana, Brackenridge, and Pickering came on board for temporary duty along with Lieutenant Lee who was under suspension for transfer home.

The *Relief's* new orders were to enter the west or Cockburn Channel entrance to the Straits of Magellan, to survey
certain harbors in the Straits, and to afford the scientists an
opportunity to explore that area. Long took an offshore course
with the idea of avoiding an opposing current and finding a
favorable wind but, instead, had to beat against a gale taking
twenty days to cover two hundred miles that Wilkes expected
him to traverse in two. Once, when about to enter Cockburn
Channel, a violent gale made it necessary to claw off again. On
another day, a calm one, a misunderstanding between the
Officer of the Deck and the Sailing Master resulted in letting
go the stream anchor without fastening the end of its chain,
thus losing both anchor and 75 fathoms of chain.

At noon of March 18 a favoring wind changed to a fierce
gale and the subsequent events of that and the following days
have been vividly described by Dana in a letter written shortly
after the event. The wind howled through the rigging "with
almost deafening violence" bringing with it driving sleet and
hail. The tops of the waves were lashed into foam. At 3 P.M.
they were alarmed to hear the cry of "Breakers under the
bows!"

A short distance ahead stood majestically the black Tower
rocks, rude towers of naked rock, one to two hundred feet in

height. The heavy surges of the southern ocean rolled in against the rocks with frightful roar and tumult, and now and then dashed the spray over their summits, veiling them in a sheet of foam, which soon disappeared, forming white, thready torrents down the black rocks. Again the cry was "Breakers on the lee bow"; and we turned a hasty glance towards our new dangers. A cliff, black and drear, was dimly discerned through the haze, and more distinctly, at its base, a line of heavy breakers. The ship was immediately put about and all possible efforts made to regain the sea to the southward. But we made no headway against the sea and wind, and rapidly drifted towards the rocks we would avoid. As a last resort we again put the ship about, and, with the Tower rocks on one side and Noir Island on the other, we ran for an anchorage under the lee of the latter. The roadstead was small and the winds were increasing in violence, endangering our masts and sails; it seemed hoping against hope—yet we hoped; and in the course of another half hour, every countenance was brightened and every heart gladdened by seeing our anchor safely down and our ship comparatively quiet.[13]

Both bower anchors had been let go in 17 fathoms of water and the chain run out to the bitter ends. The topgallant masts were housed and the yards pointed to the wind. That evening the larboard sheet anchor was also let go. Captain Long and Sailing Master Sinclair took another look at Captain King's chart which indicated that Noir Roads afforded a safe anchorage and found that in his sailing directions for the adjacent coast he warned that

No vessel ought to entangle herself in these labyrinths if she does she must sail by Eye, neither chart directions nor soundings would be of much assistance & in thick weather her situation would be most precarious—This part of the coast only requires to be known to be the more avoided.[14]

By morning of the nineteenth the wind had abated but toward noon it increased again and by night was blowing a gale with occasional squalls of extreme violence. Having shifted to the south, it struck with full force, as did the sea coming in from the open ocean. The fourth and last anchor was let go but it fell on rocky bottom and did no good. It

13 Gilman, *Dana*, pp. 99–100.
14 Sinclair Journal, Mar. 18.

became evident that the ship was dragging her anchors. The
night was dismally dark, punctuated by frequent squalls of
rain and hail. The ship moved directly towards rocks and
heavy surf about three ship lengths away.

As they awaited their fate, all speculated on the possibility of survival. Pickering was fascinated by the sight of
water shooting up the side of the black rock. "I had never
seen the like," he said, "except in pictures, where I had supposed it to be only the work of Fancy; and the idea of getting
broken bones among the surf never before occurred to me."[15]
The immediate prospect was that they would strike on the
reef, partly concealed by breakers; they could not move under
sail unless the wind shifted, and even then the chances of
threading their way on such a dark night through the profusion of rocks in this region, appropriately named the "Milky
Way," were very slight. So, too, were their chances of surviving
a wreck. As Dana envisioned it, the cold water would benumb
the most vigorous among them, and if they reached the shore
they would be dashed on the rocks or die of starvation in this
barren land — "his the happiest lot who was soonest dead . . .
I committed myself to the care of our Heavenly Father and
retired to rest. It was a night, however, of broken slumber."[16]

Upon taking bearings at dawn of the twentieth they found
that the ship had dragged off a sand strip onto shingle bottom,
diminishing their hope of hanging on. The starboard sheet
anchor chain was loose and, when the men "with deathlike
stillness and a measured tread, as if marching to their own
graves," walked it in, they found it was broken at the stock.
A stern chain parted that afternoon leaving only two of their
four anchors. At sunset the storm "wore a more angry appearance than ever" and they knew they could not survive
another night like the last.

The wind shifted again to the south-southeast with increasing violence. The ship dragged during the squalls which
were more frequent and violent than ever. As darkness descended Sinclair stood by ready to slip the cable when sail
should be set. He later recalled the noise of the cables dragging
over the rocky bottom as "the most awful I ever heard and

---

15 Pickering Journal 1, Mar. 19.
16 Gilman, *Dana*, pp. 101–102.

the Lord grant I may never hear it again."[17] Hope of survival
faded as the cable's rumble became louder and more frequent.
Realizing that the critical moment had arrived, everybody
came up from below. Captain Long stood on the foreyard,
trumpet in hand. The wind veered slightly and it appeared
they might clear the point of Noir Island, but they were
within half the ship's length of a reef over which the breakers
swept. The *Relief* rose and careened "as if half mad: her decks
deluged with the sweeping waves, which poured in torrents
down the hatches." The men were swept from their stations,
the Boatswain washed all the way from the forecastle to the
gangway. With a sudden spring the ship broke loose from her
fastenings, cleared the point and, at Long's command, the
dragging cables were slipped and the men sprang into the
yards and loosed sail. Under fore trysail and stern staysail, it
was possible to wear the ship around onto the starboard tack
and then to set the reefed courses and main trysail. They
were able to round the southern cape of Noir Island and
then, as the wind continued hauling, to head free of the coast.[18]

Captain Long won the admiration of his shipmates by
the calm and confident manner in which, from his place on
the foreyard, he had extricated the vessel from what had
seemed to be a hopeless situation. Having only a small "stream"
anchor left, he decided to open his sealed orders before ven-
turing again into the Straits. They instructed him to return
some of the personnel to the *Vincennes* at Orange Harbor,
but he interpreted the orders to give him permission to proceed directly to Valparaiso. Speaking a whaler en route he
gave her master a message for delivery at Orange Harbor,
should she put in at that place.

When Wilkes wrote his *Narrative* of the Expedition, he
gave Long and his crew and passengers due praise for their
excellent behavior in this crisis.[19] But he was extremely annoyed that Long should have permitted the *Relief* to get
caught in such a predicament, and his annoyance was augmented by the realization of the loss of time for the Squadron

---

[17] Sinclair Journal, Mar. 20.
[18] Gilman, *Dana*, pp. 102–103. Various details for the days Mar. 18–20 are taken
from the Journals of Long, Claiborne, and Sinclair.
[19] *Narrative* 1: p. 158.

and of opportunity for scientific activity.[20] Since the whaleship message never reached the *Vincennes* and the whereabouts of the *Relief*, was not known, the schooners stayed on for twenty days waiting in vain for her arrival. In Wilkes' mind this was a cause of the disaster which overtook one of them.

Long compounded his sins by reporting the incident of the near wreck directly to the Secretary of the Navy instead of through the Commander of the Expedition. Looking upon him as Captain Jones' choice rather than his own and feeling that he lacked the "determination and that fearlessness which ought to have overcome all obstacles," Wilkes made up his mind to dispense with Long's services and the store ship as soon as possible.[21]

Back at Orange Harbor, in the meantime, Lieutenant Carr, assisted by Dr. Fox and Chaplain Elliott, set up an observatory in the portable house. During their stay of two months, they recorded eleven gales. They always occurred when the barometer rose, contrary to atmospheric behavior in northern climes. The mean temperature was about 44°, the maximum 56°, and the minimum 32°. The only land animals they observed, aside from some natives' dogs, were two wolves which they shot. Fowl were plentiful, including geese, an eagle, plover, and a great quantity of ducks and the usual sea birds.

Couthouy and Drayton were the only civilians left on the *Vincennes*. There had not been room for them on the *Relief* and, in any case, they thought they could accomplish more by staying at Orange Harbor. Couthouy found the officers uncooperative in the matter of collecting shells since they were not permitted to keep even duplicates. He also found it difficult to preserve his specimens, for six glass jars tied to the ship's stern were broken and their contents lost through the carelessness of oarsmen leaving the anchored vessel. On one occasion his "boy" in cleaning the cabin threw overboard all the loose specimens in sight. Since the boats were always in use and, frequently, by officers going off for a shoot, Couthouy had only one opportunity to dredge.[22]

20 Wilkes to Long, May 25, 1839, Ex.Ex. Letters 1.
21 Autobiography 5: pp. 1042–1047.
22 Couthouy Journal, Feb. 18, Mar. 11, 17, 18, 20, 26, Apr. 16; Reynolds Journal
   1: pp. 162–163. A visiting native, nicknamed "Jim Orange," was washed, shaved,

The *Sea Gull* was the first of the exploring vessels to return to Orange Harbor and was immediately sent out to look for the *Vincennes'* launch containing ten men under Alden and Reynolds. Fitted with cutter rig, the launch had been sent to survey the islands adjacent to Cape Horn, guided only by a small incorrect chart and a few of Captain King's sailing directions. Since she had been gone for eleven days during which severe gales had been experienced, there was concern for her safety. Captain Johnson found her on March 26, snug in a cove and all well. The schooner took the launch's crew on board and attempted to tow her, but she broke loose during a gale, filled, and was lost.

Alden and Reynolds had had no opportunity to survey; the weather was so bad that for a period of eight days they remained moored close to high land and out of the wind. The best they could do was to keep a record of their runs, take bearings, and make sketches of the shore line. They had very cramped quarters, with the officers' bunks two feet apart, their "black valet" sleeping between them, and the other members of the crew stowing themselves wherever they could find room. They cooked meals ashore whenever possible, made some friendly contacts with unattractive and almost naked natives, and amused themselves at nightfall by singing and telling yarns.[23]

On the way back Reynolds had an early morning watch on the day they lost the launch. With a strong breeze blowing, he marveled at the schooner's perfect model and balance. She seemed capable of outliving the heaviest gales "so faultless was she as a seaboat, that with her helm lashed a lee, & the foresheet flat aft, *without a human being to aid or control her,* she rode, with her head offered to the Seas, in triumph & in safety."[24] An interesting comment in view of her fate.

---

clothed, and kept aboard the ship for ten days. They could not talk with him for he simply mimicked everything they said, even the sounds of Drayton's fiddle. Couthouy amused the crew by dancing with him to make him feel at home.

23 Johnson to his sisters, Apr. 2, 1839, Johnson Papers; Reynolds Journal 1: pp. 106–147. The launch measured 25′ length, 8′ beam, 5′ depth. It was decked over as far as the mast and fitted with an awning to go over the main boom when at anchor. They carried supplies for thirty days.

24 Reynolds Journal 1: pp. 155–158.

As they approached Orange Harbor they saw that the *Porpoise* had returned and those at the Harbor, seeing no launch and fearing the worst, gave her crew a most hearty welcome when they came into view.

The *Flying Fish* arrived a week later with the news that the *Peacock* had proceeded directly to Valparaiso. The schooners were now returned to their original commanders, Passed Midshipmen Reid and Knox, with orders to wait another two weeks for the *Relief* and, on April 20, the *Vincennes* and *Porpoise* set sail for Valparaiso.

When the *Relief* failed to appear by the twenty-eighth the schooners departed. The *Sea Gull* was last seen by the crew of the *Flying Fish* at midnight of that day.[25] Shortly thereafter a series of squalls were followed by a gale which was blowing furiously by 8:30 the following morning. Knox decided to run for shore but, finding his anchors dragged when under the south point of Scapenham Bay, brought the *Flying Fish* back to Orange Bay where she rode out the storm. Departing again on May 1 the schooner encountered no other vessel except a whaler whose captain was astounded to see a New York pilot boat in those waters.

During the early part of May a strong gale blew from the north for nine days without let-up. It slowed the progress of the vessels which were having to buck it. Wilkes, alarmed by the spread of dysentery and the appearance of two cases of scurvy,[26] drove the *Vincennes* with full sail on the lower yards, the bare upper masts sweeping huge circles in the sky. The taking in and setting of sail in the midst of rain and hail was killing work and left the crew with little time for rest.

For Reynolds it was a thrilling experience and he was filled with admiration for the ship and her commander.

It was startling, even to the oldest hands, to see the way in which the Captain pressed his Ship with Sail—he carried on her at a fearful rate, & the poor craft's frame, shook like an aspen leaf, in the violent encounters with the Seas. A wondrous degree

---

25 Passed Midshipman Reid was the son of the Governor of Georgia and Passed Midshipman Bacon, the second in command, came from Connecticut.

26 Wilkes Journal 1, May 1–12.

of nerve was requisite, tempered with a judgement correct
& unfailing, to wage such a strenuous opposition to the Gale & be
successful, it was well for us, that in this, there was no want & we
battled throughout that long blow with but one little accident
occurring, the loss of the jib boom.[27]

---

[27] Reynolds Journal 1: pp. 168–169.

VI

The Broad Pennant

A LL HANDS had had their fill of bleak Tierra del Fuego and Antarctic cold and were eager for a glimpse of the Cordilleras. This magnificent mountain range appeared to its greatest advantage at sunrise and sunset. Wilkes thought the view at sunrise the more striking.

> The outline is at that time of a golden hue, and may be easily traced, in a long line, running north and south. This gradually brightens, and is lost the moment the sun is seen. The evening view gives rise to disappointment. The mountains are seen at a great distance (eighty miles in a bird's flight) reflecting the setting sun, and in consequence, appear much lower than is anticipated.[1]

The wide entrance to Valparaiso harbor exposed it to strong northerly winds. Since the land rose abruptly it had the effect of lifting the wind close to shore and, as a result, the chief danger to vessels at anchor was from heavy rollers rather than from the wind. The surf was always heavy at the brief intervals of beach along the rocky shore.

The Squadron's vessels arrived one by one, the *Relief* being the first. She was able to obtain an anchor from the British naval vessel *Fly,* Captain Lock, and after sitting outside during a day of no wind entered the anchorage on April 15. The *Peacock* came in about a week later, but the *Vincennes, Porpoise,* and *Flying Fish* did not appear until about a month after that. The last to arrive, the *Flying Fish,* was twenty-two days out of Orange Bay, having been held up by the severe gale which made her lose contact with the *Sea Gull,* sprung her bowsprit, and blew away two foresails. The mild cases of dysentery among the crews of the *Flying Fish* and *Vincennes* had mostly cleared up by the time these vessels reached Valparaiso.

---

1 *Narrative* 1: p. 165.

For many Squadron members the greatest thing about Valparaiso was the receipt of mail. The supply ship, *Mariposa,* had preceded them with mail and newspapers of date up to November, 1838, and the ship *Henry Luke,* 114 days out of Boston, arrived with additional mail on April 20. Lieutenant Lee obtained passage back to the United States on the ship *Henry Lee* which, incidentally, was named after his uncle.

Everybody got shore leave in this port town of about 30,000 inhabitants which centered on a single street paralleling the bay shore. On the heights above were substantial homes of merchant families and to the south, in a ravine between two hills known as the "Main and Fore Top," were most of the grog shops and abodes of the black-eyed ladies wearing red "bayettas" who, in Wilkes' view, were an annoyance to the authorities, commanders of vessels, "and equally so to the poor sailors, who seldom leave this port without empty pockets and injured health." But he thought there was greater order-liness and more efficient policing than at the time of his visit seventeen years before.[2]

The officers and scientists went on to Santiago, the capital city, which could boast a theater, a "shingano" or amphitheatre for dance performances, a cathedral, a palace, and a library. The scientists not only saw the sights but roamed the vicinity of the two cities seeking plant specimens. Dana, Pickering, Brackenridge, and Rich hired horses and guides and went far into the mountains. Brackenridge and Rich suffered from mountain sickness, but Dana and Pickering pushed on to a height of about 10,000 feet.

Since the *Relief* still lacked adequate anchors and chains and the season for the dreaded "Northers" was approaching, Captain Hudson sent her and the *Mariposa* on to Callao, Peru. Pickering, Brackenridge, Rich, and Agate stayed with the store ship while Hale and Dana rejoined the *Peacock* and Drayton and Couthouy awaited the *Vincennes* which arrived May 15.

Dana and Couthouy seized the opportunity to make a second excursion into the interior, going the first forty miles in a gig or "velocho" and the last eighty on horseback. Their

2 *Ibid.,* pp. 167–169.

saddles consisted of layers of cloths and sheepskins under and
over wooden frames which were readily transformed into beds
at night, there being no inns. Late snows prevented them from
going far into the mountains, so they turned aside to visit a
copper mine. Dana was dividing his interests between geology
and botany and Couthouy, though his specialty was conchology, interested himself in all forms of animal life. The scientists habitually collected for each other.[3]

Both the officers and scientists enjoyed a certain amount
of social life due to the presence of President Prieto at Valparaiso. Three balls were given in his honor and in celebration
of Chile's recent victory over Peru in a battle at Yungai. The
most spectacular of these affairs took place before the arrival
of the *Vincennes*. It was held in a large open space between
two storehouses, roofed over with an awning, lined in blue
and studded with stars, and lighted by twenty chandeliers.
Rugs covered the floor and sofas and seats were ranged along
the walls which were decorated with mirrors and pictures.
Festoons of flags, flowers, and evergreens partitioned off areas
reserved for cards, smoking, dressing, and supper. Some four
hundred persons from "genteel and respectable families" attended, while sentries kept out the less genteel. The President
opened the ball by selecting a lady with whom he danced a
minuet. The general dancing which followed consisted of
"quadrilles, country-dances, waltzes, besides which they had
the lascivious dances of samacueca, cachuca, and lordean.
These partake somewhat of the bolero and fandango, or
Spanish and African dance." In the interlude marches and
national airs were played and sung. One of the bands was supplied by the British frigate *President*.[4]

It amused Captain Hudson to see the President of Chile
"with his richly embroidered coat—gold epaulets—and Field
Marshall's sash—kicking up his heels to the scrapings of cat
gut and horse hair—before that admiring crowd." In Picker-

---

[3] Dana to his brother, June, 1839 (courtesy of Miss M. T. Dana); Couthouy
Journal, May 16, 25.

[4] *Narrative* 1: pp. 171–173. The American frigate *President* was captured by the
British during the War of 1812 and this British vessel was named after her
and built along her lines. If the *Macedonian* had remained in the Squadron,
she having been captured from the British during that war, these two vessels
with similar histories would have confronted each other at Valparaiso.

ing's opinion it was a very fine affair for a new and half-barbarous country, he even doubted whether "the good city of Boston has turned out anything superior." Emmons did not think the ladies very beautiful, though richly and tastefully dressed in French fashion, and found dancing on carpets "rather heavy."[5]

As soon as the *Vincennes* arrived, official calls were made and a cottage on the hill rented for use as an observatory. Reynolds characterized it as a gathering place for fleas and the duty there "most harassing and uninteresting" until he caught a glimpse of some pretty girls living nearby which had, as he said, "an electric effect on my poor nerves." American residents entertained them in their homes and their hospitality was greatly appreciated by these men who had been away from the society of "intelligent and agreeable" American women for nearly a year.[6] The U.S. sloop *Falmouth* came into port and its officers joined in these social affairs. This was a pleasant circumstance for Wilkes because Captain M'Keever was very friendly and ready to assist the Squadron in every possible way.

The *Porpoise* sailed for Callao May 26, but the other three vessels were delayed by a succession of incidents and by a change in the weather. When, for example, the *Peacock* shifted her berth, her anchor fouled its chain and she dragged and collided with the *Vincennes* carrying away her martingale and flying jib boom and damaging her own rigging and spars. All preparations for departure had been made by June 1, but the wind became northerly bringing rain, fog, and a heavy surf, making it impossible to depart before the sixth.

Lieutenant Craven was left behind to take command of the *Sea Gull* when she arrived. Many pairs of eyes searched the southern horizon hoping against hope to see a white speck, but none was to be seen. Her young officers, Reid and Bacon, and her thirteen crewmen had many good friends in the Squadron. Their seamanship was unquestioned. From Callao, Wilkes sent a dispatch home saying that "taking into consideration the constant head winds during our passage and our stay at Valparaiso, I do not consider her out of time."

5 Hudson Journal 1, p. 194; Emmons Journal, 1, Apr. 28; Pickering to M. O. Pickering, July 12, 1839, Pickering Papers.
6 Reynolds Journal 1, p. 179.

Paulding sent this word to the Washington *Globe* hoping to allay the fears of relatives of the schooner's crew. Wilkes felt keenly the loss of their talents and enthusiasm. He surmised, later, that the *Sea Gull's* foremast must have tripped and ripped up her deck causing her to founder.[7]

Just before leaving Valparaiso, two midshipmen attached to the *Peacock,* Wilkes Henry and James L. Blair, fought a bloodless duel. This being considered a demoralizing and disreputable affair, they and their seconds were suspended and ordered home with a recommendation for dismissal from the service. The older officers, some of whom were suspected of being instigators, petitioned to have them restored to duty, laying their offense to youthfulness and inexperience. The Commander acceded to their request, doubtless much relieved that he was not forced to send his widowed sister's son home in disgrace.[8]

Callao attracted a considerable amount of shipping because of its spacious and safe harbor, but the town and the Peruvian capital, Lima, were much less attractive than Valparaiso and Santiago. By June 20 the Squadron was again assembled at anchor off the island of San Lorenzo, seven miles from Callao. The observatory was set up on the island. It took nearly a month to refit and to replenish stores in preparation for voyaging into the Pacific. The *Relief* was unloaded and, when smoked, produced three barrels full of rat carcasses.

Pickering, Brackenridge, Rich, and Agate had time for an excursion high into the mountains, where they visited a silver mine and the town of Baños, noted for its hot springs. It was an adventurous trip, for Peru was on the verge of anarchy following its defeat by Chile. They slept on dirt floors and fought fleas or slept in the open and shivered in the cold. Pickering, suffering less than the others from mountain sickness, often plodded on ahead holding his Bowie-knife pistol in readiness for bandits who were known to be roaming in the vicinity. One midnight they experienced an earthquake last-

---

[7] Wilkes to Paulding, July 1, 1839, Ex.Ex. Letters 1; *Narrative* 1: p. 230; Autobiography 5: pp. 1049–1050.
[8] *Narrative* 1: append. XXX, p. 422; Autobiography 5: pp. 1063-1064; Johnson Journal, July 12.

ing about forty seconds. It sounded to Pickering like a cannon
ball rolling on the floor overhead. The sound increased so
rapidly and approached so quickly that "before we could
spring to our feet the house was rolled and shaken as if seated
on a jumbling sea." The natives ran out of doors shrieking and
praying to the Holy Virgin for protection.[9]

Brackenridge became quite sick with ague and fever, but
kept at the task of overhauling and drying his and Pickering's
plants and seeds. Their collection filled several tin boxes when
packed for shipment on board the *Relief*.

At Callao, Pickering wrote an informative letter to his
cousin, Miss Mary O. Pickering. Since his first landing at
Valparaiso he had been "in a state of almost constant tur-
moil and excitement," and had visited places he never expected to see at this time. He had come to understand how
men could go to sea all their lives without seeing much of the
world.

Think of young Naval Officers on this station, being confined
in port for months, without liberty to set foot on shore!—and the
same happens more or less in the Merchant Service; leave to visit
the shore for a few hours at a time, being in general the most that
is granted.—Captains to be sure may have a little more liberty, but
their business will necessarily confine even them.—This is to some
extent unavoidable, and may be a good plan with those who cannot govern themselves—but there are minds that would learn, if
the opportunity were afforded—and in the Navy especially, through
which so much of the practical part of our Foreign relations is
carried on, it is all-important to have intelligent and well-informed
men. I am not aware that cultivating the understanding makes one
the less brave.

As a sort of passenger, his time was pretty much at his
own disposal, "the only trouble being to find out how long we
were going to stay a state secret of the Commander's—or often
a matter of uncertainty even with him."

Since coming to Peru, he had slept three nights at an
elevation of nearly 15,000 feet and at one of the farthest sources
of the Amazon "with a snow-storm almost every day (under the
Tropics) no fires and the thermometer near freezing point
every morning." The way of life of the country people made

---

9 Pickering Journal 1, May 16; Brackenridge Journal 1, May 16.

him think of the Dark Ages: the knife produced at the slightest affront; the mode of traveling, mostly by horseback and
everyone carrying his own provisions but the alcalde (mayor)
of each village required by law to give lodging and to provide
a cook at the cost of 12½ cents; the frequency of highway
robbery; women covering their faces; the language so much
like Latin; the forms of the Roman Catholic Religion, etc.

Lima was a walled city in decline and, in Pickering's
opinion, not comparable to Santiago "which far exceeds any
inland town we have at present in the United States; and
which, to confess my ignorance, I hardly remembered hearing
of before my visit." He had a word of praise for the market
women; if he were called upon "to personify the genius of
Independence, I think I would take the portrait of one of
these Market women, riding on a Donkey, as men do, with a
broad-brimmed hat, and a cigar in her mouth and sp-tt-g like
a Virginian."[10]

The Americans were intrigued by the Peruvian ladies'
costume called a "Saya y Manto." As described by Assistant
Surgeon Silas Holmes, who had a keen eye for feminine
beauty, it consisted of a black silk "mantos" covering the head
except for "one sparkling black eye" and the "saya" which,
made of "thick, closely pleated silk, of some bright color,
fitting to the form like a glove, hardly allowing room for a very
short step, sets off with no small taste the fine forms and
rounded outlines of youthful female beauty." There was no
lack of guides offering to show them the way to some "dam
fine gal." The most popular dances were characterized by Dr.
Holmes as "an exact and most disgusting imitation of the
generation act!"

The Doctor's chief concern, however, was with Benjamin
Holden, a marine on the *Peacock* who died of peritonitis and
whose grave became the Expedition's contribution to the
sailors' cemetery on San Lorenzo Island, and with a "boy,"
Jose de Silva, who came down with a mild case of smallpox and
had to be taken to the hospital and left in the care of Consul
Bartlett. This necessitated immediate arrangements to insure
that all on board the *Peacock* had been vaccinated.[11]

---

10 Pickering to M. O. Pickering, July 12, 1839, Pickering Papers.
11 Holmes Journal 1: pp. 115–121.

Before leaving Callao, command of the *Flying Fish* was given to Pinkney, one of the senior lieutenants, and he was ordered to take Pickering to view the ruins of the Temple of Pachacamac. An attempt was made to land through the surf with a raft made of two balsas, two India-rubber mattresses, and five oars. The raft, floated from the anchored schooner with Lieutenant Underwood its venturesome occupant, turned end over end. The watchers on the *Flying Fish* saw Underwood swim back to it just as a second roller hit and then, to their relief, saw him crawling up the beach. A boat crew then managed a successful landing and, by choosing the right moment, succeeded in passing over the rollers safely on the way back. Before long landings through the surf were to become routine. Pickering decided that a swimmer should discard clothing and life-preserver so that he might dive under the rollers in the manner of waterfowl.[12]

The Squadron reassembled at the Callao anchorage on July 4, this being one of the days of the year, along with New Year's, Christmas, and Washington's Birthday, which was always celebrated. On this occasion, in the traditional manner, the vessels dressed with flags, fired salutes, and all hands "splicing the main brace." The extra grog, however, was withheld from the *Peacock's* crew because some of them had started the day in an inebriated condition. By prearrangement a Bumboatman had floated a supply of liquor to them concealed inside a pumpkin.[13]

Drunkenness and desertion were major problems at this time. Seamen Blake and Lester, apprehended by Lieutenant Craven at Valparaiso, were brought to Callao by the *Falmouth* and charged with desertion under "very aggravated circumstances." And at Callao a detail of seamen and marine guards stole whiskey and became riotous while engaged in unloading liquor from the *Relief*. These were all court-martial offenses, usually resulting in heavy punishments, but since there was no time for a Court, Wilkes ordered twenty-four lashes, double the maximum under Navy Regulations, for all except Blake and Lester who got more, thirty-six and forty-one respectively. The Instructions under which the Expedition was operating

---

[12] Pickering Journal 1, June 29; *Narrative* 1: p. 279.
[13] Emmons Journal 1, July 4.

included the words: "you will necessarily be placed in situations that cannot be anticipated, and in which, sometimes your own judgment and discretion, at others, necessity, must be your guide."[14] These severe whippings, however, became at a later time the basis of an accusation against the Commander of inflicting illegal punishment. Five men chose this moment to desert and among them was Jacquinot, a Frenchman who had shipped at Rio as Peale's assistant.[15]

There was the usual uncertainty as to when the Squadron would sail and what it would do next.[16] One reason for delay was a reshuffle of officers among the vessels. Wilkes decided to send the slow-going *Relief* to Sydney and then directly home—to save money, as he informed the Secretary of the Navy, but also a means of getting rid of the sick and disaffected. Among the sick was the Fleet Surgeon himself, Dr. Sickles. Dr. Gilchrist, next in seniority, immediately claimed the pay and rating of Fleet Surgeon which Wilkes refused, considering him greatly overrated as a doctor and a ringleader of the "cabal," without "a spark of the 'con amore' feeling towards the Expedition." He would have shipped Gilchrist home had it not been difficult to replace surgeons. Guillou, the lowest ranking Assistant Surgeon, also sought promotion and made the mistake of writing directly to the Secretary instead of going through channels. Wilkes refused to notice his request, considering him "a novice in medicine but a very expert tailor, in which he employed a good deal of his time." The Commander liked particularly Dr. Fox, whom he made chief surgeon of the *Vincennes,* and Dr. Holmes because of his energy, cooperative spirit, and good humor. These two and Drs. Palmer and Whittle were all, in his opinion, knowledgeable in their profession, gentlemen, and useful assistants in all the departments of natural history.[17]

The transferral of certain discontented officers to the

---

14 *Narrative* **1**: p. xxviii.
15 *Narrative* **1**: pp. 232–233. Wilkes said their punishment was about a tenth of what a court-martial would have inflicted and that the crew would have considered twelve lashes no punishment at all considering their crimes. Taking "necessity" as his guide, he believed he saved "the results of the Expedition, the honour of the navy, and the glory of the country."
16 Eld to his Parents, July 12, Eld Papers.
17 Autobiography **5**: pp. 1075–1078.

Relief for return home and the consequent shifting about caused considerable excitement. Lieutenant Lee was already on his way home and Lieutenant Craven had been left behind at Valparaiso to wait for the *Sea Gull.* Craven believed that the Commander wanted to be rid of him. Wilkes, at a later time, said that "although this may have had some weight I sedulously confined it to my own breast" and, as for Craven himself, there was "apparently an unpleasantness in his doing duty under me." He made Lieutenant Carr First Lieutenant on the *Vincennes,* liking his readiness and quickness to learn, his correct notions of discipline—permitting no familiarities with other officers or crew yet always considerate and kind in manner—his modesty, his youthful appearance though manly voice, and his ability to carry out his duties without noise or confusion. Moreover, Carr set an example of neatness in his person and by attending to the needs of all the officers helped to make for good feeling and unity of purpose. The Commander's evident approval turned some of the officers against his "pet" as they called Carr.[18]

Wilkes considered suspending Lieutenant Long for failing to return to Orange Harbor but was dissuaded by Captain M'Keever who interested himself in Long's case. Anyway, there was no time for a Court of Inquiry and it would have been difficult to conduct since Long was outranked only by Wilkes and Hudson.[19]

Lieutenant Dale, though restored to duty, was now among the disaffected because the Commander, though concurring in the Court of Inquiry's findings, rebuked him publicly for his timidity, want of perseverance, and lack of skill which had resulted in delaying the Squadron. Learning that Dale had appealed to Washington and charged him with oppression and abuse of authority, Wilkes transferred him to the *Relief* for passage home.[20] Dale had been one of the first to be attached to the Expedition and in his enthusiasm had resisted inducements to change to something else. His feeling of having been treated with gross injustice and "ungenerous and cold-blooded

18 *Ibid.,* pp. 1069–1073; Couthouy Journal, Mar. 26.
19 Autobiography 5: pp. 1051–1052; Wilkes to Paulding, July 6, 11, 1839, Ex.Ex. Letters 1.
20 *Narrative* 1: append. XXXVII, p. 421; Johnson Journal, June 21.

persecution" was shared by several of his friends.[21]

The other passengers on the store ship bound for home were Lieutenant Claiborne, who had requested it, and Lieutenant Hartstein who had had an altercation with Ringgold and made a similar request.[22] To make room for these officers Lieutenants Case and Underwood were transferred to the *Vincennes* and the civilians Rich and Agate to the *Peacock*.

Requests by Passed Midshipman Gansevoort and Midshipman Clemsen for transfer to the *Falmouth* were granted as was that of Lieutenant De Haven of that vessel, for transfer to the Exploring Expedition. De Haven was made Sailing Master of the *Vincennes* in place of Acting Master North, who was sent to take Dale's place on the *Porpoise*. This caused some discontent since it prevented the promotion of Sinclair and others, in turn. Sinclair found himself designated merely as a "watch officer" on the *Porpoise*. Before long Wilkes came to feel that he had made a mistake in not sending Sinclair home along with the others and that De Haven's "education had been neglected and the requirements assigned him were entirely beyond his ability to perform."[23]

The *Relief* departed from Callao a few days after the other vessels of the Squadron. Her complement of sick sailors and disaffected officers was not sorry to be operating independently and Dale, for one, watched them go with a vehement "Thank God! They are off!"[24]

When two days out, Wilkes ordered the "coachwhip" at the mainmast of the *Vincennes* to be hauled down and the blue "Broad Pendant" hoisted in its place, signalizing the vessel as the Flagship and himself as Commander of a squadron, a responsibility ordinarily confided to an officer of the rank of Captain, the highest rank in the Navy. Gazing through his spyglass, Lieutenant Johnson could see the Commander's shoulder garnished with two lace straps but the Flagship was too far away for him to see the added buttons on his cuff.[25]

---

21 Dale, July 13.

22 Hartstein to Wilkes, May 23, 1839, Gratz Collection, Hist. Soc. Penna.

23 Autobiography 5: p. 1074; Sinclair Journal, June 15. De Haven was related to Captain M'Keever.

24 Dale Journal, July 13.

25 Johnson Journal, July 15; Whittle Journal, July 15. The uniform of a Captain included epaulettes ("straps") and four buttons on each cuff, four down each pocket fold, and four under each pocket flap.

In his Journal Wilkes mentioned the hoisting of the broad pennant as a distinguishing mark for the *Vincennes* and the assumption of a Captain's uniform as being "in obedience to order of the Secty of the Navy"—a reference to the Secretary's order of April 20, 1838, giving him command of the Squadron. He ordered Hudson to assume the uniform that his command entitled him to. His only other comment was that his reasons for not having done this before "are but known to myself."[26] His choice of this moment was apparently because of the small likelihood of encountering other American naval vessels from this point on.

---

[26] Wilkes Journal 1, July 15.

VII

Charting the Paumotu Group
of Coral Atolls

NOW THAT THE SQUADRON was headed into the Pacific it was
entering a comparatively little-known part of the world
where discoveries might be anticipated. But almost immediately this bright prospect was threatened. On the very day
that Captains Wilkes and Hudson put on epaulettes the *Peacock* ranged alongside the *Vincennes* with the news that John
Gitchell, a cooper who had shipped at Callao, had come down
with smallpox. Immediately elaborate precautions were taken
against the spread of this dread disease. Gitchell was scrubbed,
confined to a cot in a tent on the upper deck, his clothes and
bedding thrown overboard, and another check made to see
that all the *Peacock's* crew had been vaccinated. Fortune
favored the Squadron; there were no more cases and, in less
than three weeks, Gitchell, "only slightly disfigured," was
pronounced well.[1]

In general the men's health was pretty good during this
part of the cruise, except for some obstinate cases of dysentery,
diarrhea, and particularly venereal disease. However, there
were two deaths. Alexander Ogle, a Marine corporal on board
the *Vincennes,* died of "inflamation of the brain" following a
ten-days' illness, and George Reynolds, an ordinary seaman
on the *Porpoise,* succumbed after a prolonged bout with
pneumonia.[2]

During the burial service the Squadron half-masted their
flags, the crews mustered in clean clothes and uncovered as the
service was read at the gangway. Then, a sharp splash as the
marines fired three volleys and it was all over. Burials at sea

---

[1] Holmes Journal **1**, Aug. 3, 1839; Hudson Journal **1**, Aug. 5, 1839; Autobiography **5**: p. 1082.
[2] The cause of Ogle's death was not known but Wilkes decided against a post-
mortem fearing that it might create a prejudice among the men, Wilkes Journal
1, Aug. 12.

were no new experience for most of the sailors, as was indicated by the rapidity with which the dead seemed to be forgotten even though, as with these two men, they were highly
esteemed. But it shocked Assistant Surgeon Whittle, who
attended Ogle, to see how the sailors laughed and joked,
happening to be called to grog just as the marine breathed his
last. They were "as gay around the tub as if nothing had
happened." Whittle knew that they would risk their lives for,
or give their last cent to, a shipmate in distress, but three
hours after the burial they were dancing on the forecastle.
"Pray God," he said, "I may not die at Sea."[3]

During these weeks the weather was, on the whole,
pleasant and the winds moderate. It was not difficult to sail
in company, but to the Commander's annoyance the *Flying
Fish* had a way of getting off station and having to be recalled.
They averaged about 130 miles a day. The crews were kept
busy handling sails, scrubbing decks, manning boats, drilling
with small arms, and mustering weekly to hear readings of the
Articles of War and to attend Divine Service. During a calm
they enjoyed a sea bath, after donning life-preservers and
sending out a boat to scare away the sharks. The watch officers,
in addition to their nautical duties, kept hourly temperature
records, occasionally took dip readings, gauged the force and
direction of currents, and took deep-sea temperature readings.
In one area, where Arrowsmith's chart showed an island, they
spread out to sweep a path about thirty-five miles wide, but
saw nothing. During four August nights the officers and scientists observed the heavens and counted shooting stars without
seeing anything out of the ordinary.

The Commander reviewed his Instructions regarding relations with the natives and issued a general order admonish-
ing all hands to deal with them cautiously but kindly and
understandingly, reminding them that they were on a mission
of peace and should endeavor to leave behind a favorable impression "of our flag and countrymen." Copies of Admiral
Krusenstern's chart of the Low Archipelago or Paumotu
Group, which they were approaching, were distributed along

---

[3] Wilkes Journal 1, Aug. 12; Whittle Journal 1, Aug. 11; Johnson Journal, Aug.
23.

with directions for surveying islands in a minimum amount
of time.

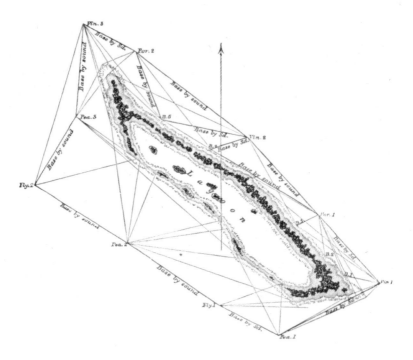

F<small>IG</small>. 9. Diagram illustrating method of charting Pacific Ocean islands by triangulation. *Narrative* 1: p. 431.

    The survey plan required the vessels to operate in pairs,
all four to start from the same point but the two pairs to work
their way around an island from opposite sides. The vessels
were to take stations offshore while their boats established
fixed points near or on shore. After hoisting preparatory signals, the vessels were to fire guns, in turn, so that their distances from each other and from the boats could be determined
by sound, the distances and angles from three points to be
recorded on "deck boards." While one vessel held its station
the other was to "leap frog" to a new one after which the
triangulation precedure would be repeated. The exact time of
each observation was to be determined by the altitude of the
sun. Series of soundings and sketches of headlands and shore-

lines were to be made and all of the data delivered to the
Vincennes before sunset; the plotting on charts to be done
on the flagship.[4]

No one was allowed to forget that Wilkes was in command. The numerous changes that had climaxed their stay at
Callao left a residue of uncertainty and discontent. The sig-
nificance of the appearance of the broad pennant was not lost
on the Squadron's members. In an attempt to discourage
familiarity among officers of different ranks, the Commander
sent a communication to the junior officers on the *Vincennes*
emphasizing that they had ample quarters of their own and
should not lounge about the quarters of the lieutenants, a habit
destructive of discipline, efficiency, and respect. The Ward
Room officers, for their part, protested vehemently saying that
the good feeling engendered by this familiarity was essential
for the success of the Expedition.[5]

On August 13 the coral island of Clermont de Tonnerre
was sighted, this being the easternmost of the Paumotu
("Cloud of Islands") Group. At first sight it resembled a fleet
at anchor, its trees seeming to bob up and down as the vessels
rose and fell, but soon its ten-mile-long white beach became
visible. The island rose to only twelve feet above sea level
and was surmounted by shrubs, cocoanut palms, and Pandanus
trees. It encircled a beautiful blue-tinted lagoon, some four
miles in width. Its abrupt rise from the ocean floor was indicated by a sounding of ninety fathoms as close as three hundred
feet from the reef and a sudden rise to seven fathoms half-way
in from that point. Clermont de Tonnerre was particularly
interesting because Admiral Krusenstern had mentioned that
the explorers Captains Beechey and Duperrey had given it
different locations. Wilkes verified the correctness of Duperrey's
observations.[6]

The island's survey was begun on the fourteenth, the
Vincennes and *Porpoise* working around the eastern side and
the *Peacock* and *Flying Fish* the western. Two boats from the

---

4 *Narrative* 1: append. XLI, pp. 429–432.
5 Autobiography 5: p. 993; Whittle Journal 1, Aug. 24.
6 Couthouy Journal, July 28; Pickering Journal 2, Aug. 13; *Narrative* 1: pp. 311,
315. Its location was twenty minutes of longitude West of that given by
Beechey.

Vincennes attempted a landing but found the surf too strong. Couthouy swam ashore and ran up the beach giving three cheers for the Expedition, believing himself the first white man to set foot upon the island; neither Beechey nor Duperrey had landed, the surf being too heavy. Blunt, Case, and Pickering also swam ashore with John Sac, a New Zealand sailor, who showed them how to reach a coral ridge standing up and then to ride the rest of the way with the next swell.[7]

Lieutenant Johnson's boat was tossed on a coral reef and had two holes torn in its bottom. He made no effort to approach some natives seen in the distance, his crew's carbines and pistols being soaking wet, but hastened to fasten a chafing mat over the holes and, by vigorous rowing and bailing, managed to get back to the *Porpoise* before the water rose above the thwarts.[8]

Landings through the surf soon became an everyday affair and a workable procedure was adopted consisting of dropping anchor just outside the reef as a means of steadying the boat until a favorable opportunity came to run in, the men jumping out in shallow water and pulling the boat onto the beach. They were soon able to land in a heavy surf, a ducking being accepted as a matter of course. Everyone wore an India rubber life-preserver even though it interfered with swimming.[9]

On the fifteenth, landings were attempted for the purpose of collecting botanical and zoological specimens and making contact with the natives. The latter stood on the beach brandishing spears and clubs, making it very evident that visitors were not welcome. Captain Vanderford, the pilot, who was familiar with this part of the world, John Sac, who spoke Tahitian, and Horatio Hale, the philologist, were now called upon to communicate with the natives and to convince them of the peaceful purposes of the Expedition—a difficult assignment.

Couthouy swam in and held out a mirror and some trinkets to the foremost native, who appeared to be a chief. When a few feet away, the chief lunged at him with his spear and Couthouy beat a hasty retreat. A second and, fortunately,

---

7 Couthouy Journal, Aug. 14; Pickering Journal 2, Aug. 14.
8 Johnson (incomplete letter, no date) , Johnson Letters.
9 Peale Journal 2, Sept. 7.

unsuccessful lunge by the chief was followed by a shower of rocks thrown at the scientist and at the nearest boat, in which John Sac stood attempting to converse. Wilkes suspected that neither the New Zealander nor the chief understood each other and that the only result of their conversation was to make both very angry. As he described the scene, John Sac became very excited,

his eyes shone fiercely, and his whole frame seemed agitated. Half naked as he was, his tattooing (that of a lesser New Zealand chief) conspicuous, he stood in the bow of the boat brandishing his boat-hook like a spear with the dexterity of a savage. It was difficult to recognize the sailor in the majestic-looking warrior before us. . . . John Sac was truly a savage, although he had imbibed some feelings of discipline, and was generally a well-disposed fellow.

Wilkes did not want the natives to think they were afraid to land and so, after firing some blanks without effect, he, Peale, and North fired charges of mustard seed which caused the natives to retreat into the bushes rubbing their legs. The officers and scientists then landed under orders not to go beyond the confines of the beach.[10]

This first and unhappy contact with natives caused considerable comment in the Squadron. Some thought the decision to fire had made permanent enemies for all white men landing there in the future and was contrary to the Commander's own orders regarding treatment of the natives. The scientists regretted that they were prevented from exploring the island. Subsequently it was learned that the natives' hostility was probably the result of having been fired upon wantonly by pearl fishermen.[11]

During the following month the Squadron surveyed or visited sixteen islands in this group.[12] Three were found to be

---

10 Autobiography 5: p. 1083; Couthouy Journal, Aug. 13. John Sac had been away from New Zealand for ten years. His face and body were tattooed and he had been exhibited in the United States. He entertained the crew by singing and dancing, had acquired civilized manners, ate cooked food and had some idea of God, Reynolds to Lydia, Aug. 30, 1838, Reynolds Letters.

11 *Narrative* 1: fn. p. 314; Eld Journal 1, Aug. 15; Johnson Journal, Aug. 15; Emmons Journal 1, Aug. 15; Whittle Journal 1, Aug. 14.

12 The names of the islands, in the order in which they were visited, were: Clermont de Tonnerre, Serle, Houden, Disappointment Islands (Wutoohee and Otooho), King, Raraka, Vincennes, Carlshoff, Wilson, Peacock, Dean, Rurick, Krustenstern, Aurora or Metia, and Tahiti.

on no chart or to be incorrectly located; one of these Wilkes
named "King," after the lookout who saw it first, and the
other two "Vincennes" and "Peacock," thus adding to a confusion of names since every discoverer added ones of his choice
to those of native origin.

August 19 was the first anniversary of their departure
from Norfolk and it set many to thinking about what had
been accomplished and speculating about what lay ahead.

Couthouy, still enthusiastic and well disposed towards
the Commander, hoped that the coming year might be more
productive and "stop the mouth of the croakers."[13] Lieutenant
Sinclair, recalling their departure "Full of ardour, unanimity
and ambition," felt that their ardor had died 'for want of encouragement and our unanimity censured as being improper"
and hoped that the next year might work as complete a change
for the better.[14] Lieutenant Reynolds had experienced a great
revulsion of feeling. Looking back at the changes that had
occurred he saw

officers dismissed, sent home with hopes blighted & prospects
blasted, for no offence, but to gratify the malignant propensities
of a *nameless man* but he will have to answer for it yet! his day of
reckoning must come—and if he expects to produce great results
from this cruise, he must not use the beings under him, as if they
were so many stones.[15]

Dr. Whittle expressed his change of feelings in even stronger
terms. Wilkes,

whom we all liked so much & who seemed disposed to behave so
honourably and even kindly toward us, has turned out to be one
of the most contemptable of petty tyrants—Instead of behaving
himself with that moderation and dignity which a man so much
elevated above his rank must do to return any of the respect & love
of his fellows, all his energies seem exerted to the exaltation of a
few favourites, the persecution of the rest of his officers the very
best & the most experienced in the Squadron, and some of them
he has taken the most contemptable means to get rid of. . . .[16]

---

13 Couthouy Journal, Aug. 19.
14 Sinclair Journal, Aug. 18.
15 Reynolds Journal 1, Aug. 18.
16 Whittle Journal 1, Aug. 19. He was much amused to have Wilkes, in great
   alarm, call for medical help having swallowed, by accident, a "Zest" powder instead of soda.

Peale regretted the time spent in places already well known to naturalists and now, having arrived where there was much that was new, was irritated at having so few opportunities for going ashore. He thought the English and French scientists had been more thorough in their investigations. At the island of Raraka he watched Captain Hudson and Lieutenant Emmons go ashore while he was left on the ship anchored close enough for him to see that the island "abounded in scientific riches, and boats were swinging idly at their davits, men were looking as to a paradise, but no, a survey is made, *nothing more* is requisite and time flees."[17]

There were, however, some bonanza days, such as that spent on uninhabited Houden or Dog Island, which abounded with bird and animal life and was free from "house flies," a pest on the islands that were peopled. The frigate birds, gannets, and sooty terns seen here were so tame they could be picked up off their nests. Wilkes joined the scientists on this island and saw "some droll sights" such as

crabs walking off with snakes, and both again seized by some stout bird and borne away.

The various snakes, the many coloured fish, the great eels, enormous and voracious sharks, shells, large molluscs, spiders, with the curious lepidopters, seemed to have quiet possession, their webs stretching in every direction, and occasioning us much annoyance; all gave a novelty to the scene, that highly interested and delighted us.

The problem that day was to get back into their boats laden with shells, birds, eggs, plants, etc., for their burdens and "gum elastic" life-preservers impeded their swimming.[18]

The scientists were concerned not only to get ashore to collect specimens but also to examine, draw, and preserve them on shipboard. Couthouy's first difference with the Commander was over his attempt to monopolize the services of Drayton to draw his specimens, a thing he couldn't do for himself. Shortly after leaving Callao, Wilkes decreed that, since there were only two artists, they should assist the scientists in turn. Couthouy could hardly object to this but had a new grievance, for when he deposited his growing coral collection on the gun

17 Peale Journal 2, Aug. 18, 27, 29.
18 *Narrative* 1: p. 318; Peale Journal 2, Aug. 20.

deck opposite the door of his cabin the smell became offensive
and he was ordered to put them in a rack on the spar deck
and to collect only single and the smallest possible specimens
of each species. He maintained that they could not be properly
examined in the noise and bustle of the spar deck and that
foreign scientists habitually made large-sized collections.
Wilkes reply was that he didn't give a damn what other expeditions did and that "he would take the responsibility of deciding all matters relative to *our* collections according to his
own views."[19]

A series of incidents took place which added to the Commander's reputation as a martinet and to the general discontent. He insisted that all boats return to the ships by sundown
to avoid the possibility of treacherous attack by the natives.
On one occasion he thought the scientists had delayed the
return of the *Peacock's* boats and sent a message to Captain
Hudson emphasizing the danger and implying that the scientists had interfered with the survey, "a service second to none
in the Expedition."[20] The reprimand was not directed at Captain Hudson, but he had been responsible for sending the
scientists ashore, believing the natives "civil and cosy," ready
to rub noses and to show the way to a water hole. It was resented by the officers as well as the scientists. Eld, usually even
tempered and well disposed towards Wilkes, expressed sarcastic wonderment that they were not all punished for "so
gross a neglect of duty and presuming to do such a thing
why did he not suspend or arrest them and send them to the
United States for trial?"[21]

A similar unpleasantness occurred when the *Flying Fish*
returned the scientists to the *Vincennes* three-quarters of an
hour after sunset and Lieutenant Pinkney received a reprimand delivered through the trumpet so that all could hear.
The next day Pinkney sent a written request that he never
again be subjected to so improper and public a reprimand
to which he received a verbal reply to the effect that the Commander would reprove him in whatever manner or place he

19 *Narrative* 1: append. XLI, p. 427; Couthouy Journal, Aug. 31.
20 *Narrative* 1: append. XLI, p. 432.
21 Peale Journal 2, Emmons Journal 1 and Hudson Journal 1, all Aug. 25; Eld
   Journal 1, Aug. 26.

pleased. The incident was not forgotten and at a later date became the basis for one of Pinkney's formal charges against his superior.[22]

The tension built up in this way was heightened by the exacting and unending character of survey duty, by the often debilitating effect of the weather, and by the uncertainty which characterized their relations with the natives. Navigating in company among these coral islands was made difficult by shifting winds and dark nights which resulted, on at least two occasions, in situations which added more fuel to the fires of discontent.

At about 3 A.M., on the night of August 15, the Squadron was sailing on and off Serle Island, which was to be surveyed in the morning. Lieutenant Underwood was Officer of the Deck on the *Vincennes* and Sinclair on the *Porpoise*. Underwood, thinking that the flagship had the right of way, began to wear around on the "larboard" tack without warning the nearby brig. The latter was on the starboard tack, which was generally accepted as having the right of way (a vessel on the larboard tack to give way "without regard to rank—Even a man of war to a merchant ship"). They approached each other on collision course and, at the last minute, both came up into the wind, but not soon enough to prevent the jib and flying jib booms of the *Porpoise* from being caught between the main and mizzen rigging of the *Vincennes*, staving her starboard quarter boat and carrying away the *Porpoise's* jib boom and springing her cathead.

Wilkes immediately suspended both officers until he could find out the facts on which they could both agree. According to Sinclair's account,

In the morning Capt. Wilkes discussed the cause of this accident in a most delicate manner thro the speaker Trumpet accusing me & all the watch of having been asleep—If I was thus negligent of my duty—If I was thus guilty of an offense the most outrageous of which any officer can be accused an offense to which the laws of the country award death . . . I ought to have been tried—not thus publicly insulted. . . .

---

22 Wilkes' Court-Martial Aug. 23–24, 1842.

He requested a legal trial which Ringgold refused to forward, saying he had already reported on the matter and was sure that justice would be done.

The following day was spent repairing the two vessels and recovering the boat which, however, proved to be beyond repair and had to be broken up. They drifted about eight miles from Serle Island and the day was lost as far as surveying or scientific work was concerned. Three days later the two officers were restored to duty, the accident being laid to ignorance and inexperience. Sinclair, however, persisted in his demand for a trial and had a stormy interview with the Commander during which he was accused of impudence and threatened with disrating.[23]

A few days later the *Vincennes* nearly ran over the *Flying Fish*. The schooner, ordered to take the scientists from the flagship to shore, luffed up alongside the larger vessel and her speed was such that she went ahead and across the *Vincennes'* bow. Wilkes ordered all sails aback which stopped the ship's way so that the schooner was able to get by with her masts about two feet away from the ship's flying jib boom. He ordered Pinkney three times to heave-to which seemed to rattle Pinkney so much that, when he did heave-to, it was under the ship's bow. The Commander stamped excitedly and shouted from the forecastle, "What do you mean, what do you mean, Sir?" The reply from the schooner was, "I have hove-to in obedience to your orders," and the shouted response from the flagship, "God damn it, Sir. I did not order you to heave under my bow." It was a miraculous escape and confirmed Wilkes' lack of confidence in Lieutenant Pinkney's nautical knowledge and skill.

Pinkney was one of Commodore Jones' selections and was commanding the *Flying Fish* only because of seniority and because Captain Hudson didn't want him as First Lieutenant on the *Peacock*. Wilkes characterized him as a lazy, "stick," that is, "one of those with an exterior of manly beauty pleasing manners and of prepossessing address" and "possessed of very considerable vanity and conceit though little to found it on." This was not a convenient time to make a change of com-

---

23 Journals of Underwood, Johnson, and Wilkes 1, all Aug. 17; Sinclair Journal, Aug. 17, 20, 22–24.

mand and the exposure of his incompetence seemed to be
sufficient punishment but the public reprimand stuck in Pinkney's memory, as it did with the other officers who felt the
lash of the Commander's tongue.[24]

Dealing with the natives was a particularly ticklish matter,
involving an effort to win their good will while remaining
constantly on guard against treachery. The language barrier
added to the difficulty of understanding people in a primitive
stage of development. In general the natives became more
friendly and communication with them easier as they came
closer to Tahiti, for the language of that island was known
to natives living nearby and, also, to some members of the
Expedition. The natives of the nearby islands were also more
used to meeting ships and dealing with traders which meant
that they would accept trinkets as presents but only calico,
tobacco, or whiskey in exchange for their own products.

An effort was made to collect information as to the
natives' physical characteristics and way of life. Pickering, in
particular, was attempting to distinguish racial differences and
Hale was looking for indications of relationships as revealed
by speech. As a clue to the reason for native habitations on
some islands and not on others, Captain Vanderford suggested
that "wherever you find a Cocoa Palm you will find an Indian." Some thought the natives were related to the American
Indians, but Pickering, after a close look at some of them,
decided they must be of Malay origin because of their dark
brown color, beards, broad flat noses, and lack of thick lips.[25]

Native customs and the kind of reception accorded the
Squadron varied from island to island. The hostility experienced at Clermont de Tonnerre was exceptional, although at
the Disappointment Islands landing parties were shouldered
back to their boats when they attempted to go beyond the
beach and in such a forceful manner that Pickering cut his
legs on the coral and lost his spectacles. However, they wanted
to trade and came out in canoes for that purpose. They paid
Hale for a pair of scissors by singing in a manner that Eld
described as harsh but more pleasing than the ordinary chant

---

[24] Wilkes' Court-Martial, Aug. 23, 1842; Autobiography 5: pp. 1079-1080, 1102–
1105.
[25] Pickering Journal 2, Aug. 15, 16, 26; Eld Journal 1, Aug. 24.

in a Roman Catholic Church. When Eld asked where their
women were, they burst out laughing as if they had found
out his intentions and offered the officers their wives if they
would follow them into the brush.[26]

At Raraka Island the Squadron came upon a large group
who had come in two big twenty-five-foot-long double canoes,
each capable of carrying from twenty to thirty people. They
were on a fishing voyage from Chain Island, a kind of depend-
ency of Tahiti and the influence of Tahitian civilization was
immediately evident in their friendliness and neat appearance.
The men had trimmed their beards and the children were so
disciplined that upon receiving presents they handed them
over to their parents. They were accompanied by native missionaries. It was felt that the crew of any ship wrecked where
these people lived would be safe and that "had the Missionaries done nothing more among these islands, they would deserve the thanks of the Civilized World."[27]

The missionaries wore cotton shirts, one had a straw hat
and the wife of another wore a blue figured gown, but the
other women and children were naked except for a piece of
cotton cloth or native tapa around the loins. Eld noticed the
pretty smiling faces and white teeth of some of the girls, "but
their intolerable accompaniment of the cocoanut oil rendered
it almost impossible to come near them." However, he gave
them some ribbons and a large old-fashioned button and was
soon surrounded by a crowd. Hale sat under a cocoanut tree
with three or four intelligent young girls who taught him the
names of things and when he spoke correctly they rewarded
him with a hearty hug.[28]

Their chief, whose hand had been bitten off by a shark
four months before, was induced to come on board the *Vincennes* where Agate drew his portrait. Before long he was
lolling on a rug with his back against an ottoman, seeming to
enjoy two enormous tobacco quids which, after a while, he
took out of his mouth and laid on the carpet beside him and
went to sleep. A ram and two yews acquired in Peru were given

26 Eld Journal 1, Aug. 24–25; Emmons Journal 1, Aug. 25; Pickering Journal 2
and Brackenridge Journal 1, both Aug. 26.
27 Pickering Journal 2, Aug. 30–31; Brackenridge Journal 1, Aug. 30–31.
28 Eld Journal 1, Aug. 30.

to these islanders with instructions not to harm them until they had increased in number.[29]

The last island before Tahiti was Metia or Aurora Island, which looked like the first "real" island, being high and solid —a relief from the low coral lagoon-centered ones. It rose abruptly to a kind of tableland about 250 feet high, was covered with woods and inhabited by about three hundred people who were friendly and enjoyed "Tahitian Civilization" —acknowledging the Queen's authority and appearing to be as licentious as her subjects were reputed to be. The women of all ages unhesitatingly offered themselves asking in return no more than a half-fathom of calico or a hatchet. The missionary influence was something of a puzzle. Eld found that one of the first things the natives asked was whether they were missionaries and, if they said "No," they were considered of no consequence. They felt obliged, therefore, to say that they were "in order to be looked upon with any kind of respect or attention."[30]

The attractions of Aurora Island were too much for two seamen who had joined the Squadron at Rio and took this opportunity to desert. They were the second loss from Emmons' boat crew; at Wilson Island a seaman, formerly engaged in the pearl-fishing trade and able to speak Tahitian, had also deserted. Emmons couldn't understand how anyone could be so lacking in common sense and forethought as to leave a comfortable ship "where little duty is required of them and every indulgence that could be reasonably asked granted" to put themselves completely at the mercy of half-civilized savages and "become beggars for their daily subsistence."[31]

On September 10 the *Vincennes* sighted Tahiti, a beautiful conical mountain clothed in luxuriant foliage. As they approached, they enjoyed a rare sight—a rainbow "embracing a large part of the island, the colours of which were distinct and beautiful beyond description and made the scene almost look like fairy land." They anchored in Matavai Bay where Captain Cook had once observed the transit of Venus. To the

---

[29] *Narrative* 1: pp. 328–330; Hudson Journal 1, Aug. 30; Wilkes Journal 1, Aug. 31.

[30] Eld Journal 1, Sept. 9.

[31] Emmons Journal 1, Sept. 10.

Commander of this latter-day expedition, "The stillness of the harbour with nothing to disturb its placid surface was refreshing as the air was with the fragrance of flowers on shore."[32]

The *Peacock*, having taken a less direct route, arrived on the following day. As she approached, the island came into plain sight, a faint ghostly mountain outline among the clouds high above the horizon, before either of her lookouts saw it, so accustomed were they to seeing only low coral islands.[33]

---

[32] Autobiography 5: p. 1085.
[33] Pickering Journal 2, Sept. 10; Emmons Journal 1, Sept. 11.

VIII
Tahiti

"E NGLISH JIM," the pilot who brought the *Vincennes* into
Matavai Bay, was an English-speaking native who wore a
white suit, black shoes, and a blue uniform cap with a gold
band but who seemed less urbane when he remarked that he
knew the Squadron was about to arrive because it had thun-
dered a few days before.

As soon as the vessels anchored they were surrounded by
canoes of all shapes and sizes, whose occupants made "a prodigious clamor." Wilkes said only chiefs could come on board
and, when all claimed that title, limited the visitors to "great"
chiefs. It became apparent that the chiefs' interest was not in
ceremonial greeting but in the solicitation of dirty linen for
their wives to wash with soap to be provided by their custom-
ers.[1]

To forestall the solicitation of business of another kind
by native women, Wilkes issued an order that no natives
would be allowed on any of the vessels unless the white flag
was at the mizzen and never before 7 A.M., or later than a
half-hour before sunset.

Another order and one which caused a good deal of discontent among the officers required all, except as permitted
by their captains, to be on board ship by sundown instead
of the usual 10 P.M. when in port. In addition, the medical
officers were required to attend constantly to the needs of
their individual ship instead of having only one medical officer
"afloat" with the Squadron in port.[2]

Some of the officers were further aggrieved by the Commander's insistence that the first oranges, bananas, and other
fruits brought to the ships should be given to the men. They
considered this an arbitrary act but he looked upon "this
monopolizing by officers as unwarrantable," for the ship's company needed fresh food the most. No fruit had been obtainable

---

1 *Narrative* 2: p. 4; Eld Journal 1, Sept. 12, 1839.
2 *Narrative* 2: append. I, pp. 419–420; Johnson Journal, Sept. 15.

97

in the coral islands and the crews now devoured it in "unaccountable quantities."[3]

The day after their arrival was Saturday, but it was considered Sunday at Tahiti because the London Missionary Society's representatives had come by way of the Cape of Good Hope and took no account of the International Date Line. The Squadron, therefore, celebrated Sunday on the following day, all officers and men not required on board ship being ordered to attend the Mission Church where Chaplain Elliott and the Rev. Mr. Pratt conducted the service. Although the great majority of the Squadron's members were Protestants and never objected to the service on board ship, some of the officers objected to being ordered to attend the service of a church that was not their own. Wilkes considered the worship of God under any sect whatever as part of an officer's duty, ignored their protests and observed that, after some hesitation, they all attended.[4]

Officers and men were soon busy with the usual tasks attendant upon arrival in port after a prolonged cruise, such as ceremonial visits, repairs to rigging, cleaning, painting, watering, and wooding.

The Squadron's vessels did not stay at Tahiti for the same length of time. The *Porpoise* departed first under orders to complete the survey of Dean's and Krustenstern's Islands, some parts of which she had passed by at night, and to rejoin the Squadron at Rose Island easternmost of the Navigator Group. The other vessels moved on to the main anchorage at Papeete where the reef afforded better protection from the strong westerly winds. On September 25 the *Vincennes* departed for Eimeo while the *Peacock* stayed on with the schooner, which required extensive repairs, until October 10.

Wear and tear on the *Flying Fish* was particularly heavy and she had sprung her mainmast and broken a number of bolts on her kelson. Her crew was transferred to the *Peacock* whose carpenters, mechanics, and sailors did the repair work under Captain Hudson's supervision. They cut two feet off the heel of the mainmast so as to bring the sprung part below

---

3 Autobiography 5: p. 1086; Eld Journal 1, Sept. 12.
4 Autobiography 5: pp. 1087–1088. The London Missionary Society was Independent or Congregationalist in origin.

deck, made a new step and fished and banded the mast. After that she was hove down, her kelson bolted, and her copper bottom repaired where needed. Various other repairs were made to her hull, rigging, and sails.[5]

After a hurried inspection of the *Flying Fish* Wilkes had reprimanded Pinkney and also Sinclair, who had just been made her First Lieutenant, for her filthy condition. Pinkney replied by asking to be relieved of his command as the only means of securing himself from the Commander's personal insults. He said that the caulkers were responsible for the mess on deck and that no attention had been paid to his request for an arms chest with the result that the muskets and pistols could not be kept in condition for use. This incident became an additional basis for charges and counter-charges at the end of the cruise.[6]

The officers surveyed the harbors of Matavai, Papaoa, Toanoa, and Papeete, and the scientists explored the interior of the island. Lieutenant Emmons was put in charge of the inland expedition which included Peale, Pickering, Brackenridge, Couthouy, Dana, Dr. Guillou, Sergeant Stearns of the Marines, two sailors, an interpreter, and four native guides. It proved to be a very strenuous excursion.

At the beginning the selection of the four guides out of some fifty applicants was a cause of confusion. About fifteen men, women, and children escorted them as far as their first encampment and partook of their dinner. They also provided some entertainment when crossing a stream, the girls taking off everything except the maro and, holding their clothes out of water in one hand, swimming easily and gracefully to the other side while the boys swam head first down a rapids, disappearing, at intervals, in the foam. The pig dinner followed by cigars and bed was a pleasant beginning, but was spoiled for Emmons when the interpreter awakened him to say that their guests had eaten all their food, making it necessary to send the native carriers back to purchase another pig and some taro.

The expedition had two objectives: one was to measure the height of Mount Orohena, the highest on the island, and

5 Hudson Journal 1: p. 301.

6 Court-Martial record, Aug. 8–10, 1842; Sinclair Journal, Sept. 15, 23, 28, and Oct. 14.

the other to measure the size and depth of Lake Waiherea. Temperatures were to be taken at different heights, in the sun and shade, and each day at three and nine, both morning and afternoon.[7] The party divided on the second day, with Emmons, Peale, Guillou, and two guides going to the lake and the others climbing the mountain. The lake's altitude was estimated to be 3,000 feet, its length a half mile and its width a third of a mile. Crossing it on a raft made of banana stems they found it was 96 feet deep at the center. It had no visible outlet and rose 5 feet during an all-night rain. The mountain party found it too precipitous to climb to the top, which they estimated to be 6,000 feet above sea level.

The two parties came together on the third day and spent that night lying in one or two inches of water because of intermittent rain and leaky tents. Breaking camp at dawn they reached the island's south shore in about four hours and in an exhausted and footsore condition. Here they could dry their clothes but, finding no horses, had to struggle along the beach on foot. The distance around the rim of the island back to Papeete was forty-five miles. Emmons, Peale, and Guillou met a missionary named Orsmond and became passengers in his whaleboat rowed by four stocky natives. It was no joy ride, however, being seated in a boat without an awning inside the reef on the side of the island known as the "frying pan" because of the merciless sun and lack of wind. In this manner the party arrived back in the five days allotted them.[8]

After a three-day rest, Pickering and Couthouy made another attempt to climb Orohena by a different route, along a steep, precipitous ridge. They got only half-way when it became necessary to descend 2,000 feet to find a place to camp for the night, leaving too little time for another try. Dana, being attached to the *Peacock*, had time to organize a party which climbed Mount Aorai, the second highest peak. Near the top they had to crawl on their hands and knees along a narrow ridge and, at the top, had hardly room to turn around. But the day was clear, the view magnificent, and Dana was able to

---

7 Their equipment included: a pocket sextant, an artificial horizon, a pocket azimuth, a sympiesometer, notebook, two thermometers, an hygrometer, a sounding line, guns and ammunition, apparatus for striking fire, and presents for the natives.

8 Emmons Journal 1, Sept. 13, 16, 18; Pickering Journal 2, Sept. 14–19.

scotch forever the rumor that corals and "screw-shells" were
to be found there. It also helped him to settle in his mind the
theory of the origin of coral islands from the submergence of
mountain ranges.[9]

The Squadron's relations with the Queen's Government
involved dealings with the missionaries who had a great deal
of political influence. Consul Blackler gave Wilkes a list of
grievances which had to do mainly with heavy fines imposed
upon American seamen and with the Government's failure to
apprehend deserters. A full-dress meeting was held at Papeete
between the Squadron's officers and the chiefs, the Queen being on another island. The Rev. Mr. Pritchard, who was both
acting British Consul and the Queen's principal adviser, presided. The chiefs promised better cooperation in the future
and were rewarded with a luncheon on board the *Vincennes*.
Presents such as calico, shawls, shoes, musical boxes, accordians,
jew's-harps, etc., were distributed and helped to engender good
feeling.

Wilkes could appreciate some of the Government's difficulties in dealing with foreigners. A law prohibited the sale of
liquor, but Hudson found that some of his men were getting
beastly drunk on gin being sold for $3.00 per jug. The native
magistrates told him that the only possible source was Consul
Blackler who had imported seventy cases for the use, he
said, of the Squadron. He had been doing a wholesale business
under the protection of the American flag. Blackler, at first,
denied the accusation, but when several dozen jugs of gin
were found under his bed he explained that since so few
whalers came to the island this was the only way he could
make a living. He was also said to have tried to induce the
American whaler captains to come by insisting upon severe
punishments for minor offenses by their seamen. Wilkes made
an official request for the removal of Blackler from office, but
the Consul died within a few years, before any action was
taken.[10]

9 *Narrative* 2: pp. 51–53; J. E. Hoffmeister, "James Dwight Dana's Studies of
  Volcanoes, and of Coral Islands," *Proc. Amer. Philos. Soc.* 82, 5 (1940) : p. 725.
10 Autobiography 5: pp. 1092–1094; Hudson Journal 1: pp. 293–294. It was reported that the American whaler *Swift*, Capt. Tobey, from New Bedford, had
  been a "Floating Grog Shop" for a time, selling 30 barrels of whiskey in defiance of the law, at a profit of $2,000.

The generally peaceable and friendly character of the natives made for good relations with them. Some of the officers were in closer contact than others, especially Surgeons Gilchrist and Holmes, who set up a temporary hospital at Point Venus, Matavai Bay, and Eld, who tended the "Obervatory" set up at the same place. The Hospital consisted of two huts or sheds of Pandanus thatch and a small cabin, said to have been built by Captain Bligh. The Observatory was in the portable house and the officers lived in two tents. During the encampment's two weeks' existence it was constantly surrounded by natives, "inquisitive and curious but always respectful." They occupied themselves eating, drinking, and sleeping. Though continually begging, they were always cheerful and gay and never angry when something was refused them.[11]

Eld was kept busy observing the transits of heavenly bodies, measuring dip intensities, variations, tidal changes, etc., some recording having to be done every hour. This was very confining work but for him "the transition from the irksome and monotonous life on shipboard to this enchanting spot we were at was delicious." The climate was delightful, there was plenty of fruit, in fact this little community drank 150 cocoanuts every day, and, at any time of day or night, there were girls. They dressed in single robes with their hair, shiny black with cocoanut oil, streaming down their backs, happily singing and telling tales. Their manners were engaging and they spoke broken English in soft voices. It was not strange that sailors were tempted to stay on at Tahiti, settle down with a native family and live in idleness. The girls made no attempt to disguise their carnal connections. Right after Wilkes and Hudson had given presents to school children who had recited from the Bible and joined in prayer, the girls went out to their men in the bushes.

The natives never attempted to steal anything, though at Point Venus they had many opportunities as only the scientific instruments were guarded by marines. One of their favorite pastimes was singing, which they frequently kept up until late at night. Purser Speiden, a religious man, taught

11 Holmes Journal 1, Sept. 12; Eld Journal 1, Sept. 13.

them several new hymns and seldom had to repeat them more
than once. They had learned sailors' songs from the whalers,
but delighted especially in their own songs, though the missionaries imposed fines in an attempt to discourage the singing
of native songs and dancing which usually built up to a kind
of frenzy, characterized by lascivious motions of the body.

Eld stayed on a few days after the instruments were
taken back on board the *Vincennes* to finish the survey of
Matavai Bay and then walked the nine miles to Papeete where
he found Nutt's Hotel a center of activity. During a two-day
stay there he met Ninito and Taii, the young daughters of
the Queen who had lunched on board the flagship. Taii, the
elder and next in succession to the throne, was about seventeen and described by Pickering as "a good-natured laughing
girl, with a good deal of propriety and very Republican in
practice." They looked awkward in European clothes which
they wore in a slovenly manner. Being fat girls and wearing
stays, to which they were not accustomed, they looked nearly
as broad as they were tall. They kept losing their shoes and
tripping on their stockings which fell about their heels.

In the evening when Eld and several others visited the
princesses and other members of the royal family they were
dressed in their native gowns of light-colored calico, had jas-
mine in their hair, and bare feet. As a result "they were not
only easy and graceful in their manners but beautiful girls."
It was an enjoyable evening passed mostly in singing and enlivened by Couthouy who demonstrated his ability to play
the jew's-harp and hummed a base accompaniment while the
girls sang "God Save the Queen" in Tahitian.[12]

At this time the young king-consort arrived at Papeete
in a small schooner which fired a confused salute from a rusty
six-pounder to which nobody paid much attention. It also
happened that the Rev. Mr. Pritchard came to Nutt's Hotel
in his capacity of pearl auctioneer and Eld bought two parcels
for $5.00 but had the misfortune to lose one of them on the
following day.

In the interest of the science of anthropology Eld and

---

12 Eld Journal 1, Sept. 13; Couthouy Journal, Sept. 30; Pickering Journal 2, Sept.
24; Reynolds Journal 1: p. 223.

Dr. Fox went about the village taking peoples' measurements. Individuals were persuaded to submit to being measured after receiving presents of tobacco or twenty-five cents and the promise that they would be mentioned "in the Book, so great a love do we all have even the savage for being perpetuated in the far famed black & white." Their research entailed some laughable scenes, particularly with

the Girls who were a little timid in being handled in so wholesale a manner & I was much pleased at the modesty . . . which displayed itself most unaffectedly & would have been an ornament to a civilized female. Many of the forms of both sexes were perfect symetry & would serve as models for an Apolo or a Venus.[13]

In "the Book" Wilkes expressed a different opinion saying that he did not see a single woman that he could call handsome. They had

a soft sleepiness about the eyes, which may be fascinating to some, but I should rather ascribe the celebrity their charms have attained among navigators, to their cheerfulness and gaiety. Their figures are bad, and the greater part of them are parrot-toed. They are exceedingly prone to prattling, or may rather be said to have a tattling disposition, for they cannot keep even their own secrets.[14]

On the whole, the Expedition's members had a high opinion of the Tahitians and recognized that foreigners were the principal cause of their troubles. Emmons contrasted the action of some drunken marines who beat up the Master's Mate and the Captain's Steward with the "uniform peaceable & good natured conduct of these people whom I have never yet seen engaged in any quarrel whatever." The liquor problem, their money consciousness and promiscuity could, in large part, be traced to the influence of unscrupulous foreigners. Couthouy thought the government's policy of imposing a light fine of $5.00 or ten yards of tapa for licentiousness compared with an $18.00 fine for drunkenness and the required restitution of ten times the value of any stolen article had much to do with determining native morals. He thought their promiscuity was explained, basically, by the genial cli-

13 Eld entered all of this account under date of Sept. 13 although he stayed ashore from that date until the first week in October.
14 *Narrative* 2: p. 22.

mate, the early physical development of the children, especially the girls, and the comparatively slow development of their intellect. Pickering, while praising the missionaries for teaching the people to read and write, blamed them for giving them nothing but translations of the Bible and Prayer Book to read. He thought the natives should not be judged by American rules and social institutions, and admired their plain-spokenness, calling things by their right names, their conversation characterized by broadness without "the *refinement* of indecent *ideas.*" As to the custom of tattooing, he noticed that many of his companions "could not rest till they had various figures delineated on their skin." He thought some of the young women were pretty and most of the men not handsome but bigger than Europeans, and this explained for him the left-handed compliment of a woman at Raraka who said "we were good-looking men for women."[15]

Although the Tahitians led a healthy if somewhat indolent life, they were not free from serious illnesses, such as syphilis and elephantiasis, which were quite prevalent. There was no doctor on the island and the missionaries often prescribed mercury treatments for venereal disease which did more harm than good. While the Squadron was there its surgeons were kept quite busy attending to the illnesses of foreigners living on the island.[16]

As a kind of final good-will offering, a few days before their departure the sailors of the *Peacock* gave an entertainment performing Schiller's play, *The Robber,* and a farce entitled, *The Village Lawyer,* plays which they had rehearsed during the long evenings while crossing the Pacific. They interspersed them with songs, such as "Jim Crow," "Rag-et-t-o," and "On the Canoe," accompanied by two drums and two fiddles. It was known that the missionaries disapproved of such amusements, but they didn't interfere. The house was full to overflowing, the foreigners and their ladies and the officers occupying the front rows. No missionaries or chiefs attended. The audience was enthusiastic and, as Emmons said,

---

15 Pickering Journal 2, Sept. 10, 21; Emmons Journal 1, Sept. 29; Couthouy Journal, Sept. 17.

16 *Narrative* 2: p. 49; Gilchrist, Sept. 28, 29; Pickering Journal 2, Sept. 10; Emmons Journal 1, Oct. 5; Holmes Journal 1: p. 179.

"The Natives were rather noisy & evidently amused, they appeared to relish the songs more than the play & the instrumental music more than all—the *final* was quite satisfactory & I presume will be remembered by these people.[17]

Altogether the Tahitian visit was a pleasant experience. It was to be expected that there would be attempts at desertion, for a life of idleness had a special appeal. Pickering marveled at the Tahitians' ability to provide for themselves from Nature's bounty. A native stripped of everything he possessed in the morning would, by night, have clothed himself from the lace of the cocoanut tree, put a garland on his head, built a house of wild bananas using the thongs and cordage from the bark of the Poorow tree, and have plaited a basket from cocoanut leaves, made a mat to sleep on, made bowls from cocoanut shells, tumblers from the joints of large bamboo, an umbrella from a banana leaf, built a fire, and have gathered enough provisions for a week to come. He concluded that it was "not the superiority of our National faculties, whether Intellectual or Physical, that is giving *our* race the advantage in some parts of the World, but our *System* of Civilization."[18]

Much as the sailors might like to desert, it was not easy to do. The natives usually captured them and brought them back; the sailors to receive lashes and their captors rewards: $8.00 per deserter, if on the same side of the island as the ship, and $10.00, if on the far side. The natives were eager to earn such pay for the average wage was $2.00 to $4.00 per month, and also they enjoyed the excitement of the chase.[19]

When the *Vincennes* anchored at Eimeo, the next island, five members of her crew made a spectacular attempt to desert. Eimeo is fifteen miles west of Tahiti and, like it, mountainous but somewhat smaller and wilder. It has a superior harbor except that, like Matavai Bay, it is open to westerly gales. Lofty hills mark three sides of the harbor and a reef stretches nearly across its entrance. The deserters rowed ashore in the dingy at night. In order to hasten matters, a reward of $30.00 per deserter was offered. On the morning of the fol-

---

17 Emmons Journal 1, Oct. 31.
18 Holmes Journal 1, Sept. 12; Pickering Journal 2, Sept. 23.
19 Emmons Journal 1, Oct. 2.

lowing day the fleeing sailors were seen climbing along the narrow and precipitous edge of a mountain ridge, with a party of natives in hot pursuit. As Dr. Whittle described the scene it was

plainly visible from the ship and all hands seemed to enjoy it very much. Sailors are much like the ancient Spartans in this respect; if they do a thing which is not exactly right, cunningly and without detection, they are thought all the better for it by their shipmates, but if they are found out and punished they are not pitied in the least.

The deserters were soon caught, offering only slight resistance as they realized that, if they pushed their captors over the edge, they would probably go with them. They also knew that the natives would not hesitate to tie their hands to their feet and carry them back slung over a pole. They duly received their twelve lashes apiece and were made to hand the rewards to their captors.[20]

Eimeo did not detain the *Vincennes* for long, its prospects for trade being slight. Sailing westward, the *Vincennes* passed more of these mostly mountainous Society Islands. They could tell from about a mile away whether an island was inhabited for, if not, a great number of birds were in evidence. Wilkes decided that, from the commercial point of view, the Paumotu Group and the Society Islands were too far off the beaten track and had too few exports to be of importance to Americans. He did not take sides in the rivalry between the English Protestant missionaries and the French Catholic interests. A few years later (1844) these islands became a French protectorate when warships were sent to Tahiti in support of Catholic missionary activity.[21]

---

[20] *Narrative* 2: p. 58; Whittle Journal 1, Sept. 25.
[21] *Narrative* 2: pp. 19, 35, 57; Autobiography 5: p. 1095; Whittle Journal 1, Sept. 30.

IX

The Samoan Islands

IT HAD BEEN EXPECTED that the Squadron would reach the Navigators' group (Samoan Islands)[1] in the spring of 1839 but it was October 7 when the *Vincennes* met with the *Porpoise* off Rose Island. This was the easternmost of this group of seven principal islands which extended from east to west in the following order: Rose, Manua, Oloosinga, Ofoo, Tutuila, Upolu, and Savaii. With the exception of very small Oloosinga and Ofoo, they increase in size when taken in that order. Wilkes planned to make observations and surveys from the *Vincennes* at Tutuila, the central island, and ordered the *Peacock* and *Flying Fish* to survey Upolu and the *Porpoise* Savaii.

Rose Island was uninhabited, but at the next island, Manua, they found natives and three English deserters who, wearing as little as the natives, came out in a canoe to beg passage. Wilkes decided they were convicts and "damned rascals" and would have none of them.[2]

At Oloosinga the Commander tried to make friends with the chief but refused to drink his ava, having seen it made by women chewing palm lilies which they spat into bowls of water which was then strained through leaves. He retreated to his boat when the natives became too familiar, borrowing his handkerchief and trying on his hat. After fish hooks were presented to the chief, the boat crew pushed the crowd aside and a hasty departure was achieved.

At Tutuila the *Porpoise* took on board Lieutenant Alden and Dr. Pickering and went on his way to Savaii while the *Vincennes* beat her way through the narrow entrance into the nearly land-locked harbor of Pago Pago. Sailing ships usually entered easily, for the prevailing wind blew into the harbor,

---

1 Pickering said that the "Navigator Islands" were called by the natives "Samoa —which name may very probably prevail hereafter." Pickering Journal 2, Oct. 8, 1839.
2 Whittle Journal 1 and Johnson Journal, Oct. 9.

but on this occasion it blew from the opposite quarter. The natives lined the shore enjoying the show as the vessel worked her way in and fired guns whose reverberations bounded from cliff to cliff "having at first the tones of rolling thunder and then gradually dying away till it blended with the moan of the heavy surf upon the beach."[3]

Unlike Tahiti, the Samoan Islands had no single ruler or central authority, each village having its own chief. The missionaries had been established here for only about three years following a confused period which ended with an agreement that the Wesleyan missionaries would concentrate on the Fijis and the London Missionary Society on the Samoans. Only a part of the native population had become "Christian," the unconverted being referred to as "Devils" and inclined to war among themselves and against the white man. Under these circumstances, the missionaries could help the Expedition establish friendly relations with the converted natives and at the same time benefit from its support of law and order. The Rev. Mr. Murray, a Scotch Presbyterian, was especially helpful and soon won the respect of all who came to know him and to observe his effective work among the natives on Tutuila. On Sunday he delivered a sermon on board the *Vincennes* which many considered the best they had heard since leaving home. The natives at Pago Pago appeared to be more "moral" than those at Tahiti; it was said that when the girls were told the missionaries would never find out if they transgressed the moral law they pointed skyward saying solemnly "mittinary there."[4]

The survey of Tutila was begun immediately and an observatory set up on the far side of the harbor with the friendly assistance of Chief Toa. When, three weeks later, the *Vincennes* rejoined the *Peacock* at Apia, on the island of Upolu, the observatory was set up again there and the local chief, Tarpoo, helpfully tabooed the area so as to keep out the curious.

The survey parties could not avoid close contact with the natives, needing their services as guides and interpreters,

---

3 Couthouy Journal, Oct. 11.
4 *Narrative* 2: p. 81; Whittle Journal 1, Oct. 11; Peale Journal 3, Oct. 18–19; Briscoe Journal 1, Oct. 20.

their help in procuring provisions, and, at times, shelter in their huts. Unlike the Tahitians, they had not been made mercenary by their contacts with white civilization. Some became genuine friends of members of the Expedition. Eld, for example, was joined on his lonely vigils at the observatory, when mosquitoes and hourly observations made sleep impossible, by Chief Tarpoo who shared with him his bountiful meals. Observing Tarpoo's apparent immunity from mosquitoes, Eld decided to adopt the native custom and smeared himself with cocoanut oil.[5]

The scenery and the people of Upolu fascinated Reynolds. He noticed in particular the natives' fondness for and care of their children and, at sundown, "the voice of men in prayer & the music of sacred hymns broke forth from every hut; surprised, pleased & wondering, we sat ourselves down, to listen & to reflect." He couldn't help thinking, "what would be the reception of these people in *our* land?" Chief Malietoa's fifteen-year-old daughter "Emma" was his favorite. She seemed to him "the image of faultless beauty, & the pearl of pure & natural innocence" with eyes that "would have melted a heart of stone." He combed her hair and taught her how to play the jew's-harp and to sew.[6]

When they traveled in the interior of the island, the Americans usually slept in the village "big house," a kind of combined inn and Council or Meeting House. They attracted attention wherever they went and were somewhat embarrassed to make their toilette with "bright eyes and pretty faces" watching every move; the natives marveled at American clothes, toothpicks, toothbrushes, cooking and eating utensils, wearing almost no clothes themselves and using leaves for plates and fingers for spoons. A spyglass fascinated them and they believed a watch could talk. In his exploration of Savaii, the big island, Pickering found the guides took so long over meals, in unnecessarily clearing paths and collecting yams, that he made better progress by himself, although he was always followed by a train of boys and, sometimes, grown-ups. He thought the Samoans more anxious to learn than American

---

[5] Eld Journal 1, Oct. 18. The chief's name was "Pea," the word "Tarpoo" or "Tupu" meant great chief, *Narrative* 2: p. 152.
[6] Reynolds Journal 1: pp. 239, 241, 253, 311.

Indians and did not consider them savages "unless the wearing of a dress suited to the Climate and ignorance of money" made them so.[7]

Whittle and Couthouy made a four and a half day excursion into the interior of Upolu, covering nearly ninety miles and passing through twenty-five villages, in a vain search for savannahs where wild sugar was rumored to grow. They met several missionaries and their wives who seemed well situated. They could employ native servants for a wage of a fathom of white cotton cloth per month, its value at home being eight cents, and could also engage in trade, directly or indirectly. Whittle thought them recruited from "the lower walks of life" and not likely to improve the moral condition of the natives by their "learning or dignity of character." The natives thought the Americans gay compared to the missionaries and noticed that they were not in the habit of praying, reading the Bible, or saying grace before meals.[8]

If the missionary influence was limited, it was due to some extent to the brief period of time that they had been established on these islands. There was even a local cult in competition with Christianity; it was started by a native known as "Joe Gimlet," once a whaler and claiming miraculous powers. The heathens or "Devils" were usually distinguished by the short fig-leaf type of tapa, by ashes or lime in their hair to make it stand out and to rid it of lice, and by being less friendly to outsiders.[9] Wilkes wanted to support the missionaries in their work and, at the same time, to pave the way for future trade by emphasizing respect for the lives and property of white men. He was careful to avoid taking sides in any inter-missionary, inter-tribal, or international rivalries.

Upon the arrival of the *Peacock* at Apia, Hudson found and arrested a native accused of murdering an American seaman, some eighteen months previous. He summoned the chiefs for a "pow-wow" at their round, thatched "faletele" or Meeting House, and tried to induce them to punish the murderer, but they excused him on the grounds that he was a heathen and didn't know any better. The *Vincennes* arrived while the

7 Reynolds Journal 1: pp. 250–253, 290–297; Pickering Journal 2, Oct. 20.
8 Whittle Journal 1, Oct. 29–Nov. 10; Reynolds Journal 1: pp. 255–256, 312–313.
9 Eld Journal 1, Oct. 18; Emmons Journal 1, Oct. 24.

meeting was in progress and, after further consultation, Wilkes
got the chiefs to agree to have the prisoner banished to some
deserted island. On the advice of Rev. John Williams, the
leading missionary in this area, an attempt was made to capture a chief named Oportuno who was accused of murdering
three American seamen from the whaleship *William Penn* and
of vowing to kill every foreigner he saw. Hudson took the
Peacock and *Flying Fish* to Savaii for the purpose, but Oportuno had plenty of warning and was not to be found.[10]

At a meeting in the Apia Council House on November 4
and 5, seven chiefs were induced to put their mark on a commercial treaty. By its terms they promised to apprehend deserters and murderers and, in return, were allowed to require
visiting vessels to pay port fees and to restrict the stay of seamen and passengers on shore. As a means of its enforcement
John Williams, Jr., son of the missionary and owner of a small
shipyard, was appointed acting American Consul.

After the signing of the treaty the people of Apia were
treated to a military display. Twenty-five marines and a hundred and twenty small-arms men were mustered on shore, each
supplied with six blank cartridges. They marched and counter-
marched to the music of fife and drum, fired in line and by
platoon, ending with a fusillade. Children kept time with the
drums "on their little pot bellies" while their elders gave
somewhat more dignified evidence of their enjoyment. It probably was, as Hudson declared, the greatest day of "Pow-wow-
ing" in the history of the island.[11]

Within the Squadron the process of disenchantment with
its Commander was growing apace among some of the officers

---

10 Hudson Journal 1: pp. 324–325. On a previous cruise of the *Vincennes* under
Capt. Aulick an attempt had been made to capture Oportuno but succeeded
only in burning his "nest." The Rev. Mr. Williams, whom Wilkes considered
"pious, cheerful, and meek, although resolute" was about to depart on the
missionary brig *Camden* to establish a new mission at the New Hebrides.
11 Hudson Journal 1: p. 331. Hudson was annoyed when the chief's wives left
grease spots wherever they sat down on the ship necessitating the scouring of
the *Peacock's* white ash combings at the hatchways. Charles Erskine, *Twenty
Years Before the Mast* (Boston, 1890), p. 82, tells how Wilkes mediated a dispute between sailors and officers of a New Bedford whaler which came into
Pago Pago flying a red shirt and the officers confined to the cabin. In his Autobiography 4: pp. 826–828, Wilkes mentions Erskine as a handsome Mizzen-top-
man who learned the rudiments of reading and writing while on board the
Vincennes.

and scientists. There was an indication of this at the unforget-
able departure of the *Vincennes* from Pago Pago for Apia on
October 25. The wind was blowing directly into the narrow
entranceway, making clawing out most difficult for, as Seaman
Erskine expressed it, the "ship's yards have to be braced chock
up in the wind's eye to keep the monkey's tails from getting
squeezed in the brace blocks."[12] She beat her way to the mouth
of the harbor, but the wind died and she missed stays as she
approached the high bluff on the western point and fell off
heading for the rocks on the other side. Lieutenant Carr stood
with trumpet in hand looking at the sails and not knowing
what to do. The pilot shouted orders and the ship came again
to the wind—nothing more could be done; it was left to the
ship to get clear if she could. Reynolds has given the best
description of this critical moment:

> We were within the influence of the rollers; the surf dashed
> and broke upon the rocks a few boat's lengths under the lee, &
> looking down beneath the Ship, the rocks *there,* were staring you
> in the face! We could not anchor, & if the Vincennes failed to claw
> off, she'd have but a rough bed to lie her bones in! We watched,
> with a suspense that was harrowing; she moved—she went ahead—
> she drew past the rocks—but it was with a sidelong drift that
> seemed to carry her nearer, yet nearer, yet nearer to destruction—
> We thought *we must go*—and then was the stillness of death, about
> the decks! the officers & many of the crew lined the lee gangway,
> looking fixedly on the foaming breakers that were so close—time
> to try the nerves! I turned to look for the Captain—he was in the
> weather gangway, leaning on the booms, with his face hidden in
> his hands—he had not the courage to look up & count the chances
> for the safety of the Ship, and instead of standing erect, observing
> the drift & progress of the Craft he commanded, inch by inch, he
> made the shamful spectacle I have mentioned, to the utter surprise
> of all who noticed it, & to his own deep disgrace. A few minutes
> decided it—the breeze freshened opportunely, *the ship just cleared
> the danger, with nothing to spare!*[13]

In the *Narrative* the Commander wrote that he had no
very precise recollection of his feelings at this trying moment

---

12 Erskine, *Twenty Years,* p. 81.
13 Reynolds Journal **1**: pp. 272–273; Whittle Journal **1**, Oct. 25. Whittle remarked
  that "'a certain personage who should have been very cool on the occasion
  showed the strongest symptoms of confusion and alarm and was in fact incompetent for some time to his duties."

except that he breathed more freely after the crisis had passed.[14] However, his state of mind was indicated by his subsequent acts; sailing far out to sea before letting the pilot off, suspending the Boatswain for swearing and growling, and suspending Reynolds because he was five minutes late in responding to a call for all hands. Reynolds had been below dressing his foot and after being told he was suspended took a couple of turns on deck, the usual "go below" order not having been given. Wilkes considered his manner disrespectful, which Reynolds denied, but his scornful feelings must have been apparent.[15]

On a dark night soon after this "Old Piner," a faithful Quartermaster of long service, sidled up to Wilkes on the quarter-deck and said he had overheard Couthouy telling some of the officers that he knew the Commander was exceeding his orders, which he had seen, and that he had decided not to obey him. He urged them to join with him and, if necessary, to help him displace the Commander. Pierce assured Wilkes that the crew was contented and glad to serve under him because they saw he knew his business. Though he made light of the matter Wilkes examined closely the journals that were handed in for inspection on the following day it being a Saturday. He had not had time to do this heretofore and it had become known that he was unaware that they contained adverse remarks concerning the Expedition and himself. He knew that his Instructions could not have been seen, unless someone had a false key to his secretary. His reading of the journals convinced him that there was some truth in what Pierce had said.

Upon arriving at Apia, he explained the situation to Hudson and called a meeting of the officers in which he included Couthouy and Dana. Ringgold was present, having come to attend the meeting with the chiefs, leaving the *Porpoise* and her officers at Pago Pago. About twenty-two persons were there. As soon as they were seated, Wilkes ordered his Secretary, Waldron, and his Clerk, Howison, to make memoranda of all that was said. He then accused Couthouy of making dis-

---

14 *Narrative* 2: p. 87.
15 Wilkes Journal 1, Oct. 25; Reynolds Journal 1: pp. 274–276.

respectful remarks about the conduct of the Expedition in "loud and rather insubordinate language" which he could not help overhearing. Couthouy denied any intention of disrespect and complained that the order making all collections government property had caused some officers to refuse to collect any more. Wilkes replied that they were collecting more rather than less and ended his talk by saying he did . not care what anyone said about him but to speak ill of the Expedition was a crime; if he heard of Couthouy doing any more of it he would land him bag and baggage on the first desert isle.

The officers appeared to be confounded by all this and Couthouy, much "taken aback," had nothing to say and, in Wilkes' view, "stood convicted before his own party." In any case, his enthusiasm for the Expedition was now gone and his usefulness ended. He lost interest in collecting, stopped keeping a journal, and was soon to be physically separated from the Squadron.[16]

The Commander did not seem to have any real fear of mutiny. In his Autobiography he commented on the famous *Somers* mutiny which took place in 1842 and involved Slidell Mackenzie who had at one time aspired to be the Expedition's historian. Wilkes was satisfied in his own mind that

mutiny is a very rare occurrence and the fault is seldom in the crew, when properly treated seamen are at all times tractable and good discipline and attention to their wants and comforts are sure to prevent any disturbance among this class of our citizens; they have very hard lives and undergo fatigues often beyond their strength to endure yet they are patient of ill treatment in many cases grumbling and discontented but seldom if ever are found to go the length of intended mutiny (as they are perfectly aware how much authority can be exercized over them and if the crime is proved on the investigation before the courts how condign the punishment is).

If this were true of seamen how much more aware must officers be of the risks they ran in any attempt to take over the command from the man to whom it was assigned unless

---

16 Autobiography **5**: pp. 963–964, 1105–1109, 1111–1114; Hudson Journal **1**: pp. 328–330.

the provocation was most extreme. At the same time Wilkes felt the inadequacy of punishment, such as suspension from duty; this might humiliate the offender and confinement in his room keep him from easy contact with his fellow officers, but it often took him away at a critical time and threw an extra burden on others. Nor was a Court Martial or Court of Inquiry very satisfactory because they took a great amount of time and kept several officers from other urgent duties. He was more than ever confirmed in his determination to rid the Expedition of troublesome persons.[17]

It was inevitable that on an expedition such as this, commanded by one of Wilkes' temperament, during periods of stress and strain there would be misunderstandings, hasty judgments, and resultant feelings of injustice and bitterness. For example, he accused Lieutenant Maury of consulting his own ease rather than the interests of the service when making tidal observations at Savaii. Maury was put ashore for nine days to record tides, temperatures, and weather conditions for every hour of the day, which he did except for the period from midnight to 5 or 6 A.M. when he slept. He was alone except for natives who knew no English and the occasional appearance of Pickering and a missionary who lived a quarter of a mile away. Since his records were incomplete it was impossible to know why the tides at Savaii appeared to be irregular compared to those at Tutuila and Upolu, and Wilkes called his work "next to valueless." But Maury was a very capable, conscientious, and reliable surveyor and under the circumstances his failure was understandable. Pickering gave his opinion, as a medical man, that it was "beyond the powers of the human constitution to keep up hourly observation for a succession of days" and emphasized that at low tide he had to wade out 200 yards to the tide-staff.[18]

Survey duty at the Samoan Islands was made difficult by incessant rains and pestiferous mosquitoes. Emmons and Eld surveyed the Northeast coast of Opolu with the aid of two boats' crews, eating salt pork and biscuits for most of their

---

17 Autobiography 6: pp. 1176–1178 and 7: pp. 1653–1654.
18 *Ibid.* 5: pp. 1115–1117; *Narrative* 2: p. 118; *Memorial of the Officers of the Exploring Expedition to the Congress of the United States* (Washington, 1847), p. 12.

meals, sleeping in the boats or, occasionally, in native huts, and having to be constantly on guard against possible attack. Eld described the duty in somewhat bitter terms in a letter to his parents: they worked from dawn to dark, half the time wading over coral reefs in water up to their waists, sometimes in rain with four men holding his cloak over his head, and sometimes under a broiling sun. He tried to combat mosquitoes by covering himself with cocoanut oil but had done it too late and was covered with sores. The vermin they encountered included "some specimens that would do credit to any civilization." Such were the "pleasures" mentioned by newspapers at home "in their sarcastic & very futile attempts to be funny." He had rheumatism "by way of heightening & rendering it perfectly delightful intoxicating as it were."[19]

The side of Upolu opposite Apia was surveyed by Perry and Colvocoressis using the *Flying Fish* as their base. Perry's boat was nearly swamped on one occasion and he became too ill to work. Colvocoressis attempted to complete the duty but was interrupted by Hudson's need of the schooner on his futile chase after Oportuno. As a result, the *Peacock* had to come back, months later, to finish the survey.

Alden and North surveyed the coast of Savaii in boats from the *Porpoise*. The brig was not a happy vessel. Ringgold had somewhat the same reputation as Wilkes as a disciplinarian and seemed to be continually at logger-heads with his Executive Officer, Lieutenant Johnson, who resented having to keep a night watch in addition to his regular duties, even after Maury's return when they were no longer short-handed. By October 29, when the *Porpoise* returned to Pago Pago, half her crew was sick owing, as the Surgeon said, to "climatical vicissitudes, without adequate protection, after severe bodily exertion." A house was chartered for their rehabilitation and, when the weather permitted, the rest of the crew were sent ashore to bathe and scrub clothes. Ringgold went to Apia to attend the meeting with the chiefs.[20]

---

19 Eld to his Parents, Nov. 1830, Eld Papers. He said he did not go to the extent of besmearing himself with turmeric but had to suffer some "pawing" by natives who did and it left him as yellow as if he had been dragged through a snuff factory, Eld Journal 1, Oct. 18.

20 Johnson Journal, Oct. 8, 17, 26.

The *Porpoise's* departure from Pago Pago was delayed by squally winds and, as she waited for favorable weather, the *Flying Fish* made a spectacular entrance before the wind under foresail and jib. Although the schooner might be a stylish sailer, her quarters were cramped and her crew was glad to be, if only briefly, out of the rough sea. In Sinclair's opinion she could not be more wretchedly uncomfortable or more ill-adapted for surveying; a prolonged stay aboard her was "enough to break down the Constitution of a horse." She had no binnacle, so the compass was kept in the cabin lighted only by a candle, and she had no arms chest, necessitating the storing of arms under mattresses. In such close quarters it was difficult for persons not to rub each other the wrong way and this became evident when, in Captain Pinkney's absence, Midshipman Harrison objected to an order of Sinclair's and used "very unofficerlike, indecorous, and insubordinate language" in front of the crew. Sinclair suspended him from duty and gave up trying to be friendly with his shipmate who was generally disliked because of his ungovernable temper and apparent hate for "the whole human race, himself included."[21]

On November 9 the wind moderated and the *Flying Fish* got out with little difficulty, but the *Porpoise* had to beat her way through the narrow entrance with the wind alternating between squalls and catspaws, tacking back and forth for four hours. She had to run out a hawser to the newly arrived whaler *Levi Starbuck* in order to get past her and almost got caught in stays when the lee main brace became fouled in some loose ropes. She finally got past the rock that had come so near to marking the grave of the *Vincennes*.

On the tenth the Squadron was reunited at Apia, and, the next day, departed for Sydney. Some officer transfers took place. Reynolds was sent to the *Peacock* following a dispute with Lieutenant Carr, who would not let him retrieve his rubber coat which someone had borrowed and allowed to be put in the Lucky Bay with dirty clothes to be auctioned off later. May, Reynold's roommate, told Wilkes he was surprised, shocked, and disgusted at this treatment of his friend and asked to be transferred also. He got his wish but was sent to

---

21 *Ibid.*, Nov. 7; Sinclair Journal, Nov. 7, 11, 13.

the schooner instead of the *Peacock*. The Commander considered his conduct rude and mutinous and threatened to prefer charges but decided to hold this over his head on pain of good behavior. May's temperament was such that it was not likely that he would finish the cruise without another run-in with its commander.[22]

The murderer taken at Upolu was put ashore on Wallace [Wallis] Island which was considered far enough away with the prevailing wind such that he would probably not find his way back soon.

As they approached Sydney on the night of November 29, the cables were bent and anchors made ready but, when opposite Port Jackson's bright revolving light, no pilot came out to meet them. None of the commissioned officers had ever been there before, but they had a favorable breeze and Wilkes, after studying Captain King's chart and with a quartermaster who had traded out of Sydney at his elbow, decided to save time by running it. With the *Peacock* following, they passed the Heads in fine style and discovered another light ahead, which they assumed had been erected at the "Sow and Pigs" on King's chart. After passing some shoal places they entered the main channel, and anchored off Sydney cove near Pinchgut Island close to H.B.M. Sloop-of-War *Blossom*.[23]

---

[22] Reynolds Journal 1: pp. 314–318; Wilkes Journal 1, Nov. 11.
[23] Wilkes Journal 1, Nov. 29; Sinclair Journal, Nov. 30; Reynolds' Critique, p. 31; Autobiography 6: pp. 1124–1126.

X

Down Under

Ten days before the Squadron's arrival at Sydney the store ship *Relief* departed from that port heading for home. She had left Callao with a complement of sixty-two officers and men of whom only two officers, Captain Long and Boatswain Black, and a minority of the crew had been with her when she left Norfolk. The rest were on board because they were sick or were leaving the Squadron at their own or Wilkes' request.

Surgeon Sickles, suffering from a severe attack of rheumatism, had had his hands full. The condition of the sick had improved somewhat en route from Callao to the Sandwich [Hawaiian] Islands, but there were two deaths. Captain Long had been ordered to work his way to a point at 16° 10′ North Latitude and 130° West Longitude and thence westward for about ten degrees in order to discover the location of the "American Group" of islands reported to exist in that general location. Needless to say the *Relief* didn't discover what was not there but this indirect route slowed her up considerably.[1]

After a fifty-day passage across this "ocean wilderness" a two-weeks stay at Honolulu helped to revive the crew's spirits. They were received cordially and honored by a visit from the King whom they greeted in the approved manner—manning the yardarms and having a collation in the cabin. Some supplies were discharged in the keeping of Consul Brinsmade who turned over to the ship twenty-two distressed seamen for return to the United States.

During the forty-one-day voyage from Honolulu to Sydney the sick list varied from six to a dozen. At Sydney four men deserted including two "distressed seamen" taken on at Honolulu. Another "supernumerary" from the Sandwich Islands died of consumption and was buried at Sydney. His coffin was placed on four oars and shouldered by a like number of sea-

---

1 Long Journal 1, July 16, Aug. 5, 13, 16, 19, 24, 1839; Sickles Journal, July 16, Aug. 6, 13, and letter to Emmons Nov. 14; Claiborne Journal, Aug. 5, 13.

men who carried it a mile and a half to the cemetery. The
little procession attracted a good deal of attention and seemed
to the Australians to be making a lot of fuss over an ordinary
seaman. Dale overheard a woman express astonishment that
the Americans did not appear to be either Negroes or Indians.[2]

The Australians with their large admixture of convicts
and "ticket-of-leave" men were, in turn, something of a curiosity to the Americans. Dale attended a theatrical performance
and found an audience that would have put the New York
"Bowery Boys" to blush with their "rable rout," cries of "Clew
up the main topsail" when the curtain fell, catcalls, etc. But
the doors of the Australian Club were opened to the officers
and here they met Captain Philip P. King, the maker of the
charts they had been using rounding the Horn and in the
South Seas.[3]

Having discharged the balance of their supplies and taken
on wood, water, and tons of rock ballast, the *Relief,* was off
again, bound at last for home. It was to be a long and uncomfortable voyage but, for the most part, speeded by favorable
winds. Before reaching Cape Horn, the sick list mounted to
sixteen. Encountering a great deal of wet weather, the men
felt the lack of charcoal and drying stoves. On Christmas Day
the weather was thick and cold and the crew obeyed the call
to receive an additional dram of whiskey with more alacrity
than the order to reef the topsails. The first day of the New
Year was an exceedingly cold, boisterous, and disagreeable one,
but they could rejoice in the knowledge that they were once
again in Atlantic waters.[4]

The *Relief* arrived at New York on March 28, 1840. She
confirmed the loss of the *Sea Gull,* extinguishing the lingering
hope that she might have turned up in Australia.

A New York *Morning Herald* reporter picked up from one
of the "distressed seamen" the information that there were
from 1,500 to 2,000 English and American sailors living on

2 Long Journal 1, Sept. 6, 11, Oct. 31, Nov. 17; Dale Journal, no date.
3 Sickles Journal, Oct. 31; Wilkes was unable to accept Capt. King's invitation to
visit him but bore testimony to the usefulness of his charts and sailing directions which he had on several occasions "been called upon to verify and trust
to in navigating the squadron," *Narrative* 2: pp. 206–207.
4 Sickles Journal, Nov. 19, Dec. 8, 25, Jan. 1, 1840.

Pacific islands, having been enticed ashore by native women
or put ashore because of mutinous conduct; that many of them
had to sleep on the ground which was "strongly impregnated
with saltpetre"; and that, after about six months these men
became lazy, wore no clothes, and drank intoxicating liquor
which caused their legs to swell like "large oblong bladders."
They were treated like dogs by the natives. The reporter
mentioned that Captain Long brought back two dogs, one from
Sydney and one from Tierra del Fuego, and a "splendid
white cock-a-too,"[5] but failed to mention that the *Relief's*
cargo included many specimens of natural history destined for
exhibition in the National Museum when that institution
came into being some years later.

According to Instructions, the Squadron should have
made a survey of the Fijis after Samoa but, because of the lateness of the season, it went directly to Sydney to prepare for a
second Antarctic cruise. They attracted no attention, not even
that of the Harbor Master, on the dark night that the two
ships entered, dropped anchor, and furled sails in Sydney
cove. The next days' newspapers commented on the vulner-
ability of the port and Wilkes, in his capacity as a naval officer,
remarked on the ease with which he could have sunk the
shipping, bombarded the waterfront, and slipped out of the
harbor unscathed. However, he hastened to call upon Governor George Gipps and to apologize for not firing the usual
salutes because of his chronometers. The Governor was very
cordial and gave him permission to use Fort Macquarie as an
observatory. The *Porpoise* and *Flying Fish* came in the next
day with the help of a pilot.[6]

Sydney was a new port to almost everyone in the Squadron. Although about a third of the population consisted of
transported convicts they were less in evidence than was expected, and free settlers were arriving in increasing numbers.
The Americans, according to Dr. Holmes, expected to find
"a den of abominations, tenanted exclusively by English crim-

5 New York *Morning Herald,* March 30, 1840.

6 Colvocoresses, *Four Years in a Government Expedition* (New York, 1852), p.
92; *Narrative* 2: p. 161; Wilkes Journal 1, Nov. 29; Autobiography 6: pp.
1125–1128.

inals, the offscouring of the earth," but found instead a flourishing colony, rapidly increasing in wealth and importance and including among its inhabitants "some of the most intelligent and gentlemanly men" he had ever met.[7]

The newness and good taste of the buildings contrasted with "the wretched style of living" at Valparaiso, a port of about equal importance. It was particularly pleasant for Americans to hear again their own language and to see this bustling city with its handsome country seats on the outskirts resembling those at home. At their first opportunity the officers hurried ashore to enjoy a good but expensive meal at Mr. Petty's Public House. They were hospitably received in private homes, the officers were made Honorary Members of the Australian Club, and the Library and Museum were opened to them for their use. There seemed to be a continual round of dinners, balls, and parties.[8]

The missionary brig *Camden* arrived December 1, bringing the sad and startling news of the murder of the Rev. Mr. Williams and his companion, Mr. Harris, shortly after landing in the New Hebrides where they were attempting to inaugerate a new mission. It was a reminder of what could happen to white men if caught by surprise on one of the less civilized Pacific islands.

The immediate business on hand was to prepare for the Antarctic voyage and to make another series of scientific observations. Wilkes established his headquarters at Fort Macquarie within easy communication with the vessels in the harbor and where he could make pendulum, magnetic, and meteorological observations assisted by Blunt, Colvocoresses, and Eld. There was already an observatory at the Fort, but it had been neglected; the building falling into ruins and the instruments covered with dirt and in disorder. Wilkes could not understand why the Australians were not more interested in astronomy, that "glorious occupation."[9]

He called the scientists together and suggested that, as there would not be much for them to do on the Antarctic

---

[7] Holmes Journal 1, Nov. 29. Soon after this convicts were sent to Norfolk Island instead of Australia.

[8] Pickering Journal 1, Emmons Journal 1, Nov. 29; Whittle Journal 1, Dec. 1.

[9] Wilkes Journal 1, Dec. 3.

cruise, they might employ themselves more profitably elsewhere keeping journals, making collections, and reporting to
him in writing after rejoining the Squadron at the Bay of
Islands, New Zealand, by March 1. Consequently, they split up
and, by going in different directions, were able to learn at
first hand a great deal about New South Wales and New Zealand.

Pickering and Dana accepted an invitation of Ward
Stephens to visit his estate at the head of the Hunter River.
This was a two-week excursion involving an overnight trip of
seventy miles up the coast to the Green Hill landing, in a
steamboat of small size and little power, after which they
traveled on horseback. On the return trip they spent three days
waiting for a gale to subside so that the steamboat could venture out of the river mouth. After their return, Pickering became ill and was mostly confined to his room at the "Club
House" from Christmas until he sailed for New Zealand in
February. In spite of pain in his ear, a stiff neck, and an attack of rheumatism, he managed visits to the Museum and
Botanical Garden.[10]

In a letter to his friend Edward C. Herrick, Dana mentioned seeing their mutual Australian friends, Alexander
McLeay, aged seventy-three, a distinguished naturalist, em-
inent in politics, science, and religion, and the Rev. W. B.
Clarke, who put geology first and theology second. Invitations
had come

from every side to visit this and that part of the Country and to
accept of their hospitality; horses were sent to our doors to aid us
in our excursions; letters of introduction forced on us to every
gentleman along our way; boxes of specimens often offered to us—
indeed, we have open door and open hearts everywhere.[11]

Rich, Drayton, and Agate visited the Illawarra district,
south of Sydney. Peale went inland and visited Lachlan Mac-

10 Pickering Journal 1, Dec. 2, 1839–Feb. 8, 1840.
11 Gilman, *Dana*, pp. 114–115. Brackenridge was in bed two weeks after a fall
   suffered when he and Rich were hurrying to pack plants and seeds in the loft
   above Consul Williams' store for shipment aboard the barque *Shepherdess*
   about to leave for the United States.

allister, a friend who had a sheep farm of 16,000 acres in the very fertile district of Argyle. On these trips the scientists saw something of the Australian natives whom they found to be very dissimilar in appearance, speech, and customs from the Pacific islanders.[12]

Hale went farthest away from Sydney, traveling as a passenger on a two-wheel mail coach about 230 miles northwest of Sydney to the Wellington Valley, on the frontier of the Colony.

Couthouy was too sick to go on an excursion and, on medical advice, took ship to Hawaii to recover his health. Wilkes wrote the Secretary of the Navy that he hoped Couthouy would be able to resume his duties later but he had, in fact, made up his mind that Couthouy was a trouble-maker and should not be permitted to rejoin the Squadron.[13]

With the exception of Couthouy and Hale, the latter being delayed on his return by heavy rains and impassable roads, the scientists took passage on the uncomfortably crowded Colonial brig *Victoria* on February 6, 1840, and arrived at the Bay of Islands, New Zealand, after a rough eighteen-day passage.

In preparing for the Antarctic cruise, the *Peacock* and *Flying Fish,* in particular, caused concern. Jonas Dibble, the *Peacock's* carpenter, gave Captain Hudson a discouraging report on her condition. He found the sheer strake, on which the channels were bolted and the gun deck ports hung, rotten in many places fore and aft and all but three or four of the stanchions supporting the bulwark on the spar deck very decayed and unable to support the rail and boats attached to it. It was estimated that repairs would take two months, necessitating a decision to leave the *Peacock* behind or to take her and be prepared "for any casualties which may occur." Wilkes and Hudson decided that the latter would be expected of them.[14]

Their Australian friends, having read of the special preparations made by Captain James Ross, marveled that they

---

12 Peale Journal 3, Dec. 21, 1839–Jan. 15, 1840.
13 Wilkes to Paulding, Dec. 23, Ex.Ex. Letters 1; Autobiography 5: p. 1114.
14 *Narrative* 2: append. XXI, p. 449; Hudson Journal 1: p. 381.

should attempt a southern cruise with vessels such as these which were not compartmented or equipped with large ice-saws or adequate means for keeping warm. They were es-pecially curious about the *Flying Fish* with its unfamiliar schooner rig. She was given new masts made of New Zealand pine an inch thicker and three feet shorter, but heavier and stiffer than the old ones which were now made into spare yards for the larger vessels. All the vessels were given a general overhaul and took on water, wood, and provisions for a period of ten months, in case they got frozen in.[15]

The physical condition and morale of the officers and men were, of course, matters of great importance. Eleven sick seamen were left in charge of the consul. The effect of a pro-longed stay in port depended in part upon the character of the port and that of a convict colony was expected to present special problems. However, Sydney was heavily policed, with constables almost always in evidence and convicts seen mainly working in chain gangs, much like the slave gangs at Rio.

Erskine, the sailor of long experience, compared Sydney with other ports he had known and thought it had the greatest intermixture of men of all nations. When he and a boat's crew dropped in at the Jolly Sailors' Inn they found a large square room with tables along the sides and national flags overhead. The tables were occupied by sailors of various nationalities joining together in a singing bee. The Americans sang "Yankee Doodle," the Russians sang with sweet soft voices, and the French with their "Marseillaise" sang with the greatest zest. They all drank together, the English their "alf and alf" out of pewter mugs, the French claret out of very thin glasses, and the Russians and Americans drank something harder out of thick small-bottomed glasses.[16]

The police were vigilant in capturing deserters but failed to find five from the *Flying Fish* who rowed ashore one night in one of her boats. Sinclair, coming on deck at 1:15 A.M., had seen three men standing about and asked one of them, a

---

15 Hudson Journal 1: p. 382; Sinclair Journal, Dec. 19.
16 Erskine, *Twenty Years,* pp. 94–96. At this time the English barque *Calcutta* cut across the *Peacock's* bows carrying away her flying jib boom which might have been a lubberly maneuver on the part of the pilot but was believed to have been an intentional reprisal for entering the port without a pilot, Em-mons Journal 1, Dec. 7, 11.

petty officer whom he trusted, what they were doing and was
told that one was relieving the watch and the other answering
a call of nature. They got away shortly after this, even managing to take the pea jacket from under the head of the cabin
boy without awakening him. A reward of $150 was offered,
boats searched the harbor and Sinclair searched every ship
about to depart, but they were not discovered. It was believed
that they were hidden by "crimps" who made a business of
kidnapping seamen and then delivering them on board another
ship short of crew and willing to pay the price.

The best the *Flying Fish* could do was to replace them
just before departure with a seaman and two ordinaries. Sinclair remarked:

I do not suppose that a vessel ever sailed under the U.S. Pendant
with such a miserable crew as we have now. We have no cook and
only 7 men, four of them are not in my opinion worth their salt,
but they are all we can get. It will be a great wonder to me if we
return from the southern cruise.[17]

The *Peacock* lost nine men by desertion, sent three to the
hospital, and was able to ship only three in their place.

The officers, too, were not anxious to leave Sydney for
the inhospitable Antarctic. Some stayed when ashore at the
Australian Club, the chief social center of the city, and wanted
to return the hospitality shown them by giving a party. They
had already printed invitations when Wilkes vetoed the use
of the *Vincennes* as interfering with preparations for departure. They then decided to drop the whole thing, but the
Commander thought it had gone too far and, taking the matter
into his own hands, secured permission to use Fort Macquarie,
appointed Ringgold to make arrangements, and footed the bill
himself.[18]

The affair was a success in spite of a shower that caused
its postponement from one to two o'clock and kept away all
but about a dozen of the ladies. A pavilion was made out of
sails and decorated with flags, those of Britain and the United

17 Sinclair Journal, Dec. 15, 23–25.
18 Emmons Journal 1, Dec. 15; Autobiography 6: pp. 1146–1149. The cost was
    $780.

States intertwined. About two hundred people sat at two long tables connected by a head table. Governor and Lady Gipps and staff were present in full uniform. The 15th Regiment Band supplied music and some of the younger people danced on the grass in spite of the recent shower. Some of the officers stayed away from the party that Wilkes had made his own, but others attended until its end at dawn.[19]

On the whole, officer morale declined during the stay at Sydney. The Commander continued to blame it on a "cabal," whose members he identified as Gilchrist, Alden, Case, Underwood, Reynolds, May, Sinclair, Pinkney, and Johnson. He considered Gilchrist and Alden the most deceitful and sneaking in their opposition and desire to see the Expedition fail as a reflection upon him. Gilchrist persisted in his claim to having been promised advancement to Fleet Surgeon. When refused permission to live ashore he wrote a letter which Wilkes considered disrespectful. Since he refused to apologize or withdraw the letter he was suspended and confined to the ship but later, for reasons of health, permitted to go ashore. Wilkes would have detached him from the Expedition at this time had he not needed his services on the southern cruise.[20]

Captain Ringgold had a dispute with Dr. Guillou which started when the latter requisitioned medical supplies in a slovenly manner and included an iron pestle and mortar to replace one which he was suspected of having thrown overboard. He was transferred to the *Peacock* where he was junior to Dr. Palmer, Dr. Holmes taking his place on the *Porpoise*. He and his friends considered this a demotion and a very high-handed act. This affair confirmed in Wilkes' mind Guillou's unworthiness for promotion, his inexperience accentuating his limited education and lack of medical knowledge.[21]

From Sydney, Reynolds wrote his family explaining, for the first time, his change of feeling towards Wilkes. The Commander had become "a false & malignant *villain*—no milder term will do." Intoxicated with power and rank, he refused

---

[19] Elliott Journal **1**, Dec. 20; Emmons Journal 1, no date; Autobiography **6**: pp. 1150–1152.

[20] Autobiography **6**: pp. 1134–1139.

[21] *Ibid.*, pp. 1130–1134, 1143–1144. The officers showed their dislike of Ringgold on one occasion by inviting him to an entertainment and then ignoring him in the presence of strangers.

to forward their respectful remonstrances to the Secretary of
the Navy and now only three officers stood by him.

The healthy feeling that was so strong and pure, is now
destroyed . . . happy hopes & prospects of every one have been
blasted & we lead a life of torment & strife, feeling that everything
we do, will be taken at an unfair advantage, confidence in the
Command is destroyed, there is none where there should be all.
Every man does his duty, but he keeps aloof from Captain Wilkes
as if he were an adder, & never trusts himself with him save in an
official manner . . . one consolation is that there is but one voice &
one feeling among us, we have suffered together & together we
have resisted. . . .[22]

In previous dispatches to the Secretary, Wilkes had mentioned the "cabal" and his determination to detach its members from the Expedition. At this time he explained the postponement of the Fiji survey and the decision to take the *Peacock* to the Antarctic in spite of her poor condition. He also
expressed the hope that the *Sea Gull* might yet turn up and
rejoin them in the spring.[23]

In a dispatch to John Forsyth, Secretary of State, he
recommended the appointment of a consul general to superin-
tend the consular representatives in the Polynesian Islands
and Australia and suggested that H. H. Williams, Consul at
Sydney, could fill the bill. He warned that foreign interests
were crowding out Americans in this area and cited the arrival
of a frigate bringing a British governor for New Zealand, the
British openly proclaiming their intention to appropriate that
important whaling center.[24]

The officers, though busy preparing for the southern
cruise, found time to make some warm friendships ashore. For
example, Lieutenant Johnson spent most of his time trying to
hurry spar makers, ship joiners, chandlers, and armourers,
finding "mechanics here, as with us, are a very independent
class," but became such a good friend of the de Maester family
that he was invited to their Christmas party and played games

22 Reynolds to Lydia, Dec. 22, 1839, Reynolds Letters.
23 Wilkes to Paulding, Dec. 22 and 23, 1839, Ex.Ex. Letters 1.
24 Miscel. Letters, Dept. of State Archives, Dec. 25, 1839.

with their children.[25] When the Squadron weighed anchor on the day after Christmas many friends waved farewell from the shore and the Consul and a few others accompanied them as far as the Heads where lack of wind held them until the tide changed. It was one of those occasions for manning the yards and giving three cheers, this time heartfelt, for the explorers were about to enter upon one of their greatest adventures.

---

[25] Johnson, incomplete letter, no date, Johnson Letters; Emmons Journal 1, Dec. 25.

XI
Wilkes Land

A S THEY SET OUT upon their second attempt to penetrate the Antarctic beyond Captain Cook's "Ne plus ultra" that intrepid explorer's words of warning were remembered. The risk was so great, he said, that "I can be bold enough to say that no man will ever venture farther than I have done; and that the lands which lie to the south will never be explored." In addition to the navigational danger from fog, snowstorms, and intense cold in that "inexpressably horrid" country never warmed by the sun's rays, there was the prospect of being frozen in forever or of coming out encased in an ice island.[1]

No one, in fact, had bettered Cook's South Pacific mark, although the *Flying Fish* had come close to it and Captain Weddell in 1819 had reached 74°15' in the South Atlantic. But more important was the sighting of land by Captain Biscoe, sailing for Enderby's of London in 1831 when south of the Cape of Good Hope and at approximately 66° South Latitude, 45° East Longitude. Accordingly, the Expedition's Instructions called for it to sail south of Van Diemen's Land [Tasmania] as far as possible and then to work westward to 45° East Longitude or "Enderby's Land."

Wilkes was in a great hurry because he was aware that both the English and French had sent out exploring expeditions and, more particularly, because the favorable season had only two months to go. The sailing directions given his captains told them to rendezvous at two points. Macquarie and Emerald Islands, before coming to the ice barrier at 160° East Longitude; then to work westward, keeping as far south as possible, to 105° or "Enderby's Land"; finally, to turn north by March 1 and rendezvous at the Bay of Islands, New Zealand.[2]

During the first few days of favorable winds preparations

---

1 Christopher Lloyd (ed.) *The Voyages of Captain James Cook Round the World* (London, 1949), p. 227.
2 *Narrative* 2: append. XXV, pp. 457–458.

were made to meet Antarctic conditions: housings built over hatchways with pulleys and weights to keep the doors closed; the ports covered with tarred canvas; charcoal stoves on sheet lead slung for warmth and for drying clothes; exploring clothing issued; loose and unessential articles stowed away and guns made doubly secure.[3]

When the weather became boisterous only the *Vincennes* and *Porpoise* managed to keep together and they missed Macquarie Island by about twenty miles and saw no sign of Emerald Island which was inaccurately located on their chart. As early as January 1 the *Flying Fish* had sail trouble and fell behind and the *Peacock* lost the others during fog and rain experienced on the third. These two vessels waited at opposite ends of Macquarie Island the required forty-eight hours without sighting each other. The flagship and *Porpoise* were stopped by pack ice at 64° 11′ South Latitude and 164° 30′ East Longitude. The *Peacock* reached the barrier at the designated point 160° East Longitude on January 15 and joined the other two vessels near that point shortly thereafter. On the seventeenth the three vessels began operating independently, since it appeared that, in this way, they might discover more and be less liable to collide in foggy weather. The *Flying Fish* reached the barrier at 161° East Longitude on the twenty-first, so far behind the others that she never made contact with them during the rest of the Antarctic cruise.

The sailors began to feel like genuine explorers as they coasted along the ice barrier, crowding the forecastle and eagerly searching the horizon at every rumor of the sighting of land. There were no maps or charts for this part of the world and it could contain a few islands surrounded by masses of ice or, possibly, a great land mass. The presence of petrels, albatrosses, and other birds which flew away every evening about eight o'clock was taken as a sure sign of the nearness of land.

The sixteenth, the day after the *Peacock's* arrival at the barrier, was remarkably clear, and at noon Eld and Reynolds

---

[3] Erskine, *op. cit.*, p. 103; Colvocoresses, *op. cit.*, p. 109; Emmons Journal 2, Jan. 7, 1840, listed clothing: "a Pea Jacket, a Macanaw Blanket, a Gurnsey Frock, a pair of Gurnsey Drawers, a pair of trousers each. Nothing to keep feet dry, Sydney's best boots were poor."

climbed to the masthead to view the ice fields. They were convinced that they could see several mountain peaks of great height and at a great distance, their summits hidden by fleecy clouds. After watching with a spy glass for about half an hour they reported what they had seen to Lieutenant Budd, Officer of the Deck, and to Captain Hudson who looked with the glass from on deck and agreed that it might be land but said they might see more in a day or two. Reynolds thought this a "singular way to receive a report of *Land*," yet he was so in doubt himself that he forgot to mention it in his own journal and it was not entered in the ship's log. Hudson was cautious because the mountains looked so white and he knew that atmospheric conditions could make distant clouds appear solid and immovable. He had no realization, at that time, that they were, in fact, in a close race with foreigners for the honor of discovering a new continent. On the *Porpoise* that day Lieutenant North, Dr. Holmes, and Captain Ringgold saw what they took to be an island bearing south-by-east. North, as Officer of the Deck, entered it in that vessel's log. Wilkes, on the *Vincennes,* saw and made a sketch of the same thing but was not sure it was land and preferred, like Hudson, to wait for later verification.[4]

The next clear day was the nineteenth and again it was Eld and Reynolds at the masthead who thought they saw land. Midshipman Clark joined them and agreed it was land and Passed Midshipman Davis, who had the Deck, entered it in the log, but Captain Hudson thought they would have a better look in a couple of days and made Davis erase the entry.[5] On the *Vincennes* Lieutenant Alden reported the appearance of land to Wilkes who wanted to confer with Hudson on the matter, but the wind was dying out and the flagship had to be towed away from the barrier by its boats and this was the last time these two ships saw each other in Antarctic waters.

The Commander did not anticipate the discovery of a continent or discuss the probability of land with anyone on his ship except the Gunner, John Williamson. Aware of the deceptiveness of appearances in high latitudes, he waited until

---

[4] Eld Journal 1, Jan. 16, 1840; Hudson's testimony during Wilkes' Court-Martial, Aug. 30, 1842.
[5] Davis' testimony during Court-Martial, Aug. 29, 1842.

he could take bearings on the peaks and promontories from three different positions. As he said in the *Narrative,* all doubt as to the reality of their discovery gradually wore away, and towards the end of the cruise the mountains of the continent became such a familiar sight that "the log-book, which is guardedly silent as to the time and date of its being first observed, now speaks throughout of 'the land.' "[6]

The last time any of the Squadron's vessels came together was the twenty-fifth, when the *Vincennes* and *Porpoise* exchanged an "all's well" and compared chronometers. Otherwise each was an isolated community undergoing experiences peculiar to itself though seeing similar sights and affected by similar weather conditions.

Spouting whales became a commonplace. The sound they made reminded Emmons of that made by high pressure steamboats on the Ohio. The schooner's crew watched anxiously when a very large and curious one came too close for comfort. On the other hand, the *Peacock's* crew watched from her high deck bleacher seats a drama of the sea: a death duel between two whales, one clinging to the jaw of the other as it churned and bloodied the water close by the ship.[7]

Penguins were a source of amusement and several specimens were captured, including a couple of large and lusty "emperor" penguins. Dr. Homes made a "sea pie" out of a huge albatross carefully skinned and parboiled, which he pronounced tender and very palatable. He also did a "taxidermy" job for Lieutenant Johnson who succeeded in shooting two crabeater seals, one of which weighed 750 pounds. These animals had to be shot in the head and at close range or they simply slid off the ice and disappeared in the water.[8]

Until the latter part of February, they experienced continuous daylight in these southern latitudes. The absence of night was a help to navigation but visibility could still be close to zero during frequent periods of fog and snow squalls. The ice fields made an awesome sight, as did the shifting shafts of light reaching to the zenith from the Aurora Australis.

Compasses were affected and sometimes rendered useless

6 *Narrative* 2: pp. 282, 295–296; Wilkes Journal 1, Jan. 19.
7 Emmons Journal 2, and Hudson Journal 1, Jan. 20; Sinclair Journal, Jan. 26.
8 Holmes Journal 1, Jan. 13 and Feb. 6.

by their nearness to the magnetic pole. On one occasion the *Peacock* had one compass heading north and, at the same moment, another heading south.

At first the wind came from the southwest, so that it appeared nonsensical to work along the barrier from east to west, but Wilkes predicted that the prevailing wind would be southeast and this proved to be true and during six days from January 28 to February 2 they experienced three severe gales, all from that quarter. Serious damage from collision with ice was constantly a matter for concern, whether sailing in a breeze with poor visability or drifting with little or no wind, as the *Peacock* was to find out. Frequent changes of direction and hurried taking in and putting on of sail was very fatiguing work and especially so in cold, snowy weather. Emmons remarked after a four-hour watch on deck in such weather that it "makes one think he has done his country a service."[9]

Wilkes described the eerie sensation experienced when sailing out of the rough sea into one of the smooth, ice-bound bays:

The ship is tossed and tumbled about by the sea & suddenly everything is perfectly still and quiet as she shoots into it under all sail as we have been—when all are awakened by it to danger, both officers and men, and everyone appears intent on looking out, here & there—the icy barrier is discovered and all anxious to acclaim from all sides, otherwise the utmost stillness, as if the ship was uninhabited . . . few can estimate it but the commander of a ship with the responsibility of the ship and crew upon him, it at times acts on me as if a weight was hung all at once on my heart strings that of one on the brink of a great accident which it is his duty to avoid & brings one to the conclusion that nothing but an all seeing eye can guide one from destruction.[10]

As the Squadron worked its way westward the vessels had their individual problems. We shall follow their separate fortunes beginning with the *Peacock,* the first to turn back.

After January 17, when the vessels went off on different

9 Emmons Journal 2, Jan. 20; Holmes Journal 1, Feb. 10.
10 Wilkes Journal 1, Jan. 16.

tacks, the *Peacock* had no further contact with either the flagship or the *Porpoise*. Eld, who believed that he and Reynolds
had seen land from the masthead, found more evidence when
he captured an "emperor" penguin in whose craw were thirty-
five big pebbles which the cook proceeded to sell at high prices.
The most conclusive evidence came on the twenty-third when,
on sounding, they found bottom at 320 fathoms. Hudson sent
the crew into the rigging to give three cheers to be followed
by "splicing the main brace."

The *Peacock* was a "happy" ship. The good feeling among
her officers was emphasized on New Year's Eve when the Cabin
Ward Room, and Steerage all dined together. The high spirits
of the crew were evidenced by their invention of games to
keep themselves warm and entertained, such as setting up a
ten pin alley on the gun deck. They could be heard "stamping
about the decks the whole day in the most merry mood—dancing and singing most of the time."[11]

On the morning of the twenty-fourth this merry mood
suddenly changed into one verging on panic. It was a clear day
with light winds and smooth water as the ship worked her way
into a bay searching, as always, for a means of reaching land.
Space for maneuvering was limited. To avoid some blocks of
ice, the head yards were squared to slow her progress and, as
she was brought into the wind, she struck a berg on the bow
and then backed into another at the stern. The first crash
threw those having breakfast out of their seats, making them
think the whole bow must be stove in, but actually the most
serious damage was at the stern where the starboard wheelrope
was carried away and the neck of the rudder wrenched so that
it became inoperable. The carpenters found that the rudder
would have to be unshipped to be repaired, and in the meantime the vessel must be steered with her sails. An ice anchor
was got out but, before the end of the hawser could be attached,
it was swept from the men's grasp by a movement of the ice.
The *Peacock* was pushed back again against the ice and this
time the rudder head broke away from two of its pintles. After
long hours of strenuous exertion the rudder was brought
amidships and ice anchors got out. All but the fore and aft

---

11 Eld Journal **1**, Jan. 22–23; Emmons Journal **2**, Jan. 1, 23, 25.

sails were furled as the vessel was held precariously by its ice anchors uncomfortably close to a mile-long ice island with perpendicular sides rising as high as the main topgallant mast-head. All had been done that could be done at the moment and dinner was piped.

FIG. 10. *Peacock* at the moment of collision with ice barrier. Drawing by A. T. Agate. *Narrative* 2: p. 302.

Near midnight the ice anchors broke loose and the vessel moved inevitably towards the towering ice. It was still light and all on deck could see what was about to happen. The *Peacock's* stern hit a piece of ice between her and the ice mass. She ground around this ice cake on her larboard quarter and then hit the ice island stern to. The crash and recoil nearly threw the men off their feet and the masts quivered like coach whips for a few moments when it looked as if the ice, which projected about twenty feet over the quarter deck at the level of the mizzen truck, would cascade upon the ship and sink her stern foremost. It seemed as if the whole stern must have been stove in and some tried to make up their minds whether to go down with the ship or die a lingering death on an ice-berg. However, the ship canted to starboard, the jib was hoisted

and the fore and main trysail sheets handed off, with the result that she moved ahead out of immediate danger. There
was considerable new damage: the spanker boom and larboard
davit carried away and the sternboat crushed; all the spar deck
bulwarks as far as the gangway loosened and a knee between
the taffrail and rail broken; and a signal gun jammed between
the head boards at the gangway. All this, however, was above
the waterline so there was no immediate danger of the ship
sinking.

She was maneuvered to an opening in the ice where all sail
that could be used to advantage was put on. All hands employed "making sail at one end of her — or taking it in at the
other — bracing in — and bracing up and — with the aid of
the ice anchors checking her into position for forcing out of
our now rather critical situation." Clear water seemed to get
farther and farther away as the wind brought in more and
more ice and by afternoon she was held hard and fast, the
north wind continuing to be light with clouds and some snow.
The rudder was got inboard and found to have its head
completely broken off at the lower part of the neck.

Toward evening the wind freshened with occasional
squalls. The ice anchor hawser broke and sail was made in an
endeavor to reach the open sea which could be seen from the
masthead. All hands were kept at work through the night
keeping the *Peacock* headed seaward. The wind continued to
be moderate but the sea swell increased and there were om-
inous signs of a gale in the northwest. Collisions with the ice
were severe enough to throw the chronometers on their sides
as they lay in their sawdust beds.

By morning of the twenty-fifth they were free of the ice
and, by 8 A.M., the threatening appearances of a gale had disappeared and it was almost calm. The carpenters, working all
night, had succeeded in getting out the broken pieces of
pintles and, by noon, had repaired the rudder sufficiently so
that it could be shipped over the side and hung.

For twenty suspenseful hours nobody had slept. Hudson
had high praise for Dibble, the ship's carpenter, who got out
of a sick bed to work on the rudder, and he congratulated the
officers and men on their cheerfulness and the alacrity with
which they performed their duty. The officers, in turn, felt
that his calm and collected manner had perhaps prevented

panic at the time of the collision and during the dreadful hours that followed.

Crowding on all sail the *Peacock* stood out of the bay, free of the drift ice still in evidence all around the compass. Since the rudder was "hanging by the eye lids — and the ship otherwise mauled" Hudson decided to return to Sydney to expedite repairs. Some thought they should work further west, keeping clear of the ice, but it was doubtful whether anything could be accomplished by this and it would only delay necessary repairs.[12]

As it was, they had to weather a strong northwest gale, reducing the strain on the rudder as much as possible by keeping it amidships and balancing the sails. For the second time the *Peacock* entered Fort Jackson without a pilot, and anchored off Sydney Cove on the morning of February 22. Upon close examination it was found that the ice had chafed the stern to within 1½ inches of the hood-ends of the vessel's planking. They ascribed their escape to Providence and to the fact that she had been built expressly for exploring service with a solid caulked bottom under her planking. She was probably the strongest vessel of her class in the Navy and it was unlikely that any other vessel in the Squadron could have survived the shocks she sustained.[13]

For the crew of the *Flying Fish* the Antarctic cruise was a nightmare. The inadequacy of the crew itself was soon apparent. Deeply laden with ten months' supplies she was wet but still able to outsail the other vessels. However, if the jib sheet had to be hauled in at night the Officer of the Deck had to take the helm and send all hands forward and, if there was a breeze, luff to get the sheet aft. The *Vincennes* sent them a cook but he proved to be unruly, negligent, and insolent, knowing that his services could not be spared. The only capable crewmen taken on at Sydney were Murray, an old Seaman, and Atkins, a boy. Pinkney had expected to rate Parker as Bo'sun, but he "ran" at Sydney, so, when fighting among the

---

12 Hudson Journal 1, Jan. 24–26; Eld Journal 2, Jan. 24; Emmons Journal 2, Jan. 24, 29; Reynolds Journal 1: pp. 282–292.

13 Hudson Journal 1, Feb. 21, 22; Eld Journal 2, Jan. 24; Emmons Journal 2, Jan. 25.

crew made it necessary to have someone swing the "cat" he gave the rating to Murray. When May caught Weaver, the cook, stealing stores and liquor, he administered twelve lashes with a rope's end himself.[14]

On New Year's Day the wind shifted to the north and became a gale. They took in the mainsail and, shortly after, the square sail split and had to be taken in. They scudded before the wind under the foresail until, after jibing several times, it carried away the jaw of the gaff. After that they proceeded under jib alone but that too got adrift "having been made fast by a Sydney Seaman" and carried away the square sail yard. In this situation with the sea breaking over them, they were signaled by the *Vincennes* to "make sail." They thought the flagship must have seen their helpless condition, for she stood down so close to them that with the glass they could recognize Knox and Captain Wilkes. However, the ship continued on her way, leaving them to their fate, and a "few deep toned curses accompanied her." Sinclair speculated as to Wilkes' motives but at a later date erased the sentence in his journal that embodied his conclusions.

Delayed by these troubles and by stopping at Macquarie Island, the *Flying Fish* didn't reach the ice barrier until January 21 and, as a result, saw none of the other vessels. She came to the bay where the *Peacock* almost met disaster on the day after that ship had freed herself and headed north.

By the time the schooner reached the barrier, four of her crew were on the sick list and the clothes of the other four were constantly wet from frequent calls on deck. Coffee was kept on tap and came to be preferred to grog. It became necessary for the officers to perform the most ordinary manual labor.[15]

As they coasted along the edge of the ice pack for the first few days the wind was moderate and the *Flying Fish* steered beautifully as they wormed in and out among the icebergs. In spite of twenty-four hours of daylight there were periods of snow squalls when they were in danger of hitting detached pieces of ice not showing much above water. Once,

---

14 Sinclair Journal, Dec. 26–31, 1839, and Jan. 28, 1840; May testimony during Pinkney's Court-Martial, Aug. 11, 1842.
15 Sinclair Journal, Jan. 1, 15, 17.

when close to and on the lee side of a mile-long ice island, the wind dropped and the schooner began to be sucked towards it. As they got out the sweeps a large mass of ice broke off with a thunderous noise, snow rising like smoke, and the swell it produced made the schooner roll so far as to take in water. Thereafter they kept farther away from ice islands. Many icebergs had caverns into which water rushed with a roar, sometimes spouting up through holes high into the air, and frequently during snow squalls this "blood-curdling" sound warned them of a berg's presence.

When the weather became thick with a gale developing on the twenty-ninth, only three crewmen were able to take the wheel. The Officer of the Deck had to divide his time between looking out from the forecastle and relieving the man at the helm so that he might go to the cabin to get warm. That night they had to put on all sail in order to work their way out from between two bergs and, lacking the manual force to reef the foresail, had to keep all sail on causing the schooner to labor heavily. They rode out the gale following along but keeping about a half mile off the barrier.

On the night of February 3 the wind freshened and again became a gale, causing the vessel to plunge furiously in a tremendous sea. On the first watch Pinkney lashed himself to the foremast as lookout and it was with great difficulty that they avoided innumerable pieces of ice big enough to stave in the bow. It was "truly a horrible night" and the next day was no better. On the midnight to four watch of the second night Sinclair lashed himself to the foremast and was frequently washed off his feet, the bow sometimes plunging under water as far aft as the heel of the foremast. They knew they had too much sail but could not reef without getting a sea into it and thereby losing the only sail under which the vessel would "lay." The three sailors capable of work were constantly on duty and one, with his foot so swollen that he could not wear shoes, stood at the helm for four hours in wet clothes and stocking feet. The schooner was leaking at every seam and, with water up to the cabin deck, the pump had to be kept going constantly.[16]

---

[16] *Ibid.*, Jan. 23, 27, 29 and Feb. 3–4.

As the gale continued and the berth deck became uninhabitable all the crew, sick and well, were moved into the officers' twelve-by-nine-foot cabin. Nothing could be cooked except on the cabin stove and that was frequently extinguished by sea water washing down the pipe. When pumping stopped for a few minutes, the water gained rapidly, the vessel lost her lively qualities and the sea broke over her with greater violence. On this day, February 5, the crew petitioned Captain Pinkney to take their condition into consideration and "relieve us from what must terminate in our death." After consulting with Sinclair, May, and Harrison, Pinkney decided to turn north. They were at 142° East Longitude having followed along the barrier from 161°.[17]

The weather moderated on the following day and they were able to make some repairs and the condition of the sick improved noticeably, but it was two weeks before they experienced a real drying sun. Sinclair discovered that his sextant had been in error since dropping it on January 1, but Pinkney would not let him correct observations recorded in the log lest someone think he was trying to claim he went farther south than he did. Progress towards New Zealand was slow because they had to reduce sail before each squall, the crew being what it was. So it was with considerable relief that they entered the Bay of Islands, on the tenth of March. Since the *Flying Fish* had not been seen by the other vessels after January 1, many assumed that she had met the *Sea Gull's* fate.[18]

As the *Porpoise* ranged along the barrier looking for an opening, her experience was similar to that of the two larger vessels. However, she alone made contact with the French exploring party which made a rival claim to the discovery of land and gave the name "Adélie Land" to a portion of the coast line. The brig had last seen the *Peacock* on the twenty-third and the *Vincennes* three days after that and so, upon seeing two sails on the thirtieth, assumed they belonged to those two vessels. They soon recognized, however, by their rake and rig the explorer Dumont D'Urville's *Astrolabe* and *Zelie*. The *Porpoise* flew the Ensign and Pendant and, in answer, the

---

17 *Ibid.*, Feb. 5; *Narrative* 2: pp. 357–359; May testimony Aug. 11, 1842.
18 Sinclair Journal, Feb. 19, 24, and Mar. 1, 10.

French vessels hoisted the Tricolor and Pendant. In deference
to D'Urville's superior rank, Ringgold attempted to pass within
hailing distance astern of the *Astrolabe*. D'Urville slacked sail to
permit the vessels to run side by side but the *Porpoise* came on
so fast that he ordered a change of course so as to fill the
mainsail and gain speed. Ringgold thought the Frenchman
was avoiding him and hauled down his flags and turned away.
The Americans were indignant at this seeming uncivil act,
especially in a region where a greeting seemed most natural
and some of the brig's crew wished they had a vessel of the
size and guns to "teach them politeness."[19] In his account of
this international incident D'Urville explained that he was
more than ready to exchange greetings and information and
mentioned that it was said at Sydney that the Americans were
very secretive about their activities.[20]

D'Urville's purpose was to locate the magnetic south pole
and so he had followed the ice barrier only from 140° to 135°
East Longitude where he met the *Porpoise*. Previous to this
meeting, he had been able to send his hydrographer in a small
boat to make magnetic observations at a place where there
was some exposed granitic rock. This was the only place where
there was nothing but ice and snow, and D'Urville had cere-
moniously planted the French flag, claimed the land in the
name of his king, and named it after his wife Adélie.[21]

After weathering the gales which came at the end of January and the first days of February without seeing any break
in the barrier, Captain Ringgold decided to take advantage
of the prevailing southeast wind and sail with it as far west as
101° East Longitude and then work back until the latter part
of February. The *Porpoise* reached her turning point on the
fourteenth and thereafter her cruise seemed to Johnson, as to
others ,"with no purpose but of obeying orders, and our cruise
is proportionately uninteresting."

The *Porpoise* reached the Bay of Islands March 26. En
route she stopped at the whalers' port on Auckland Island
with the inviting name of "Sarah's Bosom." While the crew

---

19 Johnson incomplete letter Feb. 1, Johnson Letters; Holmes Journal 1, Jan. 30;
   Narrative 2: p. 344.
20 Dumont D'Urville *Voyage au Pole Sud* (2-3 v., Paris, 1842) 8: pp. 172-173.
21 *Ibid.*, p. 170.

watered and wooded Dr. Holmes explored and found a flourishing garden with turnips and cabbages to which he contributed
by planting onions. A notice of the cruise was left on a board
and a flag planted near a bottle containing a message in case
other members of the Squadron should stop here, but none did.
It was learned later, however, that other explorers did come by
and read the message.[22]

The Commander was determined to reach southern latitudes as soon as possible and, letting the *Flying Fish* drop behind out of sight, he didn't bother to return to Macquarie
Island or search for Emerald Island, the rendezvous points.
After the vessels separated, he regretted that he could not confer with Hudson, feeling that there was no one on his own
ship in whom he could confide and believing, as he wrote in
his journal,

> that they would be as sorry to find land here because it may add
> some degree of eclat to the Expedition and myself it is provoking
> that we cant get through this interminable barrier and get over it
> —the Land that I am confident exists . . . and if I do not succeed
> it is because I cannot and an all wise Providence has otherwise
> ordered so I must be patient, altho I cannot help feeling how dis-
> gusting it is to be with such a no. of officers (one or two I must
> except) who are endeavoring to do all in their power to make my
> exertions go for nothing we shall however see how we will all come
> out of this scrape. I keep to my old motto *nil Desperandum* thus
> ends this twenty four hrs. of thought.[23]

On the twenty-third the *Vincennes* pushed far into a bay
which, like the others, proved to be enclosed by impenetrable
ice. Wilkes named it "Disappointment Bay" as an expression
of his feelings. On the following day, as the ship stood out
under light breezes, he noticed that Underwood, when Officer
of the Deck, had inserted in the log remarks to the effect that
a passage clear of ice and beyond the point where they had
turned back had been reported from the masthead. To end
all doubt in the matter the ship was immediately turned
around to spend the rest of the day beating back forty miles to
the point in question. The Commander was upset not only

---

22 Holmes Journal 1, Jan. 31, Feb. 22, 24, and Mar. 5, 7.
23 Wilkes Journal 1, Jan. 23, 1840.

FIG. 11. *Vincennes* in "Disappointment Bay," Antarctica. From sketch by Charles Wilkes. Courtesy of Peabody Museum of Salem, Mass.

by the waste of time, for it was evident that the report was untrue, but also because he considered it further evidence of efforts to discredit him.[24]

The first of three violent gales began on January 28. At times snow made it difficult to see three ships' lengths. In spite of keeping a careful watch, they narrowly missed two icebergs and it was realized that "five minutes might doom all to destruction." The gale became so severe by midnight that all hands were called on deck to work ship as they wove their way through the icebergs. The Gunner broke some ribs when he fell on the icy deck and a seaman out on the lee yardarm furling sail could not get back when the sail was blown over him. He had been there for some time before his predicament was discovered. He was rescued by throwing a bowline around his body and dragging him nearly frozen into the top. Frozen reef points could not be knotted and several men were so exhausted with fatigue, cold, and excitement that they had to

---

24 Autobiography **6**: p. 1143; Underwood Journal, Jan. 23–24.

be carried below. The Commander remained on deck during practically the whole time of the gale, sometimes having food brought to him and "how he managed to sleep was a mystery."

The night of the twenty-ninth was much like the previous one. The ship sailed under nothing but the fore storm staysail and main spencer, except when it was necessary to make sail to weather a nearby berg. The crew was divided into two watches, each two hours on duty and two off. The icebergs "could scarcely be discerned through the thick snow & *black* night, but for that indescribably *white glimmer* along the upper edge or surface, which, as we passed them appeared almost to overhang the decks."[25]

The gale abated on the thirtieth and, during a clear spell, they were able to come close to the barrier and, taking soundings, touched bottom at only 35 fathoms. Land appeared to be visible both east and west rising some five to six thousand feet. Some thought they saw a smoking volcano, but Wilkes believed it was merely drifting snow. The land was all covered with snow except for some black rocks which could be seen close to shore and apparently exposed by wind and water, but they had no opportunity to examine them closely, for a sudden recurrence of the gale made it necessary to stand out to sea once more. This was named "Piner's Bay" in honor of the quartermaster; it was the spot where D'Urville made his landing.

Convinced that they had discovered a continent, Wilkes was loath to break off the cruise but, on the thirty-first, Drs. Fox and Whittle reported that the poor health of the crew endangered the ship and Dr. Gilchrist, restored to duty, recommended an immediate return to milder climates. The Ward Room officers, for the most part, advised a twenty-four hour delay to see whether the weather improved. It did moderate on February 1, and the *Vincennes* continued westward along the barrier for another three weeks doing what, in the Commander's mind, was owed "to my country and those with whose care I have been entrusted."[26]

25 Wilkes Journal 1, Jan. 24, 28; *Narrative* 2: pp. 313–314; Alden Journal, Jan. 28; Erskine *op. cit.*, pp. 109–111.
26 Wilkes Journal 1, Jan. 31; *Narrative* 2: pp. 318–319 and append. XXVII, pp. 460–463.

Although the worst of the storm was over, the sick list increased to twenty-three, and the melting snow and ice made the ship very damp. Many of the best men were affected by coughs, their health such that the least scratch became an ulcer, incapacitating them for duty. Rheumatism was also prevalent and there were a few cases of frost-bitten fingers and toes. Another southeast gale with snow and a heavy sea was experienced on the third but the wind lessened a day later and they were by this time in an area of few icebergs.

On the fourth Wilkes himself became ill. In part, this and the illness of his three servants were caused by inhaling carbonic acid gas generated by charcoal stoves. He fainted and was unconscious for half an hour and was slow to recover from its effects.

After the fifth there were no more gales. Some squally and snowy weather was experienced, but also, some very fine days with moderate breezes. It began to get dark enough at night so that they usually shortened sail to double-reefed topsails and did not attempt to run. The ice barrier became higher and its attachment to the land more apparent and, since it was higher, Wilkes reasoned it was older and more likely to have solid ground underneath. With sunshine and smooth water, the sick improved and, although the list continued to be long, it seemed to be made up mostly of idlers whose absence did not affect the ship's efficiency.

On the twelfth the ship was laid to for three hours while they had a good look at a lofty, snow-covered mountain range, seeming to be fifteen to twenty miles away. There was no change in its form or outline during that time. They had now traced the barrier for some 800 miles and Wilkes felt there could be no doubt "of our having discovered the *Antarctic Continent* . . . I am in hopes we shall in our progress West be yet able to discover more of it. . . ." However, there seemed to be little likelihood of setting foot upon it because of the continuance of the impenetrable ice barrier. He invited all but the most disaffected officers to his cabin to celebrate with champagne and this was a pleasant occasion marked by "expressions of kindness & good will."[27]

---

[27] Wilkes Journal 2, Feb. 2–3, 8, 11–12; Autobiography 6: pp. 1141–1142; Erskine, *op. cit.*, p. 113.

On the fourteenth, a fine day, they enjoyed a kind of holiday, sending boats to a discolored ice island which was about a mile square and provided souvenirs in the form of stones and sand as well as delicious fresh water from a frozen pond in its center. They procured 500 gallons for their tanks, transporting it in leather bags. A flag was planted with messages for Hudson and Ringgold which they were never to see. Wilkes went on the ice island with his dog "Sydney" and made some drawings while the men amused themselves sliding on planks and shovels and teasing penguins.[28]

FIG. 12. Crewmen and "Sydney" enjoying recreation and filling water casks on ice island in Antarctica. Drawing by Charles Wilkes. *Narrative* 2: p. 325.

As the days passed and the interminable barrier persisted everyone became more fatigued and more anxious to break away from the constant strain of navigation among icebergs.[29]

---

[28] Wilkes Journal 2, Feb. 14; Journals of Alden and Whittle 1, Feb. 14; Erskine, *op. cit.*, p. 113.

[29] Chaplain Elliott, for the most part an onlooker, described in detail the maneuvers involved in dodging icebergs under date of Feb. 21.

Finally, at 6:30 P.M. on February 21 they reached a point where they could look westward and see the continuation of the barrier without a break, as far as the eye could see. They were at 100° East Longitude and Wilkes, deciding it would be unprofitable to continue further, gave the order to turn north. Calling the crew aft he thanked them for their uniformly good conduct during this arduous but successful cruise and expressed his belief that the Government would surely compensate them suitably for their efforts.[30]

Sydney was reached on March 11, and the misfortune that befell the *Peacock* became known. Wilkes was relieved to know that she survived the accident in spite of her poor condition. When talking with Captain Biscoe, discoverer of Enderby's Land, he learned that Captain Balleny, another British sealer, had discovered the islands which now bear his name and are located near the point where the *Vincennes* first reached the ice pack. More disturbing was the news that D'Urville had claimed the discovery of land on the *afternoon of January 19* and had coasted along the barrier for about 400 miles. It began to look as if the Americans might have been beaten by the French in discovering a continent and it became very important to establish that they had been the first to discover land. It was probable that the sightings of the thirteenth were the Balleny Islands and those of the sixteenth were doubtful, but it was possible that the sightings on the *morning* of the nineteenth were truly the mountains of a continent.[31]

After consulting the *Peacock's* and *Vincennes'* logs Wilkes felt justified in claiming the discovery of land on the morning of January 19, 1840, and sent a dispatch to the Secretary of the Navy to that effect. His claim to have discovered a continent was published in the Sydney *Herald*. In writing the *Nar-*

---

30 Wilkes Journal 2, Feb. 21; Erskine, *op. cit.*, p. 118.
31 Wilkes Journal 2, Mar. 6, 11; Wilkes to Editor of Washington *Union*, Aug. 12, 1847; Erskine, *op. cit.*, p. 128. D'Urville originally claimed discovery on January 18 but had not taken into account that his crossing of the International Date Line made it the nineteenth. The problem of priority is discussed by W. H. Hobbs in "The Discovery of Wilkes Land, Antarctica," *Proc. Amer. Philos. Soc.* **82**, 5 (1940) : pp. 561–582. Munson thought the landfall that Wilkes called "Cape Hudson" was not land. Many of the names of points along the 1,500 miles of the coast given by Wilkes have survived, see map of Antarctica prepared for the National Academy of Sciences by the American Geographical Society in 1956.

rative Wilkes gave the date as the sixteenth, based on his own sightings and the testimony of Ringgold, Eld, Reynolds, North, and Holmes. If the sixteenth was the correct date, there could be no question as to priority over D'Urville.

The logs of the *Porpoise* and *Flying Fish* could not be consulted until the Squadron reassembled in New Zealand. In any case the *Porpoise* and schooner had little to offer since neither made any landings and their deep-sea sounding apparatus was inoperable. When Ringgold turned to the north and addressed his crew, he expressed disappointment in their inability to make any hoped-for discoveries, and when the *Porpoise* arrived at the Bay of Islands Brackenridge remarked that "Officers and men looked remarkably well, but had failed in discovering anything like a Southern Continent." However, when Pickering was shown some rock samples taken from icebergs, he identified them as granitic and compact sandstone rather than volcanic and was sure that they had not come from oceanic islands but "from a large extent of land, a Continent, like Australia." All doubts disappeared with the arrival of the *Vincennes*. It was learned "with great joy that Captain Wilkes had rendered certain, what all on board the brig had always suspected, that the icy barrier so often alluded to in our southern cruise, was formed upon the coast of an immense Antarctic continent."[32]

Ever since Captain Cook's first crossing of the Antarctic Circle in 1773, only sealers and whalers had ventured so far south. Captain Balleny was one of these who, besides discovering the islands mentioned above, made a landfall at about 116° East Longitude which he called "Sabrina Land" and which corresponded roughly with what Wilkes designated on his chart as "Totten's High Land." Balleny had also seen what appeared to be open sea to the southeast of his islands and gave this information to Captain James Clark Ross whom the Admiralty sent out, at the urging of the British Association for the Advancement of Science, to locate the magnetic South Pole. When Ross found that D'Urville and Wilkes had preceded him in the area he had intended to explore, he changed his plans and used his two reenforced "bomb" warships to force his

---

[32] Brackenridge Journal 1, Mar. 28; Pickering Journal 1, "Antarctic Continent," 1840; Holmes Journal 1, Feb. 22, Mar. 30.

way through floe ice into the sea that Balleny had seen and which now bears Ross' name.[33]

At the Bay of Islands, Wilkes learned that Ross was expected soon at Hobart, but too late to go south during that season. He decided to write him regarding his experience with winds, currents, nearness to magnetic pole, etc., and to enclose a copy of his chart of the area traversed by the Squadron. Ross received this letter in August, 1840, along with a copy of the *Herald's* announcement of Wilkes' discovery of an Antarctic Continent. Since he did not believe there was enough evidence to claim such a discovery, he did not bother to acknowledge receipt of the letter.[34]

Wilkes explained to Secretary Paulding why he sent the letter and chart to Ross, contrary to his orders which explicitly prohibited giving to anyone not on the Expedition copies of "any journal, charts, plan, memorandum, specimen, drawing, painting, or proceedings of the Expedition." It was in return for assistance given him by Ross and other Englishmen when he had been abroad procuring scientific instruments and because he felt he was anticipating "the wishes of the President and yourself to afford all and every assistance in my power" for the furtherance of the objects of the Expedition.[35]

Later developments seemed to reenforce Ross in his opinion. He stopped at "Sarah's Bosom," Auckland Islands, in November, 1840, and found a sign left by D'Urville which read: "Du Janvier au 1 Février, 1840, découverte de la terre Adélie et détermination du pôle magnétique Austral." He also saw the bottle left by the *Porpoise* containing an announcement of her stopover there after coasting along the icy barrier, but making no mention of discovering a continent. In January, 1841, Ross penetrated the sea, now known by his name, located two mountains which he named after his vessels *Erebus* and *Terror,* and sailed over an area which Wilkes assumed to be the location of Balleny's islands and instead of labeling it as such simply designated it as land. This inaccuracy

33 James C. Ross, *A Voyage of Discovery and Research* (2 v., London, 1847) **1:** introduction, pp. xviii–xxv, and pp. 116–117, 269–275. In append. I, pp. 327–328, Ross describes the manner of reenforcing the *Erebus* and *Terror.*
34 Ross, *op. cit.,* pp. 116–117, 275.
35 Wilkes to Paulding, Apr. 6, 1840, Ex.Ex. Letters **1.**

led Ross to doubt the reliability of all of Wilkes work.[36] When
returning from the south, he met Captain Aulick on the U.S.S.
Yorktown at the Bay of Islands and found this American naval
officer ready to support his point of view. This seemed to Wilkes
to be adding insult to injury when he learned of it upon arriving at Honolulu in November, 1841.[37]

Ross explained his position in an account of his Antarctic
voyage published in 1847. He said that Wilkes ordinarily kept
his discoveries secret and that Sydney papers had made con-
tradictory statements regarding his findings.

I felt therefore the more indebted to the kind and generous
consideration of Lieutenant Wilkes, the distinguished commander
of the expedition, for a long letter on various subjects, which his
experience had suggested as likely to prove serviceable to me,
under the impression that I should still attempt to penetrate to
the southward on some of the meridians he had visited. . . .

From his own experience, however, he knew how easy it
was to be deluded in arctic regions where sharply delineated
clouds gave the appearance of land, and he could not agree
with the statement in the *Narrative* that the presence of Sea-
elephants and penguins, the discoloration of the water and ice,
and the sight of "something like distant mountains" should be
accepted as indicating closeness to land when in sounding they
found no bottom. In particular, he could not accept the claim
that appearances on January 16 believed to be land

were visible from all the three vessels, and the comparison of the
three observations, when taken in connection with the more positive proofs of its existence afterwards obtained, has left no doubt
that the appearance was not deceptive. From this day, therefore,
we date the discovery which is claimed for the squadron.

Making charts on this basis, Ross said, was "not only entirely
new amongst navigators, but seems to me to occasion much
confusion." In laying down the part of the coast that he had
discovered, he always took pains to include only what was

36 Ross, *op. cit.*, pp. 133–134, 279–281.
37 Autobiography 6: pp. 1173–1174.

"really and truly seen" or else marked it as "appearance of land."[38]

In 1932 the American Geographical Society reprinted Wilkes' chart and superimposed upon it the routes followed by other explorers, especially those of Sir Douglas Mawson, the Australian Antarctic explorer. This shows that Wilkes misjudged the nearness of land to the edge of the ice barrier from the point of his first contact, 165° East Longitude, to "Disappointment Bay" at 148° but that from there for a distance of over one thousand miles to "Knox's High Land" or about 105° his chart is remarkably accurate. Its accuracy has been verified by aerial mapping carried out during the International Geophysical Year (1957-1958) and since. This was a real achievement considering that the exploration was accomplished in vessels not built for combating ice and subject to the vagaries of Antarctic winds. Moreover, chart-making had to be done from shipboard, since the perpendicular ice cliffs made landings impossible. Estimates of distances to the mountains were rendered difficult by the exceptional clarity of polar air, making objects seem much closer than they actually were. The high land to the eastward designated as Cape Hudson and Reynold's and Eld's Peaks could be explained as polar mirages.[39] Whether or not the Expedition beat D'Urville by first seeing land on January 16 is of less importance than the determination that this was a continent and not a chain of islands — this was the great achievement of the Expedition and it is fitting that this portion of Antarctica should be generally designated as "Wilkes Land."[40]

---

38 Ross, *op. cit.*, pp. 115, 177–178, 278–279, 296, 299. On page 294 he quotes Wilkes as saying at Sydney, when shown an article in the *Athenaeum* telling of Balleny's discovery in November, 1839: "All our labour has been in vain." Wilkes wrote the Editor of the Washington *Union* on Aug. 12, 1847, denying seeing the article or making such a remark.

39 Hobbs, *op. cit.*, pp. 561–582.

40 Philip I. Mitterling, "America in the Antarctic to 1840," in *New York Times*, Jan. 10, 1960, gives the whole story of the controversy in its later stages. The designation "Wilkes Land" first appeared as early as 1841 on an atlas published by the Geographical Institute of Weimar.

XII

The Fijis

THE SQUADRON'S NEXT TASK was to survey the Fiji Islands and to select a harbor suitable for use by whalers and naval vessels. The *Vincennes* spent a week at Sydney before proceeding to the New Zealand rendezvous. Her officers renewed friendships and, as it happened, were on hand for the St. Patrick's Day Ball.[1] Dr. Gilchrist was sent ashore to return to the United States independently. This came as a shock to many who had assumed that his differences with the Commander had been settled.

Hudson was ordered to rejoin the Squadron at the Tonga Islands after completing repairs. Since there was no marine railway available at Sydney, the *Peacock* was taken to Mossman's Bay about four miles to the north and, to avoid the expense of heaving down, was lightened of wood, coal, sails, etc., and hove up on a bank of mud and sand at high tide. After being shored up with spare topmasts and hawsers run out to shore, her forefoot could be repaired at low tide and her copper by carpenters in diving suits. A new rudder was made on shore and new gudgeons cast at Sydney. She carried spare pintles. Australian mechanics were hired at exorbitant rates, their union having a monopoly. Stoves were unloaded and, in their place, Irish potatoes from Van Diemen's Land and the powder, canister, and grape shot which had been deposited at the Goat Island Royal Magazine were taken on board.

During this long stay there was considerable trouble with the crew. At every liberty some men would desert, most being caught and held in jail until the ship was ready to depart. Two marines, John Riley and Michael Ward, had beaten up a petty officer at Tahiti and been kept on board as prisoners-at-

---

1 Capt. Hudson made some indiscreet remarks about Catholics at a meeting of the Wesleyan Society for which he was severely criticized in Sydney newspapers. The high cost of living at Sydney was mentioned by Reynolds: eggs costing a shilling each and a chicken two dollars. He arrived $50 in debt and left owing $500 which made him glad to be going among savages again where he would not have to spend money. Reynolds Journal 1: pp. 336–337.

large subject to future court-martial and now, refusing to obey orders, were put in irons. Ward cursed and threatened Emmons who tried unsuccessfully to get Hudson to try them immediately as an example to others.[2]

The scientists reached the Bay of Islands, February 25, and, since they expected the Squadron to arrive March 1, made only short excursions at the northern end of the Northern Island. They formed a low opinion of the natives, the Wesleyan missionaries, and especially of the beachcombers and colonists. It was a confused moment in the Islands' history, when the British were hastily establishing a protectorate in order to forestall the French.

Wilkes became aware of this state of affairs when Captain William Hobson arrived at Sydney on a man-of-war, ostensibly as Consul for New Zealand but, actually, to take over as its Governor. By the time the *Vincennes* arrived at the Bay of Islands, some of the lesser chiefs had already put their mark to a treaty surrendering ownership of their lands to the British. They did not understand all that was included in the agreement, but were persuaded to accept it by the missionaries and by the American Consul, Clendon, who was an Englishman and a land speculator. The English Land Company went so far as to apportion lands to immigrants before it acquired title to them. Wilkes realized that this change-over would result in heavy port charges and other impositions upon American whalers, but it was too late to do anything about it.[3]

John Sac, the native New Zealander, was overjoyed to be home but annoyed to have to pay a month's wages to hire a canoe to take him and some of his sailor friends to his home ten miles up the Kawa Kawa River. When he met his father, who was a chief, they pressed noses, placed hands on each others' shoulders, and "purred like cats." The home-coming was celebrated with a feast and dancing. John Sac's native name was "Tuatti" and he wore native dress when he came

---

2 Emmons Journal 2, Feb. 24–Mar. 30.

3 Couthouy, before leaving Sydney, took it upon himself to write the Secretary about the *Peacock's* claim to having discovered land in Antarctica, Ex.Ex. Letters 2. Consul James R. Clendon sent the Secretary of State a copy of Hobson's Proclamation making himself Governor of New Zealand and a copy of the treaty, dated Feb. 1, 1840, ceding the Islands to Queen Victoria, *Narrative* 2: append. XXXI, pp. 473–476.

with his father to the ship hoping to persuade Waldron to purchase his family's land so that the English could not get it. Disappointed in this and somewhat saddened, he returned on board in dungarees and tarpaulin hat in time to depart with the Squadron.[4]

Most everybody, especially the scientists who had been at the Bay of Islands so long, was happy to leave this whaler port. The shore community consisted mainly of grog shops and seraglios. Several crewmen on twenty-four hours' liberty were robbed when drunk and many came back with black eyes, broken noses, and split heads. Native parents took their daughters out to the whaling ships at night and called for them in the morning. It did not seem incongruous to have the steward of a missionary brig sell to the Expedition two "beautiful specimens" of the preserved heads of New Zealand chiefs.[5]

The *Flying Fish* had arrived nearly three weeks ahead of the *Vincennes,* and Pinkney used the time to make extensive repairs and alterations including the addition of light signal topmasts which Wilkes considered unnecessary and merely to make the schooner look "flashy." He made Pinkney pay out of his own pocket $500 of the total cost of about $3,000 and reprimanded him for rating one of his crew without permission. The upshot of some acrimonious correspondence was Pinkney's suspension and replacement by Acting Master Sinclair.[6]

It was an eighteen-day passage to the Tonga or Friendly Islands. As they approached this group navigation became increasingly difficult because these waters were poorly charted, if charted at all. As the *Vincennes* approached the anchorage at Tongataboo, on the island of Ewa, she hit a coral knoll. fortunately with enough force to break it off without damaging herself. This was the first time the flagship had grounded during the cruise. She had been in these waters five years before under Captain Aulick and, in spite of some alterations, was recognized by the natives.[7]

4 Erskine, *op. cit.,* pp. 135–139.
5 Autobiography 6: pp. 1165–1169; Pickering Journal 1, Feb. 24 and Mar. 3; Clark Journal, Mar. 3; Holmes Journal 1, Mar. 26, 30; *Narrative* 2: pp. 399–400.
6 Sinclair Journal, Apr. 18.
7 Autobiography 6: pp. 1175, 1179; Pickering Journal 2, Apr. 24, 27. The *Pea-*

They were gathering, armed with war clubs, spears, and muskets, in preparation for war. The missionaries explained that these "Christians," led by "King George," were getting ready to fight the heathen or "Devils," who had started hostilities by raiding a Christian taro patch. They asked Wilkes to help them but he refused to take sides. He attempted to mediate but decided that King George was an ambitious and savage chief who should not be encouraged and that, in any case, it would be indiscreet to use military force to propagate religion; the missionaries should concentrate on converting the natives, which required patience and reliance upon setting a good example. He seemed to be justified in this opinion when, some time later, an English sloop-of-war made an effort to help the "Christians" but failed, and her captain lost his life in the attempt. Wilkes' regard for these missionaries was further reduced when he learned that two Catholic priests were allowed to sit on a ship at anchor in the harbor for three weeks without the slightest civility being extended to them. This was not setting a good example of Christian fellowship.[8]

Just as they were about to hoist anchor and head for the Fijis, on May 1, the *Peacock* came into view. She had only one new mishap to report, but a serious one from Wilkes' point of view. In attempting a deep-sea sounding 1,920 fathoms of line were let out which, upon hauling in, parted losing 1,700 fathoms of line, 200 pounds of lead, and the last of the self-registering thermometers. The scientists Rich, Dana, Agate, and Peale now returned to the *Peacock,* their former shipboard home. Hale remained on the *Vincennes* in Couthouy's place and the conchologist's duties were divided between Dana and Peale. Pinkney, under suspension, went to the *Peacock* as a supernumerary.[9]

On the night of her arrival the mosquitoes swarmed in such numbers that sleep anywhere was impossible. Some of

---

cock's only guide was a copy of a chart made by Capt. Wilson of the missionary brig *Duff* and directions shouted by officers stationed aloft, Emmons Journal 2, May 1.

8 *Narrative* 3: pp. 28–31; Autobiography 6: pp. 1179, 1182.

9 The officers of the *Flying Fish* wanted to give Pinkney three cheers when he left that vessel but Sinclair, although he thought Pinkney "a most pleasant commander and a most agreeable messmate," refused permission from "a sense of duty & respect to the authority which had placed him under suspension." Reynolds Journal, May 3.

the men climbed into the tops but even there they were not
free from these pests.[10] This night was also remembered because
of a determined effort by two Fiji women to stow away in order
to return to their home islands from which they had been taken
against their will. They first boarded the *Peacock,* having
thrown away their paddles, only to have Hudson give them new
ones and send them off. Then, after being pushed from the
Porpoise, they sank their canoe and swam to the *Flying Fish*
where they were allowed to spend the night. In the morning
they were sent to the *Vincennes* where the Commander, though
sympathizing with them, refused to interfere in native affairs
and sent them ashore.[11]

The Fiji Group, which consists of about one hundred and
fifty islands, was a difficult surveying assignment. The *Porpoise*
was sent off on a special mission to some of the outlying islands
while the other vessels established headquarters at the cen-
trally located island of Ovalou. As soon as they had anchored
in Levuka harbor on that island a white man named David
Whippy, originally from Nantucket, came out offering his
services as pilot. He had a native family, was the chief adviser
of the King of Ovalou and turned out to be not only a very
good pilot but also knowledgeable in the ways and customs
of the natives. Since these were cannibal isles the survey boats
were ordered to operate in pairs, always armed and within
sight of each other and always on guard against attack.[12]

One of the Commander's first acts was to lead the officers
and scientists up a nearby two thousand foot high mountain
peak. From the top they got a bird's eye view of the islands
and could get some idea of what lay ahead. It was a difficult
climb, in fact, too much for Captain Hudson who had been
ill and for Eld who became ill. The opportunity was taken
to give instruction in the use of instruments; at a signal from
the mountain top a gun was fired on the *Vincennes* and the
distance measured by sound. Returning to the ships in the

---

10 The nights of April 30 and May 1 are mentioned in the Journals of Peale,
   Wilkes, Pickering, and Holmes. The Surgeon said he was bitten through all
   his clothes except his hat and boots.
11 Hudson Journal 1, May 2; Sinclair Journal, May 4, said he could not tell in
   the dark whether they were pretty, but "one of them at least felt both young
   & pretty when I was wiping them off wih a dry sheet & clothing their naked-
   ness."
12 Autobiography 6: p. 1189; *Narrative* 3: append. III, pp. 402–403.

dark they became very dependent upon their native guides and, as they gave Wilkes a helping hand down the steep mountainside, he reflected on how easy it would be for one of them to push him off a cliff. He had heard many tales of their treachery and was prepared for all eventualities.[13]

A program was mapped out so that the entire group might be surveyed in the shortest possible time. The Fijis form a rough triangle with the largest island, Viti Levu, in the southwest corner, its eastern shore about fifteen miles from Ovalau. The second largest, Vanua Levu, is at the northern apex and a string of islands, known as the "Eastern Group," extends from this apex to the southeast vertex. The *Porpoise's* mission was to begin surveying at Lakemba, one of the outlying islands of that group.

The coast lines of these unexplored volcanic islands were imperfectly known. It was a more dangerous area for sailing vessels than the coral islands had been because these islands were not only surrounded by coral reefs and shoals but also, to a great extent, interlinked by them. Pilots at the masthead could usually find the channels, unless the sun was in their eyes, but the winds and currents often made progress through them difficult and dangerous. It was known that the Fiji Islanders considered a stranded vessel a gift from the gods and were habitual fighters who celebrated victories by feasting upon captured enemies. Some slight consolation was derived from the belief that cannibals considered white meat too salty, a characteristic upon which sailors prided themselves. This might have been a joking matter at first but ceased to be so before very long.

The existence of these dangers was indicated by the fact that few mariners touched at the Fijis. Few whalers came, even though whales abounded at certain seasons of the year and wood, water, and some food were obtainable. No insurance could be purchased for a voyage to these islands and it was considered foolhardy for an unarmed vessel to come among them. A few traders came seeking bêche-de-mer, turtle shells, and sandalwood for the Canton market, but by this time sandalwood had practically disappeared.[14]

---

13 Autobiography 6: pp. 1187–1188.
14 Pickering Journal 2, "Feegee Islands."

After their glimpse from the top of Mount Andulong of what lay ahead, the boats began surveying the nearest islands and Captain Hudson took the *Peacock* to Rewa, on Viti Levu, and to Mathuata and Mbau (Sandalwood Bay) on Vanua, Levu, for the purpose of persuading the principal chiefs at those places to accept commercial agreements.

The boats worked in pairs with strict orders regarding precautions to be taken in all dealings with the natives. Some felt that the Commander habitually assigned more work than could be accomplished in the time allotted. Commands were given to the ablest officers irrespective of their date of rank and, as a means to this end, they were frequently shifted. From the beginning, the boats had been designated by name instead of as belonging to particular officers. The names chosen were: *Bear, Elephant, Fox, Greyhound, Leopard, Lion, Lizard, Nightingale, Petrel, Peri, Polly, Turtle,* and *White Handkerchief.* The largest boat on a man-of-war was its launch which carried two officers, a pilot, and eight crewmen. The boats carried a commissioned and a non-commissioned officer and five men. Their equipment included sails, tents, arms, and provisions for the number of days they would be away from their base.[15]

Wilkes took personal charge of the Observatory set up on a high point of land at Levuka. This was done, of course, with the consent of the local chief, Tui Levuka (lord of Levuka, and with the help of David Whippy as interpreter. It quickly took on the appearance of a small village for, in addition to the two wooden portable houses for the pendulum, transit, and telescope, there were three tents and three native bush houses. The Commander was assisted by Perry and Eld, guarded by ten marines, a sergeant and the bos'un's mate and fed by the flagship's cook, assisted by three hired natives.[16]

Whippy was very useful since he was married to a chief's daughter and was adviser or "Royal Messenger" for Tanoa, the most powerful king of the area, who lived in Ambau Island close to the big island, Viti Levu. Having decided to assume the character of lord of all the islands, Wilkes summoned

---

15 Erskine, *op. cit.,* p. 149; Autobiography **5**: p. 1081; Emmons Journal **2**, May 12, 1840.
16 Eld Journal **2**, May 9.

Tanoa to come to him and was somewhat surprised and gratified to have the King's large canoe come into view a few days
later. Tanoa went first to the council house at Levuka where
he received an invitation to visit the *Vincennes* on the following day.

Fig. 13. Profile of Captain Benjamin Vanderford who was a pilot and trader for
the Expedition and who died in 1842 before reaching home. Courtesy of
Peabody Museum of Salem, Mass.

A great effort was made to have this a memorable occasion.
The ship was bedecked with flags and all the officers and scientists within reach were assembled on deck as the captain's gig
brought the King and part of his retinue, the rest following
in his large canoe. The moment of arrival was almost disastrous, for Tanoa was confused by the drums, marines present-
ing arms, bos-un's pipe, and especially by the fierce barking of
Wilkes' Newfoundland dog Sydney which took an instant
dislike to the visitor and had to be taken to the brig. The King
had never seen such a dog before and, since it seemed to resemble a bull and cow that Captain Eagleston of the trading

ship *Leonidas* had recently presented to the chief of Levuka, Tanoa called the dog "Bullum Cow."[17]

Fɪɢ. 14. Canoe of Tanoa, King of Ambau, Fiji Islands. The Expedition's fortified Observatory on the Island of Ovolau is in the background. Drawing by A. T. Agate. *Narrative* **3**: p. 54.

In Vanderford, the Squadron's Master Trader and Pilot, and King had an old friend. He had been on board the Salem ship *Active* which was wrecked on these islands in 1809. At that time Tanoa had taken Vanderford's property but protected his life and they now embraced each other in a most friendly manner. The natives could not pronounce Vanderford's name and called him "Put-enum" remembering the pronounceable middle name of the *Active's* captain, William Putnam Richardson. Vanderford's presence helped to put the King at ease, but he did not know the language well enough to act as interpreter, that job being performed by Whippy with the help of the King's personal interpreter.[18]

---

17 Erskine, *op. cit.*, p. 147; Autobiography **6**: pp. 1192–1193.
18 Autobiography **6**: pp. 1191–1192; Pickering Journal **2**, May 14.

The entertainment on this occasion consisted of firing double-shotted guns, whose balls skipped along the top of the water in a most impressive manner, and a drilling exhibition by the marines followed by a luncheon including such delicacies as nuts, raisins, and old Dutch cheese. Then the guests were shown about the ship and showered with presents, such as whales' teeth (the equivalent of gold on these islands, one being sufficient for the purchase of a wife), axes, accordians, boxes of Windsor soap, plane-irons, jew's-harps, red paint, and large bright brass buttons. "Old Snuff," as the whites at Levuka called Tanoa, was put into such a happy mood that he was easily persuaded to put his X on a commercial agreement after having it explained to him by the interpreter. He asked to come again the next day for an unceremonious visit and at that time was presented with a small amount of mercury which fascinated and mystified him when he attempted to pick it up off the deck.[19] It was helpful to have his friendship even though he might profess more than he really felt. "Old Snuff's" survival into old age was due in part to his being a king, for it was a custom of the Fijis to dispose of elderly and sick people by strangling or burying them alive, usually at their own request.

In accordance with his orders, Wilkes secured the use of a piece of land on which to plant a garden for the instruction of the natives, and employed twenty of them to clear it and break up the soil by means of pointed poles. Brackenridge superintended the final touches performed by two sailors using shovels, and then planted vegetable and fruit seeds himself. The natives constructed a kind of wicker fence, about ten feet high, to protect the garden from marauding animals and people.[20]

Much information about the islands and their inhabitants was obtained from a hale and hearty seventy-five-year-old Irishman named Paddy Connel who had been on the islands for forty years and who, with his strip of tapa loin cloth and dark skin, looked like a native except for his long white beard. He had three wives and claimed to have had a hundred and forty-eight children. The natives excused him and his children from

---

[19] Erskine, op. cit., p. 148; Hudson Journal 1, May 13; Autobiography 6: pp. 1194–1195.
[20] Brackenridge Journal 2, May 11–12.

eating human flesh which, he told them, his God would not permit. He had escaped from Australia after being transported there for political reasons and had no desire to return to civilization. His only ambition now was to bring the total of his children to one hundred and fifty and to kill a few more Fijis. When his last day came he hoped there would be someone around to read a bit of the Book over him. His ability to spin yarns made him a welcome visitor and he gave information about the murder of a boat's crew from the American brig *Charles Daggett* in 1834. Wilkes decided to make an example of the chief who was responsible for that savage act and sent Connel to Rewa with orders for Hudson to capture Vendovi, the chief in question, who lived there.[21]

Hudson had already made friends with the local chiefs and made his presence known by setting off fireworks, firing guns, lighting blue lights, and sending up rockets. Thokanauto, a brother of Rewa's King, was especially helpful being able to speak English "tolerably well." He had acquired the name "Phillips" as a result of making a voyage on a ship owned by that Salem merchant congressman and he prided himself on his knowledge of American phrases, such as "Salem Shags," "New York highbinders," "Baltimore mobtown," etc. When Peale, Pickering, Hale, Lieutenant Budd, and two sailors went on an excursion up the river above Rewa, they stayed overnight at his house. As Peale described the visit: "With genuine savage hospitality, a wooley headed wench was offered to each of the party for the night—all our arms were put in order and kept at hand and a guard kept at the boats."[22]

The King of Rewa showed the same kind of hospitality to Hudson, who had to ask his host to order one of his wives out of his bed since she was afraid to move otherwise. Her intrusion and the activity of the palace mice forced Hudson to sit the night out before a fire in the company of Paddy Connel. In return for the King's hospitality he invited the royal family and their retainers to visit the ship. They all came except Vendovi. Hudson resorted to the strategem of seizing and holding his visitors as hostages until Vendovi should be produced

---

21 Eld Journal 2 and Pickering Journal 2, May 20; Reynolds Journal 2: pp. 15–17.
   Pickering said Paddy once had three children born within as many days.
22 Peale Journal 3, May 17, 20; Pickering Journal 2, May 16.

FIG. 15. Vendovi, Fiji Chief. Held as hostage and brought to New York where he
died shortly after arrival. *Narrative* 3: p. 136.

and the sailors put on a theatrical performance in an effort to
make their guests' enforced overnight stay as pleasant as possible. In the morning Phillips persuaded Vendovi to give
himself up, whereupon the others were released and he was
put in irons, attended only by his Hawaiian hairdresser and
leaving behind fifty-five wives and many slaves. Vendovi was
tall and erect, scrupulously clean in his habits, and bore himself proudly. The crew treated him in a friendly manner and
after a while he was allowed on deck in the company of a
sentry. His capture took place in the latter part of May and in
July he was transferred to the *Vincennes* where he was kept
in closer confinement.

The repercussions from this act were not exactly as hoped for. It was learned through a white resident at Ovolau that an attempt might be made to capture Wilkes and hold him as a hostage for Vendovi's return. Therefore, the observatory guard was doubled, the *Vincennes* brought up so that her guns commanded the beach, and a kind of fortress built at that point of land. These preparations prevented any attempt at assault but considerable alarm was caused when Wilkes, unable to return to the ship, spent a night on an uninhabited island. The news of Vendovi's capture spread so widely over the islands that Hudson found it difficult to induce any chiefs to board the *Peacock* thereafter. She was anchored for a long time at Mathuata ("Mudwater," as the sailors called it) on Vanua Levu, but the local king would never come on board even though Hudson offered his son, Midshipman William H. Hudson, as a hostage.[23]

Wilkes considered it necessary to impress on the Fijis the inevitability of punishment for anyone harming a white man, especially because the Expedition's members were so widely scattered with as many as fifteen groups out at one time and communication so difficult. He gave strict orders to the leaders to be always on guard, to sleep in the boats, and not to go ashore on the main islands except where uninhabited. This became an impossible order when the parties were out for several days since the only way to get provisions and water was to go where there were natives. Wilkes insisted upon strict obedience to orders and this on one occasion caused Perry, one of the most intelligent and energetic officers, to hold two boats doing nothing for twelve days, waiting in vain for a rendezvous. He was reprimanded for wasting time.[24]

The Fiji Islands survey took from early May to the latter part of August. During those four months of frequent contact with the natives it was difficult not to become careless about accepting the appearance of friendship for the reality. Underwood, for example felt that over-caution induced distrust and, having acquired a smattering of the language, was inclined to

---

[23] Hudson Journal 1, May 19, 21–22 and June 20; Pickering Journal 2, May 22; Eld Journal 1, June 17.
[24] *Narrative* 3: p. 199 and append. VIII; Reynolds Critique, p. 53 and Reynolds Journal 2: p. 56.

try to parley with the natives. Pickering, who ventured alone into the interior of some of the islands, came to feel that it was perfectly safe for a white man to do so if he did not display anything to arouse the natives' covetousness. He became so confident that, on one occasion, when waiting for a boat to pick him up, he taught a chief how to shoot a pistol and romped with native boys. Dr. Holmes became lost on one of the smaller islands and was found in an exhausted condition by two natives who led and partly carried him back to where the *Porpoise* was at anchor.[25]

Wilkes, himself, frequently went ashore to take observations and worked out a system for security which depended much on the faithfulness of his dog. Upon reaching the shore, Sydney, whose place was in the bow of the boat, would be the first to land and immediately find and growl at any natives who happened to be in the vicinity. After selecting a spot from which to make observations, Wilkes' boat crew would place the sounding lines in a circle around it, too far away for a native to throw a short club or "handy billy," as they called it, with effect. Sydney would then prowl around in the circle and give warning of the approach of any natives. He was so large and strong that they were afraid of him, with reason, for he never liked the natives and, at command, would have jumped at their throats. As further security, two armed men always stood guard and Wilkes kept two revolvers at his side. Even though the observations might take from one to two hours to complete, Sydney did not stop his vigil and his master believed he owed his life to him, "the most intelligent, and faithful dog he ever knew."[26]

During these months accidents took a considerable toll. Four seamen on the *Peacock* were hurt in quick succession; one caught his hand in the chain nipper and lost part of three fingers; another fractured some ribs when he got caught between the end of a capstan bar and the muskets at the bulkhead; a third shot off his forefinger; and a fourth almost cut

[25] Sinclair Journal, May 14; Holmes Journal 2, July 4; Pickering Journal 2, July 15, 18. Pickering was considered a great chief ("Touronga") because he had four eyes and a good chief ("Touronga venaka") by the boys with whom he romped.
[26] Autobiography 6: pp. 1198–1200.

off his leg. Chaplain Elliott, who was very unpopular, happened to be temporarily on board and the *Peacock's* crew was convinced that he was a Jonas. The worst accident happened to the second mate of the trading ship *Leonidas* when he fired a cannon to help in measuring distance, and touched off some powder stuffed in his shirt. He was taken on board the *Peacock* and then to a tent on shore but suffered untold agony until he succumbed to his injuries.[27]

Day after day of survey duty took its physical toll. The day began at dawn and included pulling five or six hours on heavy eighteen- to twenty-foot oars, wading about on reefs and, after a brief rest for grog, work again until sundown. When ship-based, they returned for a scanty supper of cold tea and to sleep in their bunks. The officers were about as annoyed at Hudson's and Ringgold's ignorance of surveying as they were at Wilkes' tyranny. On the *Peacock,* in particular, everything was in such disorder that they had to run all over the ship hunting up things and were forced to shove off half supplied.

Reynolds gave his family a detailed description of a "ten day survey" that lasted for twice that length of time. He had the whaleboat, measuring 27 feet long by 4 feet wide and 2½ feet deep, with a crew of five. He never took off his clothes. It was "a matter of contrivance & ingenuity" to stow themselves away at night and they welcomed the dawn, their bones feeling as if beaten with clubs. His red flannels and whiskey saved him from rheumatism during the chilly nights. There was no more room for exercise "than a chicken in its shell. My toilette was easily made, after the fashion of dogs, by two or three good shakes, and the vigour of these, was a faint aid, to the more powerful stimulus of whiskey, in dissipating the nervous tremor, which was the natural consequence of such exposed lodgings." A salt-water wash "was neither freshening to the feelings, nor to the complexion" and often, to save the tide, they went to work before breakfast waiting hungrily until noon for their first meal. Reynolds lost his third pair of spectacles overboard with little prospect of getting another soon.

---

27 Palmer's report to Hudson Aug. 13, 1840 in Hudson Journal 1; Reynolds Journal 2: pp. 64–68.

By way of arms he carried a patent breech-loading rifle and a three-foot-long bayonet. Surveying required great concentration with a thousand things to be noticed, calling for the employment of all faculties "to an almost painful degree."

Often have I been up to my middle, screwing away with my sextant upon objects perhaps twenty miles off, with a foothold that I could scarcely preserve from the depth that I was in, & swash of the seas & surrounded by the men, who were holding books, pencils, spy glass & watch, all of which were used in time, this was deeply amusing and is but a slight specimen of the many comforts & delights which attend one on such duty as this. Nevertheless there is a strange interest & excitement in its performance despite of the dangers and privations that are incurred and one is tempted to persevere, and to surmount obstacles with a resolution that will not be baulked. It is a manly pursuit and calls into activity all the resources, that a man can well command.[28]

Along with the hardships were some memorable compensatory moments, such as when two survey boats were pulling for "Mudwater" late one night and Seaman Clark struck up an *ex tempore* song about shipwrecks among cannibals and the men all joined in the chorus keeping time with the oars. In the stillness of the night it produced an exciting and thrilling effect that reminded Emmons of similar exhibitions on the Ohio.

Another compensation was that they could give names, including their own, to places and Wilkes usually allowed these to remain on his charts. Their survival, however, depended upon the lack of native names or designations deriving from some event, such as a shipwreck, and upon acceptance by later explorers and cartographers. A scattering of names originating with the Expedition is to be found on present-day charts of the Fijis. Emmons named an island off the southern coast of Viti Levu "Storm Island," which has stuck, but islands named after his shipmates Blunt and Chaplain Elliott have not, nor has "Elizabeth Island" named after the many pretty girls he

---

28 Reynolds Journal 1: pp. 366–368 and 2: pp. 48–55, and letter to his family Sept. 21, 1840. The natives often gathered around them and were amazed to see a sailor take out and replace his false teeth.

had known by that name. He named the harbor at the location of Suva, the islands' present-day capital, after the *Peacock,* his floating home, but it did not stick any more than the names of the American states which he used to designate the numerous islands of the Yasawa Group.[29]

A Fourth of July rendezvous at Sandalwood Bay did not work out and each vessel had to celebrate separately. Wilkes made some promotions and gave the *Vincennes'* crew a holiday at the hot springs of Vanua Levu where some of the sailors played ball and Eld's scientific interest led him to determine the springs' temperature (210°) and his less academic interests to notice the prettiest girls seen in the Fijis. The crew of the *Peacock* spent the Fourth beating to windward, but had turtle to eat and wash down with an extra allowance of grog. The *Porpoise's* crew celebrated the day with a double allowance of survey duty, as Dr. Holmes remarked. Captain Ringgold had tried to do more than there was time for but did not spare himself, conning the brig from daylight to dark from a seat on her fore topgallant yard.[30]

Some satisfaction was derived from the knowledge that they had stolen a march on the British. Before the *Vincennes* left Levuka, Lieutenant Kellogg R.N., arrived in the schooner *Starling* with the information that Captain Belcher of the British survey ship *Sulphur* was at Rewa, where she had hit a reef and broken two rudder pintles. He wished to know whether the Americans had any to spare. Lieutenant Underwood was sent to get some from the *Peacock* and deliver them to Captain Belcher who then invited Wilkes to breakfast. The Commander arrived on board the *Sulphur* in time to watch grog being doled out (four-fifths water) and hear each sailor call out loudly in turn "Here's a health to her Majesty, God Bless her." Belcher was reluctant to compare magnetic needles or to give out information about navigation on the northwest coast of America where he had been surveying during part of the previous four years. He was evidently displeased to find that the Americans had preceded him here and made his departure as quickly as possible. Belcher's reputation as a tyrant

---

29 Emmons Journal 2, May 21–23.
30 Wilkes Journal 2, Hudson Journal 1, all July 4; Pickering Journal, June 27; Holmes Journal 2, July 2, 4.

was such that some of Wilkes' officers felt he was not so bad by comparison. Belcher did indicate that it was useless to navigate in the Northwest after September and before April. This was bad news for it meant that the cruise must last for two more years instead of one.[31]

The Fijians were as yet little influenced by the Wesleyan missionaries who had been on these islands only a few years. There were none at Levuka, but the white men living there wanted a mission school for their half-breed children and Purser Waldron purchased a piece of ground from Tui Levuka which he presented to the missionaries for that purpose. Up to this time Tanoa had opposed any missionary activity on his territory and those living at Rewa and Somu were only tolerated by the local chiefs because they brought vessels to the islands bringing goods of one kind or another. The missionaries led a hard life, especially their wives, and made few converts. The wives of the Rev. Mr. Cargill and Mr. Jagger at Rewa had to witness cannibalistic feasts taking place in front of their homes. The only place where Christianity had really taken hold was on the island of Oneata, one of the easternmost of the whole group.[32]

The officers and men who had little direct contact with the natives were slow to believe that they were actually cannibals. The subject ceased to be debatable after the day when some natives came alongside the *Peacock* gnawing on two skulls and a thigh bone. One was seen to be eating an eye which, with the under part of the forearm, was considered a special delicacy.[33]

After making rendezvous with the *Peacock* at Sandalwood Bay, Wilkes was able to determine what work remained to be done, and sent out parties for its completion. The *Porpoise* followed him after he started off with the *Flying Fish* and several boats to chart the Yasawa Group in the westernmost

---

[31] Autobiography 6: pp. 1201–1203. Belcher was also annoyed to have the chiefs demand port charges as a result of accepting Wilkes' commercial regulations, *Narrative* 3: p. 182. He believed the missionaries persuaded the chiefs to withhold supplies until he paid port dues, Sinclair Journal, June 15; Reynolds Journal 2: pp. 25–26.

[32] Pickering to M. O. Pickering, Aug. 18, 1840, Pickering Papers.

[33] Gilman, *Dana*, pp. 119–120; Journals of Hudson 1, Pickering 2, and Emmons 2, all July 3.

part of the Fijis. The *Peacock* and *Vincennes* were left at Mathurata under Captain Hudson's command.

On July 12 the Squadron experienced its first serious loss by theft. Perry returned from surveying at Tye, about twenty miles east of Sandalwood Bay, bringing with him Knox and the crew of the first cutter, which had run aground and been taken by the natives. Since their muskets were wet and would not fire, Knox and his men had no alternative but to retreat to the launch which was anchored a quarter of a mile away.

Previously, survey flags had been stolen but the local chief punished the thief by depriving him of his land, house, and wife. A hatchet had been stolen by a chief's companion while on board the *Peacock* and, in that instance, the chief was prepared to roast the thief, but Captain Hudson resolved the matter by giving him twelve cats at the gangway.[34]

The loss of a boat was a more serious matter, for it was valuable and its loss hindered the progress of the survey, the *Peacock* having already lost its launch which, through carelessness when being towed, had capsized and disappeared. Therefore, it was decided to act immediately and forcefully.

All the men and boats, excepting those of the *Porpoise* which had not yet arrived at the rendezvous, were collected and rowed to the town of Tye. Upon demand the cutter was surrendered but without all its contents. Wilkes decided to teach the natives a lesson and ordered Hudson to attack and burn the town. The natives fled to the hills with most of their goods and, except for firing a few ineffective shots, offered no opposition. The Commander remained with the boats and fired some rockets at natives congregated in the hills. Within an hour the flammable bamboo and straw huts of the town were reduced to ashes. Two hostages from friendly towns were released and rewarded with presents.

The next two weeks were spent surveying the Yasawa Group and checking the survey at its principal points. The last of these points was the island of Malolo and, having reached it, Wilkes could feel satisfied that this most difficult survey was nearly complete and had been achieved without

---

34 Pickering Journal **2**, May 21; Hudson Journal **1**, June 25.

loss of life or of any of the vessels under his command. With some such thoughts in mind, he went ashore on July 24 on a sand island near Malolo. After taking a round of sights, and while he and Eld were in the act of packing up their instruments they were startled to see the three other survey boats approaching with colors at half-mast and upside down.[35]

---

[35] Wilkes Journal 2, July 24; Eld Journal 2, July 15, 24.

XIII

An Act of Hostility

W HEN THE BOATS under Alden, Underwood, and Emmons
met on the leeward side of Malolo island, they were short
of food and Underwood volunteered to go to a nearby village
to bargain for something to eat. As he started off in the *Leopard*
for that purpose, Alden jocularly called to him to look out
for the Fijis and Emmons, in the same manner, advised him
to take along a life-preserver. These were their last words to
their longtime friend and fellow officer. As soon as Underwood's boat grounded it was surrounded by a dozen or so
natives. He took a chief on board as a hostage before wading
ashore with some of his men including John Sac as interpreter.
Knowing a few Fiji words, Underwood entered into a prolonged parley on the beach with a group of natives who had
two pigs but wanted to be paid with a musket and powder. In
the meantime Alden brought the cutter close to the *Leopard*
and took charge of the hostage. The two boats were anchored
about two thousand feet offshore and, since Underwood seemed
to be having trouble, Midshipman Henry was given permission to go in to help him.

About that time three natives came out in a small canoe
to communicate with the hostage who attempted to join them
when they started back but was restrained by Alden. During
the next half-hour Emmons brought his boat alongside Alden's
and Seaman Jerome Davis came out from shore to say that
Underwood needed a hatchet to get what he wanted and was
instructed to tell Underwood to get what he could and come
off without further delay. Since the tide had risen Alden
ordered the *Leopard* to move in as far as possible. After that
things happened so fast that the witnesses were in doubt as to
what came first. Alden was the senior officer present and wrote
in his journal the following account of what occurred after the
Leopard started to move in:

174

She had been gone about 10 minutes when the hostage jumped overboard & made for the beach which was the first intimation I received of anything going wrong on shore—I immediately seized my rifle & directed it at him when he slackened his pace. I then ordered 2 men to follow & secure him—he thereupon resumed his course when I determined to shoot him, but stayed my hand lest his death should bring destruction on our absent people—As I turned to direct my boat to be got underway I noticed Midn Clark in the act of firing and ordered him to fire over his head at the same time directed Lt. Emmons to pull after & take him if possible dead or alive—The report of firearms then reached us from the beach to which ensued a general mele the natives having suddenly increased to about 50—By this time my boat was flying before a brisk breeze to the stage of conflict & I called to Lt. Emmons to follow me—In a few moments we passed the Leopard shoving out, when I was informed of the death of Lt. Underwood—The boats had not yet grounded but we immediately jumped overboard & with all speed hastened to the beach opening a fire upon the Natives as soon as within range when they immediately dispersed carrying off their dead & wounded.[1]

As the story was pieced together from the accounts of witnesses the attack took them completely by surprise and seemed to have been premeditated, for the escape of the hostage appeared to be the signal for the natives to rush out from the bush. Underwood was hit in the shoulder by a spear and as he pulled it out shouted to his men to return to the boat. The natives shouted "Tu rano-u" which meant "kill the chiefs first." Underwood and Henry each shot down a native before they themselves were clubbed and fell. Seaman Dunnock and Clark killed one each and Emmons' blunderbuss brought down two or three more.

When Alden and Emmons reached the scene, Underwood lay on his back partially stripped about ten paces from the water. He breathed his last in Alden's arms. Henry was lying in the water and Emmons tried to bleed him but found he was already dead. They carried the officers' bodies to the boats expecting the natives to make a sally at any moment.

With the bodies on the deck of Alden's cutter they set out to join the *Flying Fish,* putting the ensign upside down

---

[1] Alden Journal, July 24, 1840.

and at half-mast. As they approached the schooner they were sighted by Wilkes' party which came out from the shore to meet them and, as both boats came alongside the *Flying Fish,* Alden's face was "pale as ashes and his clothes covered with Blood he frantically exclaimed, 'Great God Sir, Underwood and Henry are murdered, we have been attacked by the natives and they are both dead.'" He was wild with excitement and too incoherent to explain what had happened but the bloody and bruised bodies "told a tale that, struck through our very Souls, and made us vow within ourselves, that we would drink deeply from the sweet cup of revenge."[2]

When Wilkes and Doctor Fox jumped into the cutter the Commander almost fainted and had to be helped back to the cabin of the *Flying Fish.* Alden was there lying on the lockers with clenched fists and fixed gaze and Wilkes retreated to the cockpit and wept like a child. Eld sat beside him as the bodies were put on the larboard deck of the schooner. Then Wilkes knelt beside and kissed his nephew's body, stripped of clothing. He repeated over and over "the poor boy and his poor mother" and then patted the body of Underwood "in the most endearing manner and murmured 'poor fellow.'" After a while he was led back to the cockpit where Eld and others sat with him until he seemed to recover, along with the others, from a state of shock.

Underwood had been stripped of all but his shoes, trousers, and part of a sleeve. His skull had been smashed and he had two spear wounds. Henry had apparently been hit on the head and stunned and, falling on his face in two feet of water, had drowned. Seaman Clark was delirious with cuts on his head and a severe blow on his side. He had shot the native who speared Underwood and had his gun wrenched from him but recovered by John Sac who was unarmed. The sailor carrying the trade basket had been knocked down but escaped when the natives went after the contents of the basket.[3]

---

2 Sinclair Journal, July 24.

3 Alden's official account is in *Narrative* 3: append. XIV, pp. 426–429. The witnesses McKean and John Sac both said that the shot fired over the head of the fleeing hostage preceded the attack on Underwood and Henry, *Narrative* 3: p. 270. Alden in a letter to Emmons, Aug. 23, 1845 (Emmons 2, July 24, 1840) defended himself against Wilkes' accusation (*Narrative* 3: p. 284) that he did not obey orders and failed to keep a proper guard over the hostage.

These two young officers were men of ability and promise and among the best-liked in the Squadron. In spite of his differences with Underwood, Wilkes recognized him as one of the best surveyors. He had married only a few months before the Expedition's departure and had a child he was never to see. Henry, nineteen and the only son of Wilkes' widowed sister, had been in a very difficult situation under the command of his unpopular uncle, but handled himself so well that he won the esteem and respect of his fellow officers. Locks of hair were taken from the two bodies for their families and Agate made a miniature of Henry.[4]

Instead of a burial at sea, a small sand island was selected and the next day they were buried in a common grave by a small party. Agate read the ceremony, a volley was fired over the grave, and the sand smoothed over and dug into in other parts of the island so that the bodies would not be discovered. Wilkes named the island "Henry" and the group of islands of which it was a part, the "Underwood Group."[5]

There was no question in anyone's mind as to what to do next. The Commander's Instructions were clear in regard to a situation such as this. They called for respect for native "customs, habits, manners or prejudices" and avoidance of local disputes except as mediator, but condoned an "act of hostility" in self-defense and in protection of property.[6] While the burial service was being performed the remaining officers and men made preparations for an attack planned for the following day. Guns were cleaned, cartridges made, and Malolo patrolled to prevent any of its inhabitants from escaping. Eld was put in command of Underwood's *Leopard*. Emmons and Alden commanded the patrol boats which were followed along the shore by natives in war dress and paint who shouted defiance and occasionally fired at them, the bullets passing over their heads. It was noticed that, when the sailors returned the fire, the natives threw themselves on the ground as soon as they saw the flash. Two canoes full of natives attempting to escape were intercepted; five were killed, ten captured and put in irons, and the women and children put ashore.

---

4 Journals of Brackenridge 2, Pickering 2, Dyes, all July 31; Reynolds Journal 2: p. 115.
5 Autobiography 6: p. 1231.
6 *Narrative* 1: p. xxviii.

The *Porpoise* arrived on the twenty-fifth bringing reenforcements and, happening to have a chief and his companions
on board, held them as hostages. The desire for revenge was
strong and since, in any case, the attack appeared to have been
premeditated with robbery as its motive, it could not be allowed
to pass unpunished. They were in a mood to spare none but
women and children. The natives' mood was one of defiance
which they made plain by shouting at the patrol boats the
equivalent of "come on, we dare you."[7]

The attack was made on the twenty-sixth with a force of
about sixty men organized into three divisions with Captain
Ringgold commanding and leading one division and Lieutenants Johnson and Maury the other two. The plan was to attack
the fortified town of Sualib first and then to cross the island
and destroy the unfortified village of Arro. Wilkes directed
the activities of the cutters under Alden and Emmons and the
schooner's boat under Midshipman Clark. Their task was to
stop any escaping canoes and to embark the attacking force
after it reached Arro.

Sualib was protected by a water-filled ditch and a ten-foot
high palisade made of cocoanut trunks with interwoven wicker
work. Behind the palisade was a ditch and earthwork so that
only the natives' heads could be seen as they crouched and
shot arrows, threw spears, and fired muskets. They retreated
to this fortress rather than attempt to oppose the attackers
as they landed, and marched up the hill spreading out, cutting
down bananas, sugar cane, yams, taro, and anythings else that
came in their way as they approached the village.

When about one hundred and fifty yards from their objective they halted in the tall grass to rest and reconnoiter. As
they paused the natives grew bolder, shouting a challenge and
flourishing their spears and clubs. Then the attackers approached to within about seventy feet and began to fire whenever a native's head was seen. They were able to dodge the
spears and arrows and the natives, watching for the gun flashes,
could dodge their bullets. Occasional hits were made but the
firing kept up for half an hour without determining the out-
come of the battle. The natives apparently believed that the

7 Colvocoresses, *Four Years*, p. 161; Wilkes Journal 2, July 24; Journals of Eld
2 and Emmons 2, July 25.

charge in a musket should be in proportion to the importance
of the target (one gun was found with six to eight inches of
powder in the barrel) and they made no hits.

Ringgold's plan was to set the village on fire and he tried
to restrain the men from assaulting the gate telling them they
had come to punish the natives and not themselves. However,
Sinclair, unaware of this plan attempted an assault over the
causeway bridging the ditch. He killed the nearest defenders
with his double-barreled gun and pistol and was supported by
the Captain of the Main Top who wielded a bayonet as well as
a gun, but they found it safer to stay at the gate than to enter
or retreat back across the causeway. At an opportune moment
a rocket landed on a thatched roof and, after the native who
tried to put the fire out was shot down, the fire spread rapidly.
The men's cheers were hardly heard in the midst of volleys of
musketry, the crackling of the flames, the squealing of pigs,
and the shouting of men and women.[8]

The defenders were allowed to retreat through a rear gate
with their women, children, and wounded and, within an hour,
the village was in ashes. The bodies of four men and a child
had been left behind, and Underwood's cap and handkerchief
were found. The attackers had few casualties: one man
wounded by an arrow in his leg, another with a slight wound
in the groin, Sinclair brushed by a spent arrow that glanced
off the gate post, and one man bruised by a bullet tearing his
jacket.

Ringgold led his force the length of the island destroying
crops and huts wherever they found them and burning the unfortified village of Arro. A few stragglers fired at them and
they returned the fire killing one or two. Seventeen canoes
were destroyed and from the shore they watched a sea fight.[9]

Emmons in the lead boat containing seven men besides
himself, intercepted five canoes, each with ten warriors and
protected by temporary breastworks. He maneuvered to windward and then barged into the center of the flotilla firing his
blunderbuss and his men firing on both sides at close range.
Many natives were killed and the others were so confused
that they had little fight left in them. Three or four spears

---

8 Sinclair Journal, July 26.
9 *Ibid.,* July 24, 26; Eld Journal 2, July 26; Emmons Journal 2, July 26.

thrown at the boat were aimed at Emmons. He dodged them successfully and, having fired his last pistol, jumped into the canoe of a native about to throw another spear at him and jerked it out of his hand as "Wahoo Jack," the white interpreter, finished off his assailant with a hatchet. One canoe escaped, but the surviving occupants of the others were killed as they attempted to swim away. Emmons was the only one in his boat that was hurt, suffering severe pain in his eyes for a day or two as a result of having one of his men fire a pistol close to his face.[10]

Wilkes learned that the natives in their internecine wars did not consider themselves defeated unless they were compelled to come crawling to their conquerors, begging for mercy. When, therefore, a chief's wife came to the shore the next day offering a white cock as a token of peace, Wilkes rejected it and sent word that all of the islanders must come by noon to a nearby point of land on hands and knees and ask for mercy.

The whole force assembled at the appointed spot at noon and before long saw the islanders approaching on hands and knees with heads down, grunting somewhat like pigs. Wilkes agreed to peace on condition that they bring provisions to the *Porpoise* on the following day. In obedience to this demand, some eighty unhappy men, women, and children brought hogs, yams, cocoanuts, and water.[11]

Although the effectiveness of the white men's guns was demonstrated in this encounter, it was the rocket which started the fire and made their victory so quick and easy. Indeed, the rocket or the "fiery spirit" as the natives called it was usually resorted to when it seemed important to impress upon them the occult powers of the white man.

Shortly after this Wilkes charted some of the outlying islands from on board the *Flying Fish* and stopped at Somu Somu where a war was brewing between the natives of that place and those af Ambau. The missionaries, Messrs. Hunt and Lythe, and their wives, were very apprehensive of being caught in the middle. When the old Somu Somu chief Tui Thakau failed to live up to his promise to deliver yams Wilkes threatened to send a "fiery spirit" against him and this quickly pro-

---

10 Emmons Journal 2, July 26.
11 Eld Journal 2, July 27; Emmons Journal 2, July 28.

duced a heap of yams in addition to a present of a native drum. He was given a musket worth 1,000 yams in payment and a whale's tooth as a gift. In addition the Commander promised to send him some friendly and harmless "fiery spirits" when he departed. As it happened, one of the rockets was set off too close to one of the schooner's guns which was primed and, in spite of its having its apron on, the charge of grape and canister was fired. Fortunately, it was aimed at an angle such that the shot hit the water instead of the admiring throng on the beach. This double display astonished the natives and the sailors alike and, incidentally, made the missionaries feel more secure.

When Captain Ringgold arrived at Somu Somu a little later he met the chief's son, Tui Illa-illa, who had heard so much about the rockets that he offered Ringgold 1,000 hogs and fervently kissed his hands in a vain attempt to persuade him to make a gift of a "fiery spirit." The scientists also found that the news of the white man's fiery ally had traveled widely in the islands. On their walks they were often followed by children who would scamper in all directions when they opened their tin collection boxes expecting that one of these fearful beings was about to be released.[12]

By August 8 the Squadron, with the exception of the *Flying Fish,* had come together at Mathuata, and the first shock of the news of the murders at Malolo had been absorbed by the crews of the two ships that had remained at this anchorage. The schooner arrived the next day with Wilkes who had been on board of her since July 15. The officers held a meeting and agreed to contribute from their salaries a total of $2,000 for a monument to the memory of Underwood and Henry and such a monument was eventually placed at Mount Auburn Cemetery, Cambridge, Massachusetts, and included the names of Lieutenant Reid and Midshipman Bacon of the lost *Sea Gull.* On the tenth a special memorial service was held at which Chaplain Elliott delivered a eulogy which the officers voted to have printed, a hundred copies to be sent to the dead officers' relatives and friends.[13]

---

12 *Narrative* **3**: pp. 298–299, 301; Pickering Journal **2**, June 21.
13 Elliott Journal, Aug. 10.

The murder of their fellow officers was the greatest shock experienced by the Expedition's members. The loss of Reid and Bacon and the crew of the *Sea Gull* remained a matter of uncertainty for such a long time that it did not come as a shock. As the ships and men came together at Mathuata at the close of their Fiji activity this dramatic loss left them in a state of gloom not previously experienced. The feeling of dissatisfaction prevailing early in the cruise seemed to dissipate. Dana commented that "now things pass smoothly and pleasantly." Those who had seen Wilkes weep like a child over his nephew felt sorry for him and, in fact, it was some time before he could tend again to his duties, but when he returned on board the *Vincennes* he was seen to be "in good health, a circumstance which we were all glad to witness."[14]

---

14 Gilman, *op. cit.*, p. 121; Brackenridge Journal 2, Aug. 9.

XIV
Rendezvous at Honolulu

THERE WAS STILL some unfinished business to be attended to before the Squadron could move on to the Sandwich Islands, their next objective. Desertions took place here as elsewhere in spite of the Fijis' forbidding character and efforts had to be made to find those who had "run." It was known that the natives thought it advantageous to have a white man living in their village, and Whippy and Connel were examples of men who lived contentedly with native wives and children.[1]

The Fiji schooner *Kai-viti* had been hired from Chief Phillips for use in collecting yams and other provisions. She was commanded by Passed Midshipman Harrison, now relieved from being subordinate to Sinclair whose commission date was only slightly ahead of his. Harrison's quick temper got him into trouble with his crew, in particular with William Smith, a rather desperate beachcomber who joined the Squadron as a means of getting away from the Fijis. Smith fell asleep while on watch, the schooner being at anchor. Harrison awakened him by using strong language and hitting him with a rope's end. They grappled and both fell overboard. Harrison was not as strong as Smith but was able to break away and swim back to the vessel while Smith, who could not swim, was not seen again. Wilkes accepted Harrison's explanation, having a good opinion of him and knowing Smith as a trouble-maker; there were no witnesses.[2]

It alarmed the natives at Mathuata to have so many vessels of war in their harbor and they were relieved to have them depart on August 11 and, for its part, the Squadron had had its fill of the Fijis. Vendovi was an exception, for he was leaving home and, as it turned out, never to return. Some of the

---

[1] Hudson Journal 1, July 31 and Aug. 1, 1840; Emmons Journal 2, July 31, and Aug. 4, 1840.
[2] *Narrative* 3: append. XVI, pp. 431–432; Harrison's Court-Martial record #736 (Oct. 28–Nov. 3, 1840).

pilots and interpreters were left behind with regret, especially David Whippy who had been most helpful and whom Wilkes appointed Acting American Consul.[3]

Three months of rowing, sailing, and living in boats for weeks at a stretch and in unknown waters was a strenuous and exhausting way of life. It was estimated that during this period the *Peacock's* boats under Lieutenants Walker, Perry, Emmons, and Budd covered a total of 8,225 miles and the ship herself sailed 1,335 miles.[4] In addition to the physical strain and discomfort there was the unsettling feeling that the natives could never be trusted. But it had been an exciting and stimulating experience among these savages whose abilities and intelligence were in contrast to Polynesians. For example, their construction and handling of the chiefs' large canoes were superior to anything seen elsewhere. So, too, the authority exerted by the chiefs contrasted with the weak leadership of chiefs in more civilized areas.[5]

The scientists made the most of their limited opportunities to venture into the interior of the islands and found some interesting things such as a new species of tomato and an area not yet denuded of sandalwood trees.[6]

Dana sent his friend Herrick a kind of summary of their work. They had collected from four to six thousand species of plants. Pickering was the "heart and head in the botanical line" and "wherever we have been, he is the earliest off and latest back." Hale found much of philological interest. Couthouy, having caught a cold which settled in his lungs, had gone directly to the Sandwich Islands.

Rich has done so-so. Peale has got some fine birds and butterflies. . . . Agate is very busy, sketching and taking portraits. Unlike those of the French voyages, they may be trusted as not only characteristic but accurate likenesses of the individuals. Drayton has made an immense collection of zoological drawings. He is not in good health, but has frequent ailings which lay him up occasionally for six days or so; he smokes too many cigars and takes too

---

3 Pickering Journal 2, May 21; Brackenridge Journal 2, "Remarks on Fiji Islands."
4 Hudson Journal 1: p. 567.
5 Pickering Journal 2, Aug. 11; Wilkes Journal 2, May 20.
6 Journals of Pickering 2, and Brackenridge 2, July 20 and 30.

much medicine to be well. Brackenridge, in the botanical department is invaluable. He has suffered somewhat from fever and ague, which he took in the Peruvian Andes, but has now recovered. . . .

Dana himself had prepared some long manuscripts on geological subjects and had made a hundred sketches of mountains, craters, basic causeways and caverns, faults, dykes, etc. He also had a large collection of coral vegetation fossils from Australia and a hundred and seventy-five species from the Fijis with the animals of most of them and had figured and painted altogether about four hundred species of corals. "In geology, I shall take the liberty of disputing some of Darwin's views as to the rise of the Peruvian coast, the structure of the Andes, and also other points which I leave unmentioned, as I have dwelt long enough on self."[7]

Pickering found it difficult to classify the Fijians who would kill shipwrecked sailors, and strangle their own mothers when too old to carry two hundred pounds of yams on their backs, but would also share their fare with a white man and allow him to travel unmolested if he did not carry anything they coveted. They were not savages, for they lived in towns, were adept farmers and proficient cooks, had a theology and customs which were the equivalent of written law. They also wore a dress adapted to the climate and "the time, labour & ingenuity they expend in the art of hair-dressing is altogether beyond our ideas."[8]

We have now got through the worst part of the Cruise, and I am doing very well, not withstanding the fears of some of my friends; however we are not yet out of the woods. The opportunities for a Naturalist have been vastly greater than I anticipated, at the same time, there has been more danger than I bargained for. —A common Sea Voyage is not without danger, as you well know— Surveying in unknown districts, exposed one to an additional set of dangers, and it is not in human nature *always* to take the most prudent course—but besides these we have dangers on land, and being myself as you know rather of a curious & exploring disposition, I have at times been more exposed than others—hitherto, rating a sprained ankle, broken rib, wrenched finger, sundry bruises (for at one time I thought every place we visited would

---

7 Gilman, *Dana*, pp. 121–123.
8 Pickering to M. O. Pickering, Aug. 8, 1840, Pickering Letters.

leave its card on my unfortunate person), and an attack of **Rheumatism** at Sydney, I have come off on the whole extremely well, and am disposed to get along in future as easy as possible.—In South America I made *two trips* to the crest of the Andes . . . either of them might well form an era in the life of a Naturalist, or indeed of any intelligent person. I have drank of the waters of one of the 1,000 sources of the Amazon,—All this, which was never before done in the course of a Sea Voyage, I was enabled to accomplish by a fortunate combination of accidents, by making up my mind before hand, on never losing *an instant;* or suffering myself to be swayed by trifles. . . .[9]

Shortly after leaving Mathuata the vessels separated, the Sandwich Islands their next rendezvous. There were still a few loose ends to attend to. The *Flying Fish* was sent to trace a coral reef on the western outskirts, extending from the north southwestward until it disappeared near Round Island and the Yasawa Group. The *Porpoise* was given several tasks: to survey the shore line of Natava Bay on the northern part of Vanua Levu; to call upon the young chief, Tui Illa-illa, at Somu Somu, in the interest of the missionaries; to stop at Turtle or Vatoa Island, one of the northernmost of the Friendly Isles, to pick up some American seamen stranded there when their ship *Shylock* of Rochester, Massachusetts, was wrecked; and to return to Apia in the Samoans for the purpose of consulting with Consul Williams as to the whereabouts of the fugitive Chief Opportuno.[10] The *Vincennes* and *Peacock* sailed in company headed for the Sandwich Islands, but separated August 14 so as to make better time and to fix the location of additional islands in that part of the Pacific.

The route to the Sandwich Islands was a difficult one for a sailing ship. Helped at first by the southeast trades they soon entered the equatorial belt where the weather alternated between calms and squalls. Beyond this tiresome area were the northeast trades which were dead ahead necessitating alternate tacks to the north and east. The currents were frequently adverse and, on windless days, strong enough to carry them back a full day's distance.

The *Flying Fish* reached Honolulu first. After tracing the coral reef its full length she headed towards the northeast,

---

9 Pickering to Dr. S. G. Morton, Aug. 7, 1840, Pickering Letters.
10 *Narrative* 3: append. XV, pp. 429–431; Holmes Journal 2, Aug. 10.

crossing the equator September 2. When becalmed the schooner rolled alarmingly in the heavy swell, causing the mainmast to work nearly an inch at the step between two chocks which had been put in green and had shrunk. The whole vessel was shaken, but by using trading hatchets as wedges and placing a jack screw between the mast and the vessel's skin, the mast was kept from working. In spite of such difficulties, the *Flying Fish* made one of the quickest known passages from the Fijis. It was none too soon, for she was short of food. At Honolulu a "cargo" of letters had accumulated for the Squadron, but because its arrival was so much later than expected, very little of the mail was less than a year old.[11]

To the exasperation of the *Vincennes'* crew, she spent thirteen days surveying and making landings in the area of Gardner, M'Kean, and Enderbury Islands. Part of that time was spent searching for Sydney Island which was never reached because of contrary winds and calms. Wilkes felt in duty bound to continue the search until the shortness of provisions and water became critical, as it did by September 1 when, following a twenty-four hour calm, he decided to head north.

The second anniversary of the Squadron's departure from the United States (August 18) passed with little notice on board the flagship. In his journal Wilkes expressed the confident expectation that they would eventually be rewarded for all the hard work, exposure, and danger they had experienced and that God would continue to guide and guard them during the rest of the cruise. Some reflected, as did Chaplain Elliott, upon the sad inroads made "by dissension and death in our little company since that day when all appeared healthy and happy."[12]

At this time Wilkes examined the officers' journals and found many of them imperfectly kept. He considered it a breach of duty and faith towards the Country, the Expedition, and towards themselves when they included only routine information about winds, temperatures, and distances covered, all of which could be found in the ship's log. Entries made months after the event he considered worthless.[13]

---

11 Sinclair Journal, Aug. 15 and Sept. 19.
12 Journals of Wilkes 2 and Elliott 1, Aug. 18.
13 Wilkes Journal 2, Sept. 3.

Assistant Surgeon Whittle's journal was in contrast being both voluminous and very personal. For him making entries and composing doggerels was a pleasant way to dispose of boring hours when he was not reading, eating, or sleeping, and a way to forget how anxious he was to reach Honolulu where mail and fresh food awaited. One of his problems was to find something to write about, particularly when "sailing in the trade winds where every day passed as every other has done, without the slightest variation scarcely, even in minutiae." His plan to study French and Anatomy was spoiled by stomach and liver trouble resulting from a diet of ship's biscuit, tea, and the "saltiest beef and the brownest sugar."[14]

On September 5 it was estimated that they were 1,200 miles from Honolulu and might hope to arrive in fourteen or fifteen days, but in these uncertain latitudes it could take twice as long. Whittle's entry for that day was a comment upon the oppressiveness of the weather especially in the steerage where six men were attempting to write in a room about eight feet square and with no more fresh air than came through a single windsail. In the evening when the hammocks were slung over their only table Whittle had to write on his knee while sitting in a passageway to the Ward Room.

Two days later Whittle commented upon the suspension of his friend Blunt for not keeping a journal and his restoration to duty although he had neither written it up nor apologized. "So much for the consistency of our head of affairs." Drayton was much alarmed about an island "which some charts put down not far ahead of us." Being a middle-aged man who had lived all his life ashore, he was not to be blamed for his fears "as even we *young bloods* do not always feel entirely easy." Because of a shower Whittle missed his customary evening walk and talk with Hale. Their talk often made him forget his meteorological observations. He liked Hale extremely; he was so intelligent, well-informed, and amiable. "He does not want spirit either tho a person not well acquainted with him might think so from the softness of his manners."

It was hard to endure the constant necessity for beating

---

14 Whittle Journal **1**, Aug. 25 and subsequent excerpts from Whittle, dates as given.

against a head wind as they visualized letters and fresh food so near and yet so far in point of time. Those in debt to the Purser had the consolation of knowing that they could work it off, there being nothing for which to spend money. The ship's biscuits were becoming too hard to bite into and had enough worms to walk by themselves, as the men liked to say.

As the days passed and Honolulu was still out of reach Whittle embellished his journal with doggerel reflecting his moods, which were as changeable as the weather and, in fact, changed with the weather.

> 10 Sept. Just as our hearts were sinking to despair
> Sprung up a gentle but refreshing air
> Which by & by increased into a breeze
> And made us all as happy as you please.

The steerage was suffocatingly hot. Whittle found it fatiguing just to dress and undress. His cravat was never decently tied, he avoided pulling on and off his boots and the trouble of attaching his suspenders. He lay in bed all morning reading a book, getting up about two o'clock when he became hungry and smelled dinner. He could be lazy for there was little to do, the crew continuing to be healthy except for some slight symptoms of scurvy.

> 13 Sept. Alas! poor wanderer on the stormy ocean
> Thy lot's a hard a sad one to my notion,
> Others are snug at home, while we their betters,
> Have not the consolation even of our letters.

By noon of this date the *Vincinnes* was 480 miles from port, with little hope of arriving there in less than eight to ten days. The weather was now more balmy and the night pleasant, but the steerage continued to be hot and uncomfortable.

On the twentieth the island of Kauai was sighted about fifty miles away, but the wind was dead ahead and Oahu was not sighted until three days later and they did not reach the outer harbor of Honolulu until the twenty-fourth. It was decided that the *Vincennes* made such little progress because she was so light and had the current as well as the wind against her, so the tanks were filled with salt water and seemed to give her greater stability. When Oahu was sighted no one

among those who had been there before knew exactly where
to find Honolulu since they were approaching from the west
instead of the east. They gave Wilkes, who had never been
there, the wrong directions and soon discovered that they were
coming to the village of Wainai, under the high land of Mauna
Kaala. This was exasperating and especially so for the Commander who told himself that this was "the first time in my
life I believe that I have been taken in by relying upon others
& I think it will be the last they all looked sheepish enough
& the laugh was against them but the various excuses offered
for their ignorance were too absurd . . ."[15]

The state of mind of the Commander and crew on the
next day, when they finally dropped anchor in the outer roads
of Honolulu, was evidenced by an incident occurring at that
time. They signaled the *Flying Fish* to come out but Sinclair
was already on his way in a boat. He had selected a few letters
for some of the officers and left the rest for Consul Brinsmade
to bring out later. This mail contained the first news from
home in a year's time and Wilkes angrily ordered Sinclair off
the ship "for this breach of duty and feeling toward his brother
officers," and made him bring out the *Flying Fish* and sail on
and off the port for the next twenty-four hours.[16]

The *Vincennes* came into the inner harbor on the twenty-
fifth in the usual way, the natives walking her in by pulling
on hawsers as they waded along the reef in water up to their
necks. Honolulu with its church spires and many European
style buildings was a most agreeable sight to these voyagers
fresh from the most uncivilized area of the Pacific. A large
and colorful crowd gave the flagship a boisterous welcome, for
her arrival had been expected for the last six months and, in
any case, the arrival of a man-of-war was always an event. The
men in the crowd wore pieces of cloth in addition to the maro
and the women wore loose gowns and garlands in their hair.
The large size of the community itself was in contrast to the
Fijis.

The *Peacock* arrived on the thirtieth, having experienced
the same kind of light airs, calms, squalls, adverse currents,

---

15 Wilkes Journal 2, Sept. 23.
16 Wilkes Journal 2, Sept. 24; Sinclair Journal, Sept. 24, 25; Autobiography 6:
pp. 1243–1244.

and winds. Her empty tanks were filled with salt water and four of her guns moved into the hold in an effort to counteract her lightness. No notice was taken of the Expedition's second anniversary but they "spliced the main brace" on September 10 in honor of the twenty-seventh anniversary of Perry's victory on Lake Erie and, a day later, the officers raised a glass of wine to MacDonough's victory on Lake Champlain. Their provisions, including grog, were nearly exhausted five days before reaching port, but the crew continued to be healthy and contented.[17] The Honolulu mail had to wait until the anchor was down, sails furled, decks swept, and ropes coiled. In the Ward Room, after letters had been read, "conversation was permitted & intelligence bandied about — Anything of interest was screamed out for the benefit of all. . . ." Reynolds finished reading his mail about 10 P.M., ate a delicious watermelon and turned in about midnight too excited to sleep.[18]

The *Porpoise* arrived last, having performed various duties as she worked her way north and east. She picked up some of the shipwrecked *Shylock's* crew at Somu Somu, the rest having found passage on a whaler. At Upolu, Samoa, she procured provisions but did little else. The chiefs had not lived up to the treaty, making no effort to produce Oportuno or another chief named Tagi who had recently murdered Gideon Smith, an American seaman. Upon her arrival at Honolulu, October 7, Ringgold reported this unsatisfactory state of affairs, and its rectification entered into the Commander's plans for the winter months now that the exploration of the northwest coast of America would have to wait until spring.[19]

The "recruitment" of the crews' health and the thorough overhaul of the vessels were matters of immediate concern. It was also necessary to persuade the crews to sign new articles of enlistment. It was estimated that the cruise would have to be extended another year and a half and their articles read for three years from November 1, 1837, returning with the vessels to a port of safety in the United States. Wilkes felt no

---

17 Emmons Journal 2, Sept. 10, 11, 25; Wilkes to Secretary of the Navy Oct. 19, 1840, Ex.Ex. Letters 2.

18 Reynolds Journal 2: p. 139.

19 The Master of the trading ship *Currency Lass* bought from the natives 27 casks of oil washed ashore from the wreck of the *Shyrock*.

particular responsibility for these articles since they were drawn up before he took command. He offered the men a twenty-five per cent increase in wages, three-months advance pay, and two weeks liberty if they would sign on for a new stretch to end May 31, 1842. Otherwise, they would have three-months pay put in the Consul's hands and must work their way home as opportunity offered.

Most of them had been looking forward to going home and their immediate reaction was to leave the Squadron. When Hudson announced the terms to the *Peacock's* crew, he was startled to have two-thirds of the men cross the deck as an indication of their desire to leave. However, as Wilkes predicted, within twenty-four hours most of them changed their minds and signed the new articles.[20] The marines had signed "to serve during the term of the cruise" and, later, when three refused to do duty claiming their time was up, they were put in irons and given twelve lashes before they changed their minds.[21]

The places of twenty-three who refused to sign were filled with recruits, mostly native Hawaiians, whose articles stipulated their return to the Islands when their services were no longer needed and forbade them to draw spirit rations since they were selected on the basis of being believers in temperance. Upon his return to the United States Wilkes was accused of having contravened a law of 1813 by enlisting foreigners, but he was able to show that the law permitted the signing of foreigners in a foreign port when it was necessary to make up for a deficiency of crewmen. In retrospect, he thought it would have been better to have been weak-handed than to have these "kanakas" who, though useful in the boats and very much at home in the water, were disinclined to exert themselves and did not like to venture aloft.[22]

---

20 Wilkes to Paulding, Nov. 30, 1840, Ex.Ex. Letters 1; Emmons Journal 2, Oct. 2; Hudson Journal 2, Nov. 1–2. Many sailors resented the Government's refusal to pay their passage home, Briscoe Journal, Sept. 19 and Dec. 3. Though heartily sick of the Navy, Erskine decided not to leave the ship short-handed and got, in addition to three months advance pay, $12 grog money (for grog "tots" he had not taken), $10 for a cowry shell, and $20 for a tortoise shell, *op. cit.*, p. 203.

21 Stearns to Wilkes explaining that the marines had no written agreement, Ex.Ex. Miscel. Papers; *Narrative* 4: append. V, pp. 509–510.

22 *Laws of the United States* 2: p. 302; *Narrative* 3: p. 386; and 4: p. 112.

For two weeks the Squadron's vessels were practically empty as their crews went on liberty. About five hundred sailors paraded into town in their white frocks and trousers, black tarpaulin hats, and neckerchiefs, with money burning holes in their pockets. It was not surprising that some celebrated too vigorously and ended up in the Fort, which combined the Governor's domicile and the city prison. One night the sailors, armed with clubs, collected at the Fort with the intention of freeing some of their mates. The Governor informed Wilkes who, accompanied by Consul Brinsmade and Captain Hudson, intercepted the sailors, disarmed them, ordered them back to their boarding houses and thus succeeded in restoring peace. After that native soldiers patrolled the streets and fights between the sailors and natives were less frequent.[23]

The reaction of the populace to this sudden inundation by free-spending and exuberant men just released from long shipboard confinement and man-of-war discipline was expressed in an editorial in *The Polynesian,* the local newspaper:[24]

Jack has now been ashore for two weeks, spending in mirth, fun, and frolic according to his own interpretation of the same, the hard earned wages of many months. The streets have by day and night echoed the noise of several hundred tars, riding, dancing, reeling and shouting, parading with drums, fifes, and flags until they seem at last to have come to the conclusion that all play and no work is fully as likely to make Jack a dull boy as the reverse, and are now reshipping for the remainder of the cruise, the terms of many of them having expired when they reached this port. The scenes of noise and dissipation of which the past fortnight has been so fruitful, we should suppose were fully sufficient to bring conviction to every observer, that some radical reform is necessary to regulate and control those sources of riot and drunkenness, the grog-shops. . . .

Wilkes came to know J. J. Jarves, the young and able editor of *The Polynesian,* and may have influenced him to write a later editorial acknowledging that the sailors conducted themselves with more decorum than could be expected con-

---

23 Elliott Journal, Oct. 3; *Polynesian,* Oct. 10, 1840; Erskine, *op. cit.,* p. 205.
24 October 10, 1840.

sidering their fondness for frolic and excitement and the
temptations surrounding them, and admitting that the Squadron's visit had doubled the natives' retail trade and other
businesses in proportion.[25]

Captain Hudson presided over a Court Martial whose
members were Ringgold, Carr, Johnson, and Alden, with R. R.
Waldron acting as Judge Advocate, which tried the marines
John Riley and Michael Ward and the seaman Peter Sweeney,
all charged with having committed mutinous and seditious
acts. The Court decided that the charges were proven and sentenced all three to dismissal from the service with seventy-five
lashes for Riley, fifty for Ward, and twenty-four for Sweeney.
Wilkes kept the marines in the service and, in consideration
of time spent in confinement, reduced their sentences to fifty
and thirty-six lashes respectively. Sweeney, an Englishman, had
joined the Expedition at New Zealand and derided everything
American making himself so obnoxious that the *Vincennes'*
crew petitioned to have him dismissed, to which Wilkes acqui-
esced. At this time Acting Master's Mate A. M. Cesney was
found to have broken rules and regulations in giving out grog
and he also was dismissed from the service.

Since there had been several instances of insubordination
and mutinous acts on the part of whaleship crews it was decided to make a public spectacle of the punishment of these
three men. Officers and men were assembled October 30, but
on finding the prisoners in a drunken state, for which Cesney
was responsible, the punishment was postponed until the following day. Then the prisoners, standing on a platform, tied by
the wrists to the shrouds with their ankles tied to a grating,
and a shot-box between their legs, were towed in the *Vincennes'*
launch. Alongside each vessel of the Squadron an equal number of lashes were administered while crowds watched from
every vantage point. Finally, Sweeney, with bag and hammock,
was towed ashore in a boat stern foremost, the eagle buttons
cut from his coat and the fifer and drummer playing "The
Rogue's March."[26]

Some watchers thought this a barbarous spectacle, but

---

[25] *Polynesian*, Oct. 31, 1840; Autobiography **6**: p. 1301.
[26] Wilkes to Paulding, Nov. 2, 1840, Ex.Ex. Letters **2**; Emmons Journal **2**, Oct.
29; Erskine, *op. cit.*, pp. 207–209.

most of the officers considered it the only way to preserve discipline.[27] Emmons, who had made the charges, thought the Court's penalties should not have been reduced and that, as he watched the punishment being administered,

there appeared to be an understanding between the Prisoners & Boatswainmates that it was at least necessary to go through with the *motions*—those who witnessed the punishment will understand what I mean. . . . And here I let this matter rest—having said as little as I can in justice to my feelings—and nothing I trust, that may be construed into disrespect to my superiors.[28]

Disciplinary matters were not confined to seamen but also had to do with some officers and one scientist. The same Court tried Midshipman Harrison on charges preferred by Sinclair. Harrison opened his defense by calling the Court illegal since it was summoned by an officer (Wilkes) inferior in rank to the officer who presided (Hudson). This embarrassing technicality was, of course, brushed aside and Harrison found guilty of disrespect for a superior officer, a reprimand and dismissal being recommended. The Commander administered the reprimand and suspended him for twelve months instead of dismissing him from the service. Sinclair was transferred to the *Porpoise* and Passed Midshipman Knox again took command of the *Flying Fish*.[29]

For the previous five months Pinkney had been under suspension and in confinement on board the *Peacock*. Having prepared charges against the Commander, he planned to send them through channels to the Secretary of the Navy and, to be sure that his action would become known, had them delivered to Speiden, the Commander's Secretary, in an unsealed envelope. They were returned to him with a reprimand for the "unusual and disrespectful" manner in which they were forwarded and with the notification that this charge would be added to those already made against him. Pinkney defied

27 Elliott Journal 1, Oct. 13.
28 Emmons Journal 2, Oct. 19, 31. A man named Sweeney, known to have been discharged from an American war vessel, led a gang of beachcombers at Callao during the next few years and their object was to fleece and beat up all American sailors who came to that port, Joseph T. Downey, *The Cruise of the Portsmouth, 1845–1847* (New Haven, 1958), pp. 41–42.
29 Court-Martial records #736, Oct. 28–Nov. 3, 1840.

Wilkes further by tearing certain pages out of his journal when turning it in. Following a stormy interview he was detached from the Expedition and sought passage home.[30]

When the mercurial Dr. Guillou was summoned to explain his refusal to turn in his journal he said it contained private references and brought up again his claim to having been promised advancement and increased pay. Wilkes thought his manner impertinent and ordered him to return to the ship under suspension.[31] He was given permission to go home but refused to go unless ordered and at government expense. Since this was refused Guillou remained on board the *Peacock* and composed a letter to the Secretary complaining that he was given no trial and had been disgraced with "the stain of filling a station beneath my junior," a reference to the appointment of Dr. Fox as Acting Surgeon of the *Vincennes*. He pled to be relieved "from the clutches of a tyrant totally destitute of every principle of truth and honour." His letter was forwarded with the recommendation that he be dismissed from the service because of his conduct and because his services were no longer needed.[32]

Officer troubles extended even to Eld, who worked in the headquarters chart room along with Alden, Perry, Case, Budd, Walker, Emmons, and May. In taking the transit from its box Eld accidentally broke the level. This disturbed Wilkes as much, if not more, than his altercations with the other officers, for it would take much time to replace the level if it could be replaced at all.

I could have better have spared his services than that of the level. It is a proof what Ignorance will do, and few can tell how much I am annoyed by this officiousness and all the excuses he has to offer for it is his desire of assisting me in my duties and the consummit impudence that he could handle an astronomical Instrument of which he has no knowledge whatever. I can bear a

---

[30] Autobiography 6: pp. 1249–1250; Emmons Journal 2, Oct. 2; Pickering Court-Martial, Aug. 6–13, 1842. Dr. Palmer helped Pinkney compose the charges which were read by May and taken to Speiden by Alden who, however, did not read them.

[31] Wilkes Journal 2, Oct. 5–6.

[32] Autobiography 6: p. 1251; Emmons Journal 2, Dec. 1. A result of transferring Guillou from the *Porpoise* to the *Peacock* had been to place him below three doctors, all of later dates than himself, Court-Martial records, Aug. 3–6, 1842.

great many things but such intermeddling of ignorance surpasses all belief—in future I must have a constant eye to everything I allow none to touch the Instruments whatever may be his duty or desire. I could almost cry over it. [33]

Couthouy, his health recovered, reappeared on the scene expecting to join the Expedition. He had taken the liberty of writing to the Secretary regarding the Squadron's activities and, contrary to orders, had sent information home which had been reprinted in the *Bunker Hill Aurora*. On top of that, he had given the missionaries the impression that the Commander was a Godless as well as a difficult kind of person with whom to deal.

Wilkes' determination not to permit Couthouy to rejoin the Squadron was reenforced by the knowledge that Dana was doing a very satisfactory job as conchologist. So, when Couthouy objected to turning in his drawings and said he would ask the Secretary to be relieved from a position "whose duties I am denied the means of performing" he was sent home in spite of his protest that he had not requested it. Couthouy, Pinkney, and Lewis, a sick Midshipman, were passengers on the merchant ship *Lausanne,* which also carried a case of living plants from the Fijis.[34]

There were pleasant activities as well as sailors' drunken brawls and acrimonious controversies during this "recruitment" period. The scientists and many of the officers lodged ashore, homes were opened to them, and they found themselves looked upon with great respect, people seeming to have exaggerated ideas of their importance and wealth. It was a delight to have freshwater baths and to smell trees, grass, and flowers. Five officers rented a house for six dollars a month. It had a large flower garden and water supplied by a windmill. A hired boy took care of it and they ate their meals on board ship.[35] For some the greatest joy was to go riding in the evening and horses could be rented for fifteen dollars a month. Reynolds, in particular, found it most exhilerating after a

---

[33] Wilkes Journal 2, Oct. 1.

[34] Wilkes to Paulding, Nov. 14, 1840, Ex.Ex. Letters 2; Autobiography 6: pp. 1245–1246.

[35] Whittle Journal 1, Sept. 20; Reynolds Letter to family, Nov. 16, 1840, Reynolds Letters.

tedious voyage to find himself well mounted "scouring over a
country with companions whose spirits were as excited as my
own, and with scenery about us, that savoured more of Paradise than Earth."[36]

An official call was made upon the young King, Kamehameha III, who came from his home on the island of Maui
just to meet them. The officers wore undress uniforms and, it
was learned later, the King observing this made a hurried
change to informal attire for their reception. The meeting was
friendly. Both the King and the Governor were big, handsome,
and pleasant mannered men, and the Queen, too, was big and
impressive looking. She, as the King's principal adviser, was
generally known as the "Prime Minister," a reflection upon
the fact that royalty was based on matriarchal descent.

A missionary, the Reverend Mr. Richards, was another
adviser and acted as the King's interpreter. He consulted with
Wilkes on matters having to do with foreign relations; affairs
in which the naval officer felt the missionaries were somewhat
naive, since they kept so aloof from worldly matters. The
French two years before had threatened bombardment and by
that means got the King to annul a law against the importation
of liquor and to open the door to Catholic missionaries. The
Commander avoided involvement in these affairs but advised
the King to carry on all negotiations with foreigners in writing
and to enforce all existing laws, including one providing the
death penalty for murder. One result of this was the unpre-
cedented hanging of a chief for the murder of his wife.[37]

The Expedition was given the use of a large two-storied
stone building about a mile east of the town. An observatory,
instrument repair room, and chart room were set up on the
ground floor and Wilkes lived and worked upstairs. The officers came daily to work on charts from nine to four. The
servants were quartered in a nearby building and a horse was
kept in readiness for the Commander's early morning rides.
He became interested in a school next door which was conducted by the Reverend Mr. and Mrs. Cooke for children of

---

36 Reynolds Journal 2: p. 159.
37 Wilkes Journal 2, Oct. 9; Whittle Journal 1, Sept. 20; Pickering Journal 2,
    Sept. 30.

the royal families. The missionaries were somewhat cold towards Wilkes at first but gradually became more friendly as they recognized him and Captain Hudson as supporters of temperance, education, and piety, as well as law and order. In a letter to Boston, one wrote "a 'Boganerges' [Son of Thunder] among us & done great good — & also many of the Scientific Gentlemen. They have contributed pretty liberally to aid our schools."[38] For their part, the Expedition members found the foreign community very cliquey and rumor-mongering with themselves frequently the objects of interest.

Among the pleasanter interludes was an informal party given by the King at which the officers addressed him as "Mr. King" or just "King" and found him to be a skillful billiards player and bowler. In return for the hospitality shown them the Ward Room officers gave a picnic with cooked dog as the main delicacy; their guests included several captains of ships in the harbor and several missionaries. This was the first time the missionaries had been known to join in anything of the kind and, fortunately, nothing occurred to shock their sensibilities.[39]

By the middle of November the immediate problems having to do with personnel, ship repairs, and chart-making had been attended to and it was time to turn to other matters which were to occupy them during the winter months. Among the "loose ends" to be taken care of were the completion of the survey of the southern shore of the island of Ovalou, Samoa, and the survey of certain of the Society Islands that had been by-passed. This task was given to Ringgold who departed on the *Porpoise* on the sixteenth. The *Peacock*, with the *Flying Fish* in company, departed December 2 to survey a number of islands in the central Pacific and to make another attempt to capture the Samoan chief, Oportuno. Wilkes himself undertook the difficult task of taking scientific instruments to the top of Mauna Loa on the Island of Hawaii to make observations for comparison with those taken at sea level.

---

38 Rev. Mr. Smith to Rev. Mr. Anderson, Dec. 7, 1840. See also Armstrong to Anderson, July 7, 1840, Sandwich Islands Mission 3 and Autobiography 6: pp. 1245–1255.

39 Emmons Journal 2, Oct. 10 and Nov. 12; Pickering Journal 2, Nov. 12; Holmes Journal, Oct. 8; *Polynesian*, Nov. 28, 1840.

The *Flying Fish* made two brief excursions for the benefit of the scientists. The first was to the island of Kauai for a
five-day exploration of the interior of that interesting island.
After landing at Kola the scientists worked their way across
the island to Waidi (Halelea) where the schooner picked them
up. Dana and Agate took a northeasterly route, traveling on
horseback and part of the way by canoe, while Rich and Peale
took a middle route and Pickering and Brackenridge a westerly
one, all traveling on foot. The missionaries were helpful, providing both information and lodgings. At Waioli, Pickering
recalled that this was where the famous Crowninshield yacht
Cleopatra's Barge, which he had seen launched at Salem,
Massachusetts, his "almost native town," had been wrecked.[40]

The *Flying Fish* brought them back to Waialua on the
western shore of Oahu and they made their way from there
to Honolulu on foot. Rich and Brackenridge climbed the Kaala
range and spent a night as guests of the Reverend Mr. and Mrs.
Bishop. It happened that Chaplain Elliott and Mrs. Smith, the
attractive wife of Elliott's Seminary classmate and Honolulu
host, the Reverend Mr. Smith, also stopped at the Bishops'
the same night. They were surprised to find the Chaplain off
on an excursion "merely for pleasure." It would have been a
dull evening had it not been for Mrs. Bishop "analyzing plants
—as she called it—with as much fluency as if she had been a
Professor of one of the first Universitys of the day," as Brackenridge remarked, while everyone else "perhaps from a Godly
fear of offending each other by opening their mouths—sat like
mutes."[41]

As opportunity offered, the scientists visited the places of
interest on Oahu, such as the mountains north of the Pali, the
salt lake six miles west of Honolulu, the Punch Bowl, the
Diamond Crater hills, and the lagoon-like Pearl-River Harbour. Drayton did some dredging at the Pearl River looking
for the oyster which gave the river its name but found only a
bed of fossil oyster shells cemented together with soft lime-
stone and reddish sand.

On its second excursion the *Flying Fish* took Dana, Peale,
and Rich to the island of Hawaii. Landing at Kealakeakua Bay

---

40 Pickering Journal 2, Oct. 29 and Nov. 1.
41 Brackenridge Journal 2, Nov. 5.

they saw the stump of a cocoanut tree inscribed as a monument to Captain Cook, who was killed there. With the aid of native guides and porters they crossed the island, accompanied by a missionary named Hall and Midshipman Hudson. They were able to view the volcano of Kilauea before being picked up at Hilo and returned to Honolulu in time to sail on the cruise of the *Peacock*.

XV
Sandwich Islands Interlude

THE DAY AFTER the *Peacock's* departure, December 3, the *Vincennes* got under way for Hawaii, the "big island." Consul Brinsmade went along to get a change to mountain air and Dr. Judd, a missionary, was also on board having offered to organize a native force to carry supplies up the mountain. The doctor was thirty-six, of medium height, thick-set, very energetic, and a great favorite with his patients. He had presented Wilkes with information about the history and customs of the Islands in accordance with a suggestion made by Captain Long during the *Relief's* visit the year before. Although some mission school graduates were employed as interpreters, Wilkes' task would have been much more difficult without Judd's help.

Upon arrival at Hilo an observatory was set up on shore and the work of carrying instruments, the portable houses, and supplies up Mauna Loa began. Dr. Judd hired and organized about two hundred native porters. They and their loads were all carefully numbered, but at the moment of departure the scribe in charge could not be found and the porters became a mob, each seeking the lightest load and straggling off under the urgings of the officers who were on horseback. With considerable difficulty a bullock and forty hogs were driven ahead of the grumbling porters who were accompanied by their wives and children. Wilkes and Brinsmade brought up the rear, seated on chairs carried by four natives apiece but thinking the procession resembled moving day in New York more than the triumphal one their chairs might suggest.

On the first night the officers found shelter but no sleep in a flea-ridden hut. The second night was spent at the edge of Kilauea Crater where sleep was difficult because of the fascinating spectacle made by the huge crater and the boiling lava lake reflecting on the cloud which hovered over it. The following day was spent equalizing the bearers' packs and persuading the women and children to return home before

Fig. 16. Kilauea Crater on the Island of Hawaii. Drawing by Joseph Drayton. *Narrative* 4: p. 125.

they ate all the provisions. Dr. Judd got rid of an agitator who attempted to persuade the bearers to demand double the pay agreed upon at Hilo. Pickering, Brackenridge, and some of the officers ventured into the crater as far as the outer rim of the active cauldron. The surface was rough and, in places, so hot that Sydney, the dog, burned its feet and suffered temporary lameness. Wilkes decided that the natives could not be relied upon to take their burdens to the top of the mountain and sent a call to the ship for fifty sailors to come to their assistance.[1]

The climb from Kilauea was a fairly steady one as the mountain, formed by a succession of lava flows, had the shape of a huge rounded dome. Up to tree line the going was not too difficult, but thereafter it became increasingly so for several reasons. In the first place, the higher altitude made it very cold, especially at night, and firewood became scarce. Mountain sickness caused nausea and headaches. Wilkes felt the physical

---

[1] Wilkes Journal 2, Dec. 14, 16, 17; Pickering Journal 2, Dec. 16, 1840.

effect so much that he found it difficult to hold the sextant steady for any length of time. Water became very scarce and some of the natives took advantage of the situation to sell, at high prices, the water they carried in their calabashes. In one instance those in advance came upon a canoe containing water and, after drinking all they wanted, dumped the rest. When the sailors arrived, having been careless about conserving their supply, they had to buy some with the only coin they possessed —shirts or other parts of their wearing apparel. When snow fell it brought relief, but the ground was so porous that it quickly disappeared when the sun came out. On the desolate and bleak upper reaches Eld got some relief by eating whortleberries but had never experienced such thirst.[2]

Judd, Sergeant Stearns, and a party consisting of Brinsmade, Drayton, Midshipman Elliott, and Brackenridge reached the top on December 22. Brackenridge was the first to reach the summit and felt "not a little proud in being the second white man that had ever seen it," the first having been the scientist David Douglas. The party of four immediately started down again, since there were not enough supplies for them along with Wilkes, Judd, Eld, and Budd, who, with a few servants and sailors, were to encamp there.

On the way down Brackenridge found Longley, a seaman, in a state of exhaustion, carried him to a sheltered spot and, after covering him with a warm coat, descended to get help. Search parties were unable to find Longley but, three days later, Eld discovered him in an unconscious state, close by the trail over which many had been passing all that time. To the astonishment of his rescuers, Longley revived and recovered from his long exposure to snowstorms and severe cold.[3]

In order to establish an observatory at the edge of the crater on the top of Mauna Loa it was necessary to haul up the two portable houses, tents, supplies, and instruments, including chronometers, pendulum clock, transit, etc. The sailors who came in response to the call did most of the carrying near the top, picking up the loads dropped along the trail by the natives who could not stand the cold. By January 1 all the es-

---

2 Wilkes Journal 2, Dec. 21, 22, 28; Autobiography 6: pp. 1261–1262; Eld Journal 2, Dec. 19–21.

3 Brackenridge Journal 2, Dec. 22.

sential instruments and equipment had arrived and a series of five encampments had been established along the trail. The first known as "Saturday" station, the next, "Sunday," was at tree line about 6,500 feet altitude and where the bullock was slaughtered. The third, at 9,000 feet and about eight miles from the top, was known as the "Recruiting" station having a cave which provided shelter. The fourth at snow line, called Alden's, and the fifth, called the "Sergeant's," were used only until the apparatus was brought up. After that Sergeant Stearns moved to the summit and Alden descended to the "Recruiting" station, the men being sufficiently used to climbing in the rarified air to be able to go from there to the top in a day.

ᴸᴵᴳ. 17. Camp on "Pendulum Peak" atop Mauna Loa. Sketch by Charles Wilkes. *Narrative* **4**: p. 145.

The establishment and maintenance of the observatory were a triumph over very severe physical conditions. The cold in the upper part of the trail was too much for the natives with their sparse clothing. Their physical weakness, compared to the sailors, was due, Wilkes thought, to their vegetable diet for they appeared to have perfect physiques. The sailors, all volunteers, had started out in their usual carefree, high-spirited manner, but their enthusiasm evaporated under the hardships of cold and rarified air. Walking on the hard lava crust quickly wore out their shoes and they had to manufacture sandals out of the bullock's hide.

The first night spent at the top was Christmas and it was bleak, the wind blowing a gale and the temperature dropping to 22°. Wilkes pronounced it "No very merry Christmas for us cold, wet & with everything to discourage me." It was also a miserable one for Longley, but his discovery at this time probably saved his life. Lower down the mountain Brinsmade, Brackenridge, Drayton, and two natives spent Christmas in comparative comfort in a hut of their own making. Brackenridge related how they managed to celebrate this important day which

was calculated to be held like all the rest that have passed since we joined the Squadron in rather a mean way, but unknown to any of us—Mr. B. [Brinsmade] had dispatched a native for a Turkey which just arrived in time to be stuffed by our *Consul!!* and cooked in a steam vent by a native just in time for dinner.[4]

On the twenty-sixth Wilkes decided to go down with Judd to the "Recruiting" station to see how the men were getting along. Meeting Alden, Eld, and Pickering coming up they got a discouraging report of the men's condition. Eld thought Wilkes himself looked "quite under the weather although in good spirits."[5] The Commander and Judd were able to revive the men's spirits for, as Wilkes said, sailors

are easily encouraged and by putting a cheerful face and light heart upon the times they quickly take the contageon . . . some were looking deplorably sick others were lying about dreadfully afflicted with the mountain sickness others again exhibited to me their bleeding feet . . . all looking half savage with overgrown beards & dirty and ragged clothes altogether different from their trim and neat appearance when on board ship . . . while Dr. Judd prescribed for the sick I spoke to the well & recovering & succeeded in animating them and felt assured that I had done them some good. . . .

_____

4 Journals of Wilkes 2, Eld 2, Brackenridge 2, all Dec. 25.
5 Eld Journal 2, Dec. 26.

Longley, almost speechless, was in a makeshift tent attended by four or five of his messmates. The scene was "an affecting one no comforts and desolation itself around them a pot of tea and a measly ration of bread was all they had amongst them but they seemed contented." Indeed, the descent from 14,000 to this station at 9,000 feet was like going from winter to spring for it was possible to sit and eat outdoors.[6]

Returning to the top on the twenty-eighth Wilkes was pleased to find that Sergeant Stearns and the men had succeeded in getting the clock, a most awkward piece of apparatus, to the summit. Pickering had spent a day exploring inside the crater. Eld's face was swollen and he was suffering from a headache and pain in his gums and jaws. Pickering told him he had something like scurvy and advised him to go down but Eld was determined to stay, hoping to feel better in a few days. He joined the others in building a wall of lava blocks around their encampment and around each tent within the enclosure for protection against the wind. During these last days of December the weather was delightfully clear with little or no wind. Although the temperature at night got as low as 13°, they made themselves fairly comfortable in their buffalo robes. Wilkes and Judd discovered steam escaping through a crack in the lava within their tent which helped them to warm their hands and keep ink fluid.

By New Year's Day all was in readiness to proceed with a series of observations. The level, broken in transit, had been replaced by a new one brought up from the ship and Treble, the armourer, had succeeded in mending one of the bars of the pendulum frame, which had also broken in transit. The men still lacked rawhide with which to make sandals in place of worn-out shoes, their make-shift canvas coverings lasting for only a few hours of walking on the hard clinkers.

Although the pendulum was placed in one of the portable wooden houses which was, in turn, covered by a tent, it was affected by the changes in temperature. Therefore, straw was sent for and stuffed between the roof and tent and this kept the temperature at an even forty degrees.

After a week of favorable weather, during which observations were carried on successfully, it became raw and snowed

---

6 Wilkes Journal 2, Dec. 17.

on January 8, with more snow and a severe gale on the tenth. By the eleventh the work with the pendulum, measuring the intensity of gravity at this altitude, had been completed and the observations with the Gauss needle, measuring magnetic force, were nearly complete. The interior of the large central and two small adjacent craters had also been examined.[7]

Eld's condition improved; chewing tea helped his gums and raw potatoes helped the burning sensation inside his mouth— an antidote he had seen used by scurvy sufferers. On New Year's Eve he drank warm tea and a glass of wine and felt better. Learning that a vessel would soon be leaving for Oahu,

FIG. 18. Doctor Gerrit Parmele Judd who guided the Expedition members on their ascent of Mauna Loa, Hawaii. Courtesy of the Public Archives of Hawaii.

FIG. 19. Lieutenant Henry Eld Jr., Portrait by John Wesley Jarvis. From the collection of the New Haven Colony Historical Society.

Eld, Judd, and Wilkes spent that evening writing letters. In one, datelined "Island of Hawaii, Mauna Loa, New Years Eve, 31 Dec. 1840," Eld pictured their situation thus: four men, including Judd's native "scribe," sitting together "a la Turk"

---

[7] Eld Journal 2, Dec. 27, 28; Wilkes Journal 3, Dec. 29–31, 1840 and Jan. 5, 6, 11, 1841.

in the Commander's seven by nine foot tent on top of a fourteen thousand foot mountain and within fifty feet of an eight hundred foot deep crater, located in the tropics but experiencing a temperature of twenty degrees; shivering in spite of Pea Jacket, pilot cloth pantaloons, a comforter around his neck, a Scotch cap on his head, a "goodly quantity" of Guernsey frocks and under-flannels, and two pairs of woolen stockings, trying to warm themselves by "keeping the spirits moving"; and being amused by the most trifling thing, he and Wilkes laughing, for example, over the suggestion that Judd's scribe looked like a mutual New Haven friend.[8]

The Commander built a chimney inside his tent and managed to keep a small but smoky fire going, but water still froze less than two feet away. On the eighth the howl of the storm was so loud that they could not hear the clock, only a few feet away, and the wind blew over and broke a barometer and three thermometers. Fearing the collapse of the portable house in this near hurricane, the pendulum was temporarily put away in its box.

When the weather was good they enjoyed magnificent views from this great height and saw beautiful sunrises, sunsets, and clear moonlight nights. Since the top formed an extensive flattened dome encircling a crater of some five miles in diameter, it gave the appearance of a great plain, except for the distinctness of the horizon. The gradual slope prevented them from seeing or signaling the ship at Hilo. At sunset of the first day of the new year they noticed that the shadow of the mountain "formed a very peculiar and distinct object of a dark purple hue" giving them a vivid feeling of being at a great height.

On the twelfth, the weather having moderated and the experiments nearly completed, Wilkes and Judd made the circuit of the crater, taking four or five men and surveying instruments with them. On the far side they stopped to take in the view, as well as to measure distances and heights. It was an awe-inspiring sight which affected the Commander deeply, almost surpassing description. At that particular spot the wind had blown away the snow, except for sprinklings here and there, and the air was calm with the stillness of death. In the

8 Eld Journal 2, Dec. 31, 1840 and letter of same date, Eld Papers.

distance Maui emerged from the deep blue of the sea and
from the misty haze which connected it with the island of
Hawaii. Hualaui, the third mountain on Hawaii, rose to ten
thousand feet with white fleecy clouds creeping up its compact sides. To the right Mauna Kea, covered with a white
mantle of snow, was in bold relief against the sky and at their
feet lay the black lava plain between the two mountains. The
whole was blended and harmonized, "the like I never expect
to experience again . . . we had not time to enjoy this long,
it gave me melancholy feelings and I turned to my Instruments for relief." Mauna Kea was twenty-seven miles away
and it was determined that the highest of its nine peaks was
193 feet higher than Mauna Loa; this fact having been previously in question.   .

This was a most exhausting day for the Commander and
his party. The snow from the recent storm made walking over
crevasses dangerous and the glare gave him and two of his
men snow blindness. Returning to their encampment at sundown, they found about forty natives waiting to carry things
down the mountain. They had to be kept overnight and many,
half naked, were unprepared for the cold. To make room for
them Wilkes took down the pendulum forcing himself, although almost completely fagged out, to pack the instruments. He wrote in his journal, "I think I never suffered more
in my life, Dr. Judd did what he could for us but with little
effect & I passed a sleepless and painful night."[9]

The next day the summit party and the native carriers
started down leaving Budd, Eld, and a few men to finish recording with the Gauss needle. They had to endure two more
days of cold and gale. On a flat lava rock seaman Clark inscribed "Pendulum Peak, January 1841, U.S.Ex.Ex." On the
final day the marine Dunbar stood at the flagstaff long enough
to return their cheers as they turned to begin the descent.[10]

When the mountain expedition set out Briscoe, an
armourer on the *Vincennes*, remarked that it was no doubt
an arduous undertaking "but if it is possible for it to be accomplished by any man, Capt. Wilkes is the one who will

---

9 Wilkes Journal 3, Jan. 7–10, 12. When they fired the "Eprouvette" mortar to
    measure distance they noticed it made a peculiar noise because of the rarified
    atmosphere.
10 Eld Journal 2, Jan. 14, 1841.

succeed for a more persevering man never lived."[11] And when Consul Brinsmade returned to Honolulu he sent a dispatch to Secretary of State Forsyth which read, in part, "Captain Wilkes is now with all his pendulum Apparatus on the top of Mauna Roa at an elevation of about 14,000 feet. The undertaking is a gigantic one, and would not have been achieved by a man of less iron hearted energy and perseverance."[12]

Most of the party suffered from mountain sickness[13] and some had recurrences of asthma, rheumatism, fever, and even scorbutic symptoms. The Commander's snowblindness caused him severe pain for a time and, for the first time in his life, he felt "fairly broken down and almost past the soothing effects of the loomi-loomi, which the natives at once offered as a relief to me." This was a kind of shampooing consisting of a gentle kneading of the limbs which helped to restore the circulation and relax the muscles and joints.[14] When, however, they reached the "Sunday" station at the end of the first day of descent they experienced the salutary effect of a spring temperature, and the next morning "all nature seemed to be alive: the songs of the birds, the cheerful voices of the natives, were delightful: the green foliage gave everything an air of spring." They were so stiff that walking was painful and when they reached the place where the chairs had been left Wilkes was most relieved for he was quite unable to walk any further. They arrived at the camp at the edge of Kilauea crater late in the afternoon of January 14, having been gone twenty-eight days of which six were spent on the ascent and two on the descent.[15]

After a couple of days of rest they began a survey of Kilauea crater. Dr. Judd volunteered to procure samples of gases and of liquid lava. He descended onto the black ledge above the lava lake where he found a steam hole and was able to trap some sulphurous gas in a phial containing red-cabbage

---

11 Briscoe Journal, Dec. 14, 1840.
12 Brinsmade to Forsyth, Dec. 31, 1840, Dept. of State, Consular Letters, Honolulu.
13 Mountain sickness caused headache, giddiness, vomiting, sometimes spitting blood, and diarrhoea.
14 The natives prescribed loomi-loomi for headache, rheumatism, and all kinds of pains, but it required some skill to do it well and there could be a great difference in the way it was performed, Wilkes Journal 3, Jan. 13, 1841.
15 A native carrying their baggage became lost and could not be found by search parties. It was assumed that he perished on the mountain.

water and lime. He wore woolen stockings and sandals made
of hide over his shoes, so that he could walk over the hot
black lava rock. Coming to a small cone, which appeared to
be comparatively cool since only a small amount of smoke and
lava issued from its center, Dr. Judd dropped into it to collect
specimens of capilary glass or "Pele's hair." While absorbed in
doing this the crust broke open at the center and, with a terrific
roar, a jet of molten lava rose about forty-five feet into the
air and about fifty feet away from where he stood. He had no
time to return to the spot where he had entered the crater and
the nearby ledge was too steep and high for him to climb
out unassisted. His native helpers ran away except one, named
Kalama, who turned back at his call for help and extended his
hand over the ledge. Scorched and terrified by a second rising of the lava, Kalama shrank back but, upon the doctor's
continued call, extended his hand again and was able to help
him scramble out seconds before the molten lava lapped
beneath his feet.

Undeterred, Dr. Judd called to the natives for the frying
pan affixed to a pole which he had prepared for such an occasion. By this means he dipped up some red hot molten lava
and tried to stamp it with a navy button, but it was so
frothy that the button sank into it and the lava, becoming
suddenly cold, formed the shape but not the distinct impression
of the button. This specimen has been described as resembling
"a charred pound-cake." The party had to run back to the
edge of the black shelf because the lava began to flow out of
the crater and threatened to cut off their retreat. Judd's shirt
was scorched and he had burns on his wrists, elbows, and
wherever his shirt touched his skin. Kalama's face was severely
blistered, especially on the side most exposed to the heat.
That night the whole party spent hours at the crater's edge
fascinated by the pyrotechnic display, a sight "magnificent,
and worth a voyage round the world to witness."[16]

Alden was sent with the guide "Old Ragsdale" and five
natives to Tulani, a small peak north of Mauna Loa, to procure a set of angles connecting the crater station with the ship.
Wilkes and Judd proceeded with a party of servants, six sea-

---

[16] *Narrative* 4: pp. 172–175; Judd, *Fragments II,* Annual reports for 1840 and
1841.

men, and forty natives who had just arrived with a supply of food, on a survey eastward of Kilauea, following a line of pit-craters and a lava stream to the sea. This stream was the result of an eruption as recent as May, 1840. They returned to Hilo by a coastal route.

For Budd and Eld, the last officers to leave the summit, the descent to the point where they had left their horses, seemed like a return to paradise. As Eld said, "no natives no instruments no cursed anything to trouble me stopped when I pleased, done as I pleased and have been as happy as might be." After stopping to help survey the crater, Budd went on to Hilo while Eld with Smith, a guide, and two Kanakas went to examine the 1840 lava stream. They spent a night at a village where they found Jack Downhaul, Wilkes' native servant, who had come from the ship with some of the Commander's things. They saw him upon entering a house from which loud and boisterous noises emanated and where twenty or thirty natives of both sexes were preparing a sour potato carousal. The old chief and several of the girls began to loomi-loomi Eld

in a most violent manner on all tacks I do not think I was ever more completely abashed or felt more foolish on any occasion than I did on the present although among a parcel of savages, neither was the operation perfectly novel to me yet I had never been handled by such a number in so indescriminate a manner on any previous occasion. I soon got bravely over this however and as I knew that they were trying to pay me the greatest possible respect & attention submitted.

After sipping the sour potatoes he gave permission for a dance whereupon two men danced and sang while the drink and cooked pig were passed around. Then three girls danced and when several men became excited and noisy Eld, weary and disgusted, asked the chief to bring the party to an end.[17]

The next day he examined the sand hills and lava stream where it reached the sea. Smoke and steam came up through the crevices, at one of which Smith was able to light his pipe.

---

[17] Eld Journal 2, Jan. 19–22. The sour potato drink was made by boiling and mashing sweet potatoes and then mixing them with water and allowing them to ferment.

Eld returned to the *Vincennes* on the twenty-second. The day
after that Wilkes' party arrived and a group from the ship
set out to see Kilauea. Dr. Judd substituted for Dr. Fox, while
Wilkes and Eld set up the pendulum at the observatory on
shore.

After descending from Mauna Loa, Pickering and Brackenridge climbed Mauna Kea which, as Wilkes had determined,
was higher than the former by nearly two hundred feet. Reaching the top January 14, they found it consisted of a kind of
plateau on which were several distinct peaks composed of
scoriaceous fragments. Their stay there was short because of
the cold which froze their water jug in a few minutes, in spite
of the bright sunshine. Mauna Loa's crater was in full view,
but the hazy atmosphere obscured their view of more distant
objects. They had Chief Kanuha's permission to hunt wild
bullocks, which had been tabooed because too many were
being killed, but the only ones they saw were at a great distance. They passed the bullock pits where David Douglas
had been gored to death in 1834; it was suspected that he had
not fallen accidentally into the pit with the trapped bullock
but had been pushed into it by his guide. Pickering made a
third visit to Kilauea before sailing in the middle of February,
along with Brackenridge, Drayton, and Dr. Judd, on the native
schooner *Kahalaia* for the island of Maui.

On January 25 Wilkes and Eld, with some help from
Totten, began pendulum observations by day and star-gazing
by night. The sidereal clock maintained a very regular rate
but the pendulum showed discrepancies. Variations in temperature were reduced when the natives built a grass house
over it but this did not solve the problem. The irregularities
continued even after the pendulum was taken apart, readjusted,
and moved to a location across the bay. When the clock
stopped, it was taken apart and an enormous, industrious
spider was found, but after its removal small discrepancies in
the pendulum still persisted. On Washington's Birthday, after
nearly a month's struggle, Wilkes and Eld decided that the
pounding surf, though a thousand feet away, was the cause of
their troubles. The next day a force of sailors moved the
observatory to Mount Kanuha, three-quarters of a mile back
from the shore, and a new series of observations established
the fact that the surf had been responsible for the pendulum's

malfunctioning. It had been a most frustrating experience. Wilkes felt "completely broken down . . . I was almost ready to sit down and cry it seemed to me I had undergone days of anxiety & had had no sleep." Eld's determination had spurred him on when he was about to give up. The unending patience that this kind of work required was emphasized on the last day when Eld had difficulty making observations because the stamping of Wilkes horse set the Gauss needle undulating at a rapid rate.[18]

During the *Vincennes'* long stay at Hilo her crew became acquainted with many of the natives. On one occasion Case, Waldron, Drayton, and two or three midshipmen were invited to dine at the home of Chief Kanuha who represented the royal Governor. The chief's wife, her sister, and his five daughters were present and, upon being introduced, the ladies placed scented evergreen garlands around their guests' necks. The dinner, which included pig, pork, roast turkey, luaud fowl, sweet potatoes, taro, etc., with watermelons and bananas for dessert, lasted until three o'clock. A few days later the chief and his family dined on board the *Vincennes.* They were delighted with this attention and the ceremony that went with it, for they were never invited to dine with the missionaries or white residents.[19] Pea, the King's agent in charge of fish ponds, was also invited to dine with his family on board the flagship.

Contacts with the natives were not always so decorous. Liquor was not for sale at Hilo, an out-of-the-way port, but the journal of the somewhat illiterate assistant taxidermist John W. W. Dyes mentioned occasions during Wilkes' absence when there were visits by "yellow Hores" who "paid their respects to some of the Gentlemen's rooms in private," visited the ward room, the steerage, the berth deck, the black cooks, and gallivanted about the deck to the laughter and sneers of the crew.[20] And Abner Wilcox, a missionary teacher, when writing to Boston shortly after the *Vincennes'* departure, said he could not speak favorably of the Expedition from a religious point of view. "Some of them," he said "are pro-

---

18 *Narrative* 4: pp. 194–195; Autobiography 6: pp. 1279–1281; Eld Journal 2, Feb 2–Mar. 2.
19 *Narrative* 4: pp. 207–208; Colvocoresses, *Four Years*, p. 196.
20 Dyes Journal, Mar. 2.

fessedly pious. But some of the Officers are notoriously lewd, and while here carried on illicit intercourse with native women. What will not money do!"[21]

Chaplain Elliott habitually sought out the missionaries, frequently preaching in their chapels and inviting them to preach on the *Vincennes,* and the Commander looked to them for information, often not otherwise available, and was usually on friendly terms with them. However, he did not get along very well with Coan the principal missionary on the big island who had built up an extraordinarily large congregation in the vicinity of Hilo and whose wife conducted a girls' school. Wilkes believed that the Rev. Titus Coan sought to discourage native production of coffee and sugar and had gone to the length of uprooting coffee trees planted by Mr. Goodrich, his predecessor at Hilo.[22] He also thought Coan and the other missionaries on these islands too prone to accept outward appearance for actuality in their zeal to claim many converts and attributed the natives' readiness to stop work on Sunday to their habitual laziness and taboo-day custom.[23] It annoyed him particularly to have Coan forward, just before the ship sailed, a native complaint of damage to their sugar cane. Waldron, sent to investigate, found little damage but ten dollars was paid in settlement which Wilkes considered extortionate and an encouragement to the natives, proclivity towards acquisitiveness.

After the Squadron had gone, Coan wrote Boston in regard to its effect upon the natives on the island of Hawaii. Altogether about a thousand had been employed on the mountain and other excursions. He decried the scramble for dollars, the bewilderment of a "rude, capricious & semibarbarous people" by novelties and worldly influences accompanying the visit of a man-of-war. As a consequence, congregations were low and "the ways of Zion mourned."

Let me not be understood to assert that there was in the Commander, the officers of the Vincennes anything *peculiarly* obnoxious

---

21 Wilcox to Anderson, Mar. 25, 1841, Sandwich Islands Mission 4, #178.

22 *Narrative* 4: pp. 209–210. After the publication of the *Narrative* the Board of Missions at Boston denied that Coan had uprooted useful plants to which Wilkes replied that Mrs. Coan was his authority for the statement and that he had seen evidence of it himself, Autobiography 6: pp. 1295–1296.

23 *Narrative* 4: p. 210; Wilkes Journal 3, Mar. 4.

to the cause of religion any more than in all others engaged in the like service. On the contrary we should not expect to find, in one ship out of a hundred, more kindness, urbanity, & respect for good order than we saw in the Commander, the officers & the Scientific gentlemen of this Expedition. Capt. W. was attentive & courteous & so were most of the Gentlemen of the Ward Room & others, some of whom were professors of religion. Mr. Drayton of Philadelphia, craftsman to the Ex. made his home at our house, & was a very cherished inmate of our family, & all appeared to be on the most friendly terms. But after these concessions, which are as due to truth as to the feelings of my own heart, still, the unavoidable influence of the Ex. as a whole was to shut out the glories of heaven & to pour a flood of earthiness over the minds of the people.

Coan could report, however, that after the *Vincennes* departure the meeting house began to fill up again.[24]

When the Expedition's members compared the Sandwich Islanders with other Pacific islanders, they recognized that they had made great strides towards civilization but seemed to be very grasping and money-conscious. The Commander characterized them as idlers for "it requires some strong motive to induce them to exertions, they are obliging yet always expect a return for it; great talkers, and laughers, particularly when undergoing fatigue—easily dejected and no perseverance."[25]

In emergencies they could be relied upon. One had saved Dr. Judd's life at the cost of burning his face to a blister and, while the *Vincennes* was at Hilo, the natives on two occasions saved non-swimming members of the Expedition from drowning. The first time was when Alden's whaleboat capsized while attempting a landing through the surf and he was pulled out by the Kanakas "completely water-logged & as blue as a whet stone." The other occasion was when Vanderford capsized going out through the surf but in that case his rescuer demanded two dollars reward before helping him out. The sailors took this as an example of the falseness of the natives' Christian profession but Wilkes thought they simply could not imagine anyone drowning in the surf where they themselves felt so much at home.[26]

---

24 Coan to Anderson, June 1, 1841, Sandwich Islands Mission 4, #39, and to his wife, Feb. 17, 27, 1841, Coan Letters, N.-Y. Hist. Soc.
25 Wilkes Journal 3, Feb. 10–23.
26 Dyes Journal, Jan. 7; Alden Journal, Jan. 27; *Narrative* 4: pp. 206–207.

It took the scientists five days to make the passage to Maui, where they had time to make an excursion to the Mauna Haleakala crater before March 6 when the *Vincennes* came to anchor at Lahaina. Because of the long delay in Hilo, plans to visit the Marquesas Islands were abandoned.

The missionaries on Maui gave them a cordial reception. The Reverend Mr. Andrews and some of the boys from the mission school accompanied the scientists on their excursion to the crater. This friendly feeling was attested by Dr. Baldwin who reported to Boston that two of the scientists were accomplished botanists and "afforded me more assistance as to the vegetable productions of this part of the world than all I have had from other sources since I have been in the islands." The scientists and the officers

were often at our tables to our no small gratification. Not only their intercourse with us, but the advice they uniformly gave the rulers of this nation, & the influence they endeavoured to exert on them, stand in such delightful contrast with the advice & influence of some men of war who have been here, that the visit of the Squadron has made us quite proud of our 'Stars & Stripes'. Capt. W. is a superior man—his zeal & perseverance, in this expedition, have earned him a lasting fame. Many under him are pious . . . [27]

The Commander took this opportunity to acquire additional information about the history and customs of the Sandwich Islanders from the Reverend Mr. Richards who, as the King's adviser, was particularly well informed.[28] King Kamahameha II lived at Lahaina and accepted an invitation to dine on board the *Vincennes*. The yards were manned, blue lights lit, and rockets set off in his honor. He looked very handsome in his blue uniform with gold lace, cocked hat, white pantaloons, and boots. His manner was dignified and courtly. After a collation in the cabin he changed to a more comfortable coat and hat. Eld thought him and his suite "the most intelligent & genteel" natives he had ever seen and Wilkes, visiting him at his residence, was impressed by his friendliness and good intentions.[29]

The *Vincennes* reached Honolulu March 19 and imme-

[27] Baldwin to Anderson, Aug. 2, 1841, Sandwich Islands Mission 3, #22.
[28] Wilkes and Richards correspondence, Mar. 8, 15, Honolulu Archives.
[29] Eld Journal 2, Mar. 8; Elliott Journal 2, Mar. 10; *Narrative* 4: p. 238.

diately began preparations for departure to the northwest coast of America. At the King's request, Alden was sent with two boats to survey the Pearl River and the coast as far as Barbours Point. He found a coral bar at the river's mouth with only fifteen feet of water but inside there was ample depth for large ships and room for any number of them. It was remarked that a deepened channel into Pearl River Harbour would make it into "the best and most capacious harbour in the Pacific" but that the port of Honolulu was sufficient for all needs of the islands at that time.[30]

The most important news from home was the election of William Henry Harrison as President. His Whig administration was less likely to be interested in the Expedition than its Democratic sponsors.

Among the accounts to be settled was a payment to Dr. Judd for his important services. He and his wife, a most cheerful and hospitable couple, had seven children but owned no property, except one cow, and his pay was only four hundred dollars a year. The Sandwich Islands Mission was the only one encountered by the Expedition that had doctors and Wilkes thought the natives should be made to pay for medical services. He was determined to reward the doctor rather than the Mission and gave him the pay of a Navy Surgeon which, for the period of his service, amounted to between seven and eight hundred dollars.[31]

Judd accepted it for the benefit of his children and explained to the Board that he thought it his duty to assist in every way possible in view of the Expedition's objects and "the claims we have made on our Government for the protection of ourselves and our families from proscription and outrage." The Expedition had been short of surgeons, needed a confidential interpreter and when its Commander invited him to accompany it the Mission agreed that it was his duty to go. He had expected no reward other than "a consciousness of doing good and serving our common cause." Unforeseen circumstances had protracted his absence for double the expected six weeks.[32]

---

30 *Narrative* **4**: p. 79.
31 Autobiography **6**: pp. 1292–1294.
32 Judd, *Fragments II*, Annual reports for 1840 and 1841, pp. 127–131.

At the Mission's annual meeting this payment came under discussion when Levi Chamberlain accused Judd of breaking their rules. The matter was referred to Boston, and Judd accepted the Board's suggestion that he pay the Mission the ordinary amount payable for his services. However, it continued to be a matter for discussion until 1843 when he accepted an appointment as the King's official interpreter and financial officer. In 1849 he accompanied the two young princes on a diplomatic journey and, when in New York, had the pleasure of a second meeting with Wilkes.[33]

The Commander felt obligated to the missionaries for their helpfulness and hospitality and admired them for their strength of character. Their great influence with the chiefs led inevitably to trouble with the foreign residents and he warned them that it must lead eventually to the separation of Church and State. While avoiding involvement in local quarrels, he did what he could to encourage good feeling at Honolulu where there was much bickering not only between the missionaries and the French and English but also among the missionaries themselves.[34]

The members of the Expedition were aware of this state of affairs and found it difficult not to take sides. Alden thought the Calvinist Missionaries were ruining the islands before the French brought a reprieve. He was persuaded that they were a fanatical, intolerant, and ignorant group of zealots[35] and Emmons, while recognizing the good they had done, felt they had gone too far in discountenancing innocent games which previously had contributed to the natives' health and happiness. Their error would soon become apparent, for the newly established Roman Catholics were adopting an opposite course and would probably win over many converts.[36]

Pickering, with friends among both the missionaries and the foreign residents, saw "a great many drawbacks on a near view—or perhaps I should rather say it is not pleasant to visit the Nation in the present period of its existence. The en-

---

33 Judd to Sandwich Islands Mission, May 26, 1843, cited in G. P. Judd IV, *Dr. Judd, Hawaii's Friend* (Honolulu, 1960), pp. 102–103.
34 Autobiography 6: pp. 1297–1299.
35 Alden Journal, 1841.
36 Emmons Journal 3, Nov. 27.

grafting of the new system on the Old, does not seem to work well just now on the 'body politic.' " He thought that the native population was diminishing because the demands of commerce were reducing food supplies, money was creating new wants without providing the means of satisfying them, and the chiefs and their retainers were oppressing the people in order to gratify their personal wants. However, the natives would survive for they could live under conditions which would cause a white man to starve.[37]

Chaplain Elliott caused a coolness between the *Vincennes'* officers and the missionaries by spreading accounts of the misbehavior of some of the officers at Hilo which was a reflection upon the morals of the professed Christians among the natives. Coming from such a source the missionaries became very excited and anxious to know the truth. The Commander made enquiries and concluded that the Chaplain had believed things told him in badinage and for the purpose of irritating him, "which he had not the good sense to perceive." Elliott while acknowledging that he might have been too credulous, explained that he felt it necessary to inform the missionaries of the condition of their flocks. The officers were loud in their complaints against him and made it impossible for him to perform his clerical duties. Elliott, whom Wilkes characterized as a "spooney," had also been over-friendly with the good-looking wife of the Reverend Mr. Smith, making an enemy of his former Seminary classmate in whose house he had been a guest. During his interrogation he appeared to make several "wilful and malicious falsehoods" and was, therefore, suspended to await court martial.[38]

Wilkes professed never to have witnessed conduct or indecencies "that do not exist elsewhere in civilized places" but thought the officers had been "indecorous." It seemed to him that the missionaries could have investigated the matter more quietly. Good feeling was finally reestablished for the missionaries appreciated Wilkes' interest in their schools. The *Missionary Herald* stated that the American Navy left $65,000 whereas the French took out $20,000 and "left the deadly

---

[37] Pickering to M. O. Pickering, Mar. 10, 1841, Pickering Letters.

[38] Wilkes to Secretary of the Navy, Nov. 23, 1841, Wilkes Papers #95; Levi Chamberlain, Journal, April 5, 1841.

curse of intemperance."[39] The native chiefs showed their friendly feelings by giving the officers a luau.

On March 23 the *Porpoise* was sighted beating up for the harbor and Wilkes pushed his plans for an early departure for the northwest coast of America.

---

[39] Autobiography **6**: pp. 1282–1287; letter from Lowell Smith, Dec. 7, 1841, in *The Missionary Herald* **37**: p. 360.

XVI

Cruise of the Porpoise

T HE *Porpoise's* cruise, which began November 15, was an
exacting one. Lieutenant-Commandant Ringgold's orders
were to survey certain islands in the Paumotu Group extending southward as far as Tahiti.

The brig took on several Kanakas as crew. Their names
were so difficult to pronounce and spell that it became customary to make up names for them. For example, Jim Kahaku
became "Jim Crow" and Isaac Mahiale "Isaac Newton." At the
first muster the clerk burst out laughing when he came to "Joe
Beeswax" causing Lieutenant Johnson to select another name
for that individual.[1]

One of the vessel's assigned tasks was to land a party on a
suitable island to experiment with a boring machine to determine the character of coral rock. Carlshoff or Aratica Island
was chosen for this purpose and Johnson was deposited there
with a work-party of twelve. His orders were to keep the apparatus operating day and night for thirty to forty days. The island
had drinking water and was occupied by a friendly group of
about twenty natives who offered the landing party pumpkins,
watermelon, and cocoanuts, so they had no fear of starvation.
The Squadron's visit in 1839 was remembered and, in fact,
some of the natives were still wearing clothes given them at
that time.[2]

The boring experiment was not a success, the ground being too soft and porous. Pieces of coral prevented the pipe from
remaining perfectly perpendicular and the heavy drill tended
to hit and break it. No matter how hard they tried they could
go down only about twenty feet. Specimens for each of these
feet were preserved. Wilkes believed the attempt might have

---

1 Johnson Journal, Dec. 6, 1840; Emmons Journal 2, Dec. 2, 1840.
2 Johnson Journal, Dec. 15–16; Holmes Journal 2, Dec. 17.

been more successful if it had been made during the dry season.[3]

The *Porpoise* proceeded to survey several islands in that area and, near Saken Island, came upon a cluster of three small ones which Ringgold called the Sea Gull group and named individually after Passed Midshipmen Reid and Bacon and Quartermaster Clute. After returning to pick up Johnson's party, they sailed for Tahiti, arriving at Papeete on January 21, 1841. Very little change had taken place during their eighteen months' absence. They were impressed, as before, by the beauty and fertility of this gem of the Pacific. Old acquaintances were renewed; their friends were as contented, immoral, and immodest as ever. There was not much doing, for Queen Pomare and her entourage were visiting on another island. The quarrels between the Queen and her consort and among the chiefs persisted, as did foreigners' attempts to oppose the missionaries in internal affairs. The water front was policed more effectively. After eight o'clock at night sailors or riotous persons without a written pass from their consul were put in the stocks and held until a two-dollar fine was paid.[4]

The brig stayed only long enough to make magnetic and chronometric observations, to take on water and wood, and to refresh the crew, and hoisted anchor January 28. For the next three or four days she experienced very light winds or calms and made little progress. Heading again for the Sandwich Islands, she followed a route westward of where she had just been and surveyed the islands encountered. The supposed location of Teinhoven Island was sailed over and Penrhyn Island, which had been given two locations, was found to be thirty miles west of its position on Arrowsmith's chart.

At dawn on February 16 many canoes came out from Penrhyn Island. The natives became quite bold and climbered on board yelling so savagely and loudly that orders could not be heard. They were the wildest looking yet encountered and, frantic with excitement, began to pilfer things on the poop deck. One huge savage grabbed the manrope, pulled a

---

[3] At this point in the *Narrative* Wilkes gave his explanation of the formation of coral islands in refutation of Darwin's (and Dana's) "ingenious theory." He explained it in terms of earthquakes and the action of the sea rather than as the work of tiny zoophytes, *Narrative* 4: pp. 267–271.

[4] Holmes Journal 2, Jan. 21, 1841.

stanchion out of place and was about to pass it over the side
when he was stopped. Captain Ringgold ordered the drummer
to beat to quarters, kept the vessel under way and had the
sailors, armed with cutlasses, clear the decks. As soon as the
natives got into their canoes they began to throw coral and
shells, brandish spears, and yell defiance, paying little attention to guns fired over their heads. Some canoes were kept in
tow at the stern and, after a time, some trading was done ex-
changing knives, iron and cloth for weapons, necklaces, etc.
The natives did not know the use of tobacco, were scarified
but not tattooed or circumcised, and many were without front
teeth, the Samoan sign of bereavement. They used a few
Polynesian words but neither the Tahitians nor Hawaiians in
the crew could communicate with them.[5]

The northeast trade winds and the strong equatorial currents carried the *Porpoise* to leeward, delaying her return to
Honolulu. Her slow progress began to get on everyone's nerves.
Johnson worried about the need to repair sails, having only
thirty to forty yards of canvas left and that in five or six pieces
and of inferior quality. At dusk the officers habitually gathered
for a "cozy smoke" and, occasionally, a glass of Johnson's "good
old sherry." They talked of the necessity of putting the crew
on half allowance of bread, because of someone's oversight
when at Oahu, and speculated as to the results of the last
election: would Old Tippecanoe remain in his log cabin to
drink hard cider or would he move into the White House?

The rigging acquired a very worn appearance, parts of it
giving way in the strong wind, and the copper at the bow
acquired a ragged look. Johnson hoped they might be sent
home to refit and wondered who, in that case, would volunteer
to rejoin the Squadron. On March 14 the main topsail split
and was replaced by the only remaining good sail. Although
within a hundred and fifty miles of Honolulu, they were buck-
ing a gale which was driving them to leeward and, at that time
of year, there was little prospect of its letting up soon. Spars
were scarce as well as canvas and food. Rations were reduced
by a fourth and the sick list became unusually long. They
found it difficult to understand why they should be so short of
provisions when still within the time allowance for absence

---

[5] Holmes Journal **2**, Feb. 16; Johnson Journal, Feb. 16; *Narrative* **4**: p. 280.

from Oahu where supplies had been plentiful. The sailors believed their troubles began when they departed from Tahiti on a *Friday*.[6]

At last on the twenty-fourth the *Porpoise* beat her way to the entrance of Honolulu harbor. Ringgold pulled ashore and came back with the news of Harrison's election, the birth of a daughter to Queen Victoria, and the anticipated arrival at Honolulu of the warships *St. Louis,* Captain Forrest, and *Yorktown,* Captain Aulick, out on a general cruise for the protection of whalers. The *Vincennes'* cutter and two launches came out to tow them in but had great difficulty pulling against the wind. Square-riggers always needed help in entering this harbor, especially after the morning sea breeze had shifted to a strong one from the land. It was humiliating to have a whaler walk past, hauled by natives, and anchor a full hour ahead of them.

In spite of her difficulties, the *Porpoise* had returned only nine days after she was expected, but her copper needed to be repaired before she could proceed further. Wilkes was anxious to reach the northwest coast and to get away before the arrival of the American warships. The officers were curious to see what would happen to "the broad *swallow tail* which had *graced* the main since the moment of our separating with the *Falmouth*." They, as Johnson expressed it, could "suppose the possibility" of Wilkes having been given the authority to hoist it but could not understand why he should, "without by *intimation* (at least) of such authority, subject himself to the suspicion, which I believe to be general of an usurpation of dignities which are not his right."[7]

When the brig was hove down for repairs her back guys gave way and she fell over on the wharf. The *Vincennes* had to be brought alongside to raise her, entailing hard work for all hands since during the subsequent eleven days everything on board the *Porpoise* had to be taken out and overhauled. The men would have been kept working on Sunday if the Governor had not intervened and insisted that it was contrary to the law of the land.

Dr. Holmes sent a respectful note to Captain Ringgold

---

6 Johnson Journal, Feb. 26, 27 and Mar. 5, 12, 14; Holmes Journal 2, Mar. 6, 12.
7 Johnson Journal, Mar. 24.

pleading for a rest for the crew before setting out again, but his request was not answered. The two vessels departed on April 5. The Surgeon was probably expressing the mood of many in saying, "off we started for the W. Coast, I suppose, though I neither know nor care." He thought the *Porpoise's* crew seemed "prone to somnolency" and, as he feared, fatigue and overindulgence in the newly introduced French wines and brandies caused many to be sick. Four came down with typhoid fever but, fortunately, fair weather prevailed and there were no fatalities.[8]

Wilkes had two objectives in mind. The first was to determine whether any islands existed in the area between latitudes 33° and 43° N. and longitudes 140° and 150° W. The presence of many birds in this little-known portion of the Pacific suggested the existence of vaguely reported islands, but a thorough search was not possible because of fog, thick weather, and lack of time. The second and more important matter was the need to map the Columbia River region. Its urgency was underlined by the news received at Honolulu of the Oregon boundary question which was beginning to attract attention because the Oregon territory was being colonized by persons brought in by the Hudson's Bay Company and they were British citizens. According to the wording of Wilkes' Instructions, he was to survey and examine "the territory of the United States on the seaboard," the Columbia River, and the coast of California "with special reference to the Bay of St. Francisco."[9]

The twenty-two day voyage to the West Coast was a typical one for the *Vincennes'* crew. As Seaman Erskine described the routine:[10]

The Commodore was a great disciplinarian and always kept all hands at work when there was nothing to do. When the weather permitted he would have the quarters' beat, take charge of the quarter-deck, and would sing out through his speaking trumpet, "Silence fore and aft, wet and sand the decks, knock out your ports, take off your muzzle-bags, withdraw your tompions and cast loose your guns."[10]

---

8 Holmes Journal 2, Mar. 25, 26 and Apr. 6, 8–13.
9 *Narrative* 1: p. xxvii; Wilkes to Secretary of the Navy, May 15, 1841, Ex.Ex. Letters 2.
10 Erskine, *op. cit.*, pp. 229–230.

Fig. 20. Coxswain Charles Erskine. Member of the crew of the Brig *Porpoise* and author of *Twenty Years Before the Mast* which he published at Boston in 1890. Daguerreotype taken by Plumb at Boston in 1842.

They arrived off the Columbia on April 28. It had been a fast passage once they had reached 28° N. and passed beyond the influence of the trades and variable winds. Then the weather became boisterous, making the vessels ship water through their hawse holes and flood the gun decks. At the same time the temperature dropped from seventy-eight to forty-eight degrees.

A continuous line of breakers marked the river mouth so plainly that it was difficult to understand how Vancouver could ever have doubted that this was the entrance to a great river. The strong prevailing wind caused the breakers to be very heavy and made the Commander apprehensive, as any navigator must be when facing such a wild scene and hearing the constant roar of the waters. There was no indication of the channel entrance and they had no knowledge of the strength or direction of the currents. A Sandwich Islander, though professing to be a Columbia River pilot, was unable to point out the channel. Two quarter boats were lowered to sound for it but were recalled when the wind freshened and the weather thickened deciding Wilkes to sail up the coast to the Straits of Juan de Fuca. There was no telling how long they might have to wait for the seas to calm. The *Porpoise* was signaled to follow the flagship northward at daylight of the twenty-ninth.

At that time the weather was very thick, the wind south-southwest. At ten o'clock, with the *Porpoise* close under the *Vincennes'* lee-quarter, Wilkes was informed by the Officer of the Deck that they were in disturbed water and that the lead gave fifteen fathoms. By the time he reached the deck, land could be seen through the haze close aboard. The ship was at once brought to the wind and studding sails taken in. Both vessels had little water under their keels and were in imminent danger of stranding. As they plunged in the heavy sea, their spars were endangered and the anchor chain cables could not be bent because, for some unaccountable reason, they were not ready for use in this emergency. The only thing to do was to haul to the wind, there not being room to wear ship and the sea too heavy to tack. The lead showed five fathoms just before they passed a huge rock so close by that a biscuit could have been tossed onto it. As the cast of lead showed six, seven, eight, and nine fathoms they breathed freely again and, as the fog lifted, recognized that they were off Point Grenville and the rock known as "Destruction Isle." It appeared that they had been brought there so unexpectedly by a current setting upon the coast. It was a point where English, Russian, and Japanese vessels had been wrecked. They had had a close call. Everybody credited their escape to the good sailing qualities of the two vessels. The Commander thought it was also due to the discipline and prompt attention to orders by officers and men. By May I they had rounded Cape Flattery and were well into the Straits of Juan de Fuca.[11]

---

[11] *Ibid.*, p. 295; Journals of Alden, Eld 2, and Briscoe, all Apr. 29; *Narrative* 4: p. 295.

XVII
Oregon Territory

COMING TO ANCHOR at Fort Discovery, near the eastern end of the Straits, Wilkes noted the date, May 2, 1841, exactly forty-nine years since Vancouver, following in the track of De Fuca, had been there. After their prolonged stay in the tropics it was cheering to have a change of scenery and to realize they were only three thousand miles from home. The sandy cliffs, pine forests, and mountain peaks with Mount Olympus rising highest, were a pleasing sight. A canoe full of visiting Indians was less pleasing, for their slow gutteral talk, dirty faces and clothing contrasted with the soft Polynesian speech and the bathing habits of the Fijians. Vendovi was astonished to see so much land, but was contemptuous and would hardly deign to look at the Indians just as he would never condescend to have anything to do with Hawaiians. The Indian leader wore corduroy trousers and a coarse red cloth coat with Hudson's Bay Company buttons, while the others wore blankets or skins and conical grass hats like the Chinese. They were short, thick-set, bow-legged, muscular, and carried two-edged sheath knives. Men and women wore similar clothing, all had long hair and their babies' heads were flattened by means of tight bindings.[1] In return for fishhooks and tobacco, they brought fresh food including venison, ducks, geese, salmon, cod, flounders, herrings, crabs, clams, mussels, and oysters. It was difficult to explain to them why these large vessels were here since they were not "Bostons" nor "King Georges" nor were they trading muskets, blankets, and sheath knives for skins.

A request for a pilot, sent by Indian messenger to Fort Nisqually the nearest Hudson's Bay Company outpost, brought

---

[1] Wilkes Journal 3, May 4, 5, 1841; Alden Journal, May 1; Eld Journal 2, May 2–5; [Robinson] Journal, May 3; Erskine, *op. cit.*, p. 232. These Indians flattened their babies' heads in front to give a pointed appearance and called the Salish Indians in Montana "Flatheads" because their heads looked flat by contrast. The name stuck to the Montana Indians, Pickering, *Races of Man*, p. 24.

the First Officer of the Company's steamboat *Beaver*. He said the *Peacock* had arrived at the Columbia River, so Wilkes prepared dispatches to be forwarded to Captain Hudson. Fearing a let-down of discipline, the Commander took vigorous measures. When the men were slow about setting the studding sails he made them reset them ten times until one got torn in half. Dyes, the taxidermist, remarked that the Captain "got out on one of his tantomes" when he found spittle on the deck, swore like a trooper, and deprived some of the men of their tobacco and grog.[2]

The approach to Fort Nisqually was difficult being mostly through the narrows separating Admiralty Inlet from Puget Sound and against the wind. There was plenty of deep water, but the wind was uncertain and, at one time, the *Vincennes* careened so far that her guns were muzzle under. The scenery was delightful and reminded Wilkes of the Hudson at Poughkeepsie. To his mind nothing could be more striking "than the beauty of these waters without a shoal or rocks or any danger whatever the whole length of this Internal Navigation the finest in the world, accustomed as we are to prize that of our own country."[3]

The Fort was not visible from the water with only a path leading through the woods up a hill. They were cordially greeted by Mr. Anderson, in charge of the post, and by Captain M'Neil who commanded the steamboat. The latter was Boston-born but became a British citizen in order to trade for the Company. The English-built low-pressure steamboat *Beaver* was undergoing repairs of which she was in great need after several years of operations in these waters.

Returning Anderson's call gave Wilkes an opportunity to see inside the Fort and, during the subsequent weeks, he observed its operation. It was poorly located as regards communication by water as it was on a hill and the anchorage was confined and not protected from the prevailing southwest wind. It was being developed as a farm rather than a trading post and, since the Company's charter did not permit this activity, it was operated by the Puget Sound Company whose

---

2 Wilkes Journal 3, May 2, 8, 9; Dyes' and Robinson's Journals, May 2; Alden Journal, May 9, 12.
3 Wilkes Journal 3, May 11.

officers and share holders were the same as those of the Hudson's Bay Company.

Fort Nisqually consisted of a half-dozen log houses with bark roofs within a space of about two hundred square feet enclosed by a high picket fence with bastions at each corner. The Anderson and M'Neil families lived here, both men married to half-breeds and having several children. The farm consisted of grain fields and large barns with about 400 horses, 1,500 head of cattle, and 3,000 sheep. Two missionaries, Dr. Richmond and Mr. Wilson and their wives, lived in a log cabin in a nearby meadow from which the snowy cones of three magnificent mountains were visible. Mount Rainier to the east and Mounts Saint Helens and Hood to the south. They had never been climbed and Wilkes hoped to find time to view the terminal crater of one of them and compare it with Moana Loa.

There were few Indians in the vicinity, and such as there were Anderson considered both lazy and quite harmless and, moreover, disease was reducing their numbers. They were addicted to stealing which they did with such stealth that some of the sailors found their blankets taken from their hammocks almost under the nose of an armed guard.

At first, Wilkes was somewhat skeptical of Anderson's offer to give him all the assistance in his power, but the farm supplied the vessels with two bullocks, a daily supply of milk, and provided horses for the overland parties. The unsettled question as to ownership of the Oregon Territory caused a certain amount of suspicion on both sides. The missionaries said the Fort had been put in condition for defense when they first received news of the arrival of American warships. One of the first things the Americans did upon setting up the observatory was to raise a sixty-foot flagpole so that the Stars and Stripes might wave defiance to the British flag at the Fort. However, two yoke of oxen loaned by the Fort dragged the logs used in constructing cabins for the observatory and chart room.[4]

---

[4] Eld Journal 2, May 21. Dyes and the carpenter put a bottle under the corner of the observatory containing an 1817 one-cent piece, an 1838 dime, some verse by Robinson and the signatures of all the men present, Dyes and Briscoe Journals, June 12.

As soon as possible, the work of charting and mapping was begun. Orders were distributed for a variety of tasks: Case, aided by Totten, Colvocoresses, and May, was sent with four boats to survey Hood's Canal; Ringgold to survey Puget Sound and beyond taking the *Porpoise* as far as Fraser's River; Lieutenant Johnson to lead a party over the Cascades to map the area to the eastward; Lieutenant Carr to command the *Vincennes* at Nisqually; and Budd and Eld to take charge of the observatory. Wilkes himself accompanied by Drayton, Waldron, and two servants, planned to visit Astoria, Vancouver, the Willamette Valley, and the Columbia River as far as Walla Walla.

The *Porpoise* departed May 15, but Wilkes delayed his own departure so as to see Lieutenant Johnson's party off first. Johnson had difficulty getting organized and was made to take his paraphenalia ashore, ready or not. The Commander was impatient with his "fussing fidgeting and delaying one time no compass, then no packsaddles, then no grits, all this time wasted bargaining for horses. . . ."[5] The Indians were particularly difficult to bargain with for they habitually demanded additional pay for their horses, canoes, or services after a bargain had apparently been struck. They considered something extra as a potlatch or gift and the only solution was to feign indifference or get them competing among themselves.

Both parties finally got off on the nineteenth.

Wilkes added another servant, a Canadian guide, and two Indian boys to his group and borrowed thirteen horses from the Company. The first part of their journey was through beautiful park land with spruce trees more than six feet in diameter and some two hundred feet tall. They passed lakes with sward growing luxuriantly to the water's edge and deer feeding on its margins where every tint of wildflower grew in profusion. They also passed through extensive Butte Prairies where there were thousands of conical mounds, each about six feet high. The Indians had no explanation for their origin and the Commander decided to excavate some of them at a later date. On this first day's experience of wilderness travel they soaked their saddle bags in fording the Nisqually River, found a snake in their tent, and at its close watched with envy

---

[5] Wilkes Journal **3**, May 18.

the way the Indians rolled up in their blankets close to the fire and went sound asleep.

The Indians' horsemanship also won their admiration for, with only a rope to the animal's lower jaw and a switch, they could go at full gallop with horses that a "paleface" rider could not persuade to move faster than a walk. In Wilkes' opinion the Indian mounted was a man, but dismounted "he becomes the lazy, lounging lout insensible to anything but his own low gambling habits." As for the horses, they all seemed to have sore backs or be lamed and half starved.[6]

On the twenty-first they reached the Company's six hundred acre farm at Cowlitz and were greeted by the Superintendent, Mr. Forrest, who provided a guide and canoes. The guide. Simon Plumondon, had been a trapper for the Company but was now a farmer married to a cheerful, pretty Indian woman. At one time he had been coxswain in General Cass's canoe in the Northwest Territory. He proved to be most useful and dependable. He brought nine young Indians with him to do the paddling, the pay to be one checked shirt apiece. They were "full of merriment & laughing the live long day" but, unlike Polynesians, brought no supplies with them and had to be provided for.

It was a twenty-six mile paddle down the Cowlitz River to its junction with the Columbia. Soon after reaching that river and turning towards the sea they met the brig *Wave,* Captain Moon, which had landed the Expedition's Sandwich Islands stores at Astoria and was on her way to Vancouver to pick up a return cargo of lumber. Captain Moon informed them that the *Peacock* had *not* yet arrived, which was a great disappointment since they had been told that she had arrived some time before. At Wilkes' insistence, they continued down the river after dark. The water was calm but the tide was running against them and the going slow, the paddlers became weary and the passengers tired from sitting in a confined space. Their frequent discharge of guns was finally answered by one on shore which, along with the yelping of dogs, announced their arrival at Astoria. Mr. Birnie, in charge, came down to the shore with a lantern and greeted them cordially. They were soon in his quarters before a brightly burning fire

---

6 *Ibid.,* May 19.

and enjoying "his hospitable board spread with good cheer, although it was past midnight."[7]

Astoria, as they found out the next day, was in a decayed condition. The Company's headquarters were now at Vancouver, and Astoria was merely a convenient stopping place for its vessels. Moreover, it was on what was thought of as the American side of the river. The post included a dozen log houses and sheds, a pigsty or two, and a potato patch. But it had a fine view of the river, the ocean, and the distant mountains. The incessant roar of the ocean where the river rushed out to meet it could be heard distinctly.

Their first day here, May 23, was Sunday and a day of rest. On the next Wilkes and Birnie went to the sand hills at Point Adams for a better view of the ocean, for there had been a report that a gun had been heard, but no sail was in sight. They visited the Clatsop Indian village and had dinner with the missionary, Mr. Frost, and his wife. Frost was a shoemaker by trade and the Commander was skeptical of his real interest in bringing religion to the Indians.[8]

The departure of the Company's barque *Cowlitz* for Oahu afforded an opportunity to send letters to Dr. Judd and Consul Brinsmade and a report to the Secretary of the Navy. Then, leaving Waldron behind to await the *Peacock*, Wilkes and Drayton proceeded by canoe to Vancouver.

In contrast to Astoria, Vancouver was a village with about fifty log cabins outside the Fort which was enclosed by a twenty-five-foot-high stockade and covered about four acres. It had no bastions at the corners and no loop-holes in the wall, the only things of a military character being two old cannons and some shot placed at the steps of the Superintendent's house. In addition to this house the enclosure contained accommodations for clerks and visitors and blacksmiths' and coopers' shops. In its center was a Roman Catholic chapel and a flagstaff.

They were hospitably received by Dr. M'Laughlin, the able and energetic head of the Northwest Department of the Hudson's Bay Company. He was sixty-five but looked twenty years younger. Wilkes described him as "a tall fine-looking

---

[7] *Ibid.*, May 21, 22.
[8] *Ibid.*, May 24.

person, of a very robust frame, with a frank manly open countenance, and a florid complexion; his hair is perfectly white."
M'Laughlin was a Scot, educated in Paris, married to an Indian
and father of several grown children who were schooled in
England and France. They also met Mr. Douglass, the shrewd
and intelligent chief factor and second in command, who was
about forty years old, tall and handsome with black hair and
the florid complexion characteristic of outdoors men. The
Squadron's Commander and the head men of this semi-military
organization had several mealtime and pipe-smoking after-meal
conversations. They could converse more freely among themselves than with their subordinates and Wilkes was able to
learn a great deal about the Company's operation.

Several Protestant missionaries were at Vancouver at this
time staying as guests of the Company. Most had crossed the
Rockies along with a fur-trading party from St. Louis. They
had not found the pass too difficult nor the Indians hostile
but deplored the disposition and morals of their companions.
Wilkes found them not the best source of information as they
kept no notes and made no observations regarding soil, climate,
etc.[9]

The farm here occupied about nine square miles and included two dairies, about a hundred cows, and a large number
of sheep. Six miles farther up the river the Company had a
grist mill and two miles beyond that a saw-mill where the brig
Wave was taking on lumber. At the original site of Fort Vancouver, abandoned because of water scarcity, the Commander
found the view admirable:[10]

the noble river can be traced in all its windings, for a long distance
through the cultivated prairie, with its groves and clumps of trees;
beyond, the eye sweeps over an interminable forest, melting into
a blue haze, from which Mount Hood, capped with its eternal snows,
rises in great beauty. The tints of purple which appear in the atmosphere, are, so far as I am aware, peculiar to this country.

Wilkes and Drayton, with guide and servants, left Vancouver June 3 to visit the Willamette Valley settlement. A flat-
bottomed, shallow-draft barge, whose crew knew how to take

9 *Ibid.*, May 28–30.
10 *Narrative* 4: p. 335.

advantage of the river current, brought them to the mouth of the Willamette as speedily as they could have gone by canoe. Starting up that river they met a party of missionaries on their way to Clatsop led by the Reverend Jason Lee, who was head of the Methodist Mission in Oregon and successful in arousing interest in its activity back East. Wilkes was not impressed by his appearance or conversation and, after seeing more of the Mission's work, concluded that he lacked the capacity to manage so large an undertaking.

Farther up the Willamette they came upon a group of eight young Americans engaged in building a small schooner with which they hoped to reach San Francisco and, after selling the vessel and her cargo, to return to the East. They had decided, after a year's stay, that they did not want to marry squaws and settle down as farmers. Only one of them was an experienced shipwright and none of them had ever navigated a vessel. Wilkes liked their youthful enthusiasm and later helped them end a dispute growing out of a misunderstanding with M'Laughlin.

Proceeding to the Falls they found the salmon fishery at its height and watched the skillful manner in which the Indians trapped the fish attempting to leap the twenty-foot-high waterfall.

Here the Reverend Mr. and Mrs. Waller, whom they had previously met at Vancouver, offered them hospitality. Waller complained that the Company would not take his furs or salmon in trade. This action seemed to the Commander to come with ill grace from one who had accepted the Company's hospitality and whose duty was to convert Indians rather than to enter into commercial competition. But Mrs. Waller's housecleaning ability was admired and Wilkes declared she knew her stove better than an engineer his engine.

Her virtues were emphasized by contrast on a subsequent day when they accepted the hospitality of a farmer and former trapper named Johnson. His home was uninviting looking, but the alternative was to sleep in the rain. On the wall of their room hung a print of the capture of the *Guerrière* by the *Constitution* and it appeared that their host had taken part in that famous engagement. He had the free and easy manner of a trapper, but Wilkes thought he also had "hanging about him somewhat of the feeling of discipline that he had acquired in the service." Johnson considered his rather pretty Indian wife worth "half a dozen civilized wives," but two young rather slovenly Indian "slaves" did the housework and the guests, as they feared, spent an uncomfortable night fighting fleas.[11]

Several settlers came to see them. Wilkes thought them an idle, lounging, "uncombed, unshaven, and a dirty clothed set," but one, "Old Moore," was well-informed about some parts of the country and another, named Cannon, was thought to be the only follower of Lewis and Clark still around. They talked a great deal about organizing a government under a constitution. Some thought it unnecessary and the Commander was inclined to agree with them. When a committee of five, mainly lay members of the Mission, came to him to ask his advice, he told them that he could see little need for laws and an enforcement authority since there had been no crime other than the stealing of a horse and some pigs and, pointing out that under a constitution the Catholic majority would govern, advised them to wait until the Government of the United States "should throw its mantle over them." He suspected that their real object was to induce immigration from the East so as to increase the value of their farms and stock.

Michel La Framboise, an employee of the Company, supplied horses and saw to the portage of their provisions around the Falls. He was the most interesting member of this settlement, having come out on the *Tonquin*[12] as one of the original party landing at Astoria. He was short, rather corpulent, but possessed of "great energy and activity of both mind and body, indomitable courage, and all the vivacity of a Frenchman." He had traveled widely in the country and claimed he had a wife of high rank in every tribe, which insured his safety. He had been a trapper and was now in charge of parties going to and from California. Had it not been for his proneness to dissipation he would have risen higher in the Company's service. He, Johnson, and another settler named George Gay accompanied Wilkes' party as they proceeded up the valley past several farms of from fifty to one hundred acres owned by old servants of the Company.[13]

11 Wilkes Journal 3, June 4, 6.
12 The *Tonquin*, sent by John Jacob Astor, established his Pacific Fur Company post at Astoria in 1811, the first permanent settlement in this area.
13 *Narrative* 4: p. 349.

At the Catholic Mission they called upon the Reverend Mr. Bachelet who had been there about a year and seemed to be doing much good, legalizing the marriages of the Canadian settlers living with Indian women and caring for about ten Indian children. He advised his parishioners against adopting a constitution thinking it unwarranted for a community of only sixty settlers. The Reverend Mr. Bachelet treated his visitors to a venison dinner topped with strawberries and cream.

Michel returned to his home and the party went on to visit the Methodist Mission which consisted of log houses and workshops built by the Reverend Mr. Lee and a hospital built by Dr. White, who at this time was back East but soon to return as Indian Agent. The hospital, being used as a dwelling, was a well-built frame structure with a double piazza in front and was perhaps the best building in Oregon. They were greeted by Mr. Abernethy, the Mission's secular agent, and his wife who were evidently persons of "delicate habits." Mrs. Abernethy, a pretty and pleasant lady, seemed particularly out of place in this rough environment. They also met Dr. Babcock, the Mission's physician, and learned from him that this was considered a healthy part of the country except for the fever and ague experienced on low ground during August and September. It was proposed to move the Mission about nine miles away from the river to a healthier site where the missionaries had already selected for themselves lands amounting to about one thousand acres apiece.

Wilkes questioned the need for an extensive building program in this area where there were few Indians while the more populated Straits area in the north was neglected. He gave the subject considerable space in the *Narrative* saying that he did not wish to blame anyone but felt it "a duty I owe my countrymen, to lay the truth before them, such as we saw it."[14] The Methodist Missionary Board did consider discontinuing this particular mission but the rapid increase in population by immigration during the next few years seemed to justify its continuation so as to give spiritual help to these newcomers, if not to the Indians.[15]

---

[14] *Ibid.*, pp. 349–355; Wilkes Journal 3, June 7, 8.
[15] Report of American Board of Commissioners for Foreign Missions meeting at Rochester, N.Y., Sept. 12–15, 1843.

The party went next to the Yam Hills, the view from the top reminding Wilkes of Mount Holyoke, Massachusetts, and then returned to the Willamette Falls where it was decided that Drayton should stay to procure fish specimens and make drawings while the Commander returned to Vancouver.

At Vancouver, Wilkes made a change of plans after seeing Waldron who had come from Astoria with no news of the *Peacock*. He decided to send Drayton up the Columbia and to return directly to Nisqually so as to hurry up the completion of the survey in that area. He had the opportunity to travel as far as Cowlitz with Ogden's brigade which had just arrived from the north. Peter Ogden was the chief factor of the northern district with headquarters at Fort Saint James on Stuart's Lake. The Commander was intrigued by the brigade's "voyageurs" who lounged about

decked in gay feathers, ribands, etc., full of conceit, and with the flaunting air of those who consider themselves the beau-ideal of grace and beauty; full of frolic and fun, and seeming to have nothing to do but to attend the decorations of their persons and seek for pleasure; looking down with contempt upon those who are employed about the fort, whose sombre cast of countenance and business employments form a strong contrast to these jovial fellows.[16]

At ten o'clock on June 17, the day of departure, M'Laughlin summoned everyone to the great dining hall to drink a cup of wine to each other's health, a custom of the country. It was an old Scottish custom and carried with it "pleasing recollections, especially when there is that warmth of feeling . . . that there was on this occasion."

The river had risen to the top of its banks and rushed by with great force as one of Ogden's boats with fourteen voyageurs, decked in ribbons and plumes, stood ready to shove off. After shaking hands all around they started, paddling upstream a short distance, the voyageurs singing their boat songs, then turning around and sweeping past the spectators "with great animation." As they proceeded down the wide-flowing river each voyageur, in turn, took up the song and all joined in the chorus. They covered the thirty-five miles to the entrance of

---

16 Wilkes Journal 3, June 17.

the Cowlitz River in two and a half hours, but progress up that stream against the current was much slower. On the second day the voyageurs doffed their finery and covered their hats with oiled skins. The going became more difficult with every mile, and management of the boat in the rapids called for dexterous use of pole and paddle. It was an exciting experiance. The bowman gave direction and was responsible for the boat's safety. Their jovial singing gave them spirit, kept them awake, and made the time pass quickly. About every half-hour they would "take a spell or a smoke each one having his pouch bag ornamented a la Indian and containing his fire implements tobacco & pipe without this no one can trade in an Indian country." They reached Cowlitz on the nineteenth, Ogden and his men returning to Vancouver a day or two later.

Wilkes' party spent a rainy day as guests of Mr. Forrest. That night, before going to sleep, the Commander laid his pocket chronometer on a table and, upon awaking, was astonished to find that it agreed with a small silver watch alongside of it. His host explained that he had found the chronometer, which registered Greenwich time, wrong and had set it to Cowlitz time. He could not understand why Greenwich time should be preferred, feeling sure that his own watch was correct by the sun. Wilkes calmed himself as best he could by reading the Salmagundi Papers. Arriving at Nisqually at noon of the twenty-third, they found "all well."[17]

The Commander stirred things up. As the Purser's assistant expressed it, "The skipper has kicked up a terrible breeze all around the board, keeping everybody on the 'qui vive' and making everybody uncomfortable, as he always does." The survey parties had accomplished a good deal. A large part of the Admiralty Inlet had been surveyed by the *Porpoise* working its way north, and Lieutenant Case's boats had finished surveying Hood's Canal and begun work on Puget Sound. It was discovered that Hood's Canal extended beyond the place where Vancouver had thought it ended, its southern end within two and a half miles of Puget Sound. While encamped there Case's men heard the *Vincennes'* morning and

---

17 *Ibid.*, June 17, 18, 20.

evening guns and sent a man overland for a supply of freshly baked bread.

The Fourth of July was made an occasion for celebration and relaxation. Since it fell on Sunday, it was celebrated on the following Monday. Wilkes completed his pendulum and astronomical observations on the Fourth, and, on that day, the cooks among the crew, led by John Sac, killed, cleaned, and spitted an ox. A sappling used as a spit was suspended between tree crotches and turned by a windlass arrangement. The cooking process continued through the night, the ox being dredged with flour and basted every hour.

At sunrise of the fifth a twenty-six gun salute was fired in honor of the States of the Union. The crew was mustered in clean white frocks and trousers and the marines in their uniforms with no one on the sick list and only Vanderford and Chaplain Elliott remaining on the ship. In a jovial mood they marched single file led by flying colors and a fife and drum through the woods to the meadow, a mile away, where the ox had been spitted. After the officers came, in order, the Starboard watch, the marines, the Larboard watch, Vendovi in Fiji costume, and the Master-at-Arms with the dog Sydney bringing up the rear.

They stopped opposite the Fort and gave three cheers. A few moments later they were mightily amused to hear the Company redcoats give a few feeble cheers in return. At the meadow both officers and men engaged in games. It was most unusual for Wilkes to unbend in this manner but he lined up the two watches opposite each other, kicked the football into the air and shouted, "Sail in, shipmates." Besides "football" and "corner ball' they had horseback races and dancing on a portable floor to the tune of a fiddle, all under a broiling sun. Two brass howitzers had been brought along and a noon gun was fired to announce the beginning of the barbecue. In ramming home the charge, Daniel Whitehorn, Quarter Gunner, had his left hand and forearm nearly blown off. Doctors Fox and Richmond, who were present, feared that his arm would have to be amputated but decided to wait. Whitehorn recovered without surgery but suffered agonies as he was carried back to the ship. This put a pall upon the proceedings for a while, but men-of-war's men were used to such scenes and soon recovered their jollity. The bullock was pronounced as tender as lamb and in addition there was venison, salmon, soft bread, and they "spliced the main brace." In the afternoon the games continued although some of the men preferred to walk in the woods or talk with the Indians who stood looking on in wonderment and hunger. At sunset all returned to the ship in good order.

The Commander gave a dinner at the observatory to the officers and Mr. Anderson, Captain M'Neil, and Dr. Richmond. The "Hall of Science" was converted into a banqueting hall by decorating it with flags and using a large drafting board as a table and covering it with a fine Sandwich Island mat. Dr. M'Laughlin had been invited but missed the way and did not arrive until the next day when he dined alone with Wilkes. At his departure the yards were manned in his honor.

The Fourth of July celebration boosted the men's morale as was indicated when they gave Wilkes three cheers as he left the barbecue. Eld commented on the many "happy faces" and contrasted the "wholesome mirth, here regulated by discipline and the low drunken brawl the same circumstances would excite at home." Aside from the accident to the gunner, the only matter of serious concern at the moment was the continuing uncertainty as to the fate of the *Peacock* and *Flying Fish*. The longer these vessels became overdue the more certain it seemed that they must have met with disaster.[18]

---

[18] Eld Journal 2, July 7; [Robinson] Journal, July 4; Briscoe Journal, July 5; Erskine, *op. cit.*, pp. 236–237.

XVIII

East of the Cascades

W HILE THE *Vincennes'* crew was feasting and playing games Lieutenant Johnson's party was crossing the prairie on its return to Nisqually, having left Walla Walla on the Fourth of July headed for the Cascade range over which it had worked its way in May with great difficulty. Now, in July, the party was finding the going easier—the rivers lower, less turbulent, and the snow on the east side of the pass melted away.

Johnson had had no previous experience as an overland leader and Pickering and Brackenridge, at home in the woods, found it irritating to be under this youngster's command. In addition to the two scientists, the party included Thomas W. Waldron, Captain's clerk, Sergeant Simeon Stearns, Henry Waltham (O.S.) cook and servant, Pierre Charles guide, and Peter Bercier interpreter.

From the beginning things were at sixes and sevens. Wilkes had tried to hasten their departure but had augmented Johnson's difficulties by taking for his own party the Company's best horses, saddles, and guides. Ordered to leave May 17 they actually got off two days later and, even then, before the arrival of the guide and the interpreter.

In two months they traversed a triangular route going over the Cascades north of Mount Rainier, proceeding in a northeasterly direction to Forts Okonagan and Colville, thence south to Fort Nez Perce (Walla Walla) and finally, westward over the Cascades again and back to Nisqually. They were to collect information regarding climate, terrain, trading posts, Indians, fauna and flora.

Johnson had specific orders to keep a journal, make daily diagrams showing ground covered and natural objects, take observations of the sun at noon and the North Star at night, record thermometer readings every six hours, take bearings wherever heights of land afforded an opportunity, note the height and circumference of remarkable trees, and designate every unusual object by its native name or, if it had none, one

244

of his own choosing. Heights were to be determined by barometer, distances estimated by taking a horse's pace as a measure and timing their movements, and the velocity of river waters estimated by observing the distance a chip would move in a given time. A compass would indicate direction in open country, but in the woods "it will be better that all your party should be required to keep their own reckoning, which you will use, together with your own, in the same way as at sea." Johnson was also instructed to give the scientists every facility for the promotion of their researches, to see to the safety and comfort of his party, and to avoid disputes with the Indians [1]

They had not gone very far before they found it difficult to follow the mountain trail, not ordinarily used for horses. They had to cut their way through thick undergrowth, the packs getting wedged between trees and the horses' hoofs entangled in the roots and branches of fallen timber. Trees had to be felled across streams swollen from melting snows to make a bridge for carrying packs, the horses being made to swim across. The trail was slippery and sometimes precipitous, causing one horse to fall in the river and the food in its pack to be lost. Happening to meet a party of thirteen Indians, they hired them to help with the horses and loads. The Indians were able to carry packs weighing as much as ninety pounds.

Upon reaching the pass over the mountains on the twenty-sixth, the guide, Waldron, and the scientists went ahead with the Indians carrying the packs. Johnson stayed behind with the horses. It was an eight-mile hike over the snow-covered pass. The Indians with their loads broke through the crust but only ankle deep. They made camp on the east side of the range at the head of the Spipen River and, on the following day, the Indians brought the horses over, starting before the snow had time to melt, and the horses sank only to their fetlocks. The Indians accepted a draft payable at Nisqually instead of the usual pay in blankets, but were given part payment in food which left the party in short supply. A smart young Indian named Lashemore elected to join the party. Since four of the weaker horses were left on the other side of the pass, Pickering and Brackenridge, the "proven pedestrians" as they called themselves, walked. They made a habit of starting

---

[1] *Narrative* 4: append. XII, pp. 528–530.

ahead of the others so that they might pick up plant specimens as they proceeded. The trail followed the banks of the rushing Spipen and, when the banks became too steep and the bushes too thick, they waded along the river's edge.

On the day he crossed the pass Johnson lost the means for accurate map-making. Falling behind he became lost for three or four hours and when he finally found the camp it was on the far side of the stream. In crossing on a log, he fell in, soaking himself and causing his chronometer to stop so that, although he was able to start it again, he could only determine relative meridian distances thereafter.

On the thirty-first they came upon old chief Tidias of the Yakima tribe and, after smoking a pipe with him and having a shooting match with his companions, got down to the business of bargaining for dried salmon and horses to replace those left behind. These were paid for with a Scotch plaid, some tobacco, a canister of powder and some balls, and some of their poorer horses, so that they were still left without enough horses for everybody. They augmented their food supply a little later when they met some Indians collecting cammass roots and bought from them sun-dried root cakes. Brackenridge commented that "such bread went rather hard with us, but it was the best we had."

When they reached the Yakima River on June 2, they found it to be a hundred yards wide and too deep to ford so they inflated their gum elastic balsas (floats made of India-rubber cloth) which answered very well providing even greater safety and more carrying capacity than canoes.

Two days later their trail took them over a mountain where they experienced freezing temperatures. They started out at 4 A.M. and had to keep going through a succession of sleet storms before stopping to eat at noon. On this morning the Sergeant accidentally broke the barometer and, as Wilkes ruefully commented, "thus ended the barometrical experiments in the most interesting portion of the route."[2]

They reached the Columbia River at a point where it moved swiftly down a ravine, cut through an arid wasteland, and where, in its swollen condition, it was about six hundred

---

2 Brackenridge Journal 2, May 15–June 2, 1841. The *Narrative* and Brackenridge's Journal are the principal sources for this excursion.

yards wide and not fordable. They followed its banks northward to its confluence with the Pischous River, which they crossed with the help of an Indian and his canoe. Some Okanagan Indians helped them across the next river, the Point de Bois, as they continued northward coming at last to where the Columbia was about a third of a mile wide and placid. Here, the balsa raft and an Indian canoe got them across, the horses swimming as usual. From that point the trail was over a rolling sandy prairie.

Early on the afternoon of the eighth they came again to the river bank opposite Fort Okanagan and, leaving their horses behind, crossed in a canoe and were greeted by Le Pratt, a French Canadian in charge of the Post. Here, as at the other Company posts, French was spoken and Johnson had a chance to practice his favorite foreign language.

The Fort, located on a sandy neck of land, was similar to other Hudson's Bay Company posts, being surrounded by a palisade and containing a large house with apartments for Company officers and with trappers' families billeted in small mud houses. It was an entrepot for supplies intended for the northern posts in what the Company called "New Caledonia." Comparatively few beaver, bear, or marten skins were obtained in this rather desolate area, but the Fort was a useful stopping point where transportation changed from water to land and vice versa. It had been established by the American Fur Company some twenty-nine years before. At this time it was occupied by two Canadians and numerous half-breed women and children. Some goats and cattle provided milk and butter, but the soil was too infertile for farming. The only animal food on hand was the woodchuck, called "siffleurs" or "Whistling Rufus," which the Indians caught among the rocks on the hillside and sold for a leaden ball apiece and which the Americans found good eating.

As they overhauled their packs and the contents were disclosed, Brackenridge's disgust with their leader was heightened:

tis a fact as singular as tis true, that the party after starving for 10 days—should bring into this place not less than 25 lbs Pork, 3 whole Cheeses, 3 cases of Sardinias with some— (the Sardinias & 2 of the Cheeses were afterwards made presents of to individuals) — Had I then had the least idea that conduct would have been approved of by the Commander—or that he had direct orders to act as he did, I would certainly have taken the shortest way for the U. States, viz— across the Rocky Mountains.[3]

While at the Fort a Company party arrived from Colville. It was led by a Mr. Maxwell and consisted of forty horses bringing provisions for Ogden's brigade, which was on its way up the Columbia.

On the tenth the Expedition members recrossed the Columbia, rounded up their horses, and started off in the direction of Colville. Johnson went ahead and was soon lost to sight but, sometime later, his horse came galloping back minus rider and saddle. Thinking their leader had found a campsite, the party proceeded until sundown without finding him. After supper the Sergeant and the guide Pierre went out to look for him while those at camp fired signal guns at intervals until 11 P.M., when the searchers returned and all went to sleep. At dawn they searched again and, finally, Johnson's servant found him fast asleep at a spot three miles back where he had been since the previous afternoon. It would appear that his love of the bottle had something to do with his inadequacy as a leader.

Two days' travel brought them to the remarkable geological phenomenon known as the "Grande Coulée," a wide sunken plain with basaltic walls similar to the Palisades on the Hudson and three miles wide at their point of crossing. They decided that it had once been a lake whose waters had somehow emptied into the Columbia. Maxwell caught up with them and gave them the use of two of his horses so that, for once, the whole party could ride. This gain in mobility was counterbalanced by a further loss for science when Johnson forgot to tie his horse after dismounting and, as it ran away to join the others, the artificial horizon in his saddle bag was broken.

Pickering and Brackenridge, riding fresh horses, reached Fort Colville on the fifteenth, a day ahead of the rest of the party. The head man, McDonald, received them cordially. This post, established in 1825, was comparable in size and strength to the fort at Vancouver. The soil was rich, considerable acreage was under cultivation, and it had a grist mill. When first established a bull and two cows were brought from

---

[3] Brackenridge Journal 2, June 8.

Vancouver and the herd now numbered 196 head. The Company's northern posts and the Russian post at Sitka were supplied with cheese, butter, and pork produced here.

By the nineteenth the party was ready to start south toward Walla Walla, being better supplied than when they left Nisqually, their horses refreshed, damaged packs and saddles repaired, and each wearing a pair of moccasins made by the women at the Fort. Their supplies were paid for by a note payable at Vancouver, but Johnson felt so grateful to Maxwell for his assistance that he presented him with a Bowie-knife pistol, which Pickering had been carrying instead of a fowling piece and as a result was left without a weapon. Wilkes considered this gift of government property uncalled for and made it an official charge against Johnson.[4]

At the Chimikaine Mission they were hospitably received by the missionaries Eels and Walker who had just returned with their families from Walla Walla. This mission was well stocked with horses and cattle and had plantings of wheat and potatoes. In the morning they attended family worship held at Eels' house and, later that morning, Pickering and Johnson engaged in a heated discussion regarding the manner in which the party was being conducted. Brackenridge remarked that a sailor on shore was like a fish out of water.[5]

In a day's time the trail took them to the Spokane River through rather sterile, thickly wooded country, the rock formation changing from granite to trap and in another two days they reached the Lapwai Mission station on the Kooskooskee. This was said to have been the first river reached by Lewis and Clark after crossing the Rockies; the Indians thought those bearded men were some kind of animal. The Reverend Mr. and Mrs. Spalding had been at this mission for four years. Spalding had built a two-storied house with board floors and a combined grist and saw mill. He had also planted twenty acres with wheat, potatoes, corn, melons, pumpkins, peas, beans, etc., without neglecting his duty to teach the Indians how to farm, while his wife taught the squaws how to spin and knit. He told the Indians about the Expedition and they appeared to

---

4 *Ibid.*, June 19; Pickering to M. O. Pickering, Aug. 1, 1842, Pickering Letters; General Court Martial #26, Aug. 1, 2, 1842.
5 Brackenridge Journal 2, June 21.

listen with interest and comprehension. Many Oregon Indians had visited the United States and Spalding said he had sent letters to Boston by Indians which had reached their destination in eighty-one days from the Dalles, the slowest part of the route being from St. Louis to Boston.[6]

With fresh horses supplied by Spalding, they reached the Snake River on the twenty-sixth and two days later arrived at Fort Nez Perce, or Walla Walla, where they were welcomed by Mr. McLean who was in charge. Johnson took a two-day detour up the Spokane River as far as its Falls and Lake Cœur d'Alene.

Their route from Colville had been eastward of the one usually followed by the Hudson's Bay people, which was itself eastward of the Columbia River. Theirs was not the most direct route but it enabled them to satisfy themselves that there was no volcanic mountain in the vicinity of Walla Walla, such as appeared on maps of Oregon.

As mentioned above, Johnson's party left Walla Walla July 4, two days before Drayton reached that place as a passenger in Ogden's brigade. Having fresh horses, they made rapid progress on this last leg of their journey. The fifth of July was one of the warmest days they had yet experienced, the temperature reaching 108° in the shade. The Yakima was reached without mishap but they spent an uncomfortable night at the river's bank owing to hostile mosquitoes and curious rattlesnakes. On the eighth they camped at the same place on the Spipen River where they had been in May, and met again the chief, Old Tidias, who, this time, decided to return with them to Nisqually along with his son and four horses. The Spipen was much lower than before, but Brackenridge watched with trepidation as the packhorses carrying his precious plants swam across. The snow on the pass had disappeared and the little remaining on the west side of the range caused no trouble. It rained during the last two days and the going was difficult, but they reached Nisqually July 15, within the two months allotted. Wilkes was away on the day of their arrival

---

6 Walla Walla was on the direct post route into the interior but communication was very uncertain. Johnson's party brought to that place the first news of the Expedition's arrival in Oregon. It took nearly a year for the news of the murder of Mr. Black, the Company's factor at the northern New Caledonia post, to reach some places on the coast.

but, upon his return, appeared to be pleased with their accomplishments though annoyed that Johnson did not report more promptly and did so while on horseback. However, for the record, he had words of approval: "They traversed a route which white men had never before taken, thus enabling us to become acquainted with a portion of the country about which all had before been conjecture. They had also made a large addition to our collection of plants."[7]

It had been Wilkes' intention to send a party from the *Peacock* across the Rockies to the headwaters of the Yellowstone River, but that plan had to be abandoned because of her nonappearance. Instead Drayton accompanied Ogden's brigade as far as Walla Walla and collected information about that section of the river and its environs.

The brigade left Vancouver June 27. It consisted of nine boats rowed by sixty voyageurs, eight of whom had their Indian wives with them. Three-quarters of the boatmen were Canadians and the rest Iroquois—"all strong, active, and hardy men." These boats were equipped with square sails, since the wind was usually directly up or down the river, and measured about thirty feet in length with a beam of five and a half feet. They were flat-bottomed but sharp at both ends and clinker-built. Moreover, they were light enough to be easily transported over portages and their pine-gummed seams were easily repaired. Goods were done up in packages of varying sizes, each weighing about ninety pounds. Sixty packages made a boat's quota, its capacity being three tons.[8]

They camped the first night at the Cascades, the head of ship navigation and where the Company had a fishery. Here, the mountain range meets the river causing it to narrow and divide into swift rushing canals. At two portages most of the goods had to be landed, while the boats were tracked up through the rushing water.

At the Dalles, farther up the river, it was necessary to carry the boats as well as the cargoes A Methodist Mission had

---

7 *Narrative* **4**: p. 470; Reynolds' Critique, p. 74.
8 *Narrative* **4**: pp. 378–379. Beaver skins, costing 25¢ apiece at Fort St. James were worth $2.50 at Vancouver. Ogden's annual take was worth about £ 50,000 upon delivery in London. The voyageurs were paid only £ 17 a year but the Company gave them family allowances when they retired and took up farming.

been established here in 1838 and its head, the Reverend
Daniel Lee, received Drayton cordially. This being the salmon
season, there were about fifteen hundred Indians present but,
ordinarily, there were only a few. About seventy were hired
to carry the boats, bottoms up, a distance of about a mile. This
was accomplished on July 4 and at sunset, two days later, the
brigade reached Walla Walla. The Company flag was raised
as the boats came into view and Mr. M'Lean informed Drayton that Johnson's party had just departed two days before.
This Fort, like most of the others, was about two hundred feet
square and surrounded by a picket fence with bastions pro-
truding from two corners.

Drayton visited the missionaries, Dr. Whitman and the
Reverend Mr. and Mrs. Gray, stationed at Waiilaptu. That
station and Spalding's at the mouth of the Kooskooskee had
been established in 1837. A third station, sixty miles up the
river at Kamia, was established at the same time under the
Reverend Mr. Smith but had been abandoned because there
were so few Indians in that locality and because of Mrs. Smith's
ill health.

The Reverend Mr. Gray went with Drayton to the foot of
the Blue Mountains but they found that most of the Indians
had gone to a mountain prairie known as the "Grande Ronde"
where the Cayuse,[9] Nez Perce, and Walla Walla Indians traded
salmon and horses for the roots, skin lodges (teepees), elk and
buffalo meat of the Snake and Shoshone Indians. The missionaries had few opportunities to convert these Indians who
were mostly wanderers and seldom in the same place for more
than three or four months, but they showed them how, with
irrigation, to grow wheat, corn, and potatoes in this very dry
climate.

With the aid of his Indian boy interpreter, Drayton talked
to some of the Indians returning from the Grande Ronde and
learned that they were headed for the Shaste country to trade
horses and beaver skins for blankets or, more particularly, for
powder and ball which they could not obtain from the Company or from the Willamette settlers. He watched the incanta-
tions and manipulations of a medicine-squaw who spent many
exhausting hours extracting an evil spirit from a sick youth

9 A Cayuse chief was a very successful horse-breeder and from this circumstance
was derived the name for an Indian horse.

and, when he seemed to recover, exhibited a stone the size of a goose egg which'she claimed had caused the illness. Her reward was a basket containing eighty pounds of dried salmon and a blanket but if the boy had died his family might have killed her, just as the failure of Mr. Black, the Company factor in the north, to cure a sick Indian had been the cause of his murder. Dr. Whitman was able to win the confidence of the Indians through his medical knowledge, but after an outbreak of smallpox in 1847 the Indians raided the Weiilaptu Mission and killed him, his wife, and everyone else living there.

By joining a Company party Drayton was able to travel on horseback from Walla Walla to the Dalles, arriving there July 24. He found that the river had fallen about thirty feet during his twenty-day absence, the water now passing in a mighty torrent through a single channel between perpendicular rock walls.

He had difficulty procuring a canoe for transportation down the river because the Indians were so extortionate. However, when the Reverend Mr. Lee offered him the use of his canoe, they became more reasonable and, at the Cascades, he secured a place in a Company boat which took him to Vancouver. The information gathered by Drayton and Johnson made it possible for Wilkes to map all of the Columbia River valley. In completing his map of Oregon he also used data collected by Lieutenant Fremont in 1845 including an area extending to the Rockies. Since he dated this map 1841, although it contained Fremont's additions of a later date, he became involved in a cartographical dispute which was augmented in 1848 when Fremont published a map correcting the coast line as drawn by Wilkes.

Fremont's biographer, Frederick S. Dellenbough, comments with respect to this controversy, that none of the early surveys were strictly accurate.

They were reconnaissance maps only, and as such were extremely good. From my own experience I realize how difficult it is to do the best topographic and geodetic work in a wild, roadless country with few men, no facilities, small funds, perhaps without a base line, and with instruments shaken about for months on pack mules; above all in limited time.[10]

---

[10] F. S. Dellenbaugh, *Fremont and '49* (N.Y. & London, 1914), p. 386.

XIX

Midsummer in Oregon

AFTER THE FOURTH OF JULY and the completion of his scientific duties at the observatory, Wilkes sent Eld and Budd
with boat crews to assist Case's survey party and then joined
Anderson, the Company's head man at Nisqually, in an attempt
to discover the meaning of the mounds on Butte Prairie which
had previously aroused his curiosity. They took six sailors
armed with picks and shovels on this archaeological expedition. A day's journey brought them to the prairie where the
men were set to work digging into six of the mounds. They
appeared to have been made by scraping the surface earth into
a heap now covered with rank growth and there were at least
a thousand of them. They were regular in construction, shape,
and placement, seeming to be in groups of five. Situated as
they were on a level prairie, they could not have been made
by water-courses and appearances suggested that they had
been constructed successively and at intervals of several years,
each large enough to have required the exertions of a whole
tribe to construct. After digging to a depth of six feet the
sailors came to a kind of pavement of round stones laid on the
red gravel subsoil. There were no bones or articles of any kind,
so they did not appear to have been burial mounds. No one
could explain their purpose but, it was said, that medicine
men came here to gather herbs with which to make their
cure-alls. Anderson returned to Nisqually and Wilkes to the
survey party with the riddle unsolved.[1]

Assuming command of Case's flotilla, now enlarged to
include seven boats, Wilkes quickened its pace, beginning each
day punctually at seven o'clock and carrying on simultaneously
the placement of signal flags, triangulation, and the taking of
soundings. In five days the survey of the numerous branches of
Puget Sound was completed; all parts found to be safe for
navigation by large vessels. Pine trees predominated along the

---

1 *Narrative* 4: p. 415. The mounds are explained by geologists as resulting from
Ice Age conditions.

low-lying shore line and great quantities of seringias in full bloom scented the air, reminding them of gardens at home. Few Indians were encountered.[2]

Returning to the *Vincennes* July 16, they found that Johnson's party had arrived the day before and that Carr had prepared the ship for departure. Johnson was given new orders to lead a party down the Chickeeles River to its mouth at Gray's Harbour which he was to survey. Because Johnson had given away a Bowie-knife pistol at Colville, Wilkes inserted in the orders the admonition that no arms or other government property was to be disposed of or traded "except through absolute necessity, in which decision the officer who accompanies you must coincide." These orders were to be shown to Passed Midshipman Eld, the second in command.[3] The other members of the party were to be Brackenridge, Sergeant Stearns, Privates Rodgers and Dinsman, Seamen Thomas Ford and Henry Waltham, and "Joe," a halfbreed boy interpreter.

As the ship was preparing to sail with the tide on the morning of the seventeenth, Johnson came to Wilkes in great excitement and asked that his orders be changed so that he would not be subject to control by an officer of inferior rank. Their meeting took place on the spar deck next to the capstan and the catting of the anchor made so much noise that the Commander did not hear Johnson's reason for objecting to the orders but cut him short, giving him five minutes to go below and reconsider. In about ten Johnson reappeared—"I would not listen to him, he was dressed as I conceived very unofficer-like, having on one of the caps, or hats worn by the Indians, and showed marked disrespect in his manner, & dress to the rules of the Ship & Navy. . . ."

Johnson went below again and after five more minutes Wilkes sent word that he must leave the ship within the next five. He then reappeared "in some temper & in the dress before described" and said he would not obey the orders "or words to that effect" whereupon the orders were taken out of his hands and transferred to Eld, with Colvocoresses as second in command, and Johnson placed under arrest.[4]

---

2 Wilkes Journal 3, July 12–16, 1841.
3 *Narrative* 4: append. XIV, pp. 534–536.
4 Wilkes Journal 3, July 17.

It was dark when Eld's party made its hasty departure, Colvocoresses having barely time to collect his bedding and instruments. As they pitched their tents the *Vincennes* disappeared from view. Brackenridge was not pleased to find himself again under the orders of these young naval officers, considering them "about the poorest hands to conduct an expedition of this sort that I have ever fallen in with."[5] The next morning, after Eld and Colvocoresses had breakfasted on board the Company's schooner *Cadborough* and procured twenty days' provisions and trading goods, they set forth in two canoes heading for the portage at the most southwesterly arm of Puget Sound. Their canoes were so leaky that one man had to be kept bailing all the time and their bread and flour were almost ruined. The portage was accomplished after a day's delay, with the help of ten Indians directed by a squaw chief whose authority was unquestioned by all including her husband. She took their big canoe in exchange for a smaller and more manageable one.

After crossing Lake Sachal, they entered the river of that name where, for the first four miles, the going was very difficult. Although its width varied from twenty to sixty feet and its depth from three to twelve, the thickets along its banks and its abrupt turns made it nearly impassable. They cut their way, dragging and pulling the canoes and lost their hatchet, a serious matter, in the process.

A second portage, around an impassable part of the river took two days and after that there were sandbars, shallow rapids, and sunken snags to slow their progress. At a rapids the larger of their canoes hit a snag tearing off part of the gunwale and half filling it with water. They finally reached the entrance of the Sachal into the wider Chickeeles and a day later camped at the mouth of the Sachap, another branch of the Chickeeles. Here Eld procured an Indian guide and, taking Sergeant Stearns and two men with him in the small canoe, explored that stream. It led to some lakes and a burned-over section. Among some giant trees was one that had fallen and which Eld estimated to have been about two hundred and sixty feet tall.

Continuing down the Chickeeles the party reached the

[5] Brackenridge Journal 2, July 19.

entrance to Gray's Harbour on July 31. They were finding it hard to make headway against an incoming tide and a strong southwest wind when the squaw chief, who had preceded them from Nisqually, again came to their assistance and with the help of her large canoe got them across to the less exposed shore where they made camp.

The survey of Gray's Harbour was carried out with great difficulty. The Indians were less helpful in this matter. After bargaining for the use of one of their canoes, they, at the last moment, tried to raise the price and, since they would not take an order on the Company, had to be paid in clothing and blankets. The most efficacious pay, next to rum, was powder and tobacco, but these were in short supply. Moreover, the Indians were reluctant to go out when the water was rough, as it was most of the time.

Little was accomplished during the first ten days of August and their supplies became very low. They moved closer to the Capes, settling at South Head, and by that time were living on dead fish (a sort of hake) picked up on the beach, cammass root bought from the Indian, clams, berries, and an occasional grouse. They became sick and weak from lack of food, from physical strain, and from being continually wet.

When Wilkes reached the Columbia and found that they had not yet made their appearance, he became alarmed and sent a search party under De Haven who found them on the thirteenth, gave them some food, and brought back word of their plight. A party of Kanakas led by Boileau, a Canadian, was then sent with twenty days' food supply. The survey, completed on the twenty-fourth, indicated that Gray's Harbour had little commercial value, because its half-mile-wide entrance had dangerous breakers on both sides and, though extensive in size, was so full of mud-flats that it was not a suitable anchorage for vessels of more than one to two hundred tons. During three-fourths of the party's twenty-three-day stay a strong gale had blown from the southwest or northwest accompanied by fog which limited vision to half a mile.

At their departure they traced the shore line as far as Cape Disappointment, the Indians tracking the canoes along the shore inside the surf. After making a four and a half mile portage from shoalwater to Baker Bay they were met and taken to Astoria, arriving there on the twenty-seventh.

Boileau had brought Eld a message from Wilkes stressing how important it was that "the duty put on us be accomplished" and complimenting him and his party upon their perseverance.[6] In the *Narrative* he said,

This tour forms a part of the operations of the Expedition that I look back upon with pride and pleasure, and I feel that my thanks are especially due to Passed Midshipman Eld and Colvocoresses and Mr. Brackenridge, for their devotion to the service in which they were engaged.[7]

Wilkes' hasty departure from Nisqually and his impatience with Johnson was due, in part at least, to his conviction that something had happened to the *Peacock* now three months overdue. Along with everyone else he felt anxiety for the safety of her crew and, as Commander of the Expedition, realized that her lateness meant more work and less time to do it in for everyone else. On July 20 the *Vincennes* was joined by the *Porpoise* at their New Dungeness Roads rendezvous.

Ater leaving Nisqually on May 15, the *Porpoise* had surveyed Admiralty Sound and the outer and two inner harbors of Port Orchard, one of the most beautiful and well-protected harbors of the inland waterway, its only drawback being a rocky reef near the middle of its entrance. During June the brig surveyed Penn's Cove and Whidby's Island where members of the Sachet tribe lived in well-built timber lodges surrounded by picket fences for defense against attacks by tribes from the north. They had adopted Catholicism and shown much affection and reverence for the Mission priests who came twice a year to give instruction, baptize, and leave tokens. The priests also taught them how to grow potatoes and beans.

On the Fourth of July the *Porpoise* was near Point Roberts and the day was allowed to pass without any special effort to celebrate. She reached Fraser's River on the fifth. This river, about a mile wide at its mouth, had a serpentine channel leading through mud flats to the Company's Fort Langley, about twenty miles up river and too far for the brig to traverse at this time since she had to keep her New Dungeness rendezvous with the *Vincennes*.

Wilkes had intended to give the crews a few days rest,

---

6 Wilkes to Eld, Aug. 15, 1841, Eld Letters, folder #2.
7 *Narrative* 5: p. 134.

but the non-appearance of the *Peacock* made him decide to finish the northern survey as quickly as possible, deeming it "of too much importance to allow a day to go by unimproved." Case was sent back to complete the survey between Hood's Canal and Whidby's Island and thereby connect his survey with that of the *Porpoise*. Another division was dispatched to survey New Dungeness Bay and Protection Island. The *Porpoise* was ordered to pick up Case's party, then to proceed to Fort Langley, and after that to go through Johnson's Straits and around the north end of Vancouver Island to Nootka Sound.

Leaving the *Vincennes* at anchor in New Dungeness Bay, the Commander took seven boats across the Strait of Juan de Fuca. They had to contend with a strong wind and an ebb tide running against the wind and producing a very high sea, but the boats demonstrated their seaworthiness and the twenty miles were traversed at the cost of only one mast and a complete wetting for everybody. Once ashore fires were built, clothes dried, and the men soon restored to their "wanted good spirits."

On July 27 Passed Midshipman May arrived from the *Vincennes* with letters, dispatches, and, from Nisqually, the news of the wreck of the *Peacock* on the bar at the entrance to the Columbia. Since there was no loss of life, the Commander's first reaction was one of relief. He had made up his mind that he must go in search of her, expecting that she had been wrecked on some unknown shoal. He could not understand why Hudson had gone to Oahu when he knew that provisions and water were provided for at the Columbia which, considering the wind, was nearer than Honolulu. If Hudson had disregarded orders "without due reason he has met the fate of all those who run counter to written Instructions."[8]

New plans had to be formulated. Ringgold's orders were countermanded and he was instructed to return to New Dungeness. By strenuous exertion of officers and men a survey of the Canal de Arro was completed and the boats returned to the *Vincennes* on the evening of the twenty-eighth. Wilkes regretted that lack of time prevented the survey of the southeast end of Vancouver Island which he believed had many fine harbors.

8 Wilkes Journal 3, July 27.

The *Porpoise* returned on the following day when T. W. Waldron was sent with dispatches, via Nisqually and Cowlitz, to Astoria. These included orders to the *Peacock's* officers to prepare written reports of the circumstances which caused her loss.

With favorable wind and tide on the thirty-first, the two vessels got under way, heading down the Straits of Juan de Fuca. The *Porpoise* surveyed San Juan Harbor on the north side of the entrance to the Straits while the *Vincennes* surveyed Neah Harbor on the south; neither was found to afford a well-sheltered anchorage. While carrying out this survey, the *Vincennes* was surrounded by canoes of members of the Classet tribe. A chief named "George" who spoke a little English, came on board and obligingly posed while Wilkes made a camera lucida sketch. He was especially proud of a scar on the bridge of his nose, signifying that he had taken a whale, a great exploit. These Indians could not understand why there was no demand for their otter skins and George kept asking "what for so big ship" and "what for so many mans?"

They left the Straits on the morning of August 3 before the fog set in, but were soon so beset by it that even signal guns became inaudible. In such a situation the lead was their only resource and when it showed less than fifteen fathoms they would anchor until a favorable wind or clear weather prevailed. After two days of this, Wilkes was pleased to discover the *Porpoise* following not far astern.

At daylight of the sixth Cape Disappointment was in sight. As they approached they met the whaleship *Orozimbo* and at noon the *Flying Fish* appeared and Captain Hudson came on board the *Vincennes*.

XX
Return to Samoa

THE *Peacock* and *Flying Fish* had left Honolulu under orders to return to Upolu, Samoa, surveying particular islands en route and, afterwards, certain central Pacific islands before rejoining the rest of the Squadron at the Columbia River. More specifically, Hudson was to determine, en route to Samoa, whether the Phoenix and Birnie islands were one and the same, to fix the location of Sydney Island, to survey and contact the natives on the Duke of York and Clarence islands, and finally, to locate Quiros Island. Since the original survey notes for the southern coast line of Upolu had become lost this was to be resurveyed. From Samoa, Hudson was to take a north-westerly course so as to chart the Ellice, De Peyster, and Kingsmill groups, the Pescadores, and, finally Ascension Island; then to proceed to the Columbia River where he should arrive between April 15 and May 1.

Additional orders required him to attempt to capture Chief Oportuno at Upolu so as to "obtain ample justice" for his murder of an American seaman. This could best be achieved by holding the principal chiefs as hostages, but hostile steps were to be avoided as much as possible and Hudson was not to risk the lives of those under his command.[1]

Wilkes had little confidence that these orders would be carried out successfully, for he considered Hudson somewhat out of his element as regards survey duty because "his education had in no way been directed to this branch of his profession." Although his officers admired him as a man, they took advantage of him in performing their duties, frequently going about them in a slovenly and ignorant manner. At the outset the *Flying Fish,* departing at night, sailed past the *Peacock* unobserved, as the latter waited for her near the harbor entrance. To Wilkes this was "a sad omen" even though they

---

[1] *Narrative* 4: append. VIII, pp. 517–519.

soon found each other and bore off on a southerly course early in the afternoon of December 3.[2]

Knox and Reynolds were the only commissioned officers on the *Flying Fish,* the latter having been transferred to her two days before their departure. Reynolds was vociferously critical of Wilkes, referring to him in his private journal as either crazy or "a rascally tyrant, lier, black-hearted enough to be the Devil's brother."[3] It is probable that the Commander was aware of this and sent him to the schooner to isolate him from his like-minded cronies, Whittle and Guillou.

In about a week the two vessels reached Washington Island (New York Island on Arrowsmith's chart), and by that time it had become evident that they were not well suited for cruising in company; in a fair wind the *Peacock* was constantly shortening sail so that the schooner could catch up and, in a head wind, the tender outsailed her.

The next eight days were spent looking for but not finding five islands listed by Jeremiah Reynolds and indicated on Arrowsmith's chart. The winds and currents were so baffling that they found themselves returning to Washington Island on three separate occasions This was a waste of time in an area where Wilkes considered one day should have sufficed.[4] Heading southwestward from Washington Island, they came to Jarvis Island which turned out to be nothing more than a two-mile long sand spit containing a few shrubs and many birds.

During the last ten days of the year the vessels' progress was discouragingly slow, making only one degree of easting and six degrees of southing against variable winds and high seas with an easterly swell and current. All this time they were searching for Brooks Island or Clark's Reef on which to make magnetic observations. Christmas was duly celebrated with the steerage managing an eggnog Christmas Eve, having discovered somewhere a half-dozen eggs. Hudson conducted divine service in the morning and, together with the steerage officers, joined the lieutenants for dinner in the Ward Room. The chief topic of conversation concerned the merits of a large cake received

---

2 Autobiography 6: pp. 1305–1309.
3 Reynolds Journal 2: pp. 166, 168.
4 Autobiography 6: p. 1310.

at Honolulu baked by a lady in the United States.[5] New Year's Day was celebrated in much the same manner. Although it came on Friday, Captain Hudson held divine service, reading a sermon which Peale believed was written "by some presbiterian in *winter,* and not intended to be preached on the equator." Whittle disliked what he considered an "affectation of sanctity" and wondered where the Captain got his "horrible" pronunciation.[6]

At last on January 9 they came to Enderby Island where it was possible to land, take dip and intensity observations, and give the scientists their first chance to go ashore. Dana found a new kind of coral, Rich ten kinds of plants including two kinds of parsley, and Peale man-of-war birds, gannets, tern, petrels, golden plover, red-tailed tropic birds, and boobies. The schooner took the opportunity to send her notoriously insubordinate cook, John Weaver, to the ship to receive a dozen with the cat.

Lookouts were doubled and the officers kept a constant watch as they cruised about and passed over the locations of several islands mentioned by Jeremiah Reynolds. It appeared that whalers had sighted the same islands several times and given them different and incorrect locations. An island such as Birnie's, which was a barren coral ledge only seven or eight feet above water, could be seen in the daytime from a distance of not more than eight to nine miles or, if tree-bearing, from twelve to fifteen. On a moonlight night it could be seen about five miles away but on a dark night it might present a hazard, for no bottom could be obtained by sounding until a few hundred yards off and the color of the sea gave no warning nor did the sea birds which, on such a night, stayed close to their covey.[7]

On the seventeenth they made an island and could not decide whether it was Sydney's or Hull's. A landing was effected and it was mistakenly identified as Sydney's, on which the *Vincennes* had previously found natives hunting turtles, though none were on it now. It was actually Hull's Island,

5 Whittle Journal 1, Dec. 24, 25; Emmons Journal 2, Dec. 25, 1840.
6 Whittle Journal 1, Dec. 19, 30, 31, 1840 and Jan. 1, 4–6, 10, 1841; Peale Journal 5, Jan. 1, 1841.
7 Hudson Journal 2, Jan. 9–13, 1841; Emmons Journal 2, Jan. 10, 1841.

westward of Sydney's. As a result, they sailed seventy-five miles
farther west looking for Hull's Island which they had just left.
Not finding it at its supposed location, they decided that two
names had been attached to one island, and headed south for
Duke of York Island.[8]

They were now forty-five days out from Oahu and it
would be twenty-one more before they reached Samoa. If on
board the *Peacock,* it was hot and boring, and the food was
unpalatable, it was worse on the *Flying Fish.* Reynolds let
off steam by entering his thoughts in his journal. They had
seen only a few islands and they were all uninhabited and
uninteresting except one from which was wafted a "delicious
smell of fresh flowers & the balmy green of Earth" making
him long for "Sweet Samoa." He had never been so idle or
bored as in this "cage." Captain Knox, "Old Sam Knox" or
"Old Hard Nox" as he was familiarly called, was amiable but
they saw too much of each other. Knox sat writing on the
other side of the table two and a half feet away and they were
seldom farther apart, the schooner being only about six feet
wide abaft.

Reynolds, just twenty-five in December, was four or five
years younger than Knox who had the same date of commissioning although he had been in the service three years longer.
Knox, whose baldness and weather-worn face made him look
like a grandfather, had sailed most of his life and came from a
family of sailors. He was kind-hearted, had "a heap of shrewd
sense," and was "worth his weight in gold most any time."
They never quarreled, in spite of daily annoyances very trying
to the temper. Often they had nothing to do but stare at each
other and they grew weary of that and of talking about any
and everything. They had no books.[9]

They reached the Duke of York Island on the twenty-fifth.
The natives came out singing as they paddled, their gesticula-
tions not the usual vulgar kind. They would not come on board
but indicated their friendliness by rubbing noses with the
officers through the ports. Hale recognized some words but
their dialect was new to him. They departed in confusion when

---

8 Hudson Journal 2, Jan. 19; *Narrative* 5: p. 5; Whittle Journal 1, Jan. 18, 19.
9 Reynolds Journal 2: pp. 173–175.

the guns were fired to establish a base line, some diving and staying under water for a considerable time. Their tattooing was similar to that of Caroline Islanders, but their general appearance was that of Navigator Islanders. The schooner covered the boats as they landed, but the natives were fearful rather than warlike, sending their women and children into the lagoon in canoes and appearing to think the white men gods whose ship had descended from the sun. Their only water was collected in hollows cut into cocoanut trees, but it was sweet and good. They apparently lived on cocoanuts and fish and Hudson gave them the *Peacock's* remaining three pigs and determined to tell the Samoan missionaries about these sun worshipers.[10]

The Duke of Clarence Island was nearby but they were becalmed for two days within sight of it, and when the wind came it was too strong to permit a landing. Emmons, viewing it from the masthead, decided it was uninhabited. The wind brought a deluge and the rain water awning was spread to catch "something palatable." Water had become a serious problem, for it was discovered that they had actually more than a thousand gallons less than on daily report and the remaining supply was brackish, creating rather than slaking thirst. The shortage decided Hudson to stop hunting non-existent islands and head for Samoa.

Emmons, having the Mid Watch on the twenty-ninth, heard the sound of surf but could not see anything until at sunrise an island approached which was not on any chart. The natives who came out seemed to be friendly and resembled the Duke of York islanders in dialect, tattooing, fear of cannon fire, and desire to trade. At the village Captain Hudson was led to a seat on a mat alongside the king, an honor he did not enjoy for the king, who was apparently in a state of alarm,

embraced me—rubbed noses with me—rubbed his nose on my chin —pointed to the sun—howled—hugged me again & again—moaned— howled—pointed to the sun—put a mat around my waist—and se- cured it with a cord made of human hair—rubbed noses again— cried—howled, etc., etc. . . . [11]

---

[10] H. Hale, *Ethnography and Philology*, Ex.Ex. **6**: pp. 151–152; Hudson Journal **2**, Jan. 25; Emmons Journal **2**, Jan. 25; Peale Journal **5**, Jan. 25, 28, 29.
[11] Hudson Journal **2**, Jan. 30.

Among the sailors were some Samoans, Marquesans, and
Sandwich Islanders, but none could converse with these natives. The men were good-looking and some of the women
beautiful; only full-grown girls wore clothes. By signs and a
few words they indicated their belief that their visitors were
gods from the sun. They traded mats and canoe buckets dug
out of solid wood (the first thing of this kind the Americans
had seen) for fishhooks, knives, and beads. Peale alarmed them
by striking fire and smoking a cigar, and they were uneasy as
long as it remained lit. They stole from Purser Speiden an
article that he had just bought, and traded it over again to a
third party close by. A small windlass in their "Spirit House"
indicated that some vessel had been wrecked on their shores.[12]
Hudson thought the island might be a discovery and told Emmons it should be named for him but decided to name it
"Bowditch" island. The natives called it "Fakaafao."[13]

At sunset, February 14, they came to an uninhabited
island designated as "Queros" on Arrowsmith's chart, but
since its location and description did not agree with Arrowsmith's, Hudson called it "Swain's" after a Captain he had met
at Tahiti who told him about it. Four days were spent in the
vicinity of this island but the weather was so stormy that its
location could not be fixed with exactitude. Apia harbor on
Upolu, only a day's sail away, was reached on the night of the
fifteenth. In the morning the wind was too light and the sea
too heavy to pass over the reef at the entrance. The missionary
brig *Camden* could be seen at anchor but no canoes came out,
it being Sunday at Samoa though Saturday aboard ship.

In the calm of the afternoon the *Peacock* was warped, by
means of a kedge, past the edge of the reef. The harbor, being
on the weatherly side of the island, was unprotected from
heavy seas and a backwash out of the narrow entrance channel,
reenforced by several fresh-water streams, often caused vessels
to lie at anchor with their sterns pointed seaward, even during
the strongest blows. For a time the *Peacock* remained broadside to the heavy rollers and, through carelessness, the boat

12 Emmons Journal 2, Jan. 29; Peale Journal 5, Jan. 30.
13 Reynolds, in his Critique, denied it was a discovery. He said a Honolulu paper
  published an account of its discovery in 1836 by Capt. Smith of the *General
  Jackson* and called it "De Wolf's Island."

Petrel got caught under the accommodation ladder and was so badly damaged that it had to be broken up. Tents were set up on shore and the carpenters put to work making a new boat and repairing *Polly,* which had been damaged during an attempted landing at Quiros Island.[14]

It rained steadily during their first eight days at Apia, hampering the work of the survey parties and making it impossible to loosen sails and air ship until the weather finally cleared on February 20. However, the men had a chance to go ashore and luxuriate in fresh-water baths, and fresh water was brought to the ship. Purser Speiden tried to expedite the procurement of supplies by setting up a pig pen and trading post under a big tree in the village. This was a convenient but expensive way to operate since he had to pay for the privilege, the pen, a watchman, and for every other service requiring native help.

The most noticeable change since their previous visit was that of the seasons, the rainy season producing such luxuriant verdure that most of the village, including the new white stone church, was hidden from view. They were welcomed by their native friends as bearers of presents and by the missionaries as representatives of law and order. Reynolds was shocked to learn that his favorite, the beautiful Emma, was married to a chief old enough to be her father. The fate of Williams and Harris had had an inspirational rather than a dampening effect upon the missionaries, and their bodies had been brought here from the New Hebrides for burial.

Peale, remembered by the natives as "Good Shot," made another exploratory excursion into the interior of the island accompanied this time by Rich, Agate, and Guillou, and by his former interpreter William Cowley and carrier Papau. They happened upon "Joe Gimblet," the founder of a native religious sect. He was being waited on hand and foot by

---

14 Hudson Journal 2, Feb. 5, 6. Wilkes thought too much time was spent at Upolu correcting errors previously made by officers of this ship, Autobiography 6: p. 1310. Emmons explained the need to resurvey as due to the loss of original notes. He also mentioned the discovery, upon arrival at Apia, that the rate given the Standard Chronometer at Honolulu was too small, placing that port 29 miles too far to the east necessitating the correction of all longitudes established since leaving Honolulu in proportion of the time elapsed, Emmons Journal 2, Feb. 6, 7.

villagers, and it was said that after his two wives died Joe had disappeared into the jungle and when he reappeared said the Spirit had told him he was too old to have another wife and that his followers would see to his every want. He talked a kind of gibberish making it appear that he understood the talk to the scientists. Agate persuaded him to take a shiny red-colored railway guide in exchange for his "bible" which turned out to be a copy of the *Rambler,* a Roman Catholic monthly.[15]

Dr. Whittle made friends with the natives easily and particularly with a chief in a nearby village who took the name "Benjamin" after his conversion to Christianity. He dined with Benjamin and his sweet-faced wife Lucy more than once and they exchanged presents. Benjamin was particularly pleased to be given paper, quills, and ink.

Whittle and Hale visited Malietoa, the island's principal chief or king, who was feeble with age. They were greeted cordially by the king and his principal wife, one of two. They dined native style, eating off mats covered with banana leaves, food which was brought in a cocoanut leaf basket. Everyone ate with his fingers or with a knife if he happened to have one with him. Whittle was somewhat embarrassed for

At supper I had the honor of being fed by the Queen! As fast as I put Yam she put in Parasama which she did with a small stick and her fingers; and altho it was not very agreeable to be stuffed in this way, still as it was the Queen, I was forced by my politeness to submit.[16]

The survey on the north side of Upolu was conducted by Emmons with two boats and that on the south side by Perry with two more. The men's clothes were never dry and, since the boat awnings were not wide enough to keep all the rain out, someone had to bail constantly. As the weather improved they made more rapid progress and by the twelfth had reached the eastern end of Upolu near the town of Vailoa. Dana, who

---

15 Peale Journal 5, Feb. 6, 8, 13.
16 Whittle Journal 1, Jan. 25, 28, 30, and Feb. 2, 7–20. "Parasama," as Whittle explained, was made of tara tops, grated with cocoanut, wrapped in leaves and roasted under ground. It tasted moist and delightful "being much superior to spinach & more like it than anything I am acquainted with."

accompanied the party, went ashore to climb a nearby extinct volcano. The village chief invited him and Emmons to sleep in his house and gave them a bed of mats with mosquito bars made of thick native cloth attached to a bedstead—"no common piece of furniture even in a chief's house." Before retiring prayers were read in Samoan from missionary imprints and "a bad imitation of an old-fashioned psalm—and less musical than any of their original native songs" was sung.

Having completed his part of the survey, Emmons planted a signal flag alongside a bottle containing instructions for Perry, who was expected to reach the same point from the opposite side, and Dana engraved an Expedition mark on a large tree. Returning to Apia three days later they found the new boat finished, the ship preparing to depart, and the natives "swarming about the ship & the chiefs coming on board to admire & acquire."[17]

Perry's boats did not return until the twentieth. It had been necessary to send additional provisions and grog to them across the island. Two of his men had deserted and were kept in hiding by the chiefs, who thought a white man added prestige to their village; the deserters expecting to have a life of idleness with occasional employment as pilots. Hudson sent word via the chiefs at Apia that he would burn their villages if the men were not returned. This had its effect, for the deserters were brought back to receive their dozen lashes and the chiefs at Apia were given a lecture and then their promised reward.

Hudson now prepared to carry out his police duties, demanding of Chief Sangaputele the surrender of the murderer of the American seaman Gideon Smith in July of 1840. This was in accord with the convention the chiefs had signed in November, 1839, and was the same demand that Ringgold had made without being able to follow it up. A three-day ultimatum ended on Washington's Birthday, whereupon the *Peacock* got under way.

Arriving off Saluafata on the twenty-fourth she had to wait until late that day before there was enough wind to bring her into the harbor between two reefs where the surf was

---

17 Emmons Journal **2**, Feb. 9–17.

breaking heavily. Having surveyed the harbor, Emmons did the piloting for the ship and, in the evening, for the *Flying Fish*. To assist him with the schooner in the darkness the *Peacock* burned a blue light, fired a gun, and set off rockets causing the natives to extinguish all lights in the town.

The next day the weather was clear and the water calm. Everyone was keyed up for the attack, expecting a fight because of the natives' defiant attitude and because an American carpenter came on board for protection saying that he had been threatened and that it was rumored that native reenforcements had come from across the island. As Reynolds put fresh flints in his pistols and gave his sword a rub on the whetstone, he reflected upon the curious feeling that comes over one at such a time—the desire above all "to kill, kill, kill."

After breakfast and "a Quarter Deck Harangue" by Captain Hudson, ninety men took off in seven boats, organized into three divisions: The leading one under Lieutenant Walker supported by De Haven, the second under Lieutenant Emmons and Passed Midshipman Davis, and the third, which was to remain on the beach to protect the boats, under Lieutenant Perry and Passed Midshipman Harrison.

The *Peacock* was warped around with a kedge so that she was broadside to the town when she delivered a fifteen-minute cannonade before the boats went in. Peale was in charge of the battery which, as he wrote his brother, made a "most valorous and terrible noise" but, since the distance was about a quarter of a mile and the guns were of small caliber and double-shotted, they did little damage, the shot mostly falling short. Upon landing it was found that the natives had fled, having hidden their war canoes and valuables. The crackling of the burning bamboo was thought, at first, to be gunfire, but there was no opposition.[18]

After the men had reembarked and been refreshed, they were sent off again to burn a nearby associated town where, again, there was no opposition. About one hundred and fifty huts were burned. The men were all back on board, boats run up, kedge weighed, and waiting for a wind to take them out of the harbor by 6 P.M.

---

18 Hudson Journal 2, Feb. 25; Reynolds Journal 2, p. 202; Peale to Franklin Peale, May 25, 1841, Amer. Philos. Soc.

At about 7:30 a slight breeze sprang up and the *Peacock* began to make her way slowly through the channel in the reef. The cutter was sent ahead to tow, but a sudden wind from the northeast caused the boat itself to be towed as a heavy squall developed. The ship was taken aback and just managed to scrape past the reef, with breakers under her lee, by "shivering" the after yards and letting the head yards box her round on the larboard tack. The wind was now strong from the north-northwest and the rain came in torrents. It became so dark they could hardly see ahead the ship's length. There were shoals close by on which the sea occasionally broke heavily, but they were forced to plunge ahead or go ashore and lose the ship and all hands. The wind abated about 11 P.M., the rain continued to be heavy, and it became nearly calm but dark and cloudy. Hudson thanked God for their deliverance.

Everyone was aware of their predicament and what their fate might be if they were wrecked on a reef at the entrance to the harbor of the town they had just burned. "What fine fun it would have been for the natives" thought Whittle.[19]

Hudson's next move was to send off two secret missions to capture chiefs as hostages for the surrender of Oportuno, as had been done successfully in the case of Vendovi. By the twenty-eighth the *Peacock* was off Apia again and picked up two boats under Walker and De Haven whose mission had been to seize old chief Malietoa. But he had been warned and could not be found; indeed, the whole island and the neighboring island of Savaii knew about the burnings and watched every movement of the vessels and their boats.

Emmons was given command of the *Flying Fish* and sent to capture Chief Pare (Pea) on the island of Monona, located between Upolu and Savaii. Arriving on the twenty-seventh, he pretended to survey the shore and learned from a missionary that Pare had been forewarned and gone into hiding. As can be imagined, the deception involved in these efforts went against the grain since to hold friendly chiefs as hostages would destroy the confidence which they had endeavored to build up. The officers were not sorry to have the missions fail.[20]

---

19 Hudson Journal 2, and Whittle Journal 1, Feb. 25.
20 Emmons Journal 2, Feb. 26–Mar. 1; Peale Journal 5, Feb. 28; Reynolds Journal
    2: pp. 207–208.

The *Flying Fish* proceeded to Savaii, and Emmons finished
the survey of its south shore, where there was no good harbor,
before proceeding to their rendezvous with the *Peacock* at
Mataatu, a northern port of that island. The two vessels departed March 7, setting a northerly course with light airs
and hearts. Captain Hudson spoke for all when he said, "Lost
sight of the Navigators — glad of it."[21]

---

21 Hudson Journal 2, Mar. 7.

XXI

Survey of Central Pacific Islands

CROSSING THE 180° MERIDIAN March 13 they dropped that day from the calendar and, therefore, reached the first of the Ellice Islands on Sunday the fourteenth. Most of the low coral islands making up the Ellice, Gilbert, and Marshall Islands were in the form of circular reefs surrounding lagoons and appeared to early explorers as rings of islets so were usually referred to as Groups. Since they were so numerous, the haphazard attempts to name and locate them caused great confusion among cartographers. In turn, the Spanish, Portugese, English, French, and Russian explorers and merchant captains added names upon names as suited their fancy, frequently, of course, using native ones. Captain Hudson relied mainly upon Arrowsmith's chart which he corrected and to which he added some new names.[1] When in 1943-1944 Admiral Spruance directed the movements of the Central Pacific Force of the United States Pacific Fleet, he relied, in part, upon information derived from the Expedition's survey. At that time the native names Makin, Tarawa, and Apemana became well known to the American public.

Following Arrowsmith's lead, Hudson divided the Ellice Islands into a southern "Ellice Group" and a northern "De Peyster Group." Since they approached from the south, the first of these islands they came to was "Ellice Island" (Funafuti). To save time most of the surveying was done without landing and information about the inhabited islands gathered from natives who came out eager to trade but sometimes with nothing to offer except their women. Those from Ellice Island seemed especially poorly endowed, the inferior construction of their canoes indicating a scarcity of building materials and their only water was rain water caught in the hollowed trunks of cocoanut trees. Heavy rain squalls delayed the vessels' ap-

---

[1] Wilkes named two of these previously uncharted islands after Hudson and Speiden.

273

proach to the northern De Peyster Group, forcing them to spend two days boxing on and off.

The De Peyster natives differed from the Samoans in that they tattooed their legs, as well as the upper part of their bodies, wore long hair, long beards, and mustaches, and carried spears barbed with shark's teeth. Among them were two albinos and the sailors insisted that one having blue eyes and a red beard must be an Irishman and wanted to test him by offering him a glass of whiskey. Hale could converse with them, as their language was similar to that of the Samoans.[2]

Being between the Trades and the Doldrums, they were slowed by squally weather interspersed with calms and light winds. Realizing that they were expected to reach the Columbia River by May 7, little more than five weeks away, Hudson decided to skip some of the many islands.

By April 3 they were fairly within the northeast Trades and sighted Drummond's (Tabiteuea) Island, the first of the Kingsmill (Gilbert) group which extended northwestward to the Mulgraves. Many natives came out and boarded the *Peacock*. Their language and customs were unfamiliar. Most were entirely naked but some wore a slight fringe or girdle covering part of their abdomen but serving "no purpose of decency," and others had a kind of matted armor made of plaited and woven cocoanut husks, which were folded about their bodies above the hips. Reynolds purchased two suits of armor which he hoped to present to the Lancaster Museum in spite of Wilkes' insistence that everything—"even to a grain of sand"—be given up to the Government.[3] Ships were not new to these natives and they did not hesitate to ask for rum, whales' teeth, and tobacco, the last for eating rather than smoking.

It took two days to beat up close to this twenty-five mile long island because of a fickle wind and a strong adverse current. Since native visitors showed no alarm at the firing of a survey gun, concern was felt when all, for no apparent reason, suddenly departed. The boats were recalled and at sun-

2 Hudson Journal 2, Mar. 8, 14, 17, 18, 22, 31, 1841; Emmons Journal 2, Mar. 8, 14, 17, and 3, Mar. 18, 25, 1841; Whittle Journal 1, Mar. 21, 22, 1841; Peale Journal 5, Mar. 18, 1841.
3 Reynolds Journal 2, p. 221.

down the ship was anchored about four miles off shore. Emmons and De Haven, having taken the *Flying Fish* to the far side of the island, were beyond recall.[4]

The schooner's crew had to be careful about letting the natives come on board for, if they became sufficiently numerous, they might attempt to take possession. Reynolds found that his beard gave him distinction in their eyes and, if the *Peacock* was nearby, he would indicate that the schooner was taboo and shoo them away; when off by themselves the only thing to do was to keep armed sentries fore and aft and be constantly on the alert. Occasionally they would allow an older and milder looking individual to come on board to trade or to receive a present.[5] The experiences of the next few days showed that they had reason to be on guard.

FIG. 21. Landing of the *Peacock's* crew at the native village of Utiroa, on Drummond Island in the Kingsmill Group. In retaliation for the kidnaping of a sailor the village was destroyed. Drawing by A. T. Agate. *Narrative* 5: p. 52.

---

4 Hudson Journal 2, Apr. 3–5; Emmons Journal 3, Apr. 3, 5; Journals of Peale 5, and Whittle 2, both Apr. 5.
5 Reynolds Journal 2: pp. 228–229.

The first landing on Drummond Island from the *Peacock* was made by the cutter under Perry's command for the purpose of taking dip observations and giving the scientists an opportunity to look around. They went to the town of Utiroa to trade for fish and tough fowl. At the "mariapa" or Council House the heat was oppressive and, as the natives crowded around, the smell of rancid oil on their bodies was almost stifling and their clamor deafening. They had to repulse the natives' efforts to embrace them, to rub cocoanut oil on their faces, and to pick their pockets. Peale and Rich walked across the island, and, at one point, were surrounded by armed men whom they had to threaten with their weapons to get away. Hale and Dr. Palmer tried in vain to get information about the wreck, two years before, of the English whaler *Honduras;* it was rumored at Oahu that the captain and crew had been murdered but that the captain's widow and child were still on the island.[6]

The following day Captain Hudson led a landing party of five boats. He thought there was no real danger but warned everybody to avoid giving offense, to stick together, and to pay liberally for any purchases. Half of the boats' crews were left on the beach while the others visited the town. The native women attempted to cling to their necks while the men picked their pockets. Hudson met the chiefs and gave them presents but was not reassured when he saw an iron breast hook taken from a wrecked vessel. Dr. Guillou found himself surrounded by natives acting in a threatening manner and was saved by the timely arrival of Passed Midshipman Davis with some sailors. During the visit a disturbance took place on the far side of the village and some thought they heard a shriek. After returning to the boats it was realized that able seaman John Anderson, considered one of the "most prudent & correct" members of the crew, was missing. Walker and Davis went back with a squad of men but their shouts brought no response. A stone was thrown at Davis, and natives wearing armor and carrying spears began to assemble. The landing party shoved off a short distance from shore, fired guns in the air, and, at sundown, returned to the ship. It was hoped

<hr>

6 Mentioned in the Journal of Capt. James Float of the *Corsair* of Boston.

Anderson might yet return or the natives come asking for a ransom, but it was feared that he had been lured into a hut and murdered. This seemed more likely on the next day when their only visitors were from other parts of the island.[7]

The *Flying Fish* was also experiencing hostility. Whenever she approached the shore natives gathered and began wading out towards her. Because of calms, the crews of her two survey boats were kept at the oars most of the time and, with the thermometer registering 160° in the sun, were all, except the Sandwich Islanders, getting badly burned. Pulling into a bight to get two points in range, they were surrounded by natives asking for tobacco, and one "vociferously importuned" Emmons "for *rum* which he pronounced very plain." Emmons gave presents to two leaders as rewards for trying to keep the others back and kept the boats in four feet of water where they had an advantage over wading natives, in case of attack. De Haven bargained for three cocoanuts which they would not give him after he had paid for them. Seeing this, Emmons took the cocoanuts from their canoe. They did not attempt to stop him, but about a hundred gathered in canoes and in the water shouting taunts and shaking spears. When they began throwing pieces of coral, one of which hit a sailor in the back of the head, Emmons pointed his pistol at the thrower who hooted at him, evidently "not conscious of the effect of Firearms." To avoid a general engagement it was decided to retreat through a narrow passage in the coral, close to shore, where the natives were gathered in large numbers. Stones were thrown at De Haven who fired a pistol over their heads. As the two boats pulled through the passageway a man in each was taken from the oars to assist the officers with the guns. More coral was thrown and two pieces hit the boats, but when the oars struck some of the natives they were intimidated enough so that they did not use their weapons and it was not necessary to fire upon them. After passing through, a flotilla of canoes chased them but was lost to sight in the subsequent squally weather and darkness. At 10 P.M. the wornout boats' crews pulled through the breakers on the reef and reached the *Flying Fish*.[8]

---

[7] Journals of Hudson 2, Peale 5, and Whittle 2, all Apr. 7.
[8] Emmons Journal 3, Apr. 5–8.

Upon returning to the *Peacock* they learned of Anderson's disappearance. The boats were out finishing the survey and Agate was busy sketching a pretty native girl, one of several visitors who indicated they thought the Utiroans a bad lot. Hale went to great pains to tell those in one canoe, suspected of coming from Utiroa, that they would receive a large reward in tobacco if Anderson were returned unharmed. Plans were made to burn the town on the following day. There would be eighty-seven men in seven boats, organized in three divisions. Lieutenant Walker was to be in command with Emmons and Harrison leading one division, Perry and Davis another, and De Haven and Freeman, the Sailmaker, the third which was to stay with the boats. The schooner was to give close support. The still-fresh memory of the murder of Underwood and Henry instilled a warlike spirit.

The plan was carried out after breakfast, April 9. Since about thirty canoes had come out from other towns, the remainder of the *Peacock's* crew was kept on the alert to repel a possible attack upon the ship. It was a five-mile pull to shore. Walker estimated that six hundred warriors were waiting for them on the beach; other estimates ranged from three to eight hundred. Many natives watched the proceedings from a nearby point of land. The sailors were armed with muskets, pistols, and cutlasses and the officers with swords, pistols, and double-barreled guns. The Utiroans wore armor, shook spears, and set up a great clamor. Walker went in close with Hale standing in the bow calling to the natives to return Anderson and receive a reward, but they paid no attention and waded towards the boat shouting and splashing the water with their spears.

As Walker withdrew to the line of boats behind him, Emmons fired a rocket into the midst of the warriors causing momentary confusion. Then Walker signaled to Peale who, as prearranged, fired his double-barreled rifle hitting two chiefs in the act of rallying their followers. The incredulous manner in which the natives looked upon their dead chiefs showed their ignorance of firearms. Then a volley was fired bringing down several and causing the rest to scatter into the bushes taking about twenty dead and wounded with them. At the sound of the volley, the natives squatted in the water and dodged, making it difficult to estimate how many were hit.

Utiroa extended along the beach for about a mile. It was back about a hundred yards with a line of five-foot posts, interwoven with bamboo, about thirty paces from the beach. There was no further opposition as the landing party set fire to the town from its opposite sides. The natives could be seen, but kept out of range. The beach was narrow and the heat from the sun and fire was terrific and the smoke blowing in their faces was almost suffocating. Many canoes and cocoanut trees were destroyed along with some three hundred huts and the big council house.

The assault force had to wade out a half-mile to the boats because of the low tide and, as they departed, saw the chief and men from the neighboring town of Eita begin to pillage what was left of Utiroa. They had suffered no casualties, except one or two men wounded by their own cutlasses, and by noon were all back on board the *Peacock*.[9]

The next day they beat through the passage between Drummond's and Bishop's or Sydenham Island sighting but having no communication with natives who appeared to be out fishing. A succession of cloudy, squally, and rainy days and the lack of accurate charts made navigation difficult. Hudson, conscious of the need to hurry, remarked, after one particularly "dark, dirty & unpleasant" night, upon the difficulty of knowing "what reef or coral patch we may be thumping on before we can see it—however—I've said enough—as some of the gentry of home—*who of course know all about it*—have told the world through the public prints—'The Exploring Expedition was only a party of pleasure.' "[10]

The chart-makers seemed to have considered every hummock or detached islet as a separate island without troubling to sift and examine for accuracy such information as was available. Henderville (Nanouki) and Woodle (Kuria) Islands were found to be connected and Hopper, Harbottle, and Simpson's (Apamama) Islands were parts of a single formation, the only one affording a good harbor. By the sixteenth they were back at Woodle Island where they had been on the twelfth.

---

9 Hudson Journal 2, Apr. 8, 9; Emmons Journal 3, Apr. 9; Journals of Peale 5, and Whittle 2, both Apr. 7–9; Reynolds Journal 2: pp. 232–234.
10 Hudson Journal 2, Apr. 19.

Here they were boarded by Jack Kirby who had deserted from the English whaler *Admiral Cockburn* three years before. The island's chief had given him his eighteen-year-old daughter as a wife. He had piloted whalers and claimed to have "so civilized" the natives that they no longer urged him to cause wrecks on their shores. Tiring of this life, Kirby asked for passage to Honolulu although his wife and the chief tried to dissuade him. He promised to return and handed his wife an old rusty jackknife as a keepsake.

Through Kirby much was learned about native customs including their method of preventing over-population by infanticide. After the birth of a second child the foetus was destroyed in the uterus. Kirby's wife explained the process to Captain Hudson in the presence of her husband, father, and several male and female natives "without exhibiting the least delicacy or feeling on the subject." Incest, too, was one of their accepted customs.[11]

On the eighteenth and nineteenth they surveyed "Gilbert or Knox or Marshall Island" (Tarawa) in the usual manner, the ship going along one side and the schooner the other. Neither Gilbert nor Marshall Islands existed in the position assigned them by Arrowsmith or Duperrey, so Hudson decided that a hummock at the end of Knox Island was probably called Gilbert and finding no indication of Marshall Island "melted them into one" on his chart and named it Knox or by the native name Tarawa.

Charlotte (Apia or Apaiang) Island was surveyed next and landings made to take sights, dig wells for water, and give the scientists some relief from idleness. Lieutenant Walker ordered the cutter to take along "10 water bags, 2 buckets, 1 shovel, & Messrs Hale & Peale" which annoyed the latter as much as an order at Sandalwood Bay to "bring off the yams, hogs, & scientifics."[12]

While beating outside the reef, Hudson was astonished to see the *Flying Fish* enter the lagoon, Knox having been ordered merely to examine its entrance. She entered the northern passage under full sail, aided by a brisk breeze, headed

---

11 *Ibid.*, Apr. 16; Emmons Journal **3**, Apr. 15–17.
12 Hudson Journal **2**, Apr. 17, 19, 21–24; Emmons Journal **3**, Apr. 15–17, 22; Peale Journal **5**, Apr. 24.

across the lagoon towards its southern passage and, when the *Peacock* signaled the boats to return, answered that she was hard and fast aground. The boats returned, except Emmons' which pulled for the *Flying Fish*. It was evident that she could not be got off until flood tide but, since she was armed and reenforced by Emmons' cutter, Hudson felt she was safe from attack. The *Peacock* ran up her boats and stood along the reef until abreast of the schooner when she hove to and burned a blue light. Fires were seen burning on shore.

During the night the *Peacock* maneuvered so as to keep in position near the reef but, before dawn, ran on a sand bank. Orders were given to hoist the spanker, haul the jib sheet, square the mizzen yards, brace the head yards flat aback and let fall the foresail and in a few minutes, with the helm put to starboard, she ran off. The ship got off so easily because of the prompt carrying out of these orders and because she had been laid to shortly before touching and was not fully under way.

At daylight, to their astonishment, they found themselves back at Knox Island, having drifted eleven miles with the current. Making all sail they headed again for Charlotte Island and soon, to their relief, sighted the *Flying Fish* making for them. When Emmons returned on board Captain Hudson learned what had happened.

Captain Knox had hoped to save time by examining both passages together. After stranding, the schooner keeled over so far with the outgoing tide that her grenades were useless. She was shored up to protect her from the coral. The natives began to gather around in canoes and, when shouting at them had no effect, Knox fired at their sails and rigging. One shot cut the halyard of a canoe causing its sail to fall and its occupants to jump into the water and start to swim the three miles to shore. However, the natives continued to sail about and laugh at them until dark.

Emmons' cutter arrived about 8 P.M. and, about three hours earlier, Dr. Whittle had interrupted his reading of *Pride and Prejudice* to come aboard in response to a signal requesting medical aid. Reynolds had gone ashore and, consequently, spent the night on the *Peacock*.

The *Flying Fish* careened so far that it was impossible to walk and, much less, to sleep. Whittle wrapped in his cloak, lay on the sloping deck, almost in a standing position. The night was beautiful but disturbed by the natives who built fires and blew conch shells. At daybreak about twenty-five canoes came out but, by that time, the tide was far enough in to make it possible to haul the schooner off with an anchor. As the leading canoe came within the vessel's length and struck its sail preparatory to coming alongside, Emmons fired a bullet close to its steerman's head causing him and the others in the canoe to jump overboard. The schooner then got away and soon outdistanced the canoes. Emmons thought the natives were ignorant of firearms but "their treachery if possible surpassed that of the Feejees and whoever is unfortunate enough to fall among them in their present state—must leave a story to be told by others."[13]

Matthews (Maraki) Island,[14] examined on the twenty-seventh, had no entrance to its lagoon and squally, thick weather, and heavy seas prevented its survey. They proceeded to Pitt's Island which turned out to be two islands, the larger known to the natives as Taritari (Makin) and the smaller as Makin (Little Makin). They surveyed these on the twenty-ninth, the squalls and heavy seas having subsided.

The natives here were jolly, fat, and naked, their king so fat he could hardly climb onto the ship. A Scot named Robert Wood, who also called himself Grey, came out and offered to act as interpreter in exchange for a passage to Oahu. He said he had deserted from a Sydney whaler five years before and had not seen another ship since. The natives, a peaceful people, had treated him well but would not let him have a wife although most of them had ten or twelve, and the principal chiefs from thirty to fifty. He was the first white man they had ever seen and, for the first few months, they carried him about on their shoulders. With his beard and long hair streaming in the wind, a mat tied around his body reaching to his knees, and a kind of poncho or jacket of the same material covering the upper part of his body, Wood looked like Robinson Crusoe. At times he was so excited and incoherent that some thought him slightly deranged and he caused con-

---

13 Hudson Journal 2, Apr. 24, 25; Emmons Journal 3, Apr. 24, 25; Whittle Journal 2, Apr. 24; Gilman, Dana, p. 129.
14 This island was not on Duperrey's chart.

siderable amusement by sometimes talking in the native language and then talking English to the natives, at other times, repeating sentences as if he could not realize that this was his own language.[15]

Hale made the most of this opportunity to pump Kirby and Wood about customs and language. Hudson, having a high regard for his "talents, industry and love of research," relied on him to collect and sift this kind of information, confident that his "gatherings" would be worth more "than the united labours of the rest of us in this particular department."[16]

For several days it had been rumored that they were about to head east and that, because of the shortness of provisions, they would stop at Oahu. At general muster on the thirtieth it was announced that rations would be reduced and that they would proceed to the Pescadores (Rongerik) and then directly to Oahu, lack of time preventing visits to Strong's and Ascension Islands, where a band of desperadoes who preyed upon unarmed shipping were said to be established. They left the Kingsmill group with few regrets having corrected positions given by Duperrey and Arrowsmith, added some new islands in the group "with sufficient accuracy to answer all the purposes of navigation and withstand the test of future examination." Indeed, circumstances sometimes made accuracy next to impossible, as when at Drummond's Island Emmons had signaled the schooner to fire a gun to fix the base line, but with the sun in his eyes and the distance so great he neither saw the flash nor heard the gun. He had to guess at the length of the base line then and on other occasions when from various causes, including refraction, the surveys could be as much as a half-mile out of the way in a distance of four miles.[17]

Captain Hudson felt uneasy on May 1 as they sailed slowly under light breezes, aware of his instructions to arrive at the Columbia River between April 15 and May 1, and the emphatic wording that "it must not be later than the latter date."[18]

---

15 Peale Journal 5, Apr. 29.
16 Hudson Journal 2, Apr. 16; Whittle Journal 2, Apr. 14. Whittle considered Hale the most talented and charming man on the Expedition.
17 Emmons Journal 3, Apr. 6, 29, 30. According to Emmons, Duperrey's 1824 survey placed the reef forming the lagoon on the wrong side of Drummond Island.
18 Narrative 4: append. VIII, p. 519.

They reached the Mulgrave Islands of the Marshall group on the twenty-second and the next day with the help of a fresh breeze sighted Pedders, Daniels, and Arrowsmith Islands. They ran day and night now regardless of stormy weather; a somewhat hazardous procedure on this little-known sea. However, the islands they were passing had been fixed by Kotzebue and it was thought his chart could be relied upon.

The uninhabited Pescadores Island was surveyed on the fifth, the vessels taking opposite sides as usual. Captain Dowsett's schooner *Victoria* was presumably wrecked here, his crew murdered or carried away to another island, and his widow, living at Oahu, had asked that a search be made. On this day they also made Korsakoff (Longelap) Island which they found to be two islands instead of one, as represented by Kotzebue. Boisterous weather and a pounding surf prevented any attempt at a landing during the next two days and prevented a native canoe from reaching them. On the eighth the two vessels worked their way into smooth water on the lee side of Korsakoff Island and Captain Knox came aboard the *Peacock* for final instructions, which were to beat back to where the canoe had been seen and to find out whether any survivors from the *Victoria* were on that island, then to rejoin the *Peacock,* or, if she was not in sight, to go directly to Honolulu. As they separated, Emmons remarked, "parted company with our troublesome little pet & consort & stood to the North[d] on a wind"[19] and Reynolds, speaking for the schooner, said, "Right glad, were we all, to be rid of the Ship, with her signals & humbugging."[20]

The next day experiencing fresh breezes along with a northeast swell and rain squalls, and mindful of the scarcity of water and provision, Captain Hudson decided not to wait for the tender but to head straight for Honolulu. The *Flying Fish* sailed for two days along the reef without seeing any sign of life. The weather continued unsettled and the wind blew such a gale that heavy seas constantly broke over her, sprung her foregaff, and prevented the taking of observations. The time having expired for the rendezvous and the *Peacock* not in sight, the schooner, too, turned by the wind for the northeast.

---

19 Hudson Journal 2, and Emmons Journal 3, both May 8.
20 Reynolds Journal 2: p. 255.

XXII

The Peacock's Last Days

THE *Peacock's* ANCHORS and cables were stowed with alacrity on the ninth of May for she was headed for Oahu. If Captain Dowsett was still alive the schooner would find him. In any case it was six years since his ship was wrecked and the only reason for thinking him alive was that the survivors had not seen his body. For the past ten days they had been on and off land, usually at a great distance, and unable to make any inquiries of natives. It had seemed like a great waste of time. Now short rations and diminishing water supply were urgent reason for heading east.

Water consumption was controlled by giving everyone eight paper "checks" each day, each worth a half-pint of water when presented to the sentry guarding the scuttlebutt containing the day's allowance. The officers kept theirs in bottles which they brought to the table and used for cooking, washing, and drinking. Most of their food was of the saltiest kind, and the tropical climate added to their thirst, but they drank little coffee or tea and ate little food requiring fresh water for cooking. For a while, a store of cocoanuts acquired at the Navigator Islands provided milk for their coffee. Some could take this deprivation philosophically and agreed with Emmons that these were *"small items* in the scale of luxuries when compared to others that a *sailor* must forego."[1]

They could not go directly towards the Sandwich Islands, because this would be heading straight into the Trades. So, for the first ten days their course had to be north, then east as far as the meridian of the Islands, where they could turn south.

The higher latitudes reached in three days brought relief from the heat, the cooler, more bracing air being a welcome change for men who had been under a "vertical sun" for such a long time. The *Peacock* averaged one hundred and forty

---

1 Emmons Journal 3, May 10, 18; Whittle Journal 2, May 8, 9, 1841.

miles a day for the first few days but slowed to under one hundred as the winds became light. The smoother sea made it
possible to air bedding and clothing and very few were on the
sick list. Temperatures varying between 72° and 77° seemed
cool and the men began to wear woolen clothing and to sleep
under blankets.

In the "Variables," where wind and weather changed
frequently, progress was slow and there was not much to do,
beyond the usual housekeeping chores, and time hung heavy.
When the weather permitted, the ironwork was cleaned and
blackened and woodwork scrubbed and painted. The great
guns of the 2nd Division were no longer exercised because of
the rotten condition of their carriages, another proof, as Hudson commented sarcastically, of their "superior fit out" at Norfolk.[2] Drills and weekly readings, at muster, of the Rules and
Regulations for the better government of the Navy[3] took up
some of the time. In off hours, if the men were feeling good,
they danced to fiddle, drum, and triangle or amused themselves with games, such as "leap frog."

For the more contemplative and curious there was always
the sea and the life that it supported. They saw their first
albatross since leaving Sydney and it stayed with the vessel for
several days and was joined by others. Peale caught one with
a hook and line and shot a white one in full plumage which
he believed had never been described by naturalists. From the
surface of the sea they secured specimens of Ianthina, a kind
of snail which floats by means of an extended bladder and
whose blood answered very well for ink. Anatofa and other
crustacea and animalculae were fished from the sea and examined in detail by Dana. A school of sperm whales passed
by one day singly and in squads.

By June 1 they had reached a latitude of 35° N., and, as
the wind gradually veered to the south, they were able to take
a more southeasterly course towards Honolulu. The atmosphere which had been thick and hazy, making it damp and
unwholesome between decks, became drier.

Discovering a strange sail bearing down towards them,

---

2 Hudson Journal 2, May 18; Emmons Journal 3, May 18, 19.
3 Emmons Journal 3, July 1. These articles of War were considered largely obso-
lete and it was hoped they would have been revised by the time they got home.

they hove to and showed their colors, but the stranger hauled his wind and stood away. There was no chance of catching this "shabby fellow" and they could not help hoping that he, too, might be hungry and thirsty before the end of his voyage. They had better luck a few days later when another sail was discovered and overhauled. She was the American whaler *Magnolia* of New Bedford, Captain David Bernard, six days out of Oahu with 1,850 barrels of sperm oil and bound for the northwest coast to complete her cargo with black whale oil. She gave them some potatoes, fruit, a turkey, and twenty-two bags (250 gallons) of water for which her captain refused remuneration and "thereby proved an exception to the general rule." He also gave them newspapers, the latest dated November 11, 1840, and verifying the election of President Harrison.[4]

Still badgered by variable winds, they tacked more frequently to take advantage of every slant. At last, on June 13, there were signs that they were back in the Northeast Trades which could now be of help. Oahu was sighted the following morning, and, since they were not in position to pass on the weather side without tacking, Hudson elected to set the steering sails and pass to leeward. Upon reaching a point leeward of the mountains, though several miles off, they became becalmed except for occasional puffs coming out of the gorges and valleys. They worked their way around to the southern end of the island and before sunset sighted "Diamond Hill." The sounds made by ranging chains, getting the anchors off the bows, and bending buoy ropes were music to their ears.

It was frustrating to spend the night taking short tacks off the reef and, because of an easterly swell and a westerly current, making little progress. On the morning of the fifteenth Purser Speiden and Lieutenant Perry were sent ahead in a boat to make arrangements for procuring supplies, and, towards sunset when still about twelve miles out, they were cheered by the arrival of Consul Brinsmade bringing fresh provisions and mail.

Early in the morning of the sixteenth the *Peacock* stood in through the reef under all sail but at the entrance to the harbor the wind died out, the boats were sent to tow, and

---

4 Journals of Hudson 2, and Emmons 3, both June 5.

natives hauled on a long line as they walked along the reef. They were followed an hour later by the American whaler *Bartholomew G.* with His Majesty Kamehameha III on board. The King was received by a salute from the Fort, a band, and one hundred and fifty soldiers, in striking contrast to royal arrivals at other South Sea ports.

The *Flying Fish* had preceded them by only thirty hours. Although unable to contact the natives at the Pescadores, she had sailed between the islands determining that there were three of them. She, too, had been very short of water, especially because her supply was contaminated by dead mice and cockroaches. The hardships endured by those on the *Peacock* were compounded for the eleven men on the tender. To lack of food and water and wind under a boiling sun was added lack of space. The schooner had been on the go for six months, constantly pitching and rolling and seldom in a safe harbor. In all that time Reynolds had had only fifteen hours on shore and Knox even less, with hardly a single night of sleep undisturbed by the revels of a troop of mice, too numerous even for dispersal by Fanny, a puppy acquired at Apia. Dead mice were found in paint pots, among their clothes, and in the water. Reynolds had left most of his clothes in a tight drawer on board the *Peacock* but Knox had not and his coats and pants were eaten.[5]

Hudson was so concerned about their failure to keep up with Wilkes' schedule that he would not stay at Honolulu more than five days for watering, provisioning, and overhauling yards and rigging despite recommendations by Drs. Palmer and Whittle that the crew be given at least two weeks for recreation.[6]

Passed Midshipman Blunt was at Honolulu recovering from illness and waiting for transportation home. He refused Hudson's offer to go on the *Peacock* telling his friends that he would not dream of putting himself under Wilkes' command again. The interpreters Wood and Kirby were turned over to the British Consul, Kirby much debilitated by the sudden and complete change of diet.

They departed soon after the "Meridian" on June 21. By nine that night they were off the northern end of Oahu and

5 Reynolds Journal 2: pp. 257–265, 322.
6 Whittle Journal 2, June 14.

for the next ten days held a northerly course aided by a strong east wind. During the subsequent ten days the wind veered gradually towards the south and their course towards the east. By July 10 they had reached the latitude of 45° N., approximately that of the Columbia River, and their course had become due east.[7]

Everybody's mind turned to thoughts and speculations regarding the end of their travels. Guillou was determined to return home overland and busied himself making a poncho and hood to wear while crossing the Rockies. Whittle, convinced that the ship would afford the quickest way home, decided to stick with her saying that "Nothing short of absolute necessity would induce me to prolong my absence one moment."[8]

On the morning of July 17 the lead found ooze and sand at a hundred and ninety fathoms and, when the dense fog lifted briefly, they sighted Point Adams on low land northeast by east. Soundings at 5 P.M. brought fine gray sand at forty-one fathoms and, shortly after that, the fog lifted sufficiently to show the bold promontory of Cape Disappointment. At last, they had reached their objective, the entrance to the Columbia River.

The two vessels lay offshore during the night and on Sunday the eighteenth the weather was clearer than at any time since June 28. The *Peacock* stood in for the land, sounded at forty fathoms and at fourteen fathoms Captain Hudson wore ship, stood off, and conducted Divine Service. At 11:30 he wore ship again and stood in towards the shore. De Haven, who had the eight to noon watch, estimated Cape Disappointment to be five miles away and the schooner four or five miles to leeward. There was a light wind from the south and steerage way was much affected by the current. It seemed to be a favorable time to enter the river. Davis took the watch at noon and all hands were called at 12:33. By this time there was a moderate breeze freshening from the northwest and a heavy swell. They wore ship close in with the breakers, the water gradually shoaling to five fathoms. Emmons was sent

---

[7] Among the birds observed at this time were "Mother Cary's Chickens." They were also known as "Stormy Petrel," the name by which Wilkes became known in naval circles.

[8] Whittle Journal 2, June 30.

as lookout to the fore topsail yard and Captain Hudson stood on the forecastle and occasionally climbed onto the fore yard holding sailing directions in his hands. At 12:45 they stood in for what appeared to be the channel, but discovering a breaking sea ahead, wore ship again and proceeded farther along the breakers. The lead was constantly kept going by men in both chains. At 1 P.M. they came to a place where the water was comparatively undisturbed. Dana, standing next to Hudson on the forecastle, was as confident as the Captain that they had found the channel, this being the first spot that had no breakers. From the vantage of the masthead Emmons saw only occasional breakers, whereas elsewhere they seemed to form an unbroken line stretching from cape to cape. In answer to Hudson's repeated calls, he replied that he saw no better indication of a channel, although the water was so discolored by river sediment that it was difficult to tell. At the Captain's direction the ship stood in again and in five minutes touched bottom.[9]

The helm was immediately put down, yards braced, and every effort made to bring the ship by the wind and haul her offshore but she became unmanageable, owing to the strength of the current and force of the waves. As she went thump after thump and farther aground, the sails were clewed up and furled, dangerous work for the men aloft on swaying masts and yards. The *Peri,* the best sea boat, was lowered and Emmons went ahead to sound, but found no channel. Captain Hudson beckoned him close to the ship and, in a low voice, told him to pull for Cape Disappointment and bring off someone who knew the channel, some persons having been sighted on the bluff.

In order to lay out an anchor the first cutter was hoisted out with lines fore and aft to keep it clear of the ship, but the ebb tide meeting the ocean swell produced a combing sea which stove the boat so badly that it was of no further use. By now the ship was lifting and striking heavily and the sea had become too furious to attempt another launching. Pumps were rigged and royal and top gallant yards and masts sent

---

9 This was a channel, but only 2½ fathoms (15 feet) deep. The brig *Thomas Perkins* used it without touching although the water occasionally broke alongside, Emmons Journal 3, July 18–20.

down. Since she was making water fast the watches were divided into gangs to keep the pumps going continuously. Shot was heaved over the larboard quarter and the guns buoyed but not heaved for fear of the ship bilging on them. She was quartering to the sea, her after-body lifting with every surge of water and coming down heavily. The upper rigging was sent on deck and Hudson would have cut away the masts, except that they would then have no way of getting out the launch and the other boats. The iron tiller, which had been lashed amidships, broke off near the rudder head causing the rudder to work up and down with the motion of the ship and cut its way out, though still suspended by its pendants.

It was found possible to swing out the larboard anchor and bring her head to the sea which diminished the force of the surf, but she continued to strike on her keel fore and aft. By 6 P.M. there were only nine feet of water under the main chains and fog began to set in. Although the pumps had been kept going, the water was slowly gaining in the hold and that on the gun and spar decks was precipitated down the hatches with each roll of the vessel. At 8:45 P.M. the chain, with 45 fathoms out, broke and the ship turned broadside again and struck heavily until the starboard anchor was got out and the sea pushed the stern around so that she headed once more into the waves. It was high water a little before midnight and at that time the sea abated somewhat so that the stream anchor could be got out. Seeing a canoe in the river, three distress signals were fired.

In the meantime Emmons had pulled for the Cape but found the sea so increased that one man had to be kept bailing constantly and, when two-thirds in, they could hardly stem the flood tide and decided to turn back to the ship. The crew was nearly exhausted and the boat nearly filled, but it drifted through the outer line of breakers into smoother water where it could be bailed out. It was then possible to return to the ship with the help of an eddy where the sea seldom broke. Back at the ship they managed to whip the *Peri* on board again by means of a yard and stay tackles, in spite of the violent motion of both ship and sea. With the coming of night, no other boats were launched and the wind hauling northwest and freshening increased the sea so much that they could see a half mile of breakers inshore of the doomed vessel.

During the night the hatchways were battened down since combers occasionally rolled over the larboard bow and beam and broke down the bulwarks from the gangway foreward. Inside the water had risen to above the chain lockers. The ship's timbers and planking had worked so much that all hope of saving her was given up and the men were given a respite from the pumps. But, as Emmons said,

there was no such thing as *repose* on board for on all decks one was subject to a continual shower bath and the pitching & rolling of the ship had become so violent that there appeared but little probability of the ship holding together until daylight and *upon this only depended our safety*. In the meantime we were gradually forging farther upon the bank, when at daylight we were left for a short time stationary, the united action of the current & sea piled up the sand about us and the breakers having, owing to the low state of the ebb, receded just to seaward of us—still the water was quite rough inshore of us.

At daylight a canoe containing Wilkes' servant, John Dean, and an Indian pilot reached the ship and they learned that the *Vincennes* and *Porpoise* were in Puget Sound. The water being comparatively quiet, the boats were got out and the scientists, marines, and some of the sailors along with chronometers, charts, public papers, and survey materials were taken ashore. The canoe took Agate, Dr. Guillou, and Purser Speiden with his accounts and the hard contents of his iron case. Only the marines were allowed to take arms and no one was allowed to take any clothing except what he stood in to prevent the lumbering and swamping of the boats. Two trips were made before the breakers again became too large. By noon the ship was striking so heavily that Hudson, fearing she might go over on her beam, decided to cut away the masts. By first bracing the yards they went over cleanly and were kept clear of the ship.[10]

While all this was going on, the *Flying Fish* cruised on and off outside the breakers, which seemed to stretch from shore to shore, unable to reach the *Peacock* or to find the channel. Every time they came in close to the *Peacock* she

---

10 This account of the wreck is taken from the following sources: log entries for July 18, 19; Journals of Hudson 2, and Emmons 3, both July 17–19; Emmons' "Recollections"; Whittle Journal 2, July 18; Anonymous Journal #508; Gilman, *op. cit.*, p. 130.

signaled "Danger, you are approaching" and once when they got inside the reef Hudson refused to grant permission to anchor. Ironically, the day before they had expected Hudson to inspect the schooner and Reynolds had kidded Knox about his mouse-eaten clothes boasting that his were intact on board the ship.[11]

Knox described the scene in a letter to his father. It was horrible to behold

the huge breakers—now & then appeared to break entirely over her, she lurched heavily & often— I saw the men cut the fore & aft stays of the main & mizzen masts & knew that they were cut away but the Fore mast went of its own accord the change from a full rigged ship to a hulk was so sudden that the contrast was painful to reflect upon.[12]

The masts were going over as the boats made their third, and what would have been their last, trip. But the breakers were so huge that they were almost stood on end. Indeed, the one in the charge of Lewis, the Gunner, capsized end over end. Its crew momentarily disappeared from sight but Davis' boat was nearby and rescued all, although one was severely injured. Seeing this, Hudson hoisted the Ensign upside-down on the ten-foot stump of the mast as a signal for the boats to turn back. They obeyed but, as Emmons said, "with feelings that I will not attempt to describe nor shall I soon forget" for they did not expect those left behind to survive.

One seaman was slightly injured clearing the foremast and lucky to escape with his life, but the ship was much easier without her masts and, although the water was over the berth deck, the men left on board were piped to dinner on the spar deck.

On shore at Baker's Bay, Emmons took charge. All hands, except the exhausted members of the capsized boat, were employed erecting temporary shelters out of spruce boughs. An officer went to the top of the Cape to keep a lookout on the ship. The American Methodist missionaries, Messrs. Frost and Koen, came over from Point Adams with tents, provisions, and cooking utensils. Mr. Birnie came from Fort George, Astoria,

---

11 Reynolds Journal 2: p. 269.
12 Knox to his Father, Oct. 28, 1841, Knox Letters, Yale University Library.

Fig. 22. Wreck of the *Peacock* at the mouth of the Columbia River. Schooner *Flying Fish* attempting to assist. *Narrative* 4: p. 493.

to offer aid and Indians came from all directions offering fresh salmon for sale. Later in the afternoon it was possible to send the boats out again and they were able to take off the remaining crewmen, including about thirty seamen, the Carpenter, Boatswain, Purser's Steward, and, last to leave the hulk, Captain Hudson. By this time the ship was evidently "out of joint & working like an old basket." As they landed at Baker's Bay the others gathered around and gave them three cheers.

No lives had been lost. In fact, during the entire period since leaving the United States only two members of the *Peacock's* crew had died: Steward, who fell from the main topsail yard, and Anderson, who was probably murdered by the Drummond's Island natives. The work of the survey had been saved, as well as the instruments, and the journals of the scientists and of some of the officers along with the Purser's accounts. On her last cruise the *Peacock* had sailed upwards of nineteen thousand miles, with two hundred and six days at sea and only twenty-two in port.[13]

---

13 Hudson Journal **2**, July 19.

Rowing out to the wreck in the morning they found it had moved three-quarters of a mile to the south with only the end of the bowsprit and the stump of the mizzen mast above water. The decks were torn up with the spar deck waterway just awash. The tide was setting so fast that it was dangerous to approach too close and they were barely able to stem it on their return.

The *Flying Fish* was still hovering outside the bar and Hudson ordered Emmons to take the gig and an Indian, who called himself a pilot, to bring the schooner into Baker's Bay. This was achieved by putting her about whenever either side of the channel sounded at four fathoms. Walker and De Haven took the other boats to Astoria to obtain much needed supplies and, by the twenty-first, all the men had been moved there where, under Walker's direction, "Peacockville" was set up complete with tents and a flagstaff bearing the ship's ensign. Mr. Birnie supplied everyone with a blanket.

De Haven procured a horse and rode along the beach to Cape Lookout searching for debris and finding a few spare

Fig. 23. Temporary encampment of the *Peacock's* crew at Astoria following that vessel's wreck. Sketch by A. T. Agate. *Narrative* 5: p. 113.

spars and *Pearl,* the boat, which had capsized, high and dry on the beach and not seriously damaged. He suspected that the Indians who were prowling along the beach had picked up some clothing and bedding, but when he offered a reward they brought him only a few trifling articles among which, incidentally, was a small volume of Milton belonging to Dana.[14]

On the twenty-second Harrison relieved Emmons on the *Flying Fish* and Knox was ordered to familiarize himself with the channel. Purser Waldron was at Astoria recovering from an attack of rheumatism and through him Emmons received an order to take a party to examine the country between the Columbia River and California. The arrival on the twenty-third of Rodgers, who had been Wilkes' interpreter, with a large canoe manned by Indians, made it possible for Emmons' party to get off with the flood tide at noon of the same day. His party included Peale, Rich, Agate, Whittle, Rodgers, John Doughty (Seaman), Samuel Sutton (O.S.), Hughes, Smith, and Marsh (Marines), and Merzer (Servant). In addition to the Company canoe they used one owned by Wilkes and manned by Kanakas. Before their departure Hudson assembled all hands and thanked them for their exertions, commended them for their good conduct and prompt obedience to orders and emphasized that he would enforce discipline and regulations on shore as at sea.

Divine Service was held on Sunday the twenty-fifth with the Methodist missionaries participating, Frost preaching the sermon and Koen saying a prayer. During the following week Dana, Midshipman Clark, Crook, a marine, and Indian guides made an unsuccessful attempt to climb Mount Sualalakes, and some of the officers visited the primeval forest south of Astoria. That sleepy post was suddenly turned into a busy place by its new suburb, Peacockville. The men busied themselves making a tide staff, baking ovens, a bowling alley, and erecting signal and station staves in preparation for a survey of the river. Purser Speiden established his quarters in an abandoned chicken house and one of the jokes of the day was that it was his duty to crow at dawn. They gradually came to know the vagaries of wind and currents on the river and learned that a moderate wind at Astoria could be a gale beyond the Capes.

---

14 Dana, as told by Miss M. T. Dana; De Haven Journal, July 22.

Parties were sent out to explore the nearby branches of
the river but little real progress was made towards its survey
during the three weeks from the time of the wreck until
Wilkes' arrival. The weather was favorable and boats and men
were available, but Hudson did not know how to go about it.
On August 4 Thomas Waldron arrived bringing new orders
for Emmons to lead his party all the way to San Francisco instead of just to the California line.[15]

Three days later the *Vincennes, Porpoise,* and whaler
Orozimbo were sighted off the mouth of the river, and Hudson
went out to them in the *Flying Fish.* Wilkes threw open his
wardrobe to Hudson and congratulated him upon saving the
officers and men. After provisioning the *Vincennes* she was
left in charge of Ringgold to lie off and on while Wilkes and
Hudson, with Knox piloting, brought the *Porpoise* into the
river, the schooner following piloted by Reynolds. Plans were
made for surveying the river and the *Flying Fish* was sent out
again to the *Vincennes* with twenty-two men and orders for
Ringgold to proceed to San Francisco Bay.

After hearing Hudson's story, Wilkes concluded that the
ship was lost "by want of prudence and a due consideration of
the nature of the place he was to enter." Hudson had endeavored but failed to observe sailing directions obtained at
Oahu from Captain Spalding who had just returned from a
voyage up the Columbia in the ship *Lausanne* of about the
same tonnage as the *Peacock.* Wilkes did not doubt their accuracy but had some misgivings about their use because they
depended upon compass bearings on objects at a great distance. He assumed they came from H.B.M. survey vessels
Sulphur and *Starling,* the directions Captain Belcher would
not divulge at their meeting in the Fiji's. A slight compass
deviation, due to local attraction, might have been a cause of
error and, although there were lookouts aloft and the breeze
was moderate, the channel could not be seen because of the
discoloration of the water. Hudson's fatal error was to believe
that the channel was where the water was undisturbed. If he
had entered where there were tide ripples he would have suc-

---

15 Waldron also brought sealed letters to his brother R. R. Waldron informing
  him that the *Vincennes* would not come up the river. When this bit of news
  became spread around Wilkes knew that Thomas Waldron had opened and
  read the letters, destroying his confidence in him, Wilkes Journal 3, Aug. 15.

ceeded. He could give no reason for failing to use the schooner
to feel out the channel. Wilkes was inclined to believe

his apprehensions and imagination was the cause of his disaster
. . . I could not bring myself to find fault, and omitted any expression of my thoughts . . . all I can say [is that] the ship was
lost, through the most extraordinary blindness and folly of taking
the risk of entering without all the precautions, that were at
hand.[16]

After the ship struck, Hudson acted "in a noble manner"
and Wilkes felt it his duty, under the circumstances, to justify
him in his official report and in his recitation of the event in
the *Narrative*. In stating the case for Hudson he explained
that his course of action, under the circumstance, had been
"altogether correct, on every ground of expediency." Being
nearly three months behind schedule, he was anxious to avoid
further delay; the time seemed propitious and if the opportunity was not seized they might have to wait as much as a
week. Had the tender gone ahead and run aground she would
have been lost, then the *Peacock* would have had no alternative but to venture in by herself. The tide was too strong to
use the boats for feeling out the channel. There was no way
of determining the accuracy of his directions with cross-tides
changing every half-hour and, at times, very rapid, making
it impossible to steer by compass or maintain position. In fact,
as they discovered later, the safest time to cross the bar was
when both tide and wind were adverse and there are very
few ports in the world where this is true. Hudson had not hesi-
tated, judging the time propitious, to attempt to cross the bar
rather than subject the service to further delay, possibly as
disastrous for the Expedition as the loss of his vessel. Furthermore, there were no reliable pilots, the Indians Ramsey and
George did not deserve the name, and there was no one else
available.[17]

In his journal, however, Wilkes gave free rein to feelings
of frustration:

Before quitting this subject I owe it to myself to place it once on
record, that few or none can be aware of the difficulties I have had

---

16 Wilkes Journal 3, Aug. 5; Autobiography 6: pp. 1310–1313.
17 *Narrative* 4: pp. 490–491.

to labour under in the absence of officers to comprehend the nature of the service we are upon, & the mode & manner of acting under orders given them. I have endeavored to be always distinct, and clear, I have in conversations drawn them to my view of the duty, but they go counter to the spirit, although perhaps in their construction of it (the letter) they exceed so far my intention as to make it operate (by the waste of time) on other & more important duties they have had to perform.

Hudson's conduct of the *Peacock's* last cruise was a case in point. He was a month late in arriving at Upolu where he was overtaken by the rainy season. He then took considerable time correcting errors previously made by his own officers and, after surveying the Kingsmill Group, had no time for Ascension or Strong Islands. A month's time was wasted by stopping off at Oahu for, as he knew, there were stores brought by the chartered brig *Wave* and he could have reached the West Coast in less time than it took to reach Honolulu. Thus, the *Peacock* arrived July 17 although she had "almost imperative" orders to arrive by May 1.[18]

He would not have minded so much if he could overcome lost time by his own exertions, but this was impossible. It was not the work load but the anxiety that the delay caused that had been intolerable and it had been necessary to change all plans and come directly to the Columbia, leaving incomplete the survey of the harbors at the east end of Vancouver Island. After conferring with Hudson, Wilkes transferred his flag to the *Porpoise* and began in earnest the survey of the river.

---

18 Wilkes Journal 3, Aug. 6.

XXIII
Survey of the Columbia River

THE *Peacock's* LOSS and the consequent delays, with summer
half gone, necessitated completion of the Columbia River
survey as quickly as possible. Wilkes considered Hudson's
beginning as done "without requisite knowledge & comprehension of the duty to be performed" and started all over
again. De Haven was sent to look for Eld's party at Gray's Harbor and, at Hudson's suggestion, negotiations were begun for
the purchase of the brig *Thomas Perkins,* under charter to the
Company and anchored at Fort George, as a replacement for
the *Peacock.* An offer of $9,000 was accepted and she soon
joined the Squadron with her name changed to *Oregon.* Knox
was ordered to chart the river's mouth using, but taking no
chances on losing, the *Flying Fish.* Pondering the problem of
navigation in the treacherous cross-currents at this place, Wilkes
foresaw its easy conquest with the development of steam propulsion.

Unfavorable weather slowed the survey at first and, after
it improved, there were exasperating delays, such as when the
Porpoise ran hard aground. As the tide fell, she keeled over
on her beam ends, masts at a 45° angle and the starboard side
of her deck under water. Her crew spent a wretched night and
were unable to float her off with the incoming tide. When
the *Oregon* attempted to assist, she ran aground on the opposite edge of the channel. The *Porpoise* was in danger of
becoming so deeply embedded in the sand that it might become necessary to take out her guns and await the next spring
tides. However, by making use of the lifting power of empty
casks supplied by the *Oregon,* she was floated within twenty-
four hours.[1]

The Commander attributed this delay to the officers'
inattention to duty and thought the *Peacock's* in particular

---

1 Orders to Hudson and Sinclair, Aug. 13, 1941, Wilkes Letters; Hudson Journal
2, Aug. 12, 1841; Wilkes Journal 3, Aug. 8, 12, 13, 20, 1841.

needed disciplining and reeducation in the art of surveying; proper discipline was essential for all duty but, most especially, for surveying and it required someone with more knowledge of the duty than Hudson possessed to command respect in its performance. After three years these officers were still incapable of performing their tasks satisfactorily, deeming themselves masters when they scarcely knew the rudiments of the art.

Verily I have many things to contend with. Ignorance is not the least of them, want of proper spirit & ardor in the performance of their duties. I should be far happier and more efficient doing the work myself with but 2 assistants. Few can see how trying it is to his temper to be answered quite innocently that he had intended to take an angle but it had escaped him. My general punishment is for him to return directly, but this retards the work and sets at defiance all regularity of proceeding. A Surveyor needs more patience than Job, with all his trials I require more resignation than he did.[2]

At this juncture his relations with Hudson were very difficult. When inaugurating his regime the officers frequently told him that a particular procedure was permitted by Captain Hudson. He, therefore, found it convenient to designate to Hudson the superintendence of the inventorying and refitting of the *Oregon*. Since that vessel was inferior to the *Peacock* and even to the *Porpoise*, Hudson suggested that he be designated as a supernumerary officer without a particular command. Wilkes issued a general order on August 12 offering his "warmest acknowledgements" to Hudson and the *Peacock's* crew for their exertions during her last cruise and stating his belief that, if she could have been saved, their efforts would have achieved it; promising to make every effort to have them remembered for their personal losses; and announcing that Captain Hudson would not be attached to any vessel but, as second in command, must be obeyed by all officers and men and, in Wilkes' absence, would receive reports and approve requisitions.[3]

---

[2] Wilkes Journal 3, Aug. 20.
[3] Orders to Knox, Aug. 16, 1841, Wilkes Letters; Hudson Journal 2, Aug. 28, 1841.

The two men continued to work in close association and
in apparent harmony. Hudson had great respect for Wilkes'
ability and energy, noticing as the survey work progressed up
river that the Commander's gig was constantly in the lead—"It
is *always* with him . . . *come and not go* boys."[4] Despite their
regard for each other, it was an awkward situation which a
small circumstance could bring to the surface. One day, upon
returning to the brig, the Commander saw his broad pennant
replaced by the long "coachwhip" commission pennant.
Walker, the first lieutenant, explained that it had been done
on Captain Hudson's order which Wilkes immediately countermanded. He thought the incident showed how much Hudson
disliked his situation as supernumerary with little responsibility, even though it had been at his own suggestion. They
did not discuss the matter for he knew that Hudson had heard
him order Walker never to do it again without his permission and believed he was ashamed of it, but it indicated

the difficulties that might have occurred between us if my ship had
been the one lost in my holding the Command & taking that
of his ship, which I certainly should have done at once, that
point—I do not believe he ever contemplated or prepared himself for . . . I have had much support from him & he has
been a Friend & one in whom I could confide my crises to,
but as for actual duties other than the command & fitting of his
ship & the F.F. he has been of little or no use to me . . . I have
fully made up my mind that nothing shall occur between us that
shall mar our harmony, and I am happy to feel that he is placed
in a situation by his own choice that will not bring us in
contact. . . . [5]

Years later, when writing his autobiography, Wilkes emphasized his lack of confidence in Hudson's advice, trusting
him

only so far as I was satisfied it was within his comprehension. I
never opened my mind on the subject of my duties to him during
the whole cruise and had adopted a silence in relation to all the
intended movements or duties. I was aware this had proved unsatisfactory to him, and particularly to the officers of the Expedition

4 Hudson Journal 2, Aug. 23.
5 Wilkes Journal 3, Aug. 25.

. . . Although I must confer at times I yearned for the person I could put reliance in when I felt myself in doubt or desired to share with me the anxiety. This was at times painful, but I gradually became accustomed to reticence, and have since seen how necessary it was to keep my own counsel, and thoughts to myself.

He believed he had saved Hudson from a court martial by calling for written statements from the *Peacock's* officers regarding the wreck while events were still fresh in their minds and good feeling towards him prevailed.[6]

As the survey advanced up the Columbia the prevalence of malaria became a matter for concern. Malaria and smallpox had decimated the Indians living along the river's banks. Stringent orders were issued respecting the conduct of the survey: boats not to leave before 9 A.M. so as to give time for the men to put on clean and dry clothing, have breakfast and a smoke, and the heavy night dew to evaporate; boats to return to the ship an hour before sunset when awnings should be spread fore and aft.[7]

It was also important to maintain good relations with the Indians. This was sometimes difficult, as when they stopped to take observations at Coffin Mountain where the Indians put their dead in canoes in trees, the men carelessly failed to extinguish their cooking fire and the whole area was burnt over. Wilkes tried to explain to them that it was an accident and to placate them with presents, but felt that there would have been serious trouble if the tribe had not recently been severely weakened by sickness. The Indians themselves set fires on the prairie to clear the ground or round up game and they were so prevalent at this season of the year that the air was often smoky, so much so one day that the surveyors could not see to leave their anchorage.

They reached Vancouver at the end of August and the Commander felt better satisfied with the manner in which triangulation was performed. Sharing a tent with Hudson on shore, he made a series of astronomic and magnetic observations while Hudson supervised repairs and the laying of a berth deck on the *Oregon*. Lieutenant Walker was sent with

---

6 Autobiography 6: pp. 1321, 1325.
7 Wilkes Journal 3, Aug. 23; Holmes Journal 2, Aug. 19.

four boats to survey as far as the Cascades, the end of navigation, and Lieutenant Perry with four more to survey the Willamette up to its falls.

They happened to reach Vancouver just when Sir George Simpson, the Company's head or "God," as some called him, arrived on an inspection trip that was taking him around the world. He was about fifty-five years old, corpulent, baldish, and sandy haired with a florid complexion and an energetic and businesslike manner. He came on board the *Porpoise* together with MacLaughlin, Douglass, Rowan, and a member of the Russian Company named Von Freeman.

The officers were invited to dine at the Fort with the Company functionaries. It was a very stiff and formal affair with Wilkes and Hudson sitting on Simpson's right and left, respectively, at one end of the table and MacLaughlin at the other. According to Wilkes' account, the three at the head of the table were the only ones to carry on a conversation, the functionaries "below the salt" being as silent as in feudal times and the "officers stupid & wanting in ideas and good manners & maintaining a mawkish silence . . . there are one or two memorable exceptions who may be termed all talk." Noting the absence of wives, he supposed there must be a good reason for it but felt it degrading. If they were not considered the equal of their husbands, they should be called mistresses, if that was what they actually were. He thought highly of the Indian wives that he had met and felt that their exclusion from the table had a retarding effect upon the advancement of civilization in this part of the world.[8]

On the whole, the members of the Expedition got along very well with the officers and servants of the Company. Wilkes felt that they had been somewhat reticent towards him, at first, but became very cooperative when they found him friendly. From the beginning he indicated his determination to brook no interference with his charting and mapping projects. He assumed this to be neutral territory, as far as his and their rights were concerned, and that it must eventually become American, but this was a matter to be settled by treaty. The Com-

---

8 Wilkes Journal 3, Aug. 29, 31. Simpson had retired from active participation in the Company but was employed by its stockholders at a "huge" salary ($10,000) to prepare an objective report on its operations and general condition.

pany officials did all in their power to assist the Expedition in its mapping activities and collection of information, Hudson, at Astoria, reciprocated by sending his idle Kanakas to assist MacLaughlin when he was shorthanded for harvesting. In the *Narrative* Wilkes defended the Company from charges that it attempted to exterminate the beavers south of the Columbia and had excited Indian attacks upon the free settlers in that area. The Willamette settlers objected strongly to MacLaughlin's despotic power but could not cite instances of its wrong application. His policy seemed to be to extend every facility to all newcomers and settlers, a wise one considering the unsettled status of the territory. Many settlers and missionaries lived at the Company's expense for weeks at a time and were not always appreciative of these favors. One missionary's wife complained that MacLaughlin got out the silver plate when the Commander came to dine but considered it too good for them. In Wilkes' opinion MacLaughlin was a philanthropic, warmhearted gentleman and had done much for the welfare of the territory and the moral character of its inhabitants.[9]

As they worked their way back down the river Wilkes was annoyed to find that, because of carelessness, it was necessary to triangulate one section for the third time. Another cross to bear was the prevalence of malaria. The *Peacock's* men, the Kanakas, and the Indians seemed to be especially susceptible to ague and fever. The number of cases increased and once the Sandwich Islanders came down with the disease it seemed impossible to get them up. The Commander himself became ill but would not give in to it, feeling that he had no time to be sick and "still less inclination to lay by, I cannot without great disarrangement to the Service." However, one day he was too sick to work. Believing that salt air was the best cure for the ague, he continued to survey on Sunday, contrary to his principles and habit. On that day there were twenty-one men on the sick list.

On September 19 they had an unexpected boon that lifted everyone's drooping spirits. Sinclair had been sent back to Vancouver to pick up some articles belonging to the *Oregon* and returned with mail and newspapers. They had had no

---

[9] Wilkes Journal 3, Sept. 3, 15; Autobiography 6: pp. 1326–1329; Hudson Journal 2, July 31; Reynolds Journal 2: p. 313.

word from home for twenty-two months and this mail contained letters of as late a date as July 26 in answer to theirs sent from the Sandwich Islands in October of the previous year. The overland route had made possible a two-way communication in less than eleven months!

Anxious as Wilkes was to reach sea air, he took time to send Dr. Holmes to take a skull specimen from the graves at Coffin Rock and to go thirteen miles up the Cowlitz River. This excursion nearly ended in disaster because of the swift water; the gig almost capsized as they shot the rapids on their way downstream. Careening against a snag, two of the crew were knocked down and Wilkes, becoming entangled in its branches, was nearly strangled. The gig's oarlocks were torn away and three oars lost, but they counted themselves lucky to get away with no greater damage.[10]

They reached Fort George on September 30 and on the following day, the *Flying Fish* having completed her task of mapping the bay, arrangements were made to bring off all stores in preparation for a quick departure. Getting across the bar and to sea was sure to be a ticklish business. The Commander stirred things up in a feverish effort to be ready to depart at the first favorable moment. For some time the Company's bark *Columbia* had been hovering outside waiting to enter and its schooner *Cadborough* had been waiting three weeks at Fort George for an opportunity to go out.

Johnson and Guillou, under arrest, now rejoined the Expedition. They had rather enjoyed their stay at "Bobville," occupying themselves building a house and making friends with the Birnie family. Mrs. Birnie, a half-breed, was a motherly and simple-hearted person and her oldest child a fair-haired girl of thirteen. Only two of the children had dark skins and Indian hair and all jabbered in English, French, and Indian, as they played games with or listened to stories told them by the officers. Reynolds described an evening at the Birnie's:

It was too funny, to see a parcel of great big men, seated in a ring with this tribe of children & playing "hunt the slipper," "going to London" etc., etc.—the young ones happy beyond measure & the Mother's eyes streaming with delight, while to the Indian women,

---

10 Wilkes Journal 3, Sept. 9, 14, 17, 19, 22.

in the chimney corner, the thing was a mystery beyond their comprehension. It was a pleasant change to us, from the rough & uncouth habits of our life, to mingle thus with the young, but it only made me long the more, to be at home.[11]

Guillou, just before the Squadron sailed, accepted Hudson's invitation to come on board the *Oregon* and later transferred to the *Flying Fish*. Hale had requested and been granted permission to return home by the overland route, since it would give him an opportunity to learn more about the North American Indians, and had already departed.[12]

The tranquillity of Fort George was greatly disturbed by these preparations, the Commander "doing every thing at once, & retarding the whole," according to Reynolds. The Indian pilot, "Old George" was discharged and Knox and Reynolds, who knew the channel best, were designated pilots of the *Porpoise* and *Oregon* respectively. As they waited for the wind to change, the boats were sent to make soundings in the bay and the carpenters were busied repairing the *Peacock's* launch for which there was no room on deck. It was, therefore, presented to the Company for use as a pilot and rescue boat.

The weather cleared October 5; the wind was slight, the water comparatively smooth, and the *Columbia* seen on her way in. The Squadron's vessels, followed by the *Cadborough*, sailed safely across the bar after which the Commander transferred his flag to the *Flying Fish* and ordered the *Porpoise* and *Oregon* to wait outside while he returned to pick up the survey boats and carpenters. The survey chores were soon completed, but it was five days before there was a light west wind and smooth enough water to venture again over the bar.

During that interval Knox and Blair were sent to make additional soundings. Reynolds, left in command of the schooner, thought this was done with the intention of flattering him, but he refused to be duped by these efforts to obliterate hard feelings and regretted to see that some of the officers, influenced by smooth words, had "flung themselves into his arms,

---

11 Reynolds Journal 2: p. 310.
12 Wilkes to Hale, Aug. 17, 31, 1841, Wilkes Letters; Wilkes Journal 3, Sept. 4; R. R. Waldron wrote Mrs. Sarah J. Hale from San Francisco Oct. 30, 1841, saying that her son would return via H. B. Co., vessel to Mexico and overland to Vera Cruz, Wilkes Letters, Smithsonian Library.

without thinking that on the least cause he will trample on them again, the same as he has before." Wilkes out-Heroded Herod, in Reynolds' opinion, and his favorite name for him was "Old Bustamente," the name of the general who was at that time Mexico's reactionary President. His hatred had become such a physical thing that he felt "cold shivers" run through him when he found himself alongside the Squadron's Commander.[13]

Reynolds had no opportunity to go up the river but, during these last days, made a difficult excursion towards the Willamette, chasing and capturing a marine corporal who, with the assistance of the missionary Frost, attempted to desert. Three Negro members of the *Peacock's* crew deserted without getting caught and it was assumed they had found Indian wives.[14]

On the ninth the weather moderated and the *Flying Fish* left the river for the last time. The water, viewed from the Cape, appeared to be smooth at the bar but, when the schooner reached that critical point, the wind died out and she was caught with her bow pitching under the waves. For twenty minutes they ran along and close to the breakers and at one moment it looked as if they might have to anchor, take to the boats, and probably lose the schooner. However, by using sweeps and with a boat towing, she was brought past the danger point. Wilkes was sure that no other vessel could have passed the bar safely under these conditions and vowed he would never again take such a risk. He wanted to transfer immediately to the *Porpoise* but only the *Oregon* was in sight and the brig, to his annoyance, did not appear until dawn, two days later.

Knox was ordered to complete the survey of the bar, then to work down the coast as far as the Umpqua River and go from there directly to Oahu where the Squadron would reassemble. He was not to return to the Columbia and must do any necessary refitting at sea. The schooner's crew was sorry to miss San Francisco Bay but, like all the rest, was happy to see the last of the Columbia River.[15]

13 Reynolds Journal 2: pp. 320–321.
14 *Ibid.*, pp. 302–305.
15 Wilkes Journal 3, Oct. 10, 12.

XXIV
Overland To California

I N THE MEANTIME Emmons' party, after acquiring provisions at Vancouver and horses at the Company farm near Fort Wyeth, had recruited thirteen "mountain men" to act as hunters, packhorse men, and guides. A messenger had reached them with instructions to wait for further orders so they had camped at a spring in a ravine across the Willamette from the American Mission Settlement. The officers were in one tent and the sailors and marines in another, the mountain men preferring to sleep in the open despite a temperature drop of from thirty to fifty degrees every night. It turned out to be a longer wait than expected and the dampness and fog made this a very unhealthy location. They were well fed, however, as they were able to purchase beef, butter, and potatoes from Mr. Lee, Superintendent of the Mission.[1]

Wilkes' plans were unknown, but new orders were expected every day. A letter to Emmons from Passed Midshipman Totten written July 10 on board the *Vincennes* was not much help. He said, "opinions are very various the one most general now is that he will knock off surveying operations & return home God grant it for I am wearied to death with the never ending graph work. I am getting more and more homesick every day. . . ."[2]

The party became acquainted with some of the missionaries, settlers, and Indians. Most of them attended a Sunday Service held at Mr. Leslie's home. The Missionaries occupied much of the best land and seemed more interested in its development than in evangelizing the few remaining Indians. The settlers were contented with life in this fertile valley but anxious to establish a regime of law so as to keep the British from extending their sway into the region. A chief of the

---

[1] Emmons', Eld's, and Brackenridge's Journals are the principle sources for this excursion in addition to the *Narrative*.
[2] Emmons Journal 3, Aug. 7.

Kalapuya Indians made a speech to Emmons which, as interpreted, was to the effect that all this land belonged to his tribe.
Emmons assured him he had not come to dispute his claim.
He felt genuinely sorry for the Indians whose numbers had
been greatly reduced by diseases introduced by white men.[3]

While they waited the hunters brought in game, such as
sandhill crane and partridges, and Peale shot a deer. The
mountain men became restless and were allowed to leave with
the understanding they forfeited their pay while absent and
MacKay, the guide upon whom Emmons placed much reliance, became seriously ill and returned home. The weather,
for the most part, was hot and sultry, the temperature getting
as high as 104° in the shade.

When he learned of the arrival of the *Vincennes* at the
Columbia, Emmons sent Joseph Meek, a tall Virginian, with a
message addressed to Captain Hudson. He returned August
17 with letters, tobacco, and orders for Emmons to take his
party all the way to San Francisco and rejoin the Squadron
there.

Immediately several of the best mountain men begged
off. If they went to California, they could probably not return
until the following spring and they had their families and
harvests to consider. They were mindful of the advancing ague
and fever season and of the possibility of encounters with hostile Indians. They took away their horses, about twenty altogether. A few "foreigners" (Canadians) volunteered but insisted on receiving the same pay for returning as for going.
Because of these complications Emmons decided to return to
the Columbia and to set the facts before Wilkes. A letter from
Dana said that he expected to accompany him to San Francisco and that Wilkes had hinted that he, Emmons, might
lead a party from California home by the overland route.
Dana himself wanted to return via the East Indies, so as to
replace the coral and other sea specimens lost on the *Peacock*.[4]

Taking with him a young hunter named Black, Emmons

---

3 *Ibid.*, Aug. 8.
4 *Ibid.*, Aug. 18. Dana wrote Wilkes, Aug. 10, 1841 (Yale University Library)
saying, "I may be excused for expressing a strong anxiety to do well, what I
do at all: with this feeling I have thus far laboured, and under the same desire I have constantly looked forward to the remaining portion of the cruise
for opportunity to finish the observations commenced."

returned to Vancouver where he found Dana and Hale and learned that Wilkes was surveying the river with the *Porpoise* as his headquarters. A canoe crewed by Canadians and Kanakas took him to Astoria passing the survey vessels on the opposite bank during the night. When he finally reported on board the brig he was feeling the first symptoms of malaria and too unwell on the following day, August 23, to celebrate his birthday. For the next two days he convalesced, watching the boats go out as the two brigs went up river firing guns for base lines, running lines of soundings, and progressing about ten to fifteen miles each day.

Setting out again by canoe, Emmons reached Vancouver[5] on the 26th. Though still unwell, he conferred with MacLaughlin and met Governor Simpson, who had just arrived bringing the news of President Harrison's death and of the excitement over the arrest of the Canadian McLeod in the *"Caroline* affair." Then, confined to a room in the Fort, Emmons began a "course of Physic" under Dr. Barclay, the Company physician, and sent word to Whittle to move the encampment if it seemed essential for the men's health. When the brigs arrived two days later, he was too sick to attend the dinner in Simpson's honor. Wilkes said the California trip now depended upon the length of time involved, estimates varying from thirty-five to fifty days.

Eld's party arrived on the thirty-first, a rainy and foggy day. When they had reached Astoria, only four days before, Eld was described as looking as if he had been "dead, buried and dug up again."

Letters from the camp included one from Rodgers, the interpreter, saying that he was too sick with ague and fever to stay with the party, that Rich and Whittle had been ill but were well again, that Agate was quite sick, and that Hughes, Doughty, Smith, and Sutton had all "been down more or less." The camp's location was bad because of the dense fogs and very cold nights but it had to be near the Mission for purposes

---

5 Emmons gave some fish to Company servants who received them eagerly and told him their rations consisted almost entirely of dried salmon, tallow, and peas. Mechanics got some bread and occasionally some vegetables. He considered them worse off than any class of people east of the Rockies being ensnared by indebtedness, by their families, and by promises of a farm at the end of their service, Emmons Journal 3, Aug. 25.

of reorganization. Many had come to volunteer their services but changed their minds because of the indefiniteness of plans.[6]

With his health improved and believing that travel would improve it more, Emmons prepared to leave. His new orders emphasized the need to travel fast so as to reach the forks of the Sacramento, where the boats of the *Vincennes* would meet him, by September 30. Should the boats not be there, the party could abandon their horses, construct canoes, and proceed to the mouth of the river where they would find the *Vincennes* at anchor. Emmons was to show these orders to his subordinates Eld and Colvocoresses who were to accompany him along with Dana, Brackenridge, and Sergeant Stearns. Eld and Colvocoresses were sent off in the same precipitous manner as at Nisqually. They had arrived in time to attend the Simpson dinner and Eld worked until midnight of September 1 finishing his charts of Gray's Harbor. Emmons gave him emphatic orders to leave on the second and he did so "without being in any sort of readiness to go on such a journey."

At the Willamette they met the survey group under Perry, De Haven, and Baldwin, whom the *Peacock's* officers had not seen since their ill-fated ship left Honolulu in December, 1840. They obtained eleven horses at the Company farm and reached the encampment on the third. Several of the men were still sick with malaria which showed in their emaciated faces.

Four days were spent rounding up men and horses. Few mountain men volunteered, a principal reason being the daily reports of hostile Indians planning to ambush any party coming south. However, a half-breed guide, Baptiste Guardipii, agreed to go for $3.00 a day; the mountain men, Calvin Tibbats and Henry Black, stood fast; and the Tennessean, James Warfield, agreed to stay if his squaw, his eight-year-old daughter, and Nicholas, a Dutch servant, were allowed to go with him. Among the recruits were Wood, an American who brought two mules, Molair, a Canadian, and Ignas, a half-breed said to be an excellent hunter. In addition, the party included the Walker and Burrows families. Joel Walker, a Missourian, past middle age, had found the climate at his home too damp and brought with

---

6 Rodgers' decision was influenced by fear of the Indians and by love for a missionary's daughter. Not long after this Rodgers, his bride, her sister, and an Indian were all drowned when swept over the falls while crossing the Willamette.

him his wife, sister, three boys, and two girls. The other family included Burrows, his wife, adopted child, and a squaw servant. The party now numbered thirty-nine persons of whom twenty-eight were capable of bearing arms, and the pack train totaled seventy-six horses and mules of which forty-four were the personal property of members of the party and would, therefore, be watched over with particular care.

Relations with the Indians were sure to be a matter of concern and they experienced some difficulty with them at the portage around the Willamette Falls. They would not complete their task until given an extra shirt apiece and, even then one Indian sulked and took only a token load. Dana attempted to make him take more and a slight scuffle ensued. Eld came up and told Dana to carry his point or he would interfere. When Dana said he wished he would, Eld took the Indian's knife away from him and struck him three times with the flat of a paddle shattering it. The Indian sank to his knees "whether," as Eld said, "from pain or to excite pity I cannot positively say, but probably from the latter." Eld then cautioned the others not to follow his example in dealing with the Indians.

A hunter's dog had kept the Indians away from their camp, but after it left a number of dirty and miserably clad ones began to hang around. A bulldog was then obtained from a missionary and it immediately took over the duty of policing the camp and biting or scaring all Indian visitors.[7]

The party finally got off on September 7 and, until they reached the Elk River eight days later, their principal problem was to prevent the horses from straying so far during the night that most of the following morning was taken up in finding them. As they went farther and the horses became more tired, they strayed less and the usual procedure was to camp on the far side of a stream to discourage them. They were left unshod as long as the trail was through the woods and there were enough spare horses so that packs could be shifted when any developed sores. As provisions were consumed, packs became lighter. On the third day Boileau, the Canadian hunter,

---

[7] Eld found that he and the Abernathys had common acquaintances in Brooklyn, N.Y. They helped him procure a Spanish saddle covered with bear skin, Eld Journal 2, Sept. 4. By taking possession of the choicest tracts of land the missionaries seemed to have added an eleventh Commandment, according to Brackenridge Journal, Sept. 6.

joined the party bringing his Chinook wife and five horses.

As they progressed into the mountains, the going became more difficult. Fallen trees across the trail and overhanging boughs that sometimes swept riders off their saddles slowed their progress, and it was frequently necessary to lasso and pull mired packhorses out of creeks. Smoke was a minor annoyance, and at night there was fog and usually wolves set up a chorus around their camp. One night a grizzly bear came into camp causing considerable alarm but managing to escape before it could be shot.

During these first days they encountered few and only friendly Indians. Some dirty and poorly clad Indian acquaintances of Mrs. Warfield stayed with them one night. They were armed only with bows and arrows and one, an old Indian wearing a deerskin cape and cap and carrying a sealskin quiver, sat like a statue while Agate sketched him and appeared to be very pleased with the result. The squaws in their own party soon demonstrated their value for they were not only used to traveling on horseback, like the white women, but, unlike them, were able to carry and use guns to protect themselves and their children. Moreover, they made themselves useful around camp by mending clothes, making shot pouches, etc.

On the afternoon of September 15 they reached the Elk River which flowed southwestward to join the larger Umpqua River about two miles from its entrance into the Pacific and opposite the Hudson's Bay Company's Fort Umpqua station. The trail continued south, crossing the Umpqua about five miles upstream where the river was not so wide. They were approaching the area where hostile Indians were to be expected and Emmons decided to visit the Fort and, leaving the party encamped, took with him Agate, Sergeant Stearns, Doughty, and the guide Boileau. Before departing he read a General Order forbidding anyone to fire a gun on the camp grounds or to leave without the permission of Eld, who was left in command.

It was a difficult twenty-one mile ride over craggy ridges and it was 8:30 before they came to the Umpqua opposite the Fort where a faint light could be seen through the fog. After hobbling their horses they shouted and fired guns until the superintendent Gangriere, recognizing Boileau's voice, sent two Indians in a canoe to ferry them across. The fort was about a hundred and fifty yards back from the river and consisted of the usual picket-fence enclosure with two blockhouses at the corners and Gangriere's house, a storehouse, and quarters for Company servants inside. At this time it was occupied by five men, two women, and nine dogs. Gangriere was expecting daily to be attacked by hostile Indians who blamed the white men for spreading smallpox among them and were angered by the Company's refusal to sell them ball and powder. At the same time they were dependent upon it for clothing and tobacco. Gangriere advised Emmons to take his party across the Umpqua ten miles upsteam and to be prepared for attack when south of the river.

The superintendent was hospitable but cautious; after giving them blankets for sleeping on the storehouse floor, he locked them in for the night. In the morning Emmons was given his pick of three horses in exchange for four of his and procured several bear and deer skins, indispensable material for making trousers and shirts suitable for travel in this country.

Gangriere's wife wished to consult Dr. Whittle, so she and a servant returned with them to their camp. Eld had kept the party busy making cartridges and had distributed fifty rounds to each man. The hunters and packhorse men threatened to desert, ostensibly because of Emmons' order about firing guns and leaving camp, but really because of warnings by visiting Indians that those south of the Umpqua planned to kill all whites that attempted to pass through their territory. The guide Guardipii, the most important man among the discontented, was especially sulky and, "Indian like," would not be convinced of the necessity of Emmon's order. It developed that the hunters hoped to delay the party until the expected arrival of the larger and better equipped Company party led by the experienced woodsman Michel La Framboise, and including Guardipii's son. Boileau became so alarmed that he sent his wife back to the Fort with Mrs. Gangriere; Burrows and his squaw prepared to leave the party but in the end changed their minds.

The officers felt that once across the river no one would desert because they would be safer with the party than by themselves. They branched off from the usual route and crossed the Umpqua at an upper ford where the water was low but swift and the rocks in its bed sharp and slippery. They crossed diagonally taking the packhorses in tow but some slipped and were carried downstream until rescued by means of lassoes. They camped in an oak grove arranging tents and baggage to withstand possible attack. Packs were dried out and horses staked. Agate, Emmons, and some other suffered from fever. An Indian suspected of spying was kept from entering the camp.

The hazards, up to this point, had been those imposed by Nature, one of the worst being the cold at night, the thermometer dropping to 26° and freezing water to the thickness of a half dollar. It was so hot in the middle of the day that they wanted to wear no clothes and at night they put on all they had. They marveled at the Indians who wore only loin cloths day and night. The day they crossed the Umpqua was the first on which the air cleared sufficiently of smoke to make the sky perceptible and to rid the sun of its blood-red appearance.

It took about a week (September 20 to 28) to travel from the Umpqua River to the Rogue. This was the most difficult part of the trail as it passed over the ridge of the Umpqua Mountains and, also, through the territory of hostile Indians who were expected to attempt an ambush. On one occasion they had to pass through a prairie fire which they thought had been set to harass them, but the grass was not thick enough to make the fire dangerous.

Wild animals were often in evidence. At one time four deer suddenly crossed their path and escaped a raking fire by members of the party. On another occasion a grizzly bear, mistaken for a packhorse returning to the head of the column, stood up on its hind legs. Peale and two of the hunters fired, but it was able to turn away and escape. Emmons called off the hunt to avoid tiring the horses and burdening them with its carcass, in spite of his desire, as he said, to acquire a skin for "our *National Museum* that I trust *is to be.*"

They did not lack for venison and, from Emmons' point of view, the problem was to restrain the hunters from uselessly expending ammunition and wearing out the horses. The Mountain Men did not readily obey orders and his difficulties in this matter were enhanced by Peale's independent habits, for he seemed to enjoy hunting more than scientific work and did not hesitate to go off without permission. He shot a deer one evening, and when they went to get it in the morning the wolves had left nothing but its head and horns. Another day, when he shot a buck elk with two doe, it lunged at him and rolled after him down the mountain. Its meat was too strong to eat and its skin and horns too much to pack along at that stage of their journey.

As they worked their way into the mountains the trail became increasingly difficult. The packs made the horses somewhat top-heavy and several somersaulted down slopes, one rolling over and over for about one hundred and fifty yards down an especially steep slope without being seriously hurt. Cutlasses came in handy as they forced their way through thick overhanging boughs. Emmons, in advance, was swept off his horse by an Indian snare of boughs tied across the trail, and a rifle was discharged when its lock caught on a bush, but fortunately no one was hurt. One ridge was so steep that they had to stop every five minutes to let the horses blow and, since the mountain had been recently burned over, it was necessary to cut through or go around many fallen trees blocking the path and burnt branches cut their clothing and skin.

Upon making camp at the end of one of these particularly trying days Peale discovered that a bag carried by one of the rear packhorses had torn open and several of his possessions, including a camera lucida and his journal, were lost. Wood, an inefficient packhorseman, had been bringing up the rear, but the only thing he saw and picked up was one of Peale's boots. The party stayed in camp on the following day while Peale, Wood, and Black went back over the trail. They found only the camera lucida; Peale's drawing instruments, journal, drawings, and notes made since the wreck were lost. Meeting some "Rascal" Indians they searched their baskets and quivers, much to the Indians' alarm, but found nothing. Wood, who had been hired for his two mules as much as for himself, was discharged but remained with the party because it was unsafe to travel alone.

The horses had little to eat during these days for they had to be kept from straying, sometimes by hobbling, lest they delay early morning starts or be stolen by the Indians. They covered from twelve to sixteen miles a day during this week of travel between the rivers. Packs were lightened somewhat

by breaking up the lard kegs and putting their contents into
"parfleshes," a kind of canvas girdle. When the horses' feet
became tender they were shod, which caused one of them to
cut itself when hobbled.

Their greatest worry was possible ambush and there were
many indications that they were being followed. On the second day after leaving the Umpqua, Eld had stopped to sketch
the topography of the country and lost contact with the party.
He met a band of Indians who tried to steer him back north,
so he spurred his horse and dashed in the opposite direction.
Shortly after, when attempting to shoot a wolf, he discovered
that his gun would not go off. He finally caught up with the
party just as they were preparing to go in search of him.

The Indians usually stayed out of sight, but a few approached pretending to be friendly and asking for powder and
ball, a request never granted. One made signs to Eld, who was
bringing up the rear, and tried to lure him into the woods by
indicating a spring. Eld kept him away by pointing his rifle at
him and tried to keep out of arrow-shot distance from the
woods. At about the same time the advance party, hearing a
rustling sound ahead, dismounted and, with rifles ready, came
upon a group of squaws and dogs, and found indications that
an ambush had been prepared. The squaws, much agitated,
were allowed to depart and the warriors were seen to scatter
at a distance. That night the Indians skulked near their camp,
signaling each other with lights, so they prepared for an attack
without really expecting one, as the Indians were not known
to attack at night. It was thought that they had been incited
by the shooting of one of their dogs by Brackenridge who had
mistaken it for a wolf.

On the following day Emmons stationed the hunters a
little in advance of the column on either wing, and the Indians
could see that they were prepared for trouble and did not attack. Later that day Ignas shot a deer and, while skinning it,
was surprised by a band of about twenty Indians. His horse
warned him of their approach and, as he galloped away, they
shot arrows at him and he fired a shot at random without
turning to see whether it took effect. Since they were on foot,
he was able to escape unharmed. This incident had repercussions. It caused an immediate "heavy squall" between Emmons
and Peale, because Ignas in going off hunting by himself

without permission was only following Peale's example. Months later when Wilkes read about it in Whittle's journal, he called on Emmons for full details thinking the shooting of an Indian might become a matter for official inquiry.[8]

This incident occurred on the day they reached and crossed the Rogue River and proceeded along its banks. They were now in the country of the Klamet or, as the whites called them, the "Rogue" or "Rascally" Indians, who in previous years had made several attacks upon white travelers. Many deer and antelope were seen; the plentifulness of game was due, presumably, to the Indians' dependence upon fish. As they followed along the river, they saw Indians spearing salmon.[9]

The next day they stopped early, because Rich became too sick to travel, and a band of about twenty unarmed Indians appeared calling themselves friends but watching them cautiously from behind bushes. From the opposite bank of the river a lone Indian harangued them with words that no one understood. After he had gone, a dog appeared at the same spot and Wood, to show what a good shot he was with his long heavy rifle, killed it and could not understand why Emmons objected. During the night the Indians, about a mile down the river, shouted, war-danced, built fires, and, no doubt, pledged the extermination of the whites.[10]

Working their way southward along a branch of the river, they came to a point where the bank provided only a narrow pass between the river and rocks at the foot of the mountain. On two occasions Michel La Framboise's party had been attacked here. Some men went ahead on foot unopposed by the Indians. Eld, bringing up the rear, saw some Indians wearing Company shirts and caps. They tried to entice him into the woods, and when they had passed beyond gunshot, they showed themselves on the opposite bank and shouted taunts. Mrs. Walker and her daughter were much alarmed, but the squaws, armed with guns, were prepared for anything.

---

8 Emmons Journal 3, Sept. 25.

9 Eld mentioned seeing their first sugar pine trees whose sap forms lumps on the bark. Travelers sometimes used it in their tea and coffee. After eating it freely Eld had a stomach ache and "strong purgation" lasting two or three hours. He also mentioned pine cones sixteen inches long, Eld Journal 2, Sept. 25.

10 Emmons Journal 3, Sept. 26.

When they came out of the woods onto the prairie they saw bear, deer, wolves, rabbits, and killed their first antelope. Agate's horse developed sore feet and had to be put into the band of riderless horses, and Eld's gave out completely and had to be abandoned. There being no spare horses Eld was given one ridden by a "servant" forcing the two seamen to alternate walking and riding with one horse between them. One of them, Merzer, stubbornly lagged behind and slowed up the party. Although they were in the open prairie they could still be ambushed from rock and bush cover and the Indians were avowedly hostile and more numerous than farther north. Rich and "Colvo" were both very sick, necessitating frequent stops, and the latter became so delirious that his arms had to be taken away from him. Under these circumstances Emmons gave Merzer the choice of keeping up or being left to take care of himself.

On the night of September 28 they made their twenty-fourth encampment on a ridge at the boundary of California, which, at that time, meant Mexico. Originally this was to have been their objective but was now their halfway point. They saw a column of smoke which they took to be a signal from the Rogues to the Shasty Indians warning of their approach. At this place Michel's party had had its horses shot at night, so an unusually strict watch was set.

From a rocky peak on the ridge Emmons took observations which confirmed that they were on the forty-second parallel. Wilkes gave this peak Emmons' name.[11]

---

11 *Narrative* **5**: p. 236, note.

XXV
On To Yerba Buena

EMMONS AND ELD mapped each day's progress and every fifty to sixty miles Eld took dip and intensity observations. When Eld first took the intensity apparatus out of its box, a few days after starting, he found one of the foot screws gone which made his work more difficult, and Emmons' portable chronometer became materially affected by riding and of little use. On top of these difficulties the portable thermometer, entrusted to Whittle's care, broke when his horse fell. If some of their mapping efforts were inexact they were not entirely to blame.[1]

September 29 being a pleasant day, Whittle advised making it a day of rest, for Walker and his child were now added to the sick list. After waiting an hour while Eld went back to look for his lost journal,[2] Emmons decided to move on so as to get out of Indian country as soon as possible. Still ahead was "Bloody Pass" where Tibbats and others in the party had once been attacked by Indians. None made their appearance, however, as they went through the pass and beyond it they got their first glimpse of Mount Shasta and of the Klamet Valley. As described by Peale, the view was

of singular grandeur . . . on our right the mountains were burning and sent up immense masses of smoke; on our left was the snowy summits of Mount Chasty (Tchasty ?)—extensive plains were in front of us: In descending we had to cross rugged sandstone ridges covered with red cedar, and buckthorn bushes,—soil barren and arid,—no game, only a few wolves seen, and we had a hot and thirsty ride of about 20 miles to the Tchasty river, near to which on a small branch, we halted for the night . . . we found many curious plants and gathered their seeds—several species of Origanum were conspicuous.[3]

---

1 Eld Journal 2, Sept. 13; Emmons Journal 3, Sept. 27, 1841.
2 This day and the next are blanks in Eld's Journal.
3 Peale Journal 7, Sept. 29.

They rested on the thirtieth, the day on which they were supposed to have reached the *Vincennes'* boats. The temperature was 100° in the shade, of which there was very little in this arid region.

For the next ten days they worked their way south passing through open, dry, hot country, close to the base of Mount Shasta. Their speed was reduced by increasing sickness, especially among those who had caught malaria while encamped on the Willamette. The heat of the day and the scarcity of water were the greatest causes of discomfort. Coming to a water hole on October 2, the horses plunged in, packs and all. Emmons became so weak and faint that he often had to dismount and for the first time was unable to keep his night watch, which Eld did for him. After reaching the Destruction River it was possible to ride in the shade of trees which, along with heavy doses of quinine, was of some help to the sick. Fox grapes were abundant but did not agree with malaria.[4]

They met some friendly Indians who permitted Agate to sketch them and who demonstrated their skill with bow and arrow by shooting at a button. Their reward was the target itself and some tobacco. Buttons also bought salmon. Antelope were plentiful but too swift for the hunters who could do no better than wound a deer which was brought down by their dogs. They saw mountain sheep on Mount Shasta and its snowy summit presented a most pleasing sight in the evening when illuminated and painted pink by the rays of the setting sun.

At the end of these ten days they came to the junction of the Destruction River with the Pit,[5] the main branch of the Sacramento, this being the high point of navigation where they were to have met the *Vincennes'* boats. Wilkes' suggestion they abandon their horses and build canoes was not adopted because there was no suitable wood available and the river, becoming wider and less swift, was easily forded.

It was a great relief to come out of the mountains into the Sacramento Valley. The horses could not have lasted much longer and were giving out more frequently since the sick were

---

4 This was the region of strawberry trees (Arbutus) whose red berries were eaten by the Indians and bears, Eld Journal **2**, Oct. 5.
5 The hunters said the Pit River got its name from the Indian practice of making a concealed pit in which to trap their enemies, Eld Journal **2**, Oct. 9.

FIG. 24. Encampment of Lieutenant Emmons' expedition on the Sacramento after mapping a route from the Columbia River. Drawing by A. T. Agate. *Narrative* 5: p. 245.

less able to relieve them by walking over bad stretches. A third horse, Private Smith's, gave out completely and had to be abandoned. This made hunting more difficult as three deer demonstrated by running the gauntlet of the whole line with only one being brought down. However, the worst part of the trail and the danger of Indian attack were now behind them, but nine days of slogging down the Valley were still ahead.

Some friendly Kincla Indians traded dried salmon and bows and arrows for knives, beads, etc. Agate sketched them as Emmons attempted to get them to verify the trail by tracings in the sand. They nodded their heads in the same uncomprehending way in answer to all his inquiries. They were tattooed and they danced somewhat like South Sea Islanders. Emmons visited one of their "ranchos" or "pueblos" and thought it "much on a par with the Pig-pens in many portions of our country—in size, comforts & cleanliness." He regretted his inability to learn more about the Indians, lacking an interpreter and time, harassed by sickness and handicapped by their hostility towards the white man.[6]

---

6 Emmons Journal 3, Oct. 22.

As they progressed down the valley they saw all kinds of game and, at this stage of their journey, wild animals became one of their chief diversions. Wolves, as usual, serenaded them at night and, on one occasion, were bold enough to enter the camp and carry off a bear skin. A grizzly entered the camp one night capsizing things and causing a general commotion before departing in the darkness. On one occasion a confused herd of antelope ran ahead and "astern" of the camp. All who had guns fired at them and several shots were seen to take effect but the animals escaped. On another occasion they came upon four large buck elk and shot at least two rounds at them but they "erected heads & moved off beautifully over the prairies" although they too appeared to have been hit.

The hunters' difficulties stemmed, not only from the worn-out condition of their horses and the thick hides of the game, but also from the limitations of their rifles. Two powder kegs that fell into the water were found not to be waterproof and their contents good only for making "squibs" i.e., able to make a noise but not fire a ball. The hunters were provided with "regular bursts" but the powder may have been defective. Some of it became completely worthless, as in the case of that carried by a mule which fell down an embankment into the river with a pack including solubles, such as sugar and tea, as well as gunpowder. At times the pack animals may have seemed more trouble than they were worth, but they earned the men's admiration for their ability to keep going as long as they did. Sometimes they did amazing things as when a mule, crowded off the bank into the river, swam about three hundred yards upstream where it climbed the bank and rejoined the pack train.

Despite worn-out horses and sickness, the men made good progress, as much as twenty-five miles one day and twenty on others. Traveling was easier for the sick on cloudy days but Agate, Colvocoresses, and Emmons all suffered relapses.

In the region of the buttes two of the hunters retrieved traps they had cached when working for the Company during the previous winter. At this point, instead of following the westward bend of the Sacramento, they took a less used but more direct route south. The trail was obscure and, since their guide did not know it, reliance was placed on Warfield, but he, too, was not very sure and it was his squaw who finally showed the way, recognizing the trail by a small stone which she remembered placing in the hollow of a tree.

Coming to the Feather River, they followed along its bank to its entrance into the Sacramento where it could be crossed by means of a sandbar. On the other side they saw shoe prints—the first "civilized tracks" seen since leaving the Willamette and, across the Sacramento, horses and cows grazed, another sign of civilization. With the day nearly spent they made camp, but Wood, their detached companion, went on heading for Suter's "New Helvetia."[7]

Making an early start on September 19, they soon covered the fifteen miles to the American River[8] and, after crossing it, met a Suter employee in charge of a sheep corral and vineyard. As they approached New Helvetia Suter himself rode out with Wood to greet them. His establishment was impressive: inside a picket enclosure he was erecting a two-story home; his livestock included 1,000 horses, 3,000 cattle, and 800 sheep and forty Indians employed to tend them; thirty square leagues of land granted him by the Mexican government and, in addition, he had just purchased for $30,000 the establishment of the Russian American Company at Bodega, on the coast about ninety miles north of San Francisco Bay.[9] Suter was on friendly terms with the Indians and prepared to resist any attempt by the weak and corrupt government of California, or anyone else, to oust him.

Learning that water was not readily available and that Suter was beginning to distill liquor from his grapes, Emmons decided to make camp on the bank of the Sacramento, some two miles away, where there was water and the sick could be easily embarked. Suter came to have tea with them and had one of his men bring along a beef. He wore a kind of undress uniform with side arms and his manner was pleasant and frank. He was enthusiastic, generous, high-minded, and an entertaining talker able to converse in several languages. In need of experienced and reliable employees, having just lost fifty head of cattle when his men carelessly attempted to swim them

---

7 At this time Sutter spelled his name with one "t."

8 Dana put a footnote in his volume on geology, published in 1849, mentioning the discovery of gold on the "American fork" of the Sacramento in 1848.

9 The port at the mouth of the Russian River is now silted up.

across the American River, he took on Walker as superintendent of his farm and employed Burrows, Warfield, Wood,
and Nicholas.

A day was spent preparing to send the sick down river
and organizing a party under Eld to take the pack train to
Yerba Buena by land. Learning that Ringgold had surveyed
the river above this point, Emmons could see no reason for
further delay and, on the twenty-first, without waiting for
Suter's boat, accepted the offer of an American to take them
along with some Indian trappers. By 11 A.M. his party, which
included Dana, Agate, Colvocoresses, Whittle, Hughes, Smith,
Doughty, Sutton, and the boy Waltham, shoved off.

After landing to cook supper, they continued until their
Indian paddlers became too sleepy, when they anchored for the
night. In the morning they stopped for water at the house of
Merritt,[10] an American hunter and, when about to leave, the
Vincennes' launch came into view. Midshipman Sandford was
in charge of its crew of seventeen sailors who had been pulling
all night against a setting tide. He told them that the *Porpoise*
had arrived in San Francisco Bay only three days before.

Transferring to the launch they made sail and had to
beat against the wind, but were favored by the tide. Many
fowl, such as cranes, ducks, geese, shags, etc., were in evidence.
Later in the day the water became rough and they ran on a
shoal but were able to drag the boat off before darkness came,
when they anchored for the night. The following day was cool
and damp so that a blanket or pea jacket felt good, and their
guns became rusty, something that had not occurred during
all of their overland trip. Progress against a head wind and
an incoming tide was slow but they boarded the *Vincennes* at
about 8:30 on the evening of the twenty-fourth, happy to have
ended their long and difficult journey.

Emmons was relieved to have completed the duty under
"most harassing circumstances" which could only be appreciated by himself upon whom the responsibility fell. It would
have been easier if he had been well and could have chosen
his companions. He was, therefore, gratified to receive the
approbation of the Expedition's Commander for carrying out

---

10 Merritt could build a canoe in three days and sell it for $30 in goods or beaver
orders, Emmons Journal 3, Oct. 22.

this arduous duty "with his usual care and discretion, and served to correct many errors of the maps, especially the water courses, and ranges of the mountains." Wilkes had been concerned for the party's safety, and Emmons demonstrated that he had picked the best officer for the duty.[11]

In the meantime, Eld carried out his part of the duty, arriving at Yerba Buena four days after Emmons' group. Eld's party included Peale, Rich, Brackenridge, Sergeant Stearns, Marsh, Tibbats, Ignas, Warfield, Black, Molair, Merzer, and Boileau, who had been discharged as supernumerary. Eld made a special request for Sergeant Stearns who had shown himself invaluable in camp duties—hunting, marking time, keeping watch, etc. All the pack saddles and camping paraphernalia were taken along in case it was decided to send a party back to the United States by the overland route. The Commander, however, had decided not to do so and had dispatched a boat under Davis which attempted unsuccessfully to intercept them.

They broke camp on the twenty-first, the same day as the boat party, and progressed seventeen miles before stopping for the night near some fresh-water ponds full of fish, where there was good feed for the horses. From there on the going became progressively more difficult. They covered thirty-two miles the second day but had to leave behind one horse unable even to carry "his own miserable Carcass," and that night they had only dirty water scarcely fit to drink.

On the third day they traversed a total of forty-five miles. Eld, contrary to the advice of his Spanish guide, decided to continue beyond the San Joaquin River. Not finding water or feed for the horses where expected, they pushed on into the night. Because hides and tallow were the principal products of this area, many carcasses were left to decompose on these arid plains and, as they rode through the darkness, "the continual rattling and breaking of bones under our horses feet, had a most singular and unpoetical effect—any but Californian horses would have been frightened by it." They finally stopped at 10 P.M. at the edge of a quagmire and the exhausted men and horses lay down without food or drink. Many of the horses had ulcerous wounds and one had two broken ribs.

---

11 Autobiography 6: p. 1331.

After a late start they reached the Mission of San Jose on the afternoon of the next day. Eld presented a letter given him by Suter, addressed to Don Jose Antonio Estrade who, in a most inhospitable manner, refused his request for food. Brackenridge thought Don Jose should have noticed at least a faint trace of gentlemen beneath their buckskin. The Mission itself was in a rather delapidated condition, its Indian population reduced from about sixteen hundred to six hundred. Chancing to meet Mr. Forbes, the representative of the Hudson's Bay Company, they got a very different reception and that night the officers slept in beds and under a roof for the first time since leaving Vancouver.

On the following day they reached the Franciscan Mission of Santa Clara. At first the superintendent took them for vagabond trappers wanting to eat his fruit, but, when reproved by Rich in good Spanish, he became more hospitable, showed them around the garden, and invited them to his rooms to sample spirits distilled from pears. None of the Californians they met would believe they had come from the Columbia River until they had a good look at their horses.

Two days later they were within twelve miles of Yerba Buena but had to make camp at two in the afternoon because their horses gave out. Eld met one of the men from a boat of the Squadron which had come up a winding creek collecting red wood. The sailor insisted on speaking Spanish to him until Eld finally convinced him who he was, though dressed in buckskin and wearing a scraggly beard of fifty days' growth.

They made an early start on the twenty-eighth all in good spirits at the prospect of coming to their journey's end. They stopped briefly at the Mission of Nostra Señora de los Dolores and an hour later came upon several neatly built frame houses, and as Eld looked in a window he saw men from the Squadron playing billiards. It can be imagined what the billiard players thought when they saw who was looking in. Emmons was at Spears' house and a boat was waiting to take them to the *Vincennes*. Wilkes and Hudson also came to Yerba Buena that afternoon, having stopped at Gull (Alcatraz) Island to take some angles on their way to visit the Missions of Santa Clara and San Jose. Hudson's comment was that the men and horses looked "jaded," especially the horses. Emmons thought Eld had performed his duty faithfully, as always, and considered himself fortunate to have had a companion "that combined with the officer so many of the qualities of a gentleman.[12]

Since there was to be no overland party, the horses and equipment were advertised for sale at public auction. It attracted a considerable crowd and was conducted by the rotund "alcalde" who began by stating that all unbranded horses belonged to the government. The sale for Eld was a painful experience.

Our poor old worn out & jaded horses that had borne us faithfully, patiently thro thick & thin from Vancouver to San Francisco —a distance by the route we came about 840 miles were exposed to public vendue—their hard usage, sore backs & bare ribs held up to contempt & ridicule in English & repeated with jeers & laughs in Spanish & French.[13]

The horses brought an average of six dollars apiece, the total proceeds being two hundred and ten dollars. The hunters were paid off; some expected to trap for the Hudson's Bay Company, and others, now that the overland trip to the United States was "exploded," to work for Suter.

Eld's party had two days to get used to being on shipboard again before the signal to get underway was hoisted on Sunday, October 31. They learned with envy that the ships had been receiving fresh provisions four times a week.

----

12 Hudson Journal 2, Oct. 25; Emmons Journal 3, Oct. 28.
13 Eld Journal 2, Oct. 29.

XXVI

San Francisco Bay

THE *Flying Fish* was unable to accomplish any part of the coastal survey during the first week after leaving Fort George because of a constant gale and huge rollers. Her crew had some anxious moments when especially large ones broke under her stern. Finally, on October 21 with good weather and smooth water they completed in eight hours the survey of the bar off the Columbia. For the next two days foggy weather prevented survey work down the coast and another gale on the twenty-fifth produced a series of mishaps. To begin with, the fore stay snapped and would have taken the foremast with it had the jib not been taken in fifteen minutes earlier, its tack having given way. With the prospect of being dismasted the crew repaired the damage under showers of water that threatened to wash them overboard. The schooner rode safely through the storm but, when the worst was over, they found themselves embayed and drifting slowly towards shore under a single sail. The seas seemed higher than any they had encountered since leaving Cape Horn. As Reynolds recalled, "we watched the land, the sky, sea, & schooner, during this *longest* day, with an anxiety that was sharpened into torture: we dreaded the coming night."

They did not seem to be gaining an inch. The jib was tried but it split and had to be unbent. It was repaired in time to be used again when the foresail split. Their situation was precarious for, although the wind had died down, they were close to land, drifting under bare poles, and constantly swept by rollers. By 11 P.M. the jib was up again and, as a strong wind came from the north of west, they also hoisted the double-reefed mainsail, lowering it during each squall. The schooner's behavior exceeded expectations for she "walked" ahead at a rapid rate. By watchful and tender management of the tiller they escaped the heaviest seas. After one hour's sleep out of twenty-six Reynolds took the watch from midnight to six, determined to get out of sight of land by dawn, and did not lower the mainsail during squalls—grinding his teeth in anxiety and praying that another stay would not break. The mainsail did tear but, by that time, land was out of sight and the wind was moderate. Under bare poles all hands busied themselves mending sail; this was refitting at sea with a vengeance and they cursed Wilkes for insisting upon it.

On the thirtieth another violent wind was followed by a calm making water flow over the deck as the vessel rolled heavily. The continuance of these conditions was getting on their nerves and only their pet dogs, "Fanny Squiers" and "Kate Nickleby," were able to sleep peacefully. It was almost two weeks since they had finished surveying the Columbia bar and they had made little progress southward. Knox opened his sealed orders and learned that he was to proceed to Oahu where the schooner would be sold. Therefore, they headed southwestward favored by a nine-knot northwest wind and, with the help of the Trades, made the island of Molokai in thirteen days. On November 17 they found the *Vincennes* and *Porpoise* at anchor in the Roads off Honolulu and, to their surprise, learned that both vessels had arrived only a few hours ahead of them, having passed to the North of Molokai as they passed to the south.[1]

While the survey of the Columbia River was in progress, the *Vincennes'* crew had been enjoying a life of comparative ease. Dropping anchor off Yerba Buena (renamed San Francisco in 1848) on August 14, they found several vessels, mostly whalers, in the bay and learned from one of them of President Harrison's death. On the advice of the Captain of the Port, William A. Richardson, the vessel was moved to Sausalito or Whalers' Harbor where water was more readily procurable.

The town of Yerba Buena consisted of half a dozen one-storied "European built" houses, including the following: a large frame building where the Hudson's Bay Company's agent resided; a store run by an American named Spears; a grog shop which boasted a small billiard table and dispensed wine and "jaw breaking" cigars; a kind of "hotel," made from the poop cabin of a ship, where Captain Hinckley lived and traded in skins and hides; a blacksmith shop; some outbuildings, and a

1 Reynolds Journal 2: pp. 329–342.

dilapidated adobe building on top of the hill overlooking the anchorage. At low tide the town fronted on an extensive mud flat. The presidio or fort at the entrance to the bay was in a state of decay, occupied by one officer and one soldier who did not even bother to raise a flag on the flagstaff. This was, theoretically, a part of Mexico, but in 1836 a revolutionary government had taken over California and the only law enforcing agent was the *alcalde* who resided three miles away.[2]

Within a few days Lieutenant Carr set up an observatory on shore and Captain Ringgold started out to survey the Sacramento River with a party which included Lieutenants Alden and Budd, Passed Midshipman Sandford, Midshipmen Hammersley and Elliott, and Dr. Pickering. In three days they reached Suter's establishment where they were cordially received and four men seized the opportunity to desert, taking with them two days' rations and one of Suter's canoes.

Progressing up the Sacramento they came to a point where the rapids were too numerous and the snags and sandbars too difficult to permit further advance. As there was no sign of Emmons' party, they reversed direction.

The Indians they met appeared to be rather shy and not particularly friendly. One stole Pickering's bowie-knife pistol and an attempt was made to hold a member of the tribe as a hostage for its return, but he escaped and Ringgold, rather than shoot him down with the whole tribe looking on, let him go. This was Pickering's second pistol loss.

They saw much game including lynx, herds of elk, and foxes whose pelts were said to be worth twenty dollars apiece in China, and had to guard against wolves and bears that approached their encampments at night. Pickering had a close look at a huge grizzly when strolling along the river bank, unarmed, looking for botanical specimens. It came out of the bushes towards him. He yelled and ran towards the camp and the men went for their guns, but before they could shoot the bear had disappeared. They were back on the *Vincennes* by September 9 in a somewhat exhausted condition and several suffering from poison oak. The next week Ringgold began to survey the Bay.

---

2 Autobiography 6: p. 1336; [Robinson] Journal Aug. 15.

While he was away, the officers and men left on the *Vincennes* found plenty of entertainment. Sailors on liberty, even on Sundays, were able to purchase enough liquor for a drunken spree. The hunting was too easy for real sport. Robinson, the Purser's steward, and Sergeant Walmsley in two hours shot three bucks and a doe, losing one to the buzzards before they could round up Indians with horses to bring in the carcasses. Beef cost as little as three-quarters to one and a half cents a pound, but vegetables were scarce.[3]

The officers found social life in connection with the large family of Senor Martinez who lived with his married and unmarried children on an *estancia* or farm at Pinole, nearby. One daughter had married Richardson, the Port Captain, and another, seventeen years old, was famed for her beauty and had several avowed suitors. Parties were given for the officers and, in return, they entertained on the ship on two occasions. The first and more notable was on September 8 and included as guests seven or eight ladies and five or six gentlemen. An awning was spread over the after part of the quarter-deck, flags were used as decoration, and music was provided by a fiddler and a guitar player who, dressed in cavalier costume, also sang and recited. Wine and cake were served, the fandango danced, and dinner served in the Ward Room. Chaplain Elliott thought "one or more of our gentlemen were quite used up" and Armourer Briscoe thought the guests appeared to be half-seas over when they left, but Señora Martinez kept a sharp eye on her daughters and the party ended at the respectable hour of 10 P.M.[4]

The *Vincennes* attracted many visitors during her stay at Sausalito. Chaplain Elliott called her a kind of floating hotel, there seeming to be three or four guests on board every day and most of them staying for several days. Among the visitors were Captain Suter, the head of the Russian establishment at Bodega, two Capuchin priests, and several Padres. Some, less welcome, were deserters and especially two from H.B.M.S. *Sulphur* who were particularly obnoxious. Dr. Fox performed medical services for several persons, including the amputation

---

3 Briscoe Journal, Aug. 16, 18; [Robinson] Journal Aug. 14 and Sept. 9; Hudson Journal 2, Oct. 21, 1841.

4 Journals of Briscoe, Elliott 2, and [Robinson] all Sept. 8.

of the arm of an Indian whose hand was shattered while loading a gun for a salute.[5]

The *Porpoise* arrived October 19 and anchored close by. Boarding the *Vincennes* was, for Wilkes, like going home. The *Oregon* came in a day later. Since Emmons' party had not been heard from, Sandford was sent with the launch up the Sacramento to look for it.

Upon his arrival Wilkes "kicked up a regular dust," as the men expressed it. The *Oregon* was put into a "regular uproar" having alterations made to house additional officers and men, putting up bag and hammock racks on the berth deck, and taking on stone ballast. Ringgold's survey of San Pablo Bay was found to be faulty and he was sent out again with six boats to resurvey that bay and part of the San Joaquin River. This took nine days, but it served Ringgold well in later years for, after the discovery of gold, his charts were in great demand and he returned to California to extend their coverage.[6]

Wilkes arrived in time to attend a fete in honor of the patron saint of San Rafael, a small mission in a "tolerable state of preservation" about twelve miles north of Sausalito. Its superintendent, a Mr. Murphy, was not a good organizer and the fête was something of a disappointment. The bulls, with their sawed-off horns, had the advantage over the men and horses, tumbling them "in a ridiculous manner, until they both became quite shy." Murphy was unable to capture a bear in order to stage a projected bull and bear fight. The dancing was accompanied by hard drinking and uproarious conduct which, according to Wilkes, "may be better imagined than described."[7]

The Commander and Hudson visited the Santa Clara Mission and the pueblo of San Jose at the south end of the Bay. They were hospitably received by the inhabitants of this area and by the Padre at the Mission, but had to pay an outrageous

5 Briscoe Journal, Oct. 10; Elliott Journal 2, Aug. 4; [Robinson] Journal Sept. 18, 19 and Oct. 3, 4, 11.

6 Hudson Journal 2, Oct. 25; [Robinson] Journal Oct. 21; Ringgold, *A Series of Charts with Sailing Directions* (Washington, 1851). He made these charts in 1849–1850 with the help of Knox, Blunt, and F. D. Stuart.

7 *Narrative* 5: p. 199.

price to hire inferior horses for their return journey. With the return of Emmons' and Eld's parties, preparations were made for the Squadron's departure.

Captain Hudson remained as supernumerary on board the *Vincennes* and Ringgold returned to the command of the *Porpoise*. Wilkes gave Lieutenant Carr command of the *Oregon* but was sorry to lose him as Executive Officer of the *Vincennes* because he had kept the vessel in good order and strictly enforced rules and regulations. Both Lieutenants Emmons and Case declined the position of first lieutenant under Carr for reasons of rank.[8] Chaplain Elliott secured passage home on the brig *Don Quixote* having resigned his commission. He reached his father's house in Washington on May 6, 1842, a little more than a month ahead of the *Vincennes'* arrival at New York.[9]

The flagship weighed anchor at 3 P.M. October 31, beat up into the narrows with the ebb tide and passed the Fort at sunset. As the wind slackened, the two brigs went ahead of her. Becoming becalmed she anchored in 6½ fathoms, just beyond the 4-fathom midpoint mark of the bar. The sea was smooth. By 9 P.M., however, the flood tide brought in a dense fog and a heavier sea and the *Vincennes* began to roll and pitch as the sea increased, although there was not a breath of air stirring. Ports were secured and rolling tackle hauled taut.

By 2 A.M. of November, the rollers had increased in size with the incoming tide, beginning to break inside the bar and, occasionally, outside. An hour later the tide was in and the rollers heavier than ever. As long as the ship remained head on, she behaved well, rising on each breaker and plunging into the trough with easy and graceful movement. However, it was an anxious time and Wilkes later recalled:

There was nothing to be done in the way of seamanship, the ship kept head on—at times the roar of the advancing breakers was awful and it continued to increase until they struck the ship, not the faintest air was felt during the time we were subjected to this trial (some five hours) in a few cases, when the waves struck the bow fairly, it caused the vessel to tremble throughout . . . The spray being thrown to the height of the tops, and masthead. It was

---

8 Emmons Journal 3, Oct. 26.
9 Elliott Journal 2, Oct. 24, 1841 and May 6, 1842; Emmons Journal 3, Oct. 30.

one of the most exciting, and anxious hours I passed during the cruise.[10]

The breakers were estimated to be as much as thirty feet high. Each, as it came, filled the upper deck and some washed the running rigging out of the foretop, tore at the lashings of the booms, swept the deck and passed over the taffrail carrying with them boxes of plants and everything movable. The lanyards to the stoppers on the anchor cable were carried away, the chain whipped violently and ran out about ten fathoms until it was held by the berth-deck compressor and new lanyards.

The most critical moment was when the tide had spent itself, the ship kept head to sea by the force of the waves alone. At 4 A.M. the ebb began to make and the ship "horsed" her stern around into the trough of the waves, exposing her whole broadside to their force. While swinging, she took a combing roller, fore and aft, that flooded the spar and gun decks carrying away the lashings of the spare topmast boom, staving in two boats stowed amidships and catching Private James Allshouse who, about to go on watch, chose this moment to come up the main hatchway on the way to the head. He was caught in the abdomen between the loosened spar and the hatch combing. It was about five minutes before the spar could be moved because of the ship's pitching. Allshouse did not appear to be seriously hurt at first, because he had few bruises, but he was in agony and complained of intolerable thirst. He died of internal injuries at 7:30 that morning.

With the ebb tide the ship rode tail to the waves, heaving and setting "like the walking beam of a steamer" and with little or no strain on her cable. Occasionally she made a deep roll from a quartering sea which broke so near as to make all hands prepare to spring into the lower rigging. After daylight the sea calmed becoming a mere ground swell, but the fog persisted. When a light breeze came from the north, the *Vincennes* got under way with all sail. At 10 A.M. she fired a gun which was answered from nearby by the *Porpoise*. That vessel and the *Oregon* had been lying three miles out enjoying a perfectly quiet and comfortable night.

------

10 Autobiography 6: pp. 1335–1336.

At 2:30 Captain Hudson read the burial service as the body of Private Allshouse was committed to the deep with military honors. Then the vessels filled away, the *Vincennes* shortening sail to keep the brigs in company.

Robinson, the Purser's steward, was probably expressing the opinion of many when he said, "Capt. Wilkes was very careless in anchoring thus, and risking the lives of all hands needlessly, but it is on a par with other acts." The Commander's own comment was that this kind of phenomenon often occurs at full and at change of moon but its effects are seldom experienced or given much consideration. He had thought that being past the 4-fathom mark the vessel was secure but "the result proved otherwise."[11]

The wind was moderate and the weather pleasant on the second. Wilkes spent that day and night preparing dispatches. The letter bag was sent to the *Porpoise,* which then filled away and stood for Monterey. The flagship and *Oregon* awaited her return before heading for the Sandwich Islands. Among dispatches sent to the Secretary of the Navy was one pertaining to Oregon. Wilkes promised to make a full verbal report upon his return to Washington. Being aware of the Government's lack of information regarding the northern section of the Oregon territory and of the Straits of Juan de Fuca and realizing its importance in respect to the boundary question, he had taken time to make a thorough survey and examination of that area. This was not required by his Instructions but it was done without sacrificing any part of his orders.

I am well satisfied, after all my examination, that the proposition once made, and perhaps still entertained by the Government that the parallel of 49 degrees north should be the Boundary, never ought to have been entertained, and cannot be carried into effect without great detriment to our rights, as well as of vast injury to the territory, both as regards its defence, commercial importance, and to its ever becoming a free and independent state.[12]

Viewing the Oregon region from a political and military point of view he felt it was necessary to draw a boundary north

---

[11] Hudson Journal 2, Oct. 31–Nov. 1; Emmons Journal 3, Nov. 1, Briscoe Journal, Oct. 31–Nov. 1; Wilkes Journal 3, Nov. 1; Autobiography 6: pp. 1334–1335; [Robinson] Journal Nov. 1.
[12] Wilkes to Secretary of the Navy, Nov. 23, 1841, Ex.Ex. Letters 2.

of the forty-ninth parallel, presumably at 54° 40′ the Russian frontier. In the *Narrative* Wilkes described the weakness of all authority in California and predicted:

The situation of Upper California will cause its separation from Mexico before many years. The country between it and Mexico can never be anything but a barren waste, which precludes all intercourse except that by sea, always more or less interrupted by the course of the winds, and the unhealthfulness of the lower seaport towns of Mexico. It it very probable that this country will become united with Oregon, with which it will perhaps form a state that is destined to control the destinies of the Pacific. This future state is admirably situated to become a powerful maritime nation, with two of the finest ports in the world,—that within the straits of Juan de Fuca, and San Francisco. These two regions have, in fact, within themselves every thing to make them increase, and keep up an intercourse with the whole of Polynesia, as well as the countries of South America on the one side, and China, the Philippines, New Holland, and New Zealand, on the other. Among the latter, before many years, may be included Japan. Such various climates, will furnish the materials for a beneficial interchange of products, and an intercourse that must, in time, become immense; while this western coast, enjoying a climate in many respects superior to any other in the pacific, possessed as it must be by the Anglo-Norman race, and having none to enter into rivalry with it but the indolent inhabitants of warm climates, is evidently destined to fill a large place in the world's future history.[13]

Dana, the geologist, looking at the land from the point of view of its natural resources, concluded that, although Oregon appeared to be the best portion of Western America, the land available for the support of man was limited. Only about one-sixth, including a strip about a hundred miles in from the coast, was fit for agriculture. In that coastal section,

there is a large part which is mountainous, or buried beneath heavy forests. The forests may be felled more easily than the mountains, and notwithstanding their size, they will not long bid defiance to the hardy axemen of America. The middle section is in some parts a good grazing tract; the interior is good for little or nothing.

As to mineral production,

---

[13] *Narrative* **5**: pp. 171–172. The first edition came out in 1844.

we have only the negative fact that nothing of interest has yet been discovered within the limits of Oregon. The talcose and allied rocks of the Umpqua and Shasty districts resemble in many parts the gold-bearing rocks of other regions: but the gold, if any there be, remains to be discovered.

Just before his geology volume was printed (1849) Dana inserted a footnote recognizing that gold had been discovered and suggesting that it might be found over a wide area. He said,

The upper prairie of the Sacramento, from where we reached the Sacramento plains, was everywhere covered with the kind of quartzose pebbles that indicated a wide prevalence of the same rocks of the talcose series that we had traversed for a long distance in the Shasty Mountains and farther north.[14]

---

[14] Dana, *Geology*, Ex.Ex. **10**: pp. 625, 637–638 and note 9, p. 638. In 1849 Wilkes himself published a pamphlet entitled, *Western America, including California and Oregon, with Maps of those regions and of the Sacramento Valley*, in which he described the geographic characteristics of that area and quoted extensively from Dana's report.

XXVII

Heading For Home

THE SANDWICH ISLANDS rendezvous was necessary for reprovisioning and for procuring clothing for the *Peacock's* crew. There was not time to go into the Sea of Japan, which the Instructions permitted but did not require; this was a disappointment, for Wilkes had been looking forward to that part of the cruise.

The voyage to the Islands was uneventful, once the bar at the entrance to San Francisco Bay had been cleared. Wilkes worked on charts and Hudson made copies for distribution in the Squadron. The men were exercised at making and taking in sail, a kind of work usually performed at the beginning of a cruise to break them in; these veterans of more than three years' duty on the *Vincennes* resented this intrusion upon their leisure, but Wilkes considered it necessary for reasons of discipline and health. In fact, the malaria cases improved rapidly after going to sea; cleanliness, sea air, good food, and possibly exercise, brought about their cure.[1]

The flagship anchored off Honolulu on the seventeenth of November, the first to arrive. Consul Brinsmade brought out newspapers and some mail but most of it had been forwarded to Manila, since the Squadron had been expected to go there directly. Old friends greeted them in this now familiar port. They noticed a few changes, such as progress in the construction of the coral church and additional grog shops, the latter a result of a treaty with France permitting the import of wine. "Ardent spirits" were also obtainable, in spite of a law against their sale. Drunkenness among the natives, women as well as men, was prevalent and encouraged, if anything by the King who set a bad example before he was persuaded to take a vow of temperance. It was the practice of boardinghouse keepers and grog shop owners to organize dances for the sailors and then charge exorbitant prices for drinks and entertainment.

---

1 Wilkes Journal 3, Nov. 5, 7, 8; Briscoe Journal, Nov. 6–10, 30 and Dec. 2, 1841.

Wilkes posted a notice that he would not be responsible for debts incurred by the crews and, upon their departure, refused to pay innkeepers' demands totaling two thousand dollars.[2]

To Reynold's horror and grief it was decided not to sell the *Flying Fish*. She required considerable overhaul and was hove down, caulked, her copper renewed, and provided with a new gang of standing rigging and new suit of sails. The *Oregon* exchanged her stone ballast for some newly arrived chain cables.

The persistence of ill will in Naval circles against the Expedition again became apparent. Captain Aulick, commanding the sloop *Yorktown,* had departed from Honolulu a few days before the Squadron's arrival and while there had made disparaging remarks to the effect that letters from the United States indicated that Wilkes was crazy, the Expedition's members demoralized, and that he might have to take over its command. He also let it be known that he supported Ross's claim that there was open water in Antarctica where Wilkes had indicated land and that the Expedition had not discovered a continent but merely a chain of islands.[3]

Having endured great hardships during the Antarctic cruise, the officers were quick to refute this kind of talk. Emmons' comments were typical: if it were true that water was found where land was supposed to be, it was easily accounted for by anyone familiar with Antarctic conditions where impenetrable ice was constantly shifting and the limits of land were impossible to define, as everything was covered with ice and snow. In any case, this was an unimportant matter, but it had prejudiced public opinion and it was felt that Ross had been ungenerous in publicizing his and D'Urville's activities without mentioning those of the Americans.[4]

Wilkes called Aulick's statements humbug and regretted that he had not had an opportunity to have it out with him. He recalled that Aulick had tried to dissuade him from taking command of the Expedition, saying that he was too young and inexperienced. He had told Aulick he did not care "a fig" for his opinion "snapping my finger and thumb at the same time, and left him, we never have had a word about the Expedition

---

2 Briscoe Journal, Nov. 20, 26: Armstrong to Anderson, Oct. 18, 1841, Sandwich Islands Mission 3, #81; *Narrative* 5: pp. 258–260; Hudson Journal 2, Nov. 19.
3 Autobiography 6: p. 1338; Eld Journal 2, Nov.
4 Emmons Journal 3, Nov. 21.

after this, and so offended he was that our acquaintance ceased
at this time." He understood that when Poinsett interviewed
Aulick he had found him ignorant of the duties to be performed and totally unfit for command of the Expedition.[5]

Their Honolulu friends stood by them. For example, the
Reverend Mr. Armstrong, writing to Boston, said,

The Exploring Squadron has just left us, pointed homeward. We
had much pleasant intercourse with the commander & officers; Capt.
Aulick of the *Yorktown* and Forest of the *St. Louis* were rather
offish, were evidently prejudiced . . . [6]

Wilkes indulged in some predictions as to the future of
the Sandwich or Hawaiian Islands, seeing them destined to
persist as a neutral state in world affairs, since they had no
port that was without great expense defensible against a strong
naval force. He thought they would become economically dependent upon the power that would eventually be established
in Oregon and California and could see no possibility, as some
thought, of their domination of the Pacific coast of America.
They were not the most fruitful of the Polynesian islands but
were the most important from a locational point of view. The
belief that this circumstance would make them of great importance to any nation possessing them was largely fictitious
and due to the success of American missionaries in raising
them so rapidly in the scale of civilization. For the United
States their importance could be only as consumers of its
manufactured goods and as a convenient stopping place for
its whaling fleet which, in the future, would come to the
Islands only to rehabilitate their crews, finding their needs
otherwise better satisfied on the Pacific coast. In sum, "their
growth has already arrived at the greatest extent to which it
can ever reach."[7]

By the twenty-seventh all stragglers were back on board
their respective vessels, some "obfusticated as usual." Three
seamen were discharged and three succeeded in deserting.
Lieutenant Johnson and Dr. Guillou were left behind at their
own request to find their way back to the United States as best

5 Autobiography 6: pp. 1339–1341, 1173–1174.
6 Armstrong to Anderson, Nov. 28, 1841, Sandwich Islands Mission 3, #83.
7 *Narrative* 5: pp. 262–264.

they could, having turned in their journals, memos, writings, specimens, etc., and under orders to report themselves as arrested officers to the Secretary of the Navy. They stayed in the French Consul's cottage and, while the Squadron was in port, gave dinners for their fellow officers and were dined by them in return.

A little before noon of the twenty-seventh the flagship unmoored, fired a gun, ran up the cornet, and stood out followed by the other vessels of the Squadron. They anchored outside, waiting while the Commander finished preparing instructions. The next day Ringgold, Carr, and Knox came on board the *Vincennes* to receive them. The *Porpoise* and *Oregon* were to explore, in company, the shoals and reefs extending west-northwest from the Sandwich Islands, then to proceed in that general direction until they should fall in with the Japan current, which they were to compare with the Gulf Stream. From thence through the China Seas to the next rendezvous at Singapore where they must arrive "without fail in the first week of February [1842]."[8]

Wilkes planned to take the *Vincennes,* with the *Flying Fish* as tender, to Strong's and Ascension Islands, which the *Peacock* had been unable to reach, and to proceed from there to Manila. After that they would explore the Sooloo Archipelago on their way to the Singapore rendezvous. From there the Squadron would sail for the United States where it must arrive by May 31 which "agreeably to my promise to my crew a year previous, left me just six months to perform the duty, of which at least one hundred and forty days were required for the actual passage."[9]

The vessels now filled away on their separate courses. It was soon apparent that the *Flying Fish* was slowing up the *Vincennes* so much that valuable time was being lost so it was decided that the two vessels should proceed independently. The schooner was given additional arms and provisions and her crew augmented by two sailors and Dr. Whittle. Midshipman Blair, who had requested and been refused permission to return home directly from Honolulu, was transferred to the flagship and replaced by Passed Midshipman Sandford. The un-

8 *Ibid.*, append. X, pp. 528–529.
9 *Ibid.*, p. 265.

happy state of mind of the schooner's crew was indicated by Reynold's remark that "Old Whittle, one of the very noblest fellows in the world, made us up a most sociable mess of four, miserable, discontented wretches, as ever were seen." Their orders were to stop at Strong's and Ascension Islands and to arrive at Manila "without fail" by the tenth of January, 1842.

Proceeding under short sail the *Vincennes* pulled away from the tender as a mast was held to empty the brig of its occupants, confined because of drunkenness or for taking "French leave" while in port. Then all hands were called for three-quarters of an hour's exercise at reefing, furling, etc., which, they considered punishment since it was unheard of on a homeward bound passage.

Again a vigilant lookout was kept for suspected shoals, reefs, and islands, mostly non-existent. If they were close to the supposed location of a shoal or island at nightfall they would stay in that vicinity until daylight and they often went a considerable distance off course in order to reach such a spot. This slowed their progress and caused Wilkes to decide to by-pass Strong's and Ascension Islands.

The main object now was to have time to survey the Soo-loo Sea, so no landings were made from the *Vincennes*, except on Wake's Island which was reached December 19. This low coral island has deep blue water extending close to its shores. It had no drinking water or trees but the scientists found things of interest, such as rats, birds, crabs, etc., and Peale found a prize, an egg in the nest of a short-tailed albatross. The officers made scientific observations.

There were moments of recreation during the long monotonous days at sea. During one nine-hour period of no wind the crew enjoyed a swim. On Christmas and New Year's Day the sailors got an extra "tot" which, as one remarked "were like Angels visits — few and far between." The officers celebrated with dinners and, on Christmas, the two Captains joined in a collation in the Ward Room. This was their fourth Christmas away from home and all hoped it would be their last.

With the new year the weather became cooler and damper and, on January 8, 1842, they sighted the northern tip of the island of Luzon. They also observed their first sail since parting with the *Flying Fish*. It belonged to an East Indiaman which did not bother to show her colors until the *Vincennes* fired a gun to attract attention. The men were becoming worn out "with hard duty & exposure during this long & harassing cruise" and the officers "edgy." Lieutenant Walker, who found that being first lieutenant on the *Vincennes* was much less to his liking than on the *Peacock,* was slow in calling all hands to exercise at working ship and had the trumpet taken away from him and given to the second lieutenant, Case, shortly before reaching Manila.[10]

In mid-Pacific Wilkes scrutinized the officers' journals and found those of the midshipmen, in particular, deficient. He told them their journals were nothing more than "defective copies of the log book" and that some, not even in their own handwriting, were unacceptable. They should not expect a good recommendation if they continued to shirk this duty.[11]

The *Vincennes* ran down the coast of Luzon before a heavy northeast monsoon, with a white-capped sea tumbling about her and breaking noisily. Many towns and small craft came into view along the shore. Their entrance into Manila Bay was delayed by light winds and uncertainty as to its location but, on the twelfth, the ship beat her way in showing her colors in response to the raising of the Spanish flag on Corregidor Island. Don Juan Salomon, Captain of the Port, came out to them in a large, handsome boat pulled by sixteen oars and mounting a six or nine pounder forward and brass swivels on her quarters. The "pratique" (medical) officers also visited the ship before she was allowed to send anyone ashore. That evening the *Flying Fish* came in and anchored alongside.

The *Flying Fish* had escaped being wrecked by a hair's breadth. The day after parting with the *Vincennes* the schooner's square sail yard was carried away and, thereafter, when going before the wind she could run only under her mainsail and its heavy forty-foot boom, out at right-angles to the mast, made her uneasy and wet. In Reynolds' words, the

eternal thrashing & jumping, together with the rolling of the vessel

---

[10] Wilkes Journal 3, Nov. 16 and Dec. 31; Emmons Journal 3, Jan. 6, 1842.
[11] Wilkes to Midshipmen, Dec. 22, 1841, Wilkes Letters. Blair's Journal, for example, beginning at Honolulu, Nov. 23, 1841, and ending May 16, 1842, contains little more than the weather, changes of sail, repairs, work parties, etc., most of which would be in the ship's log.

& the floods of water that came over the deck & into the cabin,
made it utterly impossible to get a decent night's sleep, or sit, stand,
eat, or exist in any comfort—besides we were passing through an
unfrequented sea, and only had luck & a look out to trust to, to
keep from running down some Island in the dusk.

They longed for the comparative safety of the open sea.

The wind became lighter and progress slower as they
worked their way down to 10° North Latitude. At this time
Reynolds celebrated his twenty-sixth birthday with roast pig
and champagne, hating the thought that he was still a midshipman and not knowing that he had actually been promoted three
months before.[12]

The *Flying Fish* passed through the low coral southern
Mulgrave Islands, the resort of the mutineers of the whaleship
Globe. For the most part, they kept away from natives who
came out in canoes, but traded with some off Mackenzie's Islands. On December 18, with only twenty-three days left before
they were due to join the *Vincennes* at Manila, Knox decided
to take no chances on being late and headed north, by-passing
Ascension Island, despite its proximity, and following along
the northern fringe of the Caroline Islands.

On January 3, 1842, they approached Cape Espiritu Santo,
the northeast point of Samar Island, in the Philippines. Although it was a dark night, Knox insisted upon taking a course
directly for the Cape. They were only about one hundred and
fifty yards from the breakers when the lookout shouted. Sandford had the deck and ordered the helm put down to bring
the schooner by the wind as the foresheet was hauled aft. By
this time they were in the rollers and so close to shore that
they could see bottom. Since she made little heading under
foresail alone, all hands were called to hoist mainsail and jib,
for the only way to claw off was to put on a press of sail and
risk whipping out the masts. The jib had been securely tied
down to keep it from being washed off the bowsprit and was
all fouled up with the downhaul. Knox ordered Reynolds at
the bow to cut it loose, but there was no knife handy and
when one was finally procured the jib was caught and would
only go up by inches, like "hauling a ropeyarn over a nail."

---

12 Reynolds Journal 2: pp. 345–348.

The quartermaster sang out to the men, "this is no time to trust to God Almighty's interference, you must pull, *haul* for your lives!" When, finally, it was nearly up, they discovered that the halyard block had split and come out of the strap. They could distinctly see the white foam of the breakers in contrast to the surrounding blackness of land, sea, and sky. With her press of sail the schooner drove through and under the seas in a fearful manner. As Reynolds described the scene, the water came over the bow in torrents as the schooner

trembled, jumped, pitched, as if she was shaking herself to pieces: had she not have been the most glorious model of a Sea boat that ever *was* built, she could not have borne this sail, an instant, but she was true as gold, and was making a rapid progress & heading a little clear of the breakers. . . .

Yet it seemed impossible to escape striking so he went below to get a life preserver and routed Whittle telling him there was not even time to put on a shirt. Back on deck it was evident that she would not fetch past the breakers, the only thing left to do was to come about and take a chance on her getting "in stays," that is, be prevented by the heavy sea from taking another tack, there being no room to wear the vessel around. This maneuver would have been impossible with a square-rigger or even with a schooner of her class — "but wanting her qualities." All hands felt that this was the last chance,

we tried, she refused, we began to shake, there was no room to miss *often*: again, the helm was put alee, and the sails tended with all the care that we could bestow; to our infinite joy and relief she did come about, beautifully, *and we knew we were saved.*

As soon as they were far enough out from shore the mainsail was lowered. The jib had been torn to rags by the force of the water dashing against it. Having cut the downhaul they had great trouble in getting the jib down. Reynolds, at the bow, underwent a shower bath "that would not have disgraced Niagara."

Going below again they took a strong drink of brandy, dried, dressed themselves, thankful for their deliverance. It was Reynolds' worst experience, worse than when the *Potomac* ran on George's Bank, than the fire on the *Delaware,* than on the launch off Cape Horn, or than on the *Peacock* in the ice.

. . . to be roused out of a sleep, to be drowned in five minutes, without a hope, is rather appauling to any man, and the horror and dread of the time, is made, by the howling of the gale, the struggle of the vessel, the terrific aspect of the Land & Sea & darkness of night. . . .

At Oahu, Reynolds had written his family that all possible risks were fairly passed and that he expected a safe and speedy return home.

They soon passed through the San Bernardino Straits and into smooth water. One night, as they drifted with the tide in a dead calm, a scene presented itself in great contrast to their recent harrowing experience.

A more lovely night never fell from the Heavens: the atmosphere was transparently clear, not a star was absent from its place, and the waters were brilliantly illumined from the reflection of those lamps of the skies: huge fires were burning along the highest summits of the land, and the glow that arose from them, shed a vivid light down the hills.

For once, as Reynolds paced the deck the four-hour watch passed without a weary moment.

Light winds slowed their progress and caused them to arrive in Manila Bay on the twelfth of January. They anchored alongside the *Vincennes* only two days behind schedule for the rendezvous but in the effort to be on time had very nearly ended their days at Cape Espiritu Santo.[13]

The crews of the *Vincennes* and *Flying Fish* had eight days of pleasant recreation at Manila. There were the usual port duties to attend to after the anchor was dropped, cable paid out, and sails clewed up and furled. Lacking awnings for the boats, straw hats were purchased for the crews rowing under a powerful sun. Sailors not on duty were given liberty and allowed to visit other American ships in the harbor.

The mail was a disappointment, some having been sent on to Singapore and the newspapers little later than those seen at Honolulu. The latest news from China confirmed the British

---

13 *Ibid.,* pp. 350–357.

occupation of Canton.[14] There was speculation as to war between the United States and Britain over the MacLeod Affair; no British men-of-war were in the harbor, but there were several English and American merchantmen. On January 16 the American ship *St. Paul* arrived, one hundred and twenty days from Salem, bringing word that there was "No war yet." Theoretically a scientific expedition, armed only for defense, would take no part in a war and would not be subject to attack.

Consul Sturges was away but his brother and Vice Consul Josiah Moore were most hospitable. The Consul's house and billiard table were open to the officers and scientists. Wilkes, Hudson, and Waldron lived there when on shore and the change in a hot climate, after a long cruise to these "spacious and airy apartments, surrounded by every luxury that kind attentions can give, can be scarcely imagined by those who have not experienced it."[15] The others stayed at a hotel run by a friendly Senor Dios and the quarters of P. Sturges & Company, an American firm dealing in hemp, was another rendezvous, its "majordomo" a Chinese who had been on the *Vincennes* with Captain Finch and had many amusing anecdotes to tell.

Some of the officers hired a two-horse gig with postillion and joined the promenade on the Prado. They maneuvered so as to pass and repass the procession of dark-eyed, raven-haired fashionable beauties. It was two years since they had been in a city and four of separation from "womankind" and that was "too much." Evening band concerts, the illumination of churches and fireworks also brought out the beauties who came to hear, to see, and to be seen. The band music somewhat disrupted by the crowing of fighting cocks brought along by proud owners. Consul Moore introduced them to an elderly Spanish gentleman whose ladies got up a dance, which impressed Emmons by the lack of "that mock modesty" and "stiffness that often characterizes such a gathering in our country." Some found it entertaining to visit a cigar factory and watch the six thousand girls with long glossy black hair start home from work.[16]

---

[14] The so-called "Opium War" ended with the Treaty of Nanking in August, 1842.
[15] *Narrative* 5: p. 278.
[16] Emmons Journal 3, Jan. 18, 1842.

Manila had the appearance of a strongly fortified city, capable of withstanding a long siege. Emmons thought "Old Spain" appeared to better advantage here than in some of her home ports that he had visited. Wilkes was impressed with the natural wealth of the islands and thought them well located from a commercial point of view as the presence of several English and American merchantmen testified. Among them was an English steam vessel undergoing repairs, having been obliged to burn all her upper works as fuel to complete the passage. They were pleased to have the captain of an American brig, recently returned from the Fijis, report no difficulties with the natives. He said they still fought among themselves like cats and dogs but he thought the Squadron's visit had had a good effect so far as "their intercession with the Whites is concerned."

The scientists, Eld, and Russell Sturges went on an excursion into the interior splitting into two parties at Laguna de Bay. Pickering, Eld, and Sturges proceeded to a Mission beyond the town of Santa Cruz where Sturges knew the padre, F. Antonio Romana y Aranda. ·With his help Pickering and Eld secured horses, guides, and twenty natives to carry three days' supplies. Leaving Sturges at the Mission, they climbed Mount Banajoa, determining its altitude to be 6,500 feet. Six months before the rotund padre had been carried to the top by the natives and to his astonishment the Americans climbed the mountain and returned in twenty-four hours. For their part Rich, Dana, and Brackenridge were unable to secure horses and, consequently, to climb the volcano de Taal, which had been their objective. They had to satisfy themselves with a visit to the hot springs at Baños.

The *Vincennes* and *Flying Fish* departed on January 21. Warned by the Port Captain that existing charts of the Sooloo Sea were unreliable, they took along a native pilot who was also to act as interpreter in spite of scanty English. It was soon evident that he was of little use as a pilot, for he was confused by his inability to make himself understood and because this was his first experience on such a large vessel.

The *Flying Fish* was sent back to pick up Ordinary Seaman Lawrence Magill, a native of Manila who was missing. It was assumed that he wanted to return to the ship since he had $280, a lifetime saving, coming to him on the payroll.

The schooner failed to find Magill but did speak the American vessel *Ianthe* on her way in from Boston and got from her newspapers only four months old. Reynolds discovered in them a list of Navy promotions including his own and Knox's promotion to lieutenant, as of 8 September, 1841. He had not expected this for another three years and, overjoyed, called his servant from the pantry to do homage to his new rank and drew black lines around the paragraph before sending the paper to the Commander. Knox took his promotion more calmly simply remarking that it was about time he had two swabs instead of one.[17]

---

[17] Reynolds Journal 2: pp. 369–370.

XXVIII

The Last Leg

Wilkes' Instructions called for the examination of the Sooloo Sea to determine whether it provided a safe route for shortening the passage of vessels to and from China. "It may be advisable to ascertain the disposition of the inhabitants of the islands of this archipelago for commerce, their productions and resources." After a call at Singapore the Squadron was to return home by way of the Cape of Good Hope.

A matter of particular importance at this stage of the cruise was the injunction that

no journal of these voyages, either partial or complete, should be published, without the authority and under the supervision of the government of the United States, at whose expense this Expedition is undertaken, you will, before you reach the waters of the United States, require from every person under your command the surrender of all journals, as well as all specimens of every kind, collected or prepared during your absence from the United States.

Knox's orders were to examine the Apo Shoal in the Strait separating the islands of Mindoro and Palawan and to look for the flagship at two rendezvous points. On the second day out, when abreast of the high land of Mindoro, both vessels became becalmed. The *Vincennes* got a wind first and Wilkes, noticing that the *Flying Fish* continued becalmed, remarked that the officer of the deck had "so little of the true spirit" that for two hours he made no effort to sweep her out of it.[1] Probably the schooner's crew was glad to have an excuse for allowing the ship to get out of sight. However, since the native pilot was of little help and the English and Spanish charts unreliable, the *Vincennes* needed the assistance of the shallow draft and more maneuverable tender. Sometimes the angle of the sun's rays made it difficult to see coral shoals and bottom would suddenly be in plain sight under only $4\frac{1}{2}$

---

1 Wilkes Journal 3, Jan. 22, 1842.

to 9 fathoms of water. At night they boxed about, attempting to stay in a safe position.[2]

At the first of the two rendezvous points off the island of Panay there was no sign of the *Flying Fish*. Two days later, when beating against the tide, a small sail to leeward was sighted from the masthead, but soon lost to view. At sunrise of the twenty-eighth when off San Jose and near their second rendezvous, the schooner was sighted and signal guns fired, but she stood off to the westward having, this time, a favorable breeze while the ship remained becalmed. When a court of Inquiry was held at Singapore it was stated that the officer on watch failed to inform Captain Knox of the flagship's presence.

The *Flying Fish* did not reach the second rendezvous point until the thirtieth and sailed on and off until February 3, seeing no sail of any kind during those four days. Knox was anxious for their safety because of the danger of running on shoals or of encountering pirates rumored to be in this area. The lives of sixteen men depended upon one leaky boat. After leaving the rendezvous point the schooner proceeded to Singapore where she arrived February 15 and found the *Porpoise* and *Oregon* already there, but no sign of the *Vincennes*. Her whereabouts remained a mystery until she appeared three days later.[3]

The flagship, seeing no sign of the tender at the second rendezvous, made a hasty survey of San Jose harbor and proceeded to Caldera, the westernmost port of the island of Mindanao, making a "flying survey in passing" of the high and picturesque island of Panay. At Caldera there was a small fort intended as an outpost against raiding pirates and, at nearby Samoangan, a convict settlement where three regiments were stationed.

The *Vincennes'* next objective was the pirates' den, the harbor of Soung on the island of Sooloo. Because of light airs, their approach was slow. They thought the island enchantingly beautiful. As Wilkes said,

---

[2] Emmons Journal 3, Jan. 22.

[3] Reynolds Journal 3: p. 371. In his Critique (pp. 66–67) he said the *Vincennes* was not seen at all by the *Flying Fish*, but the logs of both vessels indicated a sighting at this time.

during all our wandering we most of us came to the conclusion that we had not yet met with one to equal it, it seemed to be a garden from its hill tops of very diversified surface, the clouds overhanging its lofty peaks, and the foliage in every tint of green. . . .

The ship lay still, carried by the tide with scarcely a ripple on the glassy surface of the sea and with no sound except the occasional splashing of the lead seeking bottom. The gentle slopes appeared to be well cultivated and many cottages gave the impression of a dense population and of civilized life. The picturesque bay was covered with small canoes, fishing boats, and Proas with large mat sails, passing back and forth. They anchored before sunset and before entering the bay. That evening they watched fishermen moving along the shore with lights, the water itself being sprinkled with phosphorescence. Then a delightful shower coming at the end of a hot day refreshed the air and produced on the crew "a kind of happiness or pleasure."

In the morning the boats towed the ship to an anchorage in the bay. Now they could see that a large part of the town was built on piles over the water, connected with the shore by narrow bamboo bridges, and that the houses were similar but larger and filthier than those of the Malays. Lieutenant Budd went ashore with the interpreter to call upon the Datu Mulu (Governor) to request an interview for the two Captains with the Sultan. Upon going ashore all the pleasing sights of this beautiful island seemed to disappear and it began to look more like "a filthy piratical hole."[4]

Most of the natives wore turbans and maro and carried krises—short, wave-shaped swords made of iron or indifferent steel in scabbards inlaid with silver and gold. The population was a mixture of Moors and Chinese; the men mostly small but bold, warlike, and treacherous looking, and their women kept out of sight.

The two Captains met the Datu at his home, which reminded Wilkes of a barn inhabited by a group of strolling players, filled with clothes, weapons, drums, robes, etc. The Datu, a small emaciated man with a "quick and intelligent countenance," took them to the house of Sultan Mohammed

---

4 Wilkes Journal 3, Feb. 3–4.

Damaleil Kisand where they had a formal meeting and Wilkes proposed a treaty of commerce for which the Sultan was said to have expressed a desire. It was agreed that a treaty should be drawn up to be signed the following day, giving Americans permission to carry on trade and promising to protect their persons and property in case of shipwreck or injury of any kind.

Returning to the Datu's house, the Governor tried to impress upon Wilkes the great favor he had received in being granted an interview, but the Commander insisted that it was an everyday affair with him and emphasized that he was doing the Sultan a favor for which he should be grateful. A large crowd was at the Datu's house watching Agate sketch Mohammed Polalu, the Sultan's eldest son and heir to the throne, who was about twenty-three, tall and slender, but with eyes dulled from being under the influence of opium. During their visit he took a few puffs and lay down in a listless manner, but recovered somewhat after taking betel-nut which an attendant chewed, molded into a walnut-sized ball, and put into his mouth.

The Datu treated his guests to chocolate and negus (wine) served in gilt-edged tumblers and small stale cakes made of rice and cocoanut. He was very interested in Emmons' five-barrel pistol and Dana's bowie-knife pistol which disappeared after Dana carelessly laid it on a chest. Wilkes told the Datu that he would be held responsible for its return by the next morning.[5]

It was supposed that the friendly appearance of these people was due only to the presence of the man-of-war which had boldly entered the harbor without waiting for permission. When they asked permission for the scientists to explore the interior of the island, the Sultan refused saying he could not be responsible for their safety from the mountain men, and whenever any of the officers or scientists went towards the woods or certain parts of the town they were always met by armed men who barred their way. It was suspected that objects taken from shipwrecks were hidden in these places and, in fact, Pickering saw a granite monument with markings in-

---

[5] *Narrative* **5**: pp. 336–337.

dicating its Boston origin. From later inquiries they learned
that a vessel taking such a monument to Canton had disappeared. It was rumored that the pirates enslaved their cap-
tives or held them for ransom, a padre being worth $2,000, an
ordinary white man $300, and a Filipino from $30 to $50. As a
result, nobody felt quite comfortable ashore. When the Purser's
assistant went with a party to procure beef, they were followed
by natives who mimicked and mocked them.[6]

At sunset, to insure the return of Dana's pistol, they fired
a long gun instead of the usual small brass howitzer. In the
calm of the evening its reverberations fairly shook the town
and rolled along the water to the surrounding islands. Its effectiveness was indicated by a great commotion and clatter on
shore, much shouting, beating of drums and gongs, and moving about with lights. The bowie-knife pistol was returned by
special messenger in the morning and the Commander returned it to Dana "with some suitable remarks" about his carelessness but feeling that, as it turned out, it helped their relations with these people.[7]

The scientists went to Marongas, an adjoining island,
where they gathered botanical and other specimens until a
number of fishermen appeared and became so menacing that
it was prudent to withdraw. The harbor was surveyed, Wilkes
took some astronomical and magnetical observations on the
beach, and some of the officers purchased curiosities, such as
krises, spears, shields, and shells. Soung Roads offered a good
anchorage and supplies, such as beef, vegetables, and fruits; it
could become an important commercial center, providing the
Sultan took seriously the treaty which he had signed.

The *Vincennes* departed February 6 and two days later
began a survey of the Mansee Islands at the entrance to the
Straits of Balabac. Here they were hampered by the absence of
the tender and by the prevailing heavy showers and strong
winds. It appeared that there were no serious navigational
hazards, such as reefs, shoals, winds, or currents, to prevent a
passage through the Sooloo Sea and that it would shorten, by
several days, the passage to Manila or Canton, and result in a
great saving on wear and tear. The pirates were not to be

---

6 *Ibid.*, p. 339; [Robinson] Journal, Feb. 4.
7 Wilkes Journal 3, Feb. 5.

feared unless a vessel ran aground and it was hoped that the danger of enslavement and pillage would lessen as a result of the new treaty.[8]

Helped by moderate northeast monsoonal winds, the *Vincennes* reached the Straits of Singapore on the eighteenth and anchored in Singapore Roads the following afternoon. She found the *Porpoise, Oregon,* and *Flying Fish* in the midst of many foreign vessels, the two brigs having been in port for almost a month. They had explored reefs and islands extending northwest of the Hawaiian group, including Necker Island, French-Frigate shoals, and Maro reef, but found no trace of Neva Island as laid down on Arrowsmith's chart. Because of continual bad weather and the poor condition of the vessels, Captain Ringgold had decided not to investigate the Japan current but to go directly to Singapore.

The American East India Squadron was there when the brigs arrived, departing for Manila about ten days before the *Vincennes'* arrival. It was composed of the U.S.S. *Constellation,* Captain Kearney, and the sloop of war *Boston,* Captain Long. The fact that this squadron consisting of only *two* vessels was commanded by an officer with the rank of *Captain* did not go unnoticed.[9]

Ringgold was ordered to hold a Court of Inquiry in the matter of Knox's failure to rendezvous with the *Vincennes.* This surprised and disgusted the *Flying Fish's* crew who thought that he had served faithfully and that Wilkes was incapable of gratitude.[10] In any case, Knox was exonerated.

The officers put on black armbands and colors were half-masted upon receipt of the official news of President Harrison's death. They were pleased to see H.B.M.S. *Wellesley,* a seventy-four, half-mast her colors upon her arrival from Canton. On February 22 they dressed ship in honor of Washington's Birthday which happened to coincide with the Chinese New Year so the day was celebrated on shore with processions and the beating of gongs as loud as the roar of the surf. The celebration continued for several days, for the Mohammedans also had their anniversaries.

---

8 *Ibid.,* **5**, pp. 365–366.
9 Emmons Journal **3**, Feb. 19, Kearney had the honorary title of "Commodore."
10 Reynolds Journal **2**: p. 377.

It was apparent that Singapore was a great mart for eastern commerce. Among the many vessels present were huge, hulk-like Chinese junks with their light, skipping, sampan tenders. The Anglo-Chinese War caused much of this activity since this was the only port where the junks could trade unmolested. The Squadron received letters only seventy-two days after their United States date, sent via England and by means of the newly established trans-Atlantic steamships. Projects were in the making for steam communication between India and China and banking transactions were being conducted increasingly by drafts instead of by specie. The British were using steam war vessels effectively in operations along the shallow and uncharted coasts and on the difficult rivers of China. Consul Balestier had imported a steam engine from the United States which the *Porpoise's* carpenters helped to set in motion, attracting much attention.

The great concourse of races made Singapore an exciting port of call. From early in the morning the Squadron's vessels were surrounded by innumerable bumboats bringing fruits, vegetables, eggs, live and cooked chickens, and curiosities, such as shells, birds of paradise, monkeys, parrots, corals, mats, etc. Tailors, shoemakers, and washerwomen clamored for permission to come on board making altogether a prodigious clatter. Tigers in the nearby jungle prevented the scientists from wandering very far afield, but Brackenridge managed to procure many live plants which he brought to the United States in safety. Wilkes was entertained by Consul Balestier and his lady and visited the Consul's sugar plantation. He also visited the Government's well-equipped magnetic observatory but was not impressed by the knowledge or activities of Lieutenant Elliot, its Director.

The supplies brought from America, months before, had deteriorated, the hardtack being moldy and wormy and the other food stale and musty. Flour, stored in the upper dry and hot loft of a warehouse, was destroyed by white ants which perforated the barrels. There would be a shortage of bread on the voyage home.[11]

A thorough survey was made of the *Flying Fish*. Her frame appeared to be weakened and it was estimated that re-

---

11 *Narrative* 5: p. 408; Erskine, *op. cit.,* p. 257.

pairs would be very costly in money and time. Deciding that sending her on without repairs was too great a risk to her crew, Wilkes reluctantly put her up for public sale. He had a strong attachment for the schooner because of the efficient aid she had occasionally afforded and because he thought that "as a vessel of her class, she was almost faultless." After the removal of her stores and armament she was sold for $3,700 to a Mr. Whitehead who said she would make a beautiful yacht, but it was suspected that he intended to use her to smuggle opium. Her crew left her reluctantly and was saddened at the sight of her going out under the British flag. Emmons thought she deserved to be retained and was entitled "to a place in our National Museum *if* we ever have one." Although he was glad to be transferred to the *Porpoise,* Reynolds thought she could be trusted to round the Cape of Good Hope and had a regard for her such as "a man must entertain for a gallant horse, that has carried him safely through the fight."[12]

At five in the morning of February 26 the Squadron was under way, assisted by the land breeze. The most direct route to the Straits of Sunda was through the Straits of Rhio and Bangka which were navigated in company without difficulty. As usual in confined water, they kept the lead going with good lookouts aloft and the officers observing ranges and angles. In the Straits of Bangka they met a bark flying Dutch colors and when she made no response to their hail the *Vincennes* wore around upon her and fired a gun across her bow as the brigs astern maneuvered to cut her off. She let go all halyards, clewed up, and furled all sails except her jib. Lieutenant Budd boarded and found her malay crew unable to speak English. It was suspected that there were white men in hiding and that she was a pirate ship, but no effort was made to investigate further. They followed the light of another vessel through the Straits and discovered, in the morning, that she was the English bark *Java* bound for Singapore but returning to Batavia having lost twelve of her native crew by dysentery leaving hardly enough hands to work ship. The Captain's wife had just given birth to a child and so Dr. Fox went aboard with medical supplies and food and brandy contributed by the officers' mess.

---

12 Emmons Journal 3, Feb. 24; Reynolds Journal 2: p. 378; Wilkes Journal 3, Feb. 25.

This was a notable day for other reasons. The Commander issued a General Order regularizing the acting lieutenancies which had been in effect from the beginning of the cruise and recognizing the promotions to lieutenant, as announced in the newspapers, for Sinclair, Baldwin, Knox, Totten, Davis, and Reynolds. He also gave appointments as Acting Masters to Passed Midshipmen May, Sandford, and Harrison. On the other hand, it became known on this day that Ringgold and Carr were given a "diabolical" order to go home via Rio de Janeiro with a stop at St. Helena. The ostensible reason was to pick up some boxes of specimens and to take certain dip and intensity observations, but it was immediately assumed that the real reason was to assure the arrival home of the *Vincennes* well in advance of the brigs. Some felt ready to do anything short of mutiny to avoid this additional delay. When they signed the new Articles at Oahu, Wilkes promised that the cruise would not extend beyond May 31, 1842, "unless prevented by an Act of God, or some unforeseen accident" and now the chances were that it would extend beyond that date.[13]

It felt good, however, to pass through the Straits of Sunda and head across the Indian Ocean towards America. But time passed slowly, especially when the wind was contrary or dropped out. The ships sailed independently, the brigs dropping out of sight astern of the *Vincennes*. The *Porpoise* and *Oregon* sailed along together "cozily" for some time but the latter developed a lead of some eighty miles by the time they doubled the Cape and she was a day ahead of the *Porpoise* at St. Helena.

The *Vincennes* lost two of her crew before reaching the Cape. On March 3, George Porter (O.S.) died of dysentery contracted at Singapore. He it was who had survived being hung by the neck at the very beginning of the cruise. He had a reputation for bravery and a robust appearance but, in spite of warning, did not protect himself from the heat and ate and drank excessively. About three weeks later Benjamin Vanderford, Master's Mate, pilot and interpreter, died. He had been sick for several days during the last of which he was "crazy as a Bedlamite," kept under opiates, and held in bed by his mess-

---

13 Emmons Journal 3, Feb. 24; Wilkes Journal 3, Feb. 28.

mates who took turns watching him. Vanderford was considered a worthy man, with a reputation for reliability, industry, and honesty, and had been most useful in the Fijis which he knew well, having made several voyages there in command of Salem vessels in the sandalwood and bêche-de-mer trade. He was sixty years old, was said to have decided to join the Expedition after the wreck of a vessel of which he was a principal owner, and was looking forward to rejoining his family, but seemed to have a premonition that he would not live to see home again. Some thought intemperance caused his death and an autopsy indicated a diseased brain. The person most affected by his death was Vendovi who could talk to him in his native language and counted on his help in America. The Fiji chief had been mortified to have the ship's barber crop his great mat of hair but had become friendly with many of the crew and was passionately fond of music, striving mightily to extract a tune from his favorite instrument, the jew's-harp. However, after Vanderford's death he seemed to lose interest in life, taking to his cot more and more.[14]

The voyage across the Indian Ocean took days and weeks that one seaman characterized as "the blank leaves of a sailor's life." They were impatient to be home and the change to damp weather caused much catarrh and influenza. The officers occupied themselves making charts and writing up their journals. It was April before they approached the African coast when turbulent seas and high winds made the vessels uncomfortable and charting impossible; their attention was again directed to the familiar problems of a sailing vessel under stress and strain.

Near Cape Town they were becalmed but the sea remained high and irregular, influenced by a strong westerly current. When a breeze came up they hauled to the northward and almost immediately passed from a warm to a cold current. By April 12 they were off Table Bay with anchors off the bows and chains bent but unable to enter because of fog and it was two days before they picked up a fisherman who could pilot them into the harbor.[15]

The *Vincennes* stayed at Cape Town three days. Consul

---

14 Wilkes Journal 3, Mar. 22, Briscoe Journal, Mar. 22.
15 Emmons Journal 3, Apr. 5, 11.

Isaac Chase was ill but attended to their needs. Wilkes made an official call upon Governor Sir George Napier and visited the Royal Observatory where he was pleased to see that their chronometers agreed with his. He was highly displeased, however, to see a chart made by Ross showing his own South Polar Expedition tracks and those of D'Urville but omitting those of the U. S. Exploring Expedition even though it appeared that Ross had used information that Wilkes had sent him.

H. B. M. S. *Sulphur* came to Table Bay while they were there and the Commanders exchanged civilities but the Americans could not forget that Captain Belcher had not offered them his chart of the Columbia River when they gave him rudder pintles for which he had a critical need. It was said that most of Belcher's officers had deserted him.[16]

Some of the *Vincennes'* officers hired a carriage and four and drove to High Constantia, about ten miles out of Cape Town. Several ladies and gentlemen visited the ship, curious to see an American frigate and a Fiji chief, but Vendovi did not show to advantage since he lay on his cot all day feeling sick and mournful. Some of the crew of a wrecked American sealer were taken on board for return to the United States.

As they departed, April 17, they observed a curious mirage, reminiscent of the one seen near Cape Horn and, like that, caused by differences in the temperature of the air at two levels. A ship appeared to be two ships, one on top of the other.

It was a thirteen-day passage to St. Helena where Wilkes hoped to meet the brigs, but they had already gone on their way to Rio. A one-day stop at this famous island gave the officers an opportunity to visit Longwood where Napoleon had lived in exile and been buried until 1840 when his bones were returned to France. They were shocked to find Longwood falling to pieces, part of it used as a stable, and were annoyed to have to pay fifty cents for admission and to be importuned to buy water from Napoleon's spring.

At last, May 1, the *Vincennes* headed for New York. Weather conditions added an extra ten days to the promised return date of May 31. South Atlantic temperature readings, taken at the ocean's surface and at one hundred fathoms, led

---

16 Wilkes Journal 3, Apr. 15.

Wilkes to some conclusions regarding submarine polar currents trending toward the Equator and their effect upon the feeding habits of whales which he enlarged upon in the final chapter of his five-volume *Narrative*.[17]

In accord with Instructions, all officers' and scientists' journals, writings, specimens, curiosities, etc., were called for to be listed, packed, and sealed in the presence of Hudson, Emmons, and Pickering. The Commander was very explicit in regard to this matter:

> The above order is to be construed in its *spirit* as well as *literal* construction; & they will particularly enquire of each person if he has given up all, & everything connected with the Expedition, or that may be important to it in the illustration of any part of it or facts relative to it—whether gathered by himself, or derived from others. . . . [18]

It caused quite a commotion, even though everyone would be repaid for anything they had purchased. May wrote on his box of shells, "Purchased at Public Sale after the Comdr of the Ex. Ex. had refused them" and was called to the Cabin for an explanation:

> when asked if he intended it as a mark of disrespect he rudely replied *"to state a fact,"* on my asking him if I had ever refused to purchase any shells, he said in an impertinent manner *"not you but your Agent or Agents on board the Currency Lass at Ovalu."* I told him he was mistaken, and that I requested if there was no disrespect meant on his part in thus marking his box, that he would have it erased to prevent that impression on the Officers and crew, to which he answered *"he would do no such thing"* in a highly disrespectful manner and tone and I ordered him to leave the Cabin & consider himself under suspension.[19]

May had a good record as an officer and had been promoted Acting Master not long before this, but his temperament was as excitable and touchy as that of the Commander. As this was his second offense, charges were preferred and he was slated for a court-martial along with Johnson, Guillou, and Pinkney.

---

[17] *Narrative* 5: ch. XII.
[18] Emmons Journal 3, May 16.
[19] Wilkes Journal 3, May 23.

The other officers reluctantly surrendered all their souvenirs and mementoes, so dear to the heart of voyagers in distant lands. Emmons thought such a sweeping demand most importunate but bowed to the inevitable and listed the following articles: the skull of a Flathead Indian, a bundle of bows and arrows, a shark's tooth sword, Shasty Indian armor, a Manila mat, some coral, and copper coins. He particularly prized a Fiji bow and arrow which Maury had given him after his canoe fight at Malolo.[20]

It was rumored that Wilkes had a valuable collection of shells and curiosities in a cabinet in his cabin given him by Consul Balestier at Singapore. He found it necessary to disabuse the officers of the idea that he intended to keep this as a private collection.[21]

The call for journals also caused concern. Dr. Whittle, whose journal was filled with personal reflections, including unfavorable judgments of his Commander, claimed in vain the right to send it sealed to the Secretary of the Navy. It was from his journal that Wilkes first learned of the Indian attack upon Emmons' guide in California, about which he made further inquiries.[22]

Case, in his entry for April 28, 1841, the day before the *Vincennes'* near disaster off the California coast, made no mention of the anchor cables being bent and Wilkes made a notation to the effect that he had inadvertently neglected to do so. In high dudgeon Case replied that a closer reading of his journal would show that he rarely mentioned whether cables were bent or not and, if they were bent on the twenty-eighth they were unbent on the twenty-ninth when there was critical need for them. He requested that, in the future, any alleged inaccuracies be pointed out to him and he would correct them himself if necessary.[23] Several of the journals have words

---

20 Emmons Journal 3, May 16.
21 Autobiography 6: p. 1352.
22 Wilkes to Whittle, May 28, 1842, Wilkes Letters.
23 Case Journal, May 9; Wilkes Journal 3, May 17; Wilkes correspondence with Case and Knox, May 16, 17, and June 4, 1842. He gave Case considerable responsibility because of his rank but thought him "incapable of making the commonest observations correctly" and lacking in proper interest or desire to learn. Both were reprimanded for destroying government property: Case for tearing down shelves to make boxes and Knox for cutting down a washstand.

and phrases erased here and there and it is likely that these changes were made shortly before their final surrender.

Wilkes showed more confidence in Emmons than perhaps any other officer, except Eld, but found fault with him, too, during these last days. He thought Emmons careless in making observations and gave him a two-day suspension because, when he had the deck, the Master's Mate threw the log aft creating a noise while dip observations were being made in the cabin below. Emmons was suspended again when with a northeast wind and a choppy head sea they entered the Gulf Stream. The ship seemed to be straining. Emmons, who had the deck and was aware of a general order not to shorten sail without first informing the Commander, sent an officer to tell him that something might give way if they continued under the same sail. The answer was an order to put on more sail and shortly after that the bobstay parted. Emmons then began reducing sail and sent word to Wilkes who came on deck giving orders that caused confusion and divided the work force so that nothing could be accomplished in a proper manner. According to Emmons,

This rather embarrassed than relieved him—& did not at all satisfy me—I however did not partake of his excitement and continued to repeat his orders—that he might not accuse me of disrespect—and at the same time see what a mess he had got everything in—until he finally ordered me below & sent for the 1st Lieut. when he reduced sail as I had previously suggested. . . .[24]

It is evident that everybody's nerves and especially the Commander's were on edge during these last days when obdurate weather conditions frustrated their efforts to reach New York by May 31. Wilkes worked on charts and official papers such as letters recommending promotions for some and pensions for Longley, whose exposure on Moana Loa had left him with chronic rheumatism, and for Whitehorn, whose Fourth of July accident made him permanently unfit for service or for earning a living. In anticipation of the publication of the Narrative he engaged Frederick Stuart, his Clerk, to return

[24] Emmons Journal 3, Apr. 28 and June 1; Wilkes Journal 3, May 26.

to Washington as draughtsman and Drayton to help prepare drawings and paintings for publication.[25]

On June 2 a strong favorable wind veered becoming a head wind and then died out leaving them becalmed for two days. As they waited impatiently for the northeast Trades, they met the schooner *Exchange,* five days from New York, and got from her newspapers and potatoes. A spell of dirty weather caused the ship to tumble about and reduced her fair-weather rate of ten to eleven knots to eight or nine. However, when sounding on the evening of the eighth they got sand at thirty-seven fathoms and knew it was time to bend anchor cables. In the morning of the ninth they experienced thick fog but saw and then lost sight of a pilot boat. Wilkes made the last entry in his journal which reads, in part:[26]

At 2½P.M. our guns were answered and shortly afterwards we were boarded by a Pilot who took us in charge—thus is my [command] given up, but I cannot close the pages of this Journal without rendering thanks to Almighty God for his preservation of me and enabling me to conduct this Expedition to a successful issue. . . .

The state of excitement I now feel under renders it impossible for me to sum up the cruize as it is my intention to do after I can be settled and hear that all those I love dearly are well.

The fog lifted on the tenth which became a beautiful day as the *Vincennes* sailed in fine style to Quarantine. After a short stop, she was towed by a steamer through the Narrows into the harbor. The officers watched with keen interest to see what would happen to the broad blue pennant as the ship approached the Navy Yard commanded by a "real" Captain. The problem was solved neatly. The crew was mustered on deck and Wilkes thanked them for their good behavior and stated again his belief that the government would reward them suitably for their successful completion of such a perilous cruise. Then a national salute was fired, the broad pennant hauled down, the command turned over to Captain Hudson, and the Expedi-

---

25 Letters of recommendation, Wilkes Letters, June 4, 7, 8, 10 for Amos Chick (Carpenter), John W. Dyes (Master's Mate), Samuel Hawkins (Sailmaker), and Midshipmen Clark, Thompson, Hammersly, and Elliott.
26 Wilkes Journal 3, June 5, 9.

tion's commander entered a boat to be pulled to a landing at the Battery while the crew gave him three cheers.[27]

---

27 Reynolds' Critique, p. 69.

XXIX

Home Again

THE BATTERY was crowded with "the fashion of the city" when the *Vincennes* came up the harbor, but Wilkes received no ovation as he landed at White Hall. He went to the Astor House before going on to Washington and learned with relief that his family was all well, not having heard from them for the past fourteen months. His youngest daughter, a newborn babe when the Expedition started, was now four and his son Jack, having received a warrant in the Navy, was in Brazil under Commodore Morris.[1]

As soon as the *Vincennes* was moored, all the men who could be spared were allowed to take their bags and hammocks and go ashore. Their eagerness to be released from long confinement on shipboard under man-of-war discipline can be imagined. Many "went to quarters" at New York's then famous or infamous "Five Points" where boardinghouse keepers gave them a cordial reception and acted as their bankers (for a percentage) until they received their pay two weeks later.

The public was much less interested in the Expedition upon its return than it had been at its departure. The officers were interviewed and New York newspapers enumerated the highlights of the cruise. Vendovi, the Fiji chief, was a source of curiosity but he was apathetic and caught a severe cold during the last few days of the cruise which settled in his lungs and caused his death three days after the *Vincennes'* return.[2]

Nineteen days after the flagship's arrival the *Oregon* came in and the *Porpoise* three days after that. The new arrivals augmented the forces of opposition to the Expedition's Commander. They could not forgive him for sending them to Rio, delaying their return home by a month beyond the date promised at the time of reenlistment. The five small boxes of specimens picked up at Rio hardly required the services of two

---

1 *Autobiography* **6**: pp. 1368–1370.
2 *Ibid.*, pp. 1235–1238.

vessels. The officers were also annoyed to have their orders include the requirement that in addition to the daily recording of air and surface water temperatures they should determine that of the water at a depth of a hundred fathoms.[3] This enraged Alden who, as Executive Officer of the *Porpoise,* must see to the carrying out of this duty. He let off steam in his otherwise very scanty journal saying, "every day between this & the U.S.! ! ! ! Can it be for *punishment?* Ans. No. Scientific purposes. Bah!"[4]

Their ten-day stop at Rio was not unpleasant for they saw several of their friends stationed there with the Brazil Squadron, but on the final passage home they were bedeviled by contrary winds and calms which agonizingly prolonged their voyage. Arriving at New York June 29 and July 2, respectively, they had little to report that was newsworthy since the flagship had preceded them. They yearned to be free of their vessels and were tired of each others' faces and conversation. Reynolds thought of himself as thin, wrinkled, and gray and, going ashore July Fourth to see the processions and fireworks, was self-conscious about his "horrible, longtailed, greasy antiquated uniform coat." As soon as possible he procured new clothes and leave of absence to visit with his family in Lancaster.[5]

The controversy with Ross was one of the first things about which they were questioned. When the brigs were at Rio the British bomb ketch *Arrow* came in, having completed a survey of the Falkland Islands. At Port Louis, on those islands, she had met one of Ross's Antarctic vessels and Dr. Holmes, by talking with some of the *Arrow's* crew, ascertained that Ross never passed over any points of land laid down as actually seen by Wilkes.[6]

More sensational were the rumors of charges and counter-charges that preceded the Squadron's arrival. Shortly after the *Vincennes* reached New York the *Herald* said:[7]

We understand that there is to be a nice mess dished up in a short time in the shape of court martials, courts of inquiry, arranging of specimens, rock, etc., in the eating of which nearly all of the

---

3 *Narrative* 5: append. XIV, p. 533.
4 Alden Journal, Mar. 8, 1842.
5 Reynolds Journal 3: p. 32.
6 Holmes Journal 3, May 17; *New York Sun,* June 13, 1842.
7 New York *Morning Herald,* June 13, 1842.

officers of the Exploring Expedition are to participate with finger glasses and napkins. It is said that there are at least a bushel and a half of charges already preferred against Lieut. Wilkes, the commander-in-chief, and that several officers of the squadron have come home under arrest. It took four or five years to start this expedition, four years for it to catch Vendovi, knock down a mud village, discover Symmes' Hole, and survey the Sandwich Islands, and five years are yet to elapse before all is satisfactorily settled with the officers who had command of the fleet. Verily it is a pity that poor Vendovi is dead.

Wilkes made an immediate effort to scotch the rumor that he had solicited, directly or indirectly, the command of the Expedition and procured testimony on the matter from Poinsett, Paulding, ex-President Van Buren, Dickerson, B. F. Butler, Amos Kendall, and Levi Woodbury: Paulding acknowledged that the appointment was made before he took office and that he had always believed his selection was made on grounds highly honourable to his professional character and scientific attainments;[8] Poinsett said it was conferred by the President on his recommendation "given without any solicitation whatever, and before you or any persons connected with you could have been aware of my intention to propose you for this service;"[9] Van Buren knew of no effort made in his behalf and said that the Department's embarrassment, due to the refusal of several officers, was obviated "by the spirit with which you entered upon the command and the capacity you was supposed to possess for a successful execution of its highly responsible duties."[10]

Upon his arrival in Washington, Wilkes made an official call upon Secretary Upshur to report the completion of his task in accordance with Instructions. In his autobiography he gave the following account of this visit:[11]

His reception of me was very cold he never offered to shake hands with me nor requested me to take a seat. I felt indignant at such treatment and my spirit rose. I took a seat unasked and expressed to him my astonishment at the course he was pursuing re-

---

8 Paulding to Wilkes, Aug. 3, 1842, Court-Martial Records.
9 Poinsett to Wilkes, June 14, 1842, Poinsett Papers.
10 Van Buren to Wilkes, July 22, 1842, Court-Martial Records.
11 Autobiography 6: pp. 1374–1376.

specting me, and towards the Expedition, that he was entirely mistaken as respected myself, and the great results the Expedition had achieved and all and every examination into my conduct, and that of the conduct of the Expedition would prove it. I was fully aware the course he had attempted to pursue, and I was entirely independent of him and well knew I had friends, who would have justice done me, and closed by saying that his attempt to wreck the Expedition would fail, and he would lose the brightest feather he could put into his bonnet in the course of action he had and was about to pursue. I took my leave, and prepared for war to the knife. . . . he had not a word to say and showed his agitation by putting on and taking off repeatedly his spectacles, particularly when I told him I was not to be crushed by his machinations. . . .

His only other interview with Upshur was when he was summoned to be asked who had written an anonymous communication containing charges against Brackenridge and some of the officers. The document in question was a closely written foolscap sheet which lay on the Secretary's desk.

I asked him if he expected me to do such an act, that I should treat it, if he desired me to tell him in the way I always treated such anonimous communications, he asked me how, I threw it upon the floor and put my foot upon it, & gave it a kick saying that was the way I treated all such papers or letters, and I immediately got up. I requested to know if there was any other business on which he wished to see me, he said no, so I took my departure leaving him somewhat abashed. I felt he deserved this rebuke and my feeling of repugnance at such a request that I did not hesitate to return his untoward act as I conceived was due to him.

When he recounted this incident to friends they laughed heartily, but Wilkes realized that Upshur had the power to give him much annoyance "but I had no idea of permitting him to act ungentlemanly towards me, I was an officer in the Navy, and was entitled to be shown all the respect my rank, and services entitled me." He relied upon the influence of these friends who applauded him although "they judged I was able to take care of myself, as they frequently told me."[12]

His official call upon President Tyler served to increase his disgust with the Whig Administration.

---

12 *Ibid.,* pp. 1377–1378.

I found him on entering seated in the center of a semi-circle around the fire, and about a dozen of the messiest looking fellows, all squirting their tobacco juice into the fire, and over the white marble hearth. Mr. Tyler got up and extended his hand to me and the attendant who had ushered me found me a chair, I was literally struck with surprise to find myself in such company at the President's House, it was exactly like a Virginia or North Carolina bar room, and after the chair was brought forward, the President said be seated Sir! and this was all the recognition I got of my presence, of course I felt obliged to tarry a short while, and then took my leave, and I have very great doubts if the President knew who I was, and am inclined to believe he did not, or was determined to ignore all that had anything to do with the Expedition; he continued his talk, and jokes with these boorish visitors, as soon as I could I made my escape, and glad to get beyond the vulgarity and boorishness of this squad of politicians, who had not the least idea of the respect due our chief magistrate, and I must add neither had the President any idea of the position he occupied as the head of the country.[13]

Indeed the President's situation was not a happy one. He had succeeded President Harrison after the latter had been in office for only a month. He was at odds with his own party because of his veto of the national bank bill favored by Clay and other Whig party leaders. He was more interested in the annexation of Texas than in remote California and more concerned about the settlement of the Maine boundary than the future of Oregon. Wilkes' friends told him that the President did not appear to believe in the discovery of an Antarctic continent. Believing that it was the Administration's policy to play down the Expedition's achievements, Wilkes became alarmed at the rumor that Robert Greenhaw, Librarian of the State Department, whom he characterized as a "half crazy individual" might be appointed to write the Expedition's history.[14]

In 1840 Greenhaw had written a *Memoir* on Oregon which a Senate Select Committee on Oregon had had printed. It described the geography and resources of that territory together with a statement of the basis for American claims to its possession. Wilkes decided to keep the journals and other documents in his own possession so as to prevent anyone but himself from

---

13 *Ibid.*, pp. 1379–1380.
14 *Ibid.*, pp. 1378–1379.

writing the history. He decided to accept Poinsett's invitation
to lecture on the subject of the Expedition before the National
Institute which had been formed largely in the expectation
that it would become depository for its collections. For three
evenings in June, Wilkes lectured in the hall of the Patent
Office, illustrating his talks with maps, drawings, etc. About
four hundred persons attended, including such notables as
J. Q. Adams, Benton, Upshur, Wickliffe, and other members
of the Cabinet and of Congress.[15]

He began by stating his surprise that so little was known
of such a highly creditable national undertaking.

I did not hesitate to throw the blame where it belonged, and
on those who were present, & seated near me—this drew the whole
attention of the audience and I gave a succinct view of all that was
interesting to be known, throughout the account there was a marked
interest and an audible approval when I closed—this brought Mr.
Wickliffe to his feet who endeavored to take me to task for having
stated very many things that the department considered that I was
not at liberty to divulge, he was followed by Mr. Preston in more
eloquent remarks & took strong ground in favor of my right, and
there was no right in the Navy Dept. to suppress what was truly the
public, Mr. Adams followed complimented me highly, and spoke of
the results in glowing terms and replied to Mr. Wickliffe's remarks,
as did many others among them Mr. Benton. The audience was
much interested in these remarks and complimentary. . . . [16]

Upshur offered a resolution of thanks and a request that
Wilkes prepare a synopsis of his remarks; the resolution was
accepted unanimously. The lectures made it possible for him
to thwart Upshur's order to deliver to his Office the journals
and logs as soon as practicable, for he needed the material in
order to make the synopsis. Eventually the House passed a
resolution favoring the retention of the records by the Joint
Committee of the Library and Upshur was persuaded to rescind
his order. Furthermore, the lectures and the synopsis helped
to persuade Congress to let Wilkes write the history. This was
due, particularly, to Judge Tappan, Senator from Ohio, and a

---

15 Wilkes to Poinsett, June 16, 1842; Washington *National Intelligencer*, June 25,
1842.
16 Autobiography 6: pp. 1388–1391.

member of the Library Committee, who interested himself in
the Expedition. He introduced a bill to have the superintendence of the collections and of the history and reports put into
the hands of the Committee. It became law August 26, 1842,
whereupon Upshur was persuaded to order Wilkes to prepare
a history and reports on hydrography, magnetism, and meteorology.[17]

The matter of most importance for Wilkes was that of
promotion. Believing that there was a movement on foot to
prevent it and knowing that Pinkney and Guillou had preferred charges against him, he requested a Court of Inquiry
to clear him in time to receive promotion before the Senate's
adjournment. Upshur refused this request and ordered his
court-martial along with the officers against whom he had preferred charges. This court was summoned to meet on board the
man-of-war *North Carolina* at the Brooklyn Navy Yard beginning July 25. When he asked whether he might expect to be
promoted as a "constructive and implied pardon for any alleged
offense" if acquitted, the Secretary replied in the negative.[18]

17 D. C. Haskell, *The Wilkes Expedition and its Publications*, pp. 34–35; W. J.
Rees, *The Smithsonian Institution*, pp. 219–220; Minutes of Joint Library Committee, Aug. 26, 1842, Tappan Papers **18**; Autobiography, pp. 1380–1382, 1392.
18 Upshur to Wilkes, June 21, 30, 1842, Ships of War, Letters **32**.

XXX
The Courts-Martial

CAPTAIN CHARLES STEWART was President of the Court and its other members were Captains Jacob Jones, Biddle, Ridgely, Downes, Barron, Read, Bolton, and Turner, Commanders Tatnall and Cunningham, and Lieutenants Gerry and du Pont. Noting that there were only two of his rank and only three with whom he was acquainted, Wilkes called it a picked court and thought most of its members indisposed to do him justice. The Court was charged with twenty-three cases altogether. At Wilkes' request it was agreed to take up his case after those of his subordinate officers May, Johnson, Guillou, and Pinkney.[1]

The Judge Advocate was Charles H. Winder of Baltimore, whom Wilkes characterized as "a young man without any knowledge of law, and destitute of character, and devoid of truth, who was a pet of the Secretary, and ready to do his bidding." Lieutenant du Pont thought him clever and likable but with little understanding of what was a military offense and what could or could not be substantiated by witnesses. Wilkes was represented by his friend Philip Hamilton.[2]

The Court was organized on July 25 and du Pont thought "a good mood & general cordiality" marked its opening session. He had a young man's reaction to serving with so many venerable and high-ranking officers who blocked his chances for promotion as long as they remained on active duty and confided to his friend Pendergrast that, "It is melancholy to see . . . the high physical condition of these old cocks, they look better & fresher than I remember any of them ten years ago." He thought half the charges and half the officers to be

---

1 Navy Dept. Archives, General Courts-Martial **43**, #823–26 and **44**, #827, Microfilm Columbia University, **51**, #26–27. Hereafter cited as G.C.M. Records.
2 Autobiography **6**: p. 1383; S. F. du Pont to Pendergrast, July 25, 1842, and Aug. 25, 1842, Samuel Francis du Pont Papers in Henry Francis du Pont Winterthur Collection, Eleutherian Mills Historical Library, cited hereafter as EMHL W9.

tried could have been disposed of by the Department and that the Expedition's officers appeared to be "the finest body of young men I have yet seen in the Navy."[3]

The charges against Passed Midshipman May were the first to be taken up and the first of these was for "insubordination and mutinous conduct" when, after Reynolds' transfer to the *Peacock*, May had applied for transfer for himself in a rude and disrespectful manner. It was quashed on May's plea that it occurred over two years before and the statute of limitations applied. A second charge of "disrespect to his superior in the execution of his office" arose from his manner of labeling a box of shells and his subsequent stormy interview with Wilkes. He had written a letter of apology but charges were preferred because it was his second offense. The Court decided that he had been disrespectful and sentenced him to be publicly reprimanded by the Secretary of the Navy.[4]

Johnson's trial followed on August 1-2 and, like May's, was quickly concluded and dealt with comparatively trivial matters. He was accused of giving away public property, a bowie-knife pistol, and of refusing to obey orders that made him subject to control by Eld, his inferior in rank. Wilkes emphasized that the Expedition was distinct from the regular Navy and that "when on Special duty by my Private instructions—Rank was not to be regarded." He justified sending Johnson home by reading a letter from Secretary Paulding, dated 14 December, 1839, saying that in this great undertaking whose results were being watched by the civilized world and, if successful, would redound to the credit of the United States.

you are in a great degree personally responsible, and are in my opinion fully justified in enforcing those measures, which you believe best qualified to ensure the attainment of the great objects of the Expedition. Cabals of discontented officers, must be promptly arrested, and their leaders, either kept in Subjection, or detached from the Squadron, as it is not to be endured that the purposes you are sent to attain, are to be defeated by the fantastic claims of rank, which I shall never recognize to the extent of preventing any Commanding officer from selecting such as he deems best qualified for a particular and special organization of his own Ship.

---

3 S. F. du Pont to Pendergrast July 25, to Sophie July 27, and to Charles Henry Davis July 29, EMHL W9–722, 724, 725.

4 G.C.M. Records **43**, #823.

Johnson was acquitted of both charges.[5]

Assistant Surgeon Guillou's trial lasted from August 3 to 6 and was more complicated than the first two. His troubles stemmed from his claim that Wilkes had given him a verbal promise of promotion to Acting Surgeon before the Expedition started and that, when there was a vacancy, the duty and pay of Surgeon was given to Dr. Fox, his junior. At Sydney he had refused Ringgold's order to make requisitions for medicine on the grounds that it was not his duty and, at Honolulu, he had cut pages containing personal matter from his journal.

Of the six charges against Guillou, the Court decided he was guilty of four, including disobedience, neglect of duty, disrespect, and disobedience to orders. He was sentenced to dismissal from the Service.

Secretary Upshur accepted the Court's decision but suggested that the Service would not be hurt if the President restored him to duty. Guillou collected letters attesting his good moral character, assiduous attention to duty, and professional skill. Some excused him because of his inexperience in naval matters or, as Emmons expressed it, "a misconception of his rights & duties." Dr. Fox thought he was contending for right in the abstract and if there was error it was because "we were all young and inexperienced." His parents, refugees from the insurrection in Santo Domingo, had many friends in Philadelphia and his brother, Constant Guillou, a respected member of the bar, made a special appeal asserting that he had only refused to perform the duty of a Surgeon when not holding that rank. Guillou objected to being tried by sea officers instead of his peers i.e., medical officers, and claimed that he had been sufficiently punished by being kept under arrest for two years in strict confinement on board ship. In consideration of Guillou's good moral character and long confinement, President Tyler commuted the sentence to "suspension without pay or emoluments for twelve months from the date of the sentence."[6]

Pinkney's trial was also complicated and lasted from August 6 to 13. He had been disgruntled to have officers of inferior rank command the schooners and, when finally given

---

5 *Ibid.*, #824.
6 *Ibid.*, #825.

command of the *Flying Fish,* felt that her needs were disregarded while Wilkes thought he failed to keep her in good condition. At New Zealand he had had $3,000 worth of unauthorized repairs including work which was considered unnecessary and merely for convenience. His relations with the Commander had come to a climax at Honolulu when he attempted to forward charges against him unsealed so that they could be seen by others.

In his defense Pinkney said that he, like the other officers, had started out with great enthusiasm. His friends recommended Wilkes — "But, alas! gentlemen, I forgot that he who had once violated the chastity of rank, must have made himself its enemy forever." In belatedly granting him command of the *Flying Fish,* Wilkes had tacitly admitted his error in not doing so earlier and his mortification was the sole cause to which Pinkney could trace his strange animosity. As to his failure to keep a journal, he had decided after a few months' effort that his observations were "such an idle affectation of research, that I destroyed a record of which I felt thoroughly ashamed."

The Court found him guilty of two out of six charges, namely, "treating superior with contempt" and "disobedience of orders." He was sentenced to public reprimand by the Secretary of the Navy and to six months' suspension from duty.[7]

Wilkes' trial lasted from August 17 to September 7. There was one change in the Court, Captain Barron being replaced by Captain Cassin. Guillou made seven charges and Pinkney four, these were set forth in thirty-five specifications of which seven were striken out at the outset and two during the trial.

From the beginning Wilkes felt that the Court was more interested in trying him than his officers. The prosecutor had all the witnesses testify as to his character and reputation when trying the others. In turn Reynolds, Emmons, Blunt, Couthouy, North, Maury, Walker, and Perry expressed a general opinion that Wilkes was harsh, overbearing, insulting, easily excited and offended, and, when excited, his manner was violent and his tone of voice frequently disrespectful. Alden, who had served with the Commander over a period of nearly five years, said he had seen him when he was "exceedingly kind and

---

7 *Ibid.,* #826.

attentive" and the opposite "just as much one way as the other."

There was also favorable testimony: Ringgold said Wilkes was "very prompt and energetic, and decided in his manner," courteous and gentlemanly towards his officers; Carr knew nothing of his being "harsh, overbearing, and insulting personally"; and Fox testified as to his devotion to duty, averaging about five hours a day for sleep and even going without sleep for such a long time as to affect his health.

Hudson said that,

Mr. Wilkes is of an excitable character, and he wishes every officer to move when he gives him an order. His manner is like that of every other active officer—he wishes things to be done promptly, when he orders it to be done . . . I have never seen him excited without cause.[8]

The bitter feelings of many of the officers towards Wilkes was evident. Du Pont mentioned, in a letter to his wife, that during May's trial,

One of the witnesses examined today showed by his manner & tone, as well as the force of his words, that bitter & heartburning hostility which pervades the officers of the Exploring Exp. against their commander—the Court is crowded with them, hanging on every word that is said with an intensity of interest & feeling that I have never seen equalled—I have seen frequently excitement on ship board, & in squadrons, but the indignation which seems to pervade these young men, must have sprung from some cause not usual in the Service—they are the handsomest & most prepossessing fellows you can ever conceive, but there does not seem a man of any experience or knowledge to contend with such difficulties, among them.

On the other hand Wilkes seems perfectly self-possessed, he was examined today as a witness—he looks broken & very old however. Hudson was also in court; poor fellow, he seems universally condemned for the loss of his ship, & his having waved his rank to go with Wilkes of whom he is said to have been much afraid.[9]

Du Pont thought the officers gave evidence in clear, positive, and spirited manner and even those who were calm and

8 *Ibid.*, #823.
9 S. F. du Pont to Sophie July 27, EMHL W9-724.

received no injury from Wilkes said there was just cause for the asperity of the others. He was particularly impressed by Perry's testimony, "the best delivered in tone & manner that has yet come before us." He was becoming more and more convinced that the charges against the officers were trivial or arose from trivial circumstances, that those against Wilkes himself were not much more serious, and that the whole affair did not justify a court-martial. The Expedition by its composition, special character, and orders was more civil than military and all amenability to martial law should have been ruled out. He heard that at one time consideration was given to putting a merchant captain in command. Wilkes was a "disagreeable, overbearing, & disgusting commander," but he doubted that he had transcended his authority and "the whole matter could easily have been arranged by the Secretary."[10]

After witnesses had been examined and cross-examined, Wilkes made a long and detailed statement in his own defense. He asserted that upon arriving home, after having successfully carried out the objects of the Expedition, he found himself condemned in absence and an effort made to prejudge him which was so far successful

that the press has teemed with that unqualified denunciation of me personally, and of my actions yet undivulged in the form of legal evidence, as would seem to have been intended to overawe this court and force from it by the power of that mighty engine, a verdict in opposition to the dictates of their own consciences.[11]

He emphasized that he had not sought the command, was surprised and flattered to have it offered, and had requested Poinsett to offer it to all those above him on the Navy list, particularly those attached to the Expedition. At his insistence the scientific objects connected with the "education of an accomplished seaman or within the scope of the medical profession" were given to the naval officers, namely: astronomy, hydrography, physics, and meteorology. Had these been given to civilians, as originally planned, the sea officers would have

---

10 S. F. du Pont to Davis July 29 and Aug. 31, and to Sophie July 29, EMHL W9–725, 737, 726.

11 Wilkes' "Defence" as submitted to the Court has been printed separately along with the "Record of Proceedings." Cited, hereafter, as "Defence," and in this instance p.1.

had nothing to do but keep watch and attend to ordinary shipboard duties. Some of the officers were lax in the performance of these extra duties and some avoided them, in fact, a "cabal" existed and its members attempted "to thwart all the objects of the Expedition, which were not consistent with the ease of the gentlemen who composed it." Yet the officers were all volunteers and were paid extra compensation for scientific work at the same rate as those on coast survey. He had not spared himself and did not spare others in the performance of this public service.

In his summation Wilkes said that charges of cruelty and disobedience to orders were based on attacks made on Pacific islanders and he should be tried for murder, arson, and robbery, or not at all. His orders recognized that there would be times when necessity must be his guide.

He admitted that the charge of illegal punishment of men under his command was the only one that caused him the least anxiety, and averred that it was infrequent and necessary for the good order and discipline of the service. Navy Regulations stated that "any theft, not exceeding twenty dollars, may be punished at the discretion of the captain, and above that sum, as a court martial shall inflict." The six men who stole liquor from the *Relief* at Callao committed a court-martial offense, but there was no time to hold a court and, therefore, they were given more than the legal twelve lashes. The other illegal punishments were inflicted upon deserters at times when courts-martial could not be held.

A charge of "scandalous conduct tending to the destruction of morals" was based on his official claim of having discovered land in Antarctica on January 19, 1840, when the sightings were so doubtful that none were entered in the ships' logs. Eld and Reynolds, however, testified that subsequent sightings convinced them that they had seen land on that day and indications of land as early as the fifteenth.

Guillou's final charge was that Wilkes committed "Scandalous conduct unbecoming an Officer" in mounting the blue broad pennant, in wearing a coat with four buttons on each cuff, four down each pocket fold, four under each pocket flap, and two epaulet straps, the uniform of a Captain, and in signing himself "Captain." Wilkes admitted the truth of the allegation, but denied the charge. With respect to the pennant he quoted Navy Regulations which stated that "No officer shall wear a broad pendant of any kind, unless he shall have been appointed to command a squadron, or vessels on separate service" and, in regard to the uniform, cited a new Regulation which said that "When an officer shall receive an acting appointment to fill a vacancy . . . he may assume the uniform, and annex his acting rank to his signature." He, therefore, pleaded usage with respect to an act nowhere forbidden and, as to assuming the title of Captain, considered the charge entirely frivolous "when every skipper of a North River sloop bears it, and a midshipman, if in command of a tender, would be called by it."

Pinkney charged "scandalous conduct unbecoming an officer and gentleman" when on two occasions he was reprimanded within the hearing of all, the commander using the phrase "God Damn it." Wilkes denied using that language on either occasion and cited the testimony of witnesses who did not mention it, except Blunt who said he shouted through the trumpet, "God Damn it Sir, you have disobeyed my orders; I ordered you off at sunset, and now it is a quarter or half an hour after it. Don't do it again, Sir; don't do it again." He argued that Blunt could not have heard him because he stood at the starboard gangway while the schooner was on the larboard quarter and the trumpet directed away from him. In a letter to his sister Johnson remarked that "One thing he [Wilkes] should be d - - - d for is abusing Simon in his defense— trying to impugn his testimony when he knew that he himself was lying at the time."[12]

Pinkney's other charges were: "neglect of duty" with respect to the long delay in forwarding to the Secretary his letter of complaint; "oppression" in regard to his arrest and long confinement on shipboard; and "cruelty and oppression" in refusing to discharge four marines whose terms of enlistment had expired.

Wilkes accused Pinkney of insinuating that the *Sea Gull* was lost because Reid and Bacon were incompetent and said,

I might contrast the intelligence, attention to duty and untiring activity of the lamented Reid and Bacon with all that is opposite

---

12 Johnson to his sister, Sept., 1842, Johnson Letters.

in the character of Lt. Pinkney. He has told you that he is no surveyor, his own evidence . . . must have satisfied you that he is no sailor. I shall content myself in vindication of the memory of the dead, with saying, that two finer or more talented young men were not to be found in the Squadron, nor do I know of their superior in the whole navy.

He criticized the Attorney General for acting as if he were in a "common law" court acting as counsel for the prosecution in adducing evidence against him and suppressing favorable evidence, instead of acting impartially. He disavowed any personal reflection on the Secretary of the Navy. Although Upshur had signed the charges against him, he, at the close of Wilkes' lecture before the National Institute, had commended him and his officers in the warmest terms saying that the report on Oregon was by itself ample compensation for the whole cost of the Expedition and that its results were highly valuable and honorable, not to this country alone, but to the whole world. He erred, however, in not permitting a court of inquiry which would have obviated the need of a court-martial.

In his final appeal Wilkes told the members of the Court that they held in their hands "the honour, dearer than life, of a brother officer" made conspicuous by circumstances and whose condemnation would reflect discredit on the Navy itself. He should be acquitted of all charges and

may I not venture to say that a bare verdict of not guilty is far less than the nation has a right to require at your hands? Its honour, its glory, the untarnished lustre of its unconquered flag, have all been assailed through me. With you rests the power of vindicating that honour, exalting that glory, and wiping off any stain which these proceedings have cast upon that banner.[13]

He felt strongly about newspaper misrepresentations, believing that a *Herald* reporter was given "the most outrageous misrepresentation of the evidence and paid for it as I discovered afterwards through my friends." He also believed that several of the Court had positions held out to them to which they were ordered immediately after its adjournment.[14]

---

13 Defence, pp. 50–53.
14 Autobiography 6: p. 1384.

Du Pont, writing "Pender" September 22, the day on which the verdict was announced, said the papers had grown tired of the trials and the *Herald* had even stopped reporting, Bennett coming out for Wilkes "having it is said received seventy $ for his recanting article." As soon as Wilkes knows his sentence "a grand intrigue, public & private will be entered into, to raise him to a port Captaincy—we have had the *Commercial* already out, telling what was done in like case for Parry, RN, Vancouver, etc." He thought, however, that Wilkes and Hudson had "used themselves up" and though the sentence might seem astonishing it would "be no assessment of the way the man is estimated *as a man.*" He felt, as a junior member of the Court, that the old Captains were behind the times, alive to questions of discipline and respect for a superior but not to moral delinquencies.[15] Wilkes had emphasized that he derived his ideas regarding discipline from the senior officers whose methods had been the means of achieving "the proudest laurels of which our country can boast" and which he had found all-sufficient under the most trying circumstances, a source of contentment far more than of complaint. He avowed himself opposed to the new idea "that authority is to be derived from the *steerage* and *wardroom,* and that officers are to be shown the instructions of their commander, and be civilly asked if they will perform their duty."[16]

On the other hand, du Pont remarked that "twenty years ago, if Lieuts. had given such testimony, I believe they would have been sent to jail—& the court would have turned around to try them." But he was in agreement with the Court's decisions believing the sentences, on the whole, not far from the mark.[17]

The scientists were not involved in the trials, except that Couthouy testified regarding the attempted landing at Clermont de Tonnere against native opposition. Pickering expected to be called in connection with Johnson's giving away the bowie-knife pistol, which he considered a trivial matter, and was relieved that he was not questioned regarding Johnson's ability as an overland leader. He did not enjoy being in

---

15 S. F. du Pont to Pendergrast Sept. 22 and Oct. 6, EMHL W9–742, 747.
16 Defence, p. 4.
17 S. F. du Pont to Pendergrast Oct. 6, EMHL W9–747.

New York and idle, denied access to his notes when he wanted to be preparing them for publication before many things faded from memory.[18]

Wilkes was found not guilty or the charges not proven in every case except that of illegal punishment of seamen and was sentenced to be publicly reprimanded by the Secretary of the Navy. Upshur carried it out immediately writing Wilkes as follows:[19]

Sir: you have been duly tried by a Court Martial, found guilty of illegally punishing or causing to be punished, men in the squadron under your command, and sentenced to be publicly reprimanded by the Secretary of the Navy, at such time and place as he may deem proper. This sentence is approved.

The country which honored you with a command far above the just claims of your rank in the navy, had a right to expect that you would, at least, pay a scrupulous respect to her laws. The rebuke, which by the judgment and advice of your own associates in the service, she now gives you for having violated those laws in an important particular, involving the rights of others of her citizens, will be regarded by all, as the mildest form in which she could express her displeasure.

This did appear to be a mild punishment but to Wilkes, according to du Pont, the sentence and the wording of the reprimand "cut to the very soul" for "Wilkes extreme arrogance, & conviction that he would not only be acquitted, but it would be accompanied with a flourish of trumpets & a swipe at his accusers, has thus rendered his sentence doubly severe to himself—he writhed severely under it, & swears vengeance against Upshur."[20]

[18] Pickering to M. O. Pickering Aug. 1, 1842, Pickering Papers.
[19] Upshur to Wilkes Sept. 22, 1842, Tappan Papers 17.
[20] S. F. du Pont to Pendergrast Oct. 6 and to Davis Oct. 14, EMHL W9-747, 750.

XXXI
First Fruits

WHILE THE COURTS-MARTIAL were taking place little could be done in the way of arranging specimens, preparing scientific reports, or writing a narrative. The Courts' findings were not momentous nor the punishments severe, but the ill-feelings vented during those hot summer days were not quickly forgotten.

Almost immediately salt was rubbed into open wounds by the Treasury Department's 4th Auditor who disallowed extra pay for scientific work as being contrary to law. Paulding, on one of his first days in office, had sanctioned the extra pay on Wilkes' assurance that Poinsett had agreed to it. The officers petitioned Congress and, upon the recommendation of the Senate Committee on Naval Affairs, the pay already received was allowed, but it still depended upon the Commander's certification, which he refused to give in the case of Pinkney and of Guillou,[1] that scientific work had been performed.

There was a prolonged bout with the Treasury Department over the matter of Wilkes' own pay because he had directed Purser Waldron to credit him with the pay of a captain plus that of a superintendent of Coast Survey. The 4th Auditor said it should have been that of a lieutenant-commandant plus that of a lieutenant instead of a superintendent. The overpayment for the period of the cruise amounted to $12,000 and was owed to the Government. The matter eventually came before Congress and Wilkes' claim was accepted, but only after it had been in abeyance for ten years.[2]

The matter of promotion was foremost in the minds of the three leaders of the Expedition and the two youngest

---

[1] House Committee on Naval Affairs, *Report*, #270, Feb. 25, 1843, and Senate *Report* #71, Jan. 16, 1843, both 27 Cong., 3 Sess.: Upshur to Wilkes, Apr. 23, 1843, Ships of War, Naval Archives. In the end Pinkney and Guillou received this extra pay.

[2] Autobiography 7: p. 1403. A Captain's pay was $4,000 and that of a Lieutenant Commandant $1,800.

passed midshipmen. Hudson, having seniority, was promoted to commander in November, 1842, and Wilkes, to his chagrin, had to wait until July, 1843. Ringgold did not receive that rank until 1849. Eld and Colvocoresses were both promoted to lieutenant in February, 1843.

The cold reception given the members of the Expedition was keenly felt. There was no official word of commendation and public apathy was in contrast to the great interest at the time of their departure. Upshur dismissed the scientists, informing them that there was no authorization for their further employment. The Whig Administration seemed to consider that they had had their share of employment and glory and it was now time to give way to someone else. Couthouy, arriving home early, went to Washington to see what was being done about his specimens to which he had attached numbered metal tags corresponding to descriptions in his notes. He found that J. K. Townsend, a retired clergyman, had been employed to arrange them and had taken all the tags out of the jars because they discolored the alcohol, and had not substituted any other means of identification.[3]

The first shipment of specimens went to the Peale Museum at Philadelphia under the care of Titian's brother Franklin, and the first Congressional appropriation for their care was $500 as part of an appropriation for the Army in July, 1840. A year later $5,000 was voted to pay for their care and transfer to Washington, this time as part of an appropriation for the Navy. The transfer was engineered by the National Institute which assumed control of the collections after their placement in the Great Hall of the Patent Office alongside its own collection. After that $20,000 was appropriated for their care but the first custodians were political appointees, including Townsend and a couple of taxidermists, who proceeded to unpack and dry specimens in preparation for their exhibition. When Dana finally saw his crustacea he found many small ones dried and transfixed with pins obliterating their "characters" and making the larger ones unfit for dissection.[4]

---

3 *Proceedings of Biological Society*, Washington, **4**; Couthouy to Tappan, Jan. 15, 1842, Tappan Papers **17**.
4 Haskell, *Wilkes Expedition*, p. 7.

At Wilkes' suggestion, Judge Tappan called back Pickering to arrange the collections and he, in turn, called back the
other scientists.[5] Pickering assumed that the collections were
the responsibility of the National Institute and it was not clear
to Peale, Rich, Agate, Brackenridge, or Dana, when they arrived, whether it was the Institute or the Library Committee
that was in charge. Dana described the confused state of affairs
to his friend Redfield. He had assumed that the Institute had
authority but soon after Congress opened "there was a sudden
change in affairs." Judge Tappan and Wilkes were determined
to prevent the expenditure of any part of the Congressional
funds for the particular interests of the Institute. In the Institute's view the Scientific Corps should give way to others;
however, without Congressional help, the Institute's "castle-
building" was coming to an end. Dana predicted that it would
slide down hill rapidly "with a smack to nothing at the bottom," for it had proceeded on too grand a scale, was already
in debt, and its members had quarreled among themselves
and with the Patent Office. Its meetings consisted mainly of
reading the minutes of previous meetings with little new business to record except lists of specimens received. Judge Tappan,
something of a conchologist and interested in the sciences, was
their Captain now and was determined to have their publication "a splendid one, and his ideas and plans with regard to it
are what they should be." Wilkes, to his mortification, had no
control over any but his own departments which he was push-
ing and had already sent Drayton off to see about making engravings.[6]

It should be said for the Institute that it served the Expedition well in preventing the wide dispersal and possible loss
of some of its collections, and it also secured the initial appropriations for their care.

Peale shared Dana's view of the Institute. In addition to
his scientific interest in the collections he was in need of employment to support his family since the Philadelphia Museum was on the rocks. He was paid $120 a month and had
Tappan's assurance that he might expect an increase. He wrote
his friend George Ord that, as the Institute had been rebuffed

---

5 *Ibid.*, p. 7; Wilkes to Tappan, Aug. 25, 1842, Tappan Papers **17**.
6 Dana to W. C. Redfield, Feb. 1, 1843, Yale University Library.

in its effort to take control, they could now look forward to finishing their task quietly and in poverty.[7]

As a member of the American Philosophical Society, Peale was invited to give a report on the Expedition at its centennial meeting scheduled for May, 1843, but there was not time to get permission from the Library Committee whose members were absent from Washington. He took the opportunity, however, to let that Society's officers know about developments in Washington—how the scientists had been dismissed and then recalled

in a more humble and subdued capacity, and under a different organization; with the loss of much valuable time, and some pecuniary inconvenience.

The specimens in natural history which have been our pride, can no longer be pointed to as the monuments of our labor; They have been stuffed into miserable effigies for the want of working drawings, dimensions, and a knowledge of their characteristic attitudes, and proportions; And have become "bones of contention" among persons not connected with our researches; Men who have not dared the elements, or exposed their lives to seek them like the members of the Expedition; but sitting comfortably by their firesides, boldly assert that *"these collectors were amply paid* for their labors!"

The *pay* we rec'd in the Expedition barely sustained our anxious families during four years that we were absent and it is quite needless, now to distress, or insult us.

He thought the Philosophical Society should have been given control of the collections, for it had given scientific advice, helped to select the Scientific Corps, and had a hundred years' experience in scientific matters.[8]

The Patent Office was located in a large building bounded by Seventh and Ninth and F and G Streets, Northwest Washington, and the collections were deposited in its upper Hall. Every month Pickering reported to Tappan on the state of affairs. In April, 1843, he stated that he had arranged for the services of Brackenridge, that Dana and Hale were both "indefatigable in preparing their materials for publication," that Rich "seems really to be at work in earnest," that Peale worked

---

7 Peale to Ord, Mar. 14, 1845, Amer. Philos. Soc.
8 Peale to Bache and Ludlow, May 8, 1843, Amer. Philos. Soc.

in his own rooms but was frequently in the Hall busily engaged with his specimens, and that he himself had been unpacking shells.[9]

Couthouy still hankered to have a part in writing the report on crustacea and wrote Tappan that he hoped to be released from a business engagement "now a worse than Egyptian bondage," but he was not happy at the prospect of receiving a paltry $120 a month with a wife and two children to support and, in the end, decided not to come to Washington.

By June, Pickering had selected shells for exhibition and packed duplicates in boxes, planning to arrange them in two sets, one geographic and the other by genera. His sympathies were with the Institute—Tappan called him its showman—and in July he asked to be relieved of his curatorship so that he might devote himself to preparing his notes for publication.[10] After his abdication, Pickering decided to go abroad for further study along anthropological lines before undertaking the writing of a volume on the "Races of Man." His absence during the subsequent year and a half slowed up the preparation of the scientific volumes because he had interested himself in several of the sciences and his journal was the fullest of any of the Corps.

Upon his departure, the supervision of the collections was turned over to Wilkes who immediately pressed Tappan to put an end to the Institute's attempts to have the Expedition "do work for it." He was scornful of its claim to having an *"immense* and *valuable"* collection of its own and repeated the remark of Ellsworth, Director of the Patent Office, that they had "two or three oyster bottles and a double headed calf or two." At the same time, he expected that, eventually, the Expedition's collections would be turned over to the Institute. But for the present he wanted it kept apart, believing that the Institute would neglect it and, in fact, some of its members had helped themselves to exhibits.[11]

A large sign was placed over the door of the Hall reading in gold letters, "Collection of the Exploring Expedition" and

---

9 Pickering to Tappan, Apr. 25, 1843, Tappan Papers **17**.

10 *Ibid.,* July 23, 1843, **18**.

11 Wilkes to Abert, Sept. 16, 1843, and to Tappan, Sept. 22, 1843, Tappan Papers **18·**

notices to the same effect were posted for the guidance of visitors. As Peale said, from the time Wilkes took charge, "the National Gallery assumed rank among the places worthy of being visited by citizens and strangers in the metropolis."[12] It became necessary to provide for policing since the Hall attracted idlers who walked about smoking and chewing and spitting.

A greenhouse was built in back of the Patent Office for the living plants under Brackenridge's care. Eventually, these were removed to the Botanical Garden below the Capitol. Visitors requesting plant specimens and cuttings became troublesome and, as the collection could not be enlarged if this was permitted, Wilkes instructed Brackenridge to refuse all requests, thus producing some altercations, sometimes involving Congressmen. On one occasion, President Tyler's lady left in a huff and complained of Brackenridge's action to the Commissioner of Patents, referring to him as "one of the workmen."[13]

As a result of these acts, Wilkes acquired some new enemies, especially among some members of the Institute who now "cut" his acquaintance and he felt hampered at every step by his enemies in the Navy Department. Whenever he asked for a document, the file clerks seemed unable to locate it or were very slow in delivering it. His request for the assistance of Lieutenants Budd, Carr, and Totten, his clerk Stuart, purser Waldron, and Drayton, was granted, but Eld was ordered to sea the very day his services were requested. Upshur said it would be against public interest to change his orders, to which Wilkes replied there were plenty of officers capable of performing sea duty but none who could replace this young man in scientific work.

Eld was not anxious to go out again on sea duty, especially on the "cockle-shell" *Wave*, and came to Washington just at the time, as it happened, that Upshur took Webster's place as Secretary of State, and Henshaw, the new Secretary of the Navy, permitted the change. By the end of August, 1843, Eld was installed at Mrs. Kennedy's boarding house and continued in this shore duty for the next two years. Wilkes wanted

---

12 Peale to Ord, July 3, 1845, Amer. Philos. Soc.
13 Autobiography 6: pp. 1395–1399. To the amusement of the ladies Wilkes had a guard follow chewers around carrying a "kit" of water and a sponge.

him because he understood the work, was anxious to improve himself, asked no favors, and was determined to do his duty at whatever cost to himself.[14] Along with other members of the Expedition, Eld had sacrificed his physique during the strenuous days of surveying under all kinds of adverse conditions. He had had a first attack of rheumatism in 1833, a recurrence in 1839, and every year thereafter. Its effects did not wear off easily, its piercing throbs continuing for weeks at a time. He wrote his father in June, 1846, that he was unable to work for three days and, when he had a few moments' lull, he would crawl into town, so that his room could be put in order and he could get away from its four walls. Asked how he was and where he had been, he would try to answer amiably; the questioners were always surprised to hear that he had been sick, he looked so well, and how could he have rheumatism at his age? The Navy doctor gave him phosphate ammonia in sarsaparilla and burgundy pitch plaster which brought relief.[15]

By the summer of 1846 Eld and the officers working on charts had had enough of this duty and, with the country at war with Mexico, applied to go to sea. Their Washington days had not been all work and no play. Eld had become very friendly with Wilkes' daughter Janie. His career was cut short by yellow fever which caused his death in 1850.

The charts were one of the first and most valued products of the Expedition. Several copies were made of each, so as to leave nothing to the discretion of the engravers and to insure against loss by fire. A controversy with Senator Benton arose over the Columbia River charts for he was convinced that that river provided one of the most favorable harbors in the world and secured statements from Knox, Reynolds, and Blair in support of his view, which Wilkes refuted in newspaper statements. To Wilkes' further annoyance some of the Columbia River settlers claimed credit for the Expedition's survey.[16]

---

14 Wilkes to Tappan, Apr. 30, 1843, Tappan Papers **18**.

15 Eld to his Father, June 28, 1846, Eld Papers.

16 When two officers (probably Reynolds and Blair) asked to borrow the *Flying Fish's* log for the Columbia River period Wilkes refused to let it out of his office fearing they might try to change it in their own handwriting, Wilkes to Jack, Aug. 2 and 9, 1846, John Wilkes Letter Book; Drayton to Wilkes, Sept. 11, 1850, Ex.Ex. Miscel. Papers.

The Fiji Islands charts were particularly useful because so little was known of that area and, as Dana told Asa Gray, they were far superior to D'Urville's, the work of a few days, since they represented three and a half months' survey. Dana thought some of the officers were excellent surveyors and, whatever might be said of Wilkes and his *Narrative*, the hydrographical department was well carried out.[17]

The *Narrative* became Wilkes' immediate concern and he produced this five-volume history in remarkably short time, writing mostly at night. His driving force and self-confidence were exhibited in this as in everything else he undertook. He wanted the world to know about the Expedition's achievements and felt he could do the job better than anyone else.

The Act of Congress which gave the direction of the publication of the *Narrative* to the Library Committee limited the number of copies to one hundred.[18] The reason for this was not so much to hold down expenses, for the printing and binding were to be of the finest quality, but rather to emphasize their value by making them scarce, this being a national undertaking and the copies meant for presentation to foreign governments. It was to be modeled after an excellent set of ten volumes printed by the French government describing the scientific achievements of the voyage of the *Astrolabe* under D'Urville during the years 1826-1829 and distributed during the years 1830-1835.[19]

Wilkes was well aware that Greenhow and others would like to write the narrative if he did not. J. N. Reynolds, the original aspirant for that honor, showed up in Washington late in 1842 offering his services to Judge Tappan and suggesting that the publication could be "easily made, if rightly begun and put in and kept in proper hands."[20] But as long as

---

17 Gilman, *op. cit.*, p. 149.

18 Haskell, *op. cit.*, p. 9. By a Resolution of Feb. 20, 1845, Congress determined that the hundred copies should be distributed as follows: one to each State in the Union; two each to France, Great Britain, and Russia; one each to twenty-five designated countries, one to the Naval Lyceum, Brooklyn; one each to Wilkes, Hudson, and Ringgold; two to the Library of Congress; the balance to to be held for later distribution to new States and Territories and additional Nations.

19 Gilman, *op. cit.*, p. 144; Autobiography 7: p. 1436.

20 J. N. Reynolds to Library Committee, Dec. 25, 1842, Tappan Papers 17.

Wilkes had possession of the journals he was the only one in
a position to do the writing. They and the ships' logs were his
primary sources and the extensive descriptions of places and
peoples were derived from information from a variety of
sources, especially from consuls and missionaries. In reviewing
the journals he noticed many misstatements and malicious
remarks but declared himself more amused than angry. Lieutenant Lee requested that his journal should not be used as it
contained things he regretted having written, so Wilkes returned it with the seal unbroken. This helped to indicate to
the other officers that he did not consider their journals of
great importance and was relying mainly on his own.[21]

Drayton was of great assistance in the selection of illustrations and in superintending the making of engravings. Wilkes
was determined that none of the engravings or scientific writings should be done by foreigners and Drayton, an experienced engraver and colorist himself, found the means of having
all such work done in this country. He was on very good terms
with the Commander who had confidence in his ability and
good taste and admired him because he was "economical of
time, and showed an example of industry that is seldom to
be met with."[22] In fact, they were on such friendly terms that
Drayton could safely converse and correspond with him in a
bantering tone—a kind of court jester and handyman. He contributed his own drawings and traveled about arranging for
the printing and negotiating with scientists. Although Wilkes
did not rate himself as an artist, twenty-one woodcuts, six
full-page plates, and nine vignettes were made from his
sketches.

The *Narrative* was completed in January, 1844—a hercu-
lean task, the five volumes totaling about 2,500 printed pages.
His wife helped and Judge Tappan read and approved the
manuscript. Wilkes aimed to be truthful and to avoid vitu-
peration. When it came to the printing he found he had much
to learn. He sent the first chapter to the printer with instructions to conform exactly to his spelling and punctuation and
saw it come back covered with corrections and accompanied by a letter from Mr. Sherman, the printer, pointing

---

21 Autobiography 5: p. 1038 and 7: pp. 1455–1458.
22 *Ibid.* 7: pp. 1407–1408.

out gently the absurdity of his instructions. Wilkes then visited the printing office to learn the operations involved and employed a proofreader recommended by Fenimore Cooper. Sherman did the work carefully, using the best hand-made paper and taking four months to print the five volumes and atlas.[23]

A reason for Wilkes' haste was the publication in book form in 1844 of Greenhaw's *Memoir* enlarged and now entitled *The History of Oregon and California and other Territories in the North-West Coast of North America*. It contained a footnote mentioning the Expedition and the *Narrative* soon to be published.

Although Congress provided for only 100 copies the contract with the printer called for a "token" of 250 copies. Wilkes requested the right to purchase for himself the 150 extra copies and the copyright for the *Narrative* and *Atlas*. The Committee granted his request and also gave him the right to publish a larger edition, at his own expense except for the free use of the government-owned engravings. This larger edition of 1,000 copies was to be octavo instead of quarto and to have less expensive black cloth covers instead of dark green morocco ones.

The two editions came out almost together at the end of 1844. Wilkes was accused of breaking the law in publishing for private benefit and Congressman J. W. Davis was made chairman of a Select Committee to look into the matter. The Commander prepared a long statement explaining that his official report to the Secretary had already been printed, in part at least, in the newspapers and that the *Narrative* gave his own individual views and observations which the copyright made his property. He needed the copyright to prevent the publication of a garbled edition and hoped that a less expensive edition might "diffuse a full knowledge of the results of the Expedition."

The demand for the *Narrative* was such that three additional printings were made in 1845 and a total of fifteen editions made before the last one in 1858. Of these editions two were condensations into single volumes and two were two-volume condensations. Of the latter, one was published in

---

23 *Ibid.*, pp. 1440–1443.

London and the other, translated into German, was published in Stuttgart. The *Atlas* appeared in only three editions.

To reassure the Davis Committee, Wilkes had Waldron estimate the total cost of the Expedition, beginning when he took command. The figure arrived at was $750,000 and he claimed that this was $100,000 less than it would have cost to operate the Squadron's vessels on coastal duty and in port during an equal period of three years and ten months. That difference would nearly pay for the cost of the publication of the charts, the *Narrative,* ten scientific and nine folio atlas volumes.[24]

The publication of the *Narrative* brought Wilkes both "good & ill blasts" and, as he wrote Jack, he believed he was hardened to both abuse and praise and that neither could throw him off balance.[25]

Philip Hone thought it worth the twenty-five dollars it cost and that, besides the value of its contents "and the very respectable style, it is superior in print, paper, and embellishments to any work of an equal size ever published in the United States."[26]

It was a remarkable achievement to write such a lengthy work in such a short time even though it was largely a compilation. The author was elated at the way it sold and wrote Jack that he felt he had gained his end in having it published in such a creditable manner and "financially I may reap some advantages though not the extent it was first supposed." Commander and Mrs. Wilkes celebrated with a large party at the end of 1845 and he told Jack that all the elite of Washington had been invited, that it was a magnificent affair and written up in the papers.[27]

The Expedition's members read the *Narrative* with mixed feelings. Eld, closer to Wilkes than most of the others, wrote his father before its publication that he thought it would be first rate or, at least, beautifully gotten up and would reflect credit on everybody.

---

24 *Ibid.,* pp. 1446–1451; Wilkes to Davis, Jan. 28, 1845, Tappan Papers **20.**
25 Mrs. Wilkes to John with postscript by Com. Wilkes, June, 1845, John Wilkes Letter Book.
26 Nevins (ed.) *Diary of Philip Hone* (New York, 1927), Mar. 31, 1845.
27 Wilkes to Jack, Jan. 8, 1846, John Wilkes Letter Book.

W. will come off in flying colours having literally trampled down
all opposition to his views from the President of these United States
and his Cabinet down. The more I see of him the more I am impressed with his indomitable perseverance & tenacity "like a cork
he cannot be sunk."

After publication he sent his father a copy and said that the
Commander

has soft soaped me occasionally which by the bye I would not have
wished asked or expected — all I require is a simple statement of
facts. Wilkes appears to have my welfare at heart and when it does
not clash with himself & others he makes all very well.[28]

In January, 1847, thirteen officers presented a Memorial
to Congress requesting the expurgation from future editions
of a number of critical remarks reflecting upon the Expedition's
members. It was signed by Walker, Johnson, Alden, Dale,
De Haven, Baldwin, Sinclair, Reynolds, Blunt, May, Sandford,
Blair, and Colvocoresses. A draft of the Memorial is among
Reynold's papers and it is likely that he was its author, but
Wilkes seems to have considered Walker the prime mover.
Alden was particularly upset because the *Narrative* pointed
to him as being responsible for the murders at Malolo. Most
of the officers believed that Wilkes was using the *Narrative*
to get back at them for their criticism of him during the Court-
Martial.[29]

He wrote Senator Pearce that the Memorial was the work
of a cabal which had opposed him and the other principal
officers, especially Ringgold, during the entire cruise. All but
three had been suspended at one time or other for neglect of
public property, inattention to duty, or disobedience to orders.
He was surprised to find the names of De Haven, Baldwin, and
Colvocoresses included, having counted them among his warm
friends, and presumed they had been coerced into signing. The
meaning of some of the quotations used in the Memorial had
been misconstrued by italicizing or by taking them out of
context. Wilkes said he would welcome an inquiry by the

---

28 Eld to his Father, Mar. 16 and May 2, 1845, Eld Papers.
29 *Memorial of Officers of the Exploring Expedition to the Congress of the United
   States*, Washington, Jan., 1847.

Library Committee. Congress took no action when he expressed a willingness to erase or modify the statements in question in future editions.[30]

Criticism of the *Narrative* came from far-away Honolulu. The *Polynesian* gave it a friendly reception, but objected to Wilkes' praise of the Rev. Mr. Goodrich for planting coffee trees which, he said, the Rev. Mr. Coan had uprooted. The trees had in fact flourished and increased, except for ten old and valueless ones that Coan had cut down. "Had Capt. Wilkes known more," the *Polynesian* said, "he would have misjudged less. . . .[31] *The Friend,* a missionary journal, was more emphatic in its criticism pointing to other inaccuracies, such as a description of a well-trodden trail over soil as an indistinct trail over lava. This led *The Friend* to question the accuracy of everything in the *Narrative*.[32]

John Pickering, Charles Pickering's uncle and a philologist of note, congratulated Wilkes upon the *Narrative* which he thought was written "in a style so appropriate to the subject" and which communicated "numerous results that will be interesting to readers of every class." At the same time he reminded the Commander that the reports of the scientists were the important part yet to come and which, he knew, were eagerly awaited abroad. He emphasized that foreign savants would only be satisfied if these volumes were published under the personal direction of their authors, who were the responsible parties and who gave them authority.[33]

30 Wilkes to Pearce, Jan. 15 and 23, 1847, Wilkes Papers.
31 *Polynesian,* June 6, 1846.
32 *The Friend,* Honolulu, Feb. 1, 1847.
33 Jno. Pickering to Wilkes, May 20, 1845, Tappan Papers 20.

XXXII

Destiny Made Manifest

THE REPORTS of the scientists were one of the most enduring achievements of the Expedition. They were published, one by one, over a period of several years. Congress became increasingly reluctant to appropriate funds for this purpose. The scientists were hampered initially not only by the damage done to some of the specimens but also by a decision of the Library Committee that only new discoveries could be included in their reports. The limit of a hundred copies per volume meant that the results of their labors would reach very few of the savants who eagerly awaited their publication.

The cost was estimated in 1845 at $89,370 but the final total was nearly $300,000. Audubon, one of the Expedition's well-wishers, guessed the cost of publication would be half a million and wished he had the wealth of the Emperor of Russia or of the King of France to ensure its completion and distribution to every scientific institution here and abroad.[1] The work consisted of twenty-four volumes. Three of these were never printed but most of them had unofficial as well as official issues.

Publication was suspended in 1874 at which time the list of volumes was as follows:

v. 1-5. *Narrative*. By Charles Wilkes. 1844.

v. 6. *Ethnography and Philology*. By Horatio Hale. 1846.

v. 7. *Zoophytes*. By James D. Dana. 1846, and atlas, 1849.

v. 8A. *Mammalogy and Ornithology*. By Titian Peale. 1848.

v. 8B. Republished as revised by John Cassin. 1858.

v. 9 *Races of Man*. By Charles Pickering. 1848.
       as revised by John Cassin. 1958.

v. 10. *Geology*. By James D. Dana. 1849.

v. 11. *Meteorology*. By Charles Wilkes. 1851.

v. 12. *Mollusca & Shells*. By A. A. Gould. 1852 and atlas, 1856.

v. 13-14. *Crustacea*. By James D. Dana. 1852-53 and atlas, 1855.

---

[1] Haskell, *Wilkes Expedition*, p. 8.

v. 15.   *Botany. Phanerogamia.* Part 1, Asa Gray. 1854 and atlas 1856.

v. 16.   *Botany. Cryptogamia. Filices.* By William D. Brackenridge. 1854 and atlas, 1855.

v. 17.   *Botany, Cryptogamia. Musci,* by William S. Sullivant. *Lichenes,* by Edward Tuckerman. *Algae,* by J. W. Bailey and W. H. Harvey. *Fungi,* by M. A. Curtis and M. J. Berkeley. *Phanerogamia of Pacific North America,* by John Torrey.1874. (Never officially distributed.)

v. 18.   *Botany. Phanerogamia.* Part 2. By Asa Gray. (Never printed.)

v. 19.   *Geographical Distribution of Animals and Plants.* By Charles Pickering. (Printing never completed.) Parts 1 and 2 issued by the author privately in 1854 and 1876 respectively.

v. 20.   *Herpetology.* Charles Girard and Spencer F. Baird, 1858.

v. 21-22. *Ichthyology.* By Louis Agassiz. (Never printed.)

v. 23.   *Hydrography.* By Charles Wilkes. 1861 and two volumes of charts, 1850-58.

v. 24.   *Physics.* By Charles Wilkes. (Never printed.)

During the thirty-odd years while these volumes were being prepared for publication many things happened. In public affairs the notable developments were the settlement of the Oregon boundary, the Mexican War, the annexation and discovery of gold in California, and the Civil War. Matters of personal concern to Wilkes included the explosion on the warship *Princeton* which killed Upshur and Secretary of the Navy Gilmer; the death of his wife as a result of a railroad accident; his marriage to the widow of his friend Commodore Bolton; and the death of Drayton, his chief assistant and intimate friend. Congressional interest in the scientific publications ended when the Civil War began. Wilkes himself returned to active duty and was sent to the Caribbean in command of the screw-sloop *San Jacinto.* In November, 1861, he intercepted the British mail steamer *Trent* and took off the Confederate Commissioners Mason and Slidell causing an international incident for which he is chiefly remembered.

The volume on physics was to have been the final one of the series. According to John Wilkes, it was going to press

when appropriations ended and the Library Committee refused to do anything about it. He said his father considered
the calculations resulting from astronomical, geographical, and
meteorological observations would have made this the most
valuable volume of all. The portion on the "Theory of the
Zodiacal Light" was printed in 1857 and that on "The Circulation of the Oceans" read at a meeting of the American Association for the Advancement of Science two years later.[2]

Many of the pendulum data were mislaid for so long that
they were superceded by subsequent observations and some of
Wilkes' theories regarding the formation of dew and fog and
the circulation of the atmosphere did not stand the test of
time. However, they indicated an independent and searching
mental attitude which served to stimulate discussion and lead
to sounder theories. In the opinion of Commander F. W.
Reichelderfer of the Weather Bureau, expressed in 1940,

> It is scarcely to be expected that a man with the ability and
> excellent general qualifications of Wilkes should also be a profound
> physicist and mathematician, even in the science of his day. Perhaps
> his greatest scientific error was in trying to demonstrate that the
> earth's rotation has no effect upon atmospheric circulation, a fact
> not generally understood at that time .... The portion giving "Sail-
> ing Directions" for a voyage around the world proved to be far
> more enduring in accuracy and value ....
> He was a pioneer in charting sailing routes and his observa-
> tions still are represented in the averages shown on the Pilot Charts
> published monthly by the Hydrographic Office, charts which, dur-
> ing the days of sailing vessels, led to enormous savings in time of
> ocean passage and to great benefits to shipping of all nations.[3]

Matthew Fontaine Maury is usually thought of in this
connection. He succeeded Wilkes as head of the Depot of
Charts and Instruments, taking office in the year of the Expedition's return. He was, in fact, following his predecessor's
lead.

The Commander's efforts to add to scientific knowledge
did not pass unnoticed in academic circles. When the Associa-

---

2 *Ibid.*, pp. 109–110.
3 Cmdr. F. W. Reichelderfer, "The Contributions of Wilkes to Terrestrial Magnetism, Gravity, and Meteorology," *Proc. Amer. Philos. Soc.* **82**, 5 (1940): pp.
   583–600.

tion of American Geologists and Naturalists met in Washington
in May, 1844, Wilkes read a paper explaining how icebergs and
ice floes increase in size mainly by the freezing of atmospheric
moisture and consequently provide a source of pure fresh water.
The Association's members inspected the exhibits at the Patent
Office and were invited to see some of the drawings, illustrations, native costumes, etc., that were not on exhibition. Their
Proceedings mention the achievement of the Squadron and its
"distinguished commander":[4]

A general expression of surprise was heard at the vast amount
of valuable labor performed by the Expedition in all its departments; and in no field will the value of these labors be more generally felt than in the minute and accurate surveys of the groups of
Pacific islands visited by the squadron, mostly regions heretofore
known to mariners only conjecturally. A beautiful specimen of this
sort of work was shown on the large chart of the Feegee group.

In 1853 and after this group became the American Association for the Advancement of Science, Dana became its president. He was one of the youngest but also, one of the most industrious and knowledgeable, of the Expedition's scientists.
His opinion of the Commander was about as fair-minded as
could be expected from anyone under "Bustamente's" command during those long and arduous years. As he told Asa
Gray, Wilkes,

although overbearing with his officers, and conceited, exhibited
through the whole cruise a wonderful degree of energy, I much
doubt if with any commander that could have been selected we
should have fared better, or lived together more harmoniously, and
I am confident that the navy does not contain a more daring explorer, or driving officer.[5]

In any case, his name has become permanently implanted
upon the face of the globe. Maps of Antarctica indicate the
portion of the coast where the vessels of the United States Exploring Expedition followed the ice barrier as Wilkes Land.
Recognition in academic circles provided a measure of
solace but came late and was muted. The indifference of the

4 Abstract of *Proceedings of the Association of American Geologists and Naturalists,* May 1844, p. 43.
5 Gilman, *op. cit.,* p. 149.

Whig government is understandable, if inexcusable. The Expedition was not of its doing. The public, too, was unimpressed for several reasons: the false start under Captain Jones; naval opposition to Wilkes' selection; the belief that it was a pleasure cruise; the dispute with Ross; the return of members under arrest; the rumors of disruption and tyrannical leadership; and, finally, the series of courts-martial that marked its return.

Moreover, more momentous matters engaged the attention of the Administration and the public. At the time of the Expedition's return, negotiations over the Maine boundary were in a critical stage, the Webster-Ashburton Treaty being signed in August of 1842. In his annual message President Tyler explained that a protracted discussion of the Oregon boundary had been avoided in order to conclude the Maine agreement. He mentioned, however, that there had been increased migration of Americans into that western territory. The Expedition found only about sixty American households in the Willamette Valley, but a hundred and thirty-seven settlers came in 1842 and more followed, in rapidly increasing numbers, in subsequent years.

Secretary of State Webster had a New Englander's interest in the acquisition of trading centers on the Pacific coast and and in 1842 instructed the American Minister in Mexico to sound out that government in regard to securing the port of "St. Francisco" in exchange for the settlement of claims of American citizens against it. Nothing came of this. Wilkes argued that Oregon's northern boundary should be above the forty-ninth parallel so as to insure control of the magnificent inland waters of Puget Sound, and President Tyler in his message of December, 1843, averred that the United States had always claimed the right to the coastal region extending to the Russian boundary at 54° 40'. This claim became the Democratic party's slogan in the election of 1844 with an "or Fight" added. Consequently, Mexico delayed making any concessions south of the forty-second parallel believing that Britain and the United States actually would fight over the Oregon question.[6]

---

[6] James D. Richardson (ed.), *Messages and Papers of the Presidents* (10 v., Washington, 1903) **4**: pp. 196, 258. See also, Albert K. Weinberg, *Manifest Destiny* (Baltimore, 1935).

By the time Polk and the Democrats rode into office with the aid of the slogans "Reannexation of Texas" and "Reoccupation of Oregon," the preliminaries in regard to Texas had already taken place making it easier for Polk to compromise on the forty-ninth parallel for Oregon. The greater concession was, in fact, made by the British since there were practically no Americans north of the Columbia River where the Hudson's Bay Company had a considerable establishment. The annexation of Texas led to the Mexican War and, at its conclusion in 1848 the Treaty of Guadalupe-Hidalgo handed over the California territory to the United States. In the latter part of that year gold was discovered and triggered the large-scale movement of people into that region.

This flow of American people over the Rockies to the shores of the Pacific came to be looked upon and justified as "manifest destiny." It seemed obvious that this contiguous region, unoccupied except for a few savages and ungoverned except for a British trading company and a few unstable Mexican revolutionaries, should be taken over by the vigorous, fast-growing United States. Yet a very few years before, the attention of the American people and government was centered upon the boundary of Maine and the annexation of Texas. The land beyond the Rockies was little known and little wanted. The sudden adoption of this new vision of destiny was due in large part to the work of the first United States Exploring Expedition. Its charts and reports pointed up the value of Puget Sound and San Francisco Bay and the *Narrative* gave detailed information regarding the interior region. Unlike Greenhaw's *History,* this was a first-hand account and the interest it aroused is indicated by the several editions through which it passed. The Rocky Mountains had seemed for many years to be a natural boundary but now they were replaced by the Pacific Ocean. The Wilkes Expedition had much to do with making destiny manifest as it had not been before 1842.

Appendix
The Scientific Reports

THE FIRST of these publications was Hale's *Ethnography and Philology* which came out in the spring of 1846. He had returned via Mexico arriving home in May, 1842, when he began to write, unhampered by the necessity of having to arrange collections of specimens. Upon completing the manuscript, he went abroad leaving proofreading to his novelist mother, Mrs. Sarah J. Hale, and Professor Hart, neither of whom was very familiar with geographical names. They had to call upon Drayton for help and this delayed publication.

Asa Gray reviewed the volume favorably declaring it had "a certain classical completeness. . . . The style of this volume is marked by rare excellences, and those of the highest order. It is elegant, terse, compact, and business-like, to a remarkable degree." He predicted that it would take its place in the foremost rank as a contribution to general philology and criticized the government for its foolish policy of authorizing only one hundred elegantly printed and bound copies instead of more at less cost for wider distribution. The printer made an extra 150 "token" copies, but it was still a too limited issue.[1]

The American Philosophical Society in 1940 published a centennial review of the Expedition's achievements, in which Harley H. Bartlett commented that in his opinion, Hale's conclusions, after tracing the migrations of the Polynesian peoples through their vocabularies, "have not since been improved upon, although they have been only too often neglected" and his Fijian grammar was "remarkably in advance of its time, in that it presents an analysis of the language unmarred by any preconceptions, based upon European philology, of what such a language ought to be like, but isn't."[2]

---

[1] *Proc. Amer. Philos. Soc.* **82**, 5 (1949) : p. 636. This issue celebrated the centenary of the Expedition and included a series of papers on the subject. Cited, hereafter, as A.P.S. Cent.

[2] A.P.S. Cent., pp. 636–637.

Dana's volume on *Zoophytes,* the second of the scientific works spawned by the Expedition, also came out in 1846. His response to the Library Committee's attempt to reduce costs by limiting the scientists to the description of *new,* heretofore undiscovered species, was to say that he could not undertake the work unless he was permitted to recast the classification of genera and species in the light of his own researches and in accord with all known specimens. Of 483 species of corals collected on the cruise, only a little more than half were previously known, and Dana had to correct and amplify their descriptions because few had been examined in a living state. Tappan was persuaded to approve Dana's manuscript by Gray, who said, "If the volumes of the Scientific part of the Exploring Expedition equal this both in its fine generalizations and in accurate detail, our country may be truly proud of the results of the Expedition," and predicted that it would long remain an authority on this previously most obscure and difficult department of the animal kingdom.[3]

Dana made most of the sixty-one plates in the atlas that accompanied this volume, the remainder being made by Drayton. Agate died of consumption in 1844 and this set back the preparation of drawings. His death was felt as a personal loss by members of the Expedition who greatly respected him as a man as well as an artist.

Dana also wrote and made many of the plates for the volume on *Geology* (X) published in 1849 and the two volumes on *Crustacea* (XIII and XIV) which came out in 1852-1853. The latter were made difficult by the careless treatment given the specimens and by the loss of many month's work when the *Peacock* was wrecked. Furthermore, after the engravings for the atlas were completed, a large part of the original drawings were lost by a fire in Philadelphia. Of the 680 crustacea described, 500 were new. This was the first time any considerable number of crustaceans had been described making his classification, for the most part, permanent.[4]

At the beginning of his labors Dana felt handicapped by the dearth of books and libraries in Washington. As he told a

---

3 Gilman, *Dana,* pp. 144, 147; Gray to Tappan, Mar. 11, 1846, Tappan Papers **21** (hereafter cited as T.P.) .

4 Drayton to Tappan, Feb. 3, 1845, T.P. **21**.

friend, "It is perfectly absurd! that I should be able to prepare my reports in a city where there are no books!" Returning to New Haven in 1845, he wrote Tappan that he felt he would be leaving his post of duty if he returned to Washington.[5] Another reason for his wanting to be in New Haven was his marriage in June, 1844, to Henrietta Silliman, the nineteen-year-old daughter of Professor Benjamin Silliman, whose assistant he had been before joining the Expedition. Dana, twenty-nine at the time of his marriage, had already achieved recognition through his widely used textbook *System of Mineralogy,* published in 1837.

In the centennial review of Dana's work Bartlett mentioned the parallelism in the lives of Dana and Darwin: both profiting by joining a naval exploring expedition; both interesting themselves in crustacea; both, in the field of geology, concentrating on volcanic and coral islands; and both, in spite of long invalidism, becoming gigantic figures in the world of science.[6]

Dana learned at Sydney that his subsidence theory regarding the origin of coral islands and reefs and the evidence in support of it reenforced a similar theory proclaimed by Darwin whose voyage on the *Beagle* corresponded, with respect to the coral islands, with that of the Expedition. Darwin's monograph on *Coral Reefs* was printed in 1842 while Dana's work was still in manuscript. Working independently they arrived at similar conclusions i.e., that coral grows best on the outer edge and keeps pace with the rising sea level as the land subsides and the lagoon develops. Dana reasoned that a subsiding island would have an embayed shore line, a conclusion that came to him during his ascent of Tahiti's Mount Aorai. They disagreed mainly in their explanation for the absence of corals from certain coasts. It is said that Darwin remarked when he first saw Dana's volume, "To begin with a modest speech, I am astonished by my own accuracy!"[7]

Bartlett believed that Dana's observations led him to think along evolutionary lines, but for religious reasons he would not allow himself to break with conventional thought.

5 Gilman, *op. cit.,* p. 145.
6 A.P.S. Cent., pp. 638–639.
7 Gilman, pp. 209–210, 662–663.

He was Darwin's equal in accuracy of observation and power of systematization. The *Origin of Species* was published in 1859, at which time Dana was suffering from a physical break-down, and it was some time later that he avowed himself an evolutionist.[8]

Dana and Peale took over Couthouy's work on crustacea, in addition to their own specialties, just as the Expedition arrived at the Fijis where the opportunities for geological investigation were limited; as Dana explained, "we were shut out from the interior of the islands by the character of the natives; at the same time coral reefs spread out an inviting field for observations, hundreds of square miles in extent." So for their three months' stay they explored the "groves of the ocean" wading over reefs at low tide, bucket in hand, or floating over deeper but clear water in a canoe with natives who would dive down and bring up any choice piece of coral at which they might point. Four-fifths of the observations on coral were made in the Fiji Islands.[9]

The third scientific volume was Pickering's *Races of Man,* which did not come out until 1848 because of his absence abroad and because Tappan would not accept it until many references to areas not visited by the Expedition, such as Africa, Arabia, and India, were deleted. Pickering was a slow worker, characterizing himself as "a very slow coach" in contrast to Dana whom he called "a racer." Bartlett called Pickering's writing "slovenly, discursive and unsystematic" and the contents "a medley of narrative and miscellaneous observations upon all sorts of subjects." However, it broke new anthropological ground, since Pickering named eleven races of man whereas the generally accepted view was that there were only three, namely white, yellow, and black derived from Noah's sons Shem, Ham, and Japheth. Linnaeus, however, had distinguished a fourth by separating the American Indians from Asiatics. Wilkes thought the volume contained much valuable information but was disappointed in it as a whole — "perhaps

---

[8] A.P.S. Cent., pp. 658–659, 721–732. Dana acknowledged his support of the theory of evolution in the last edition of his *Manual of Geology.*

[9] Gilman, pp. 150–151. Dana charged Couthouy of plagiarism when the latter wrote an article on the influence of temperature on coral distribution but, later, exonerated him. See *Boston Journal of Natural History* 4: pp. 66–105 and *The American Journal of Science and Arts* 46: pp. 129–136.

expected too much from him. It is difficult for him to let his
information leak out unless he is tapped." He told Tappan in
1848 that he would rejoice when he could "see him fairly out
of sight" but was concerned to have his cooperation because
of the usefulness of his journals.[10]

Of the one hundred authorized copies of the *Races of
Man*, thirty were destroyed by fire and not replaced, but Pickering had a hundred and fifty copies printed in London and
from 1848 to 1890 seven reprints were made in England. His
absorbing interest during the latter part of his life was the
history and migration of peoples as demonstrated by the uses
and names of plants and one of the last of the Expedition's
publications was the partial printing of his *Geographical Distribution of Animals and Plants* (XIX) privately produced by
the author himself.

When Titian Peale came to Washington, he was not in a
happy mood, for the failure of the Philadelphia Museum had
put him in financial straits and he found his specimens had
been maltreated. As he wrote a friend,

> my two birds (male & female) made into one,—the legs of one put
> on another body—hundreds of fine insects put in "families" without
> localities, although they came from all parts of the world.—arrows
> in another, with their ends sawed off to make them fit into fancy
> stands, etc.—all for the great end,—promotion of science.[11]

He found that he had to teach assistants how to prepare
specimens and to make drawings of new species all for pay that
was less than that of many clerks in and about the offices. Like
Eld, he suffered from rheumatism which deprived him of sleep.
He, too, felt the lack of library facilities and was further annoyed to lose credit for discoveries since they were not permitted to send descriptions to scientific publications and, as a
result, foreigners often published first.[12]

On top of these lesser troubles, Peale suffered grievous
losses in his family from the deaths of an infant son in 1844 and
of his wife, who died of consumption two years later, and his

---

[10] Wilkes to Tappan, May 28, 1845, Wilkes Papers; A.P.S. Cent., pp. 646–647;
Haskell, *Wilkes Expedition*, p. 64.

[11] J. Poesch, *Titian Ramsey Peale*, Peale to Prof. J. F. Frazer, May 15, 1844, p. 96.

[12] Peale to C. Waterton, Aug. 25 and to Ord, Nov. 26, 1844, Amer. Philos. Soc.

eldest daughter, who died of the same disease a year after her
mother. Titian was left with two teenage children, a son Francis and a daughter Sybilla.[13]

When Congress finally, in December, 1846, established
the Institution for which the Englishman Smithson had left a
most generous bequest, Peale applied for the position of cur-
ator, but none was appointed at that time. His troubles with
respect to his report accumulated and Wilkes began to doubt
his ability to produce a volume of sufficient scientific accuracy,
since he lacked Dana's analyzing ability and knowledge of
Latin.[14] Peale wrote an introduction in which he apologized
for the volume's shortcomings due to causes beyond his control: its publication delayed by the disbandment of the Scientific Corps upon its arrival home; the loss of his personal library
and butterfly collection on the *Peacock;* and the scarcity of
reference books in Washington. He acknowledged indebtedness to the faculty of Georgetown College for his Latin descriptions and concluded with the following paragraph referring
to his relations with naval personnel:

> A civilian on board a ship of war has much to contend with,
> particularly where the officers are young and inexperienced, as was
> the case in our Expedition. Rank and command afford the only
> standards of comparison; and as a naturalist is not supposed to have
> either the one or the other, it gives me the greater pleasure as such
> to record that there were but few occasions during our long and per-
> ilous voyage, when I was obliged to feel the dependence of my situa-
> tion. Collectively, it is rare to find a band equally possessed of the
> cool perseverance, and upright and generous feeling, which with
> other good qualities, characterized the members of the late "South
> Sea Surveying and Exploring Expedition" to which I shall always
> feel proud of having been attached.[15]

Wilkes considered the introduction irrelevant and its tone
"very objectionable & not borne out by the facts to my knowledge." Moreover, neither Hale nor Dana had been allowed
prefaces and so, with the Library Committee's consent, it
was suppressed and the volume's title changed from *Zoology*

---

13 Poesch, *op. cit.*, p. 98.
14 Wilkes to Tappan, May 28, 1845, T.P. 21.
15 Reprinted in Haskell, pp. 59–60 from rough draft in Amer. Museum of Natural
   History; copy among Wilkes Papers.

to *Mammalia and Ornithology,* which seemed more appropriate to its contents.

There was also trouble with the plates to accompany Peale's volume. He had made fifty with approximately thirty-eight still to complete when the engravers gave up their contract deciding that the work involved was too much for the price paid. To finish the atlas without increasing the cost, it was necessary to leave out non-essential backgrounds and Peale would not agree to this change.[16] He was dropped as a member of the Scientific Corps in June, 1848, but told that he would be paid twenty dollars for each plate that he completed. About this time Congress authorized the appointment of additional examiners in the Patent Office and he became an Assistant Examiner and made no more plates. He informed a friend that he would now perform duties "not so congenial" but "more harmonious" and he continued in that occupation for the next twenty-five years.[17]

Wilkes considered his departure "good riddance," but found it difficult to get the drawings finished satisfactorily. A hundred or possibly fewer copies of the text were printed without an atlas and, since Peale did not have any printed privately and those not sent abroad were destroyed by fire in 1851, this particular issue is the rarest of the whole series.

With Drayton doing most of the negotiating, Wilkes set out to find someone to finish the plates and, after some hesitation, to rewrite the text which he decided was deficient. The young up-and-coming "closet naturalist," John Cassin, was approached and, after a long delay, agreed to do the work for a thousand dollars a year over a five-year period. This issue, also entitled *Mammalia and Ornithology,* was published in 1858.

Bartlett, with the perspective of a century, thought that if latinity was a test of scholarliness Peale's volume was superior to Cassin's, its defects those of haste, inexperience in editing and proofreading, rather than knowledge.

---

16 Wilkes to Pearce, Dec. 30, 1847, Letter Book, 1841–1847; Peale gave an account of these developments in an article entitled, "The South Sea Surveying and Exploring Expedition" in *American Historical Record* 3 (1874) : pp. 307–308; Haskell, pp. 64–65 illustrates the manner in which background material was eliminated.

17 Poesch, p. 99.

His book has blemishes to be sure, but not such serious ones that
Wilkes or the country had any reason to be ashamed of it. However,
it was a time when Americans were very sensitive about any scientific or literary shortcomings that they might have. Anything European was *a priori* good: anything American probably bad . . . .[18]

The volume on *Mollusca and Shells* presented a special
problem since this was to have been Couthouy's department.
Dana and Peale were too busy with their own specialties to
undertake this additional volume and the shells were such attractive souvenirs that some members of the National Institute
dipped into the collection before it could be described.

Wilkes wanted Drayton to undertake it since he had
helped to make the collection and done some of the drawings
and descriptions, but he was classified as an "artist" and "drafts-
man" and Tappan decided in favor of Augustus A. Gould who
was a professional. It was agreed that some shells would be
sent to him at Boston where he could make use of the libraries
and have the help of Amos Binney, co-founder with him of
the Boston Society. It was also agreed that he could publish a
short Latin character of each discovery so as to assure its
claim to priority and these descriptions appeared in a series
of articles in the *Proceedings of the Boston Society of Natural
History*. Gould followed Lamarck's system and used Couthouy's names as far as possible, giving him credit for his
notes although they were somewhat lacking in precision and
very few were made after the Expedition rounded Cape Horn.
The shell collection was probably the largest made by any
similar expedition. Most of them were gathered from beaches
and coral reefs since there were few opportunities to dredge
in deep water because of the constant employment of men and
boats on special hydrographical duties.[19]

The shells were too great a temptation for Judge Tappan.
Being something of a conchologist, he could not refrain from
helping himself to a few choice ones. When the Library Committee was informed of this by Pickering it rescinded, on May
16, 1846, a previous resolution permitting the disposition of

---

18 A.P.S. Cent., p. 642.
19 Gould's correspondence with Wilkes, Drayton, and Tappan from October 1843
   through October, 1845, in Tappan Papers, **18–20**; Haskell, pp. 72–75; Wilkes
   to Tappan, Sept. 26, 1843, Letter Book,, 1841–1847.

the specimens by its agents. Judge Tappan immediately resigned and shortly after left Washington. By another resolution the Committee thanked him for his valuable services,
recognizing that it was through his endeavors that the publications had been launched so successfully. It turned over the
direction of the remainder of the publications to Wilkes, who
found Senator Pearce less amenable than Tappan.[20]

It became evident that botany was too big a subject for
Rich to handle by himself. He had joined the Scientific Corps
originally as assistant to Asa Gray, becoming its botanist when
the latter resigned. Gray, in a letter to Sir J. D. Hooker a
botanist friend, expressed lack of confidence in both Rich and
Tappan.

The botanist who accompanied the expedition is no doubt
perfectly incompetent to the task, so greatly so that probably he has
but a remote idea how incompetent he is. I have not seen him nor
the plants. Certainly I would not touch them (any but the Oregon
and Californian) if they were offered to me, which they are not
likely to be. I consider myself totally incompetent to do such work
without making it a special study for some years, and going abroad
to study the collections accumulated in Europe. Of course if they
are worked up at all in this country, they will be done disgracefully.
. . . The whole business has been in the hands till now of Senator
[Tappan] the most obstinate, wrong-headed, narrow-minded, im-
practical ignoramus that could well be found . . . .[21]

Wilkes decided to divide the subject into six parts leaving
only one part (the flora of the Fijis, Samoa, Tahiti, and East
India) to Rich; the other parts to be distributed as follows:
Pickering to take South America and New Zealand; Brackenridge, the subject of ferns; Sullivant, mosses, which were to be
sent to him at Columbus, Ohio; Professor Tuckerman, lichens,
the work to be done at Cambridge, Massachusetts; and the
Sandwich Islands and descriptions of algae still undetermined.

Rich completed his manuscript in 1846 and, on the com-
mencement of the Mexican War, joined the army. Wilkes told
Senator Pearce that Rich's manuscript was incomplete and

20 Wilkes to Jack, Sept. 28, 1845, John Wilkes Letter Book; Pearce to Tappan,
May 16, 1846, T.P. 21.
21 Haskell, p. 85.

took no notice of intertropical plants which were considered among the most valuable results of the Expedition and "if published as it is would bring disgrace upon the Expedition as well as himself." Brackenridge and Pickering agreed with this opinion. Dr. John Torrey, Professor of Chemistry and Natural History at Princeton, agreed to describe the Oregon and California plants and advised turning over part of the rest to European monographists, but Wilkes would not consider this.

Asa Gray, who was consulted next, insisted that the only way to avoid having the work done by foreigners was to send an American botanist abroad. He agreed to go himself when allowed five years in which to complete the task. He began immediately to familiarize himself with the collection which he found less ample than he had supposed, many specimens being represented in fruit or flower only. The collections from Oregon, California, and the Sandwich Islands were very fine but the rest was meager and too much of an along-shore and roadside collection to be of great interest. He was not familiar or particularly interested in tropical forms but found a good deal that interested him in the Compositae, especially those of Río Negro, Patagonia, and the Andes.

Doubt as to localities resulted from Rich's having muddled over the collection for years trying to describe it and "doing some harm and no good." He had forbidden the annexing of labels and remarks to specimens at the time they were gathered—the very thing that ought to have been done.[22]

The scientists had occasionally named new plants after themselves, such as Calandrinia Pickeringii, Malvastrum Richii, and Pittospium Brackenridgei. Gray, in turn, dedicated some new finds to them, for example:

As the Ancients garlanded the graves of their deceased friends with violets, so I dedicate this new genus of Violacea to the memory of Alfred T. Agate, the Botanical Artist of the Expedition, who died in Washington shortly after its return. (Agatea).

With much satisfaction I dedicate this genus (Draytonia Rubicunda) to Joseph Drayton Esq., the principal of the Scientific artists of the Expedition, of no small attainments in natural history

---

22 *Ibid.*, pp. 84–87.

especially in conchology, to whose pencil and superintendance the illustrations of the whole invertebrate zoology of the Expedition owe their high perfection.

The first *Botany* volume, edited by Gray, was printed in 1854 and its atlas two years later. In 1855 Brackenridge's volume on *Ferns* (XVI) was printed but twenty-four of the official copies and all but ten of the unofficial ones he had had made for himself were destroyed by fire. As Brackenridge had no knowledge of Latin, his descriptions were in what Gray called "a loose ungrammatical lingo" and had to be retranslated before publication. Because of its rarity, this volume has been little known.[23]

Brackenridge's horticultural contribution was of great importance. The original small greenhouse in back of the Patent Office had to be enlarged three times between 1843 and 1845. Congress, responding to a petition of the National Institute, founded the National Botanic Garden and set aside six acres in the Mall near the Capitol where, in 1850, conservatories were constructed. Brackenridge was in charge as long as Wilkes had supervision, after which he moved to a farm near Baltimore where he operated a nursery and became horticultural editor of the *American Farmer*.

He reported to the National Institute in 1842 that the Expedition had brought or sent home 684 species of seeds and 254 species of live plants and received several additional plants in return for the distribution of seeds. When the dried specimens in the herbarium became the nucleus of the Division of Plants of the United States National Museum, they totaled 9,674 species.[24]

A second botanical volume, also edited by Gray, was a kind of miscellany having several authors and, because of lack of appropriations, was not published until 1874. William S. Sullivant, who wrote the section on mosses thought the col-

---

[23] A.P.S. Cent., pp. 672–679; Haskell, pp. 89–91.

[24] A.P.S. Cent., p. 678. The Norfolk Island pine was an example of a living plant belonging to the Expedition that was lost and later recovered. It was sent home in the brig *Lydia* from New Zealand, stolen at Salem, and bought from a shoemaker by a friend of Wilkes. When Wilkes discovered it, it had grown from 18 inches to 15 feet in height and become so large that the friend had sent it to Hogg's greenhouse in New York. Upon its identification, it was returned to Washington. Autobiography 5–6: pp. 1400–1401.

lection a very poor one considering the places visited and the time occupied. The section on lichens was written by Edward Tuckerman who found eight new species. Algae were described jointly by Professor Bailey of West Point and William H. Harvey and fungae by the Rev. M. A. Curtis and the Rev. M. J. Berkeley. Harvey was an Irishman and Berkeley an Englishman and to that extent it became necessary to call upon foreigners for help, but each was associated with an American and the American's name came first.[25]

Torrey's manuscript, entitled *Phanerogamia of the Pacific North America,* was finished some twelve years before Wilkes called for it and when he did Torrey was mortally ill. By that time practically everything in it was known whereas it would have been of great interest if published earlier. The greatest American plant find of the Expedition was the California pitcher plant or *Darlingtonia californica.* The first specimens had leaves and scapes but no flowers or fruit and were found by Brackenridge in marshes at the head waters of the Sacramento River near Mount Shasta.[26]

Gray wrote a second part to this *Phanerogamia* but it was never called for and has remained in the Gray Herbarium at Cambridge, Massachusetts.[27]

The authors of these publications were very annoyed to have them so limited that they did not have any free copies. Dana appealed to his scientist friends to petition Congress for additional copies for donation to scientific, college, and public libraries. In 1849 he wrote to Dr. S. G. Morton, Vice-President of the Academy of Natural Sciences at Philadelphia, saying, "Congress, as you know, requires frequent efforts, before even a good object can be secured. There is need of influence in behalf of the Exped. & Science at the present time, for there is much opposition to us."[28]

[25] A.P.S. Cent., pp. 679–682; Haskell, pp. 92–97; F. S. Collins, "The Botanical and other Papers of the Wilkes Exploring Expedition" in *Rhodora* **14**: pp. 57–68.

[26] A.P.S. Cent., p. 682.

[27] Haskell, p. 97.

[28] Dana to Morton, Jan. 26, 1849, Academy of Natural Sciences, Philadelphia. In 1858 a friend of Dana sent him a copy of his *Geology* which he had purchased in Canton, it having been sent to the Emperor of China and received by the Governor General of Canton but not forwarded because it required presentation by an ambassador, as tribute. It was stolen and sold, escaping the sack of Canton by the British, Gilman, p. 143.

Congressmen, at best, were lukewarm in the matter of completing the scientific volumes and some, irritated by the continuing requests for funds, wanted to chuck the whole thing. Every year the Commander prepared estimates and argued in support of them before the Library, the House Appropriations, and Senate Finance Committees. Frequently the Committees took no action, making it necessary to rush through amendments to appropriation bills and, if a bill went to Conference, there might be further difficulties. To Wilkes' disgust, Pearce resorted to log rolling instead of defending the expenditures on the floor of the Senate. The hundred-copy limit meant that the Government had beautiful gifts to present to foreign rulers but nothing for congressmen to present to their constituents and, consequently, they lost interest.[29]

This indifference would have been erased if popular interest had been sustained and pride in the Expedition's achievements widely felt, somewhat as present-day enthusiasm for astronautical achievements helps legislators and taxpayers forget about costs. Whalers and South Sea traders, the instigators of the Expedition, were well served by it, as were the navigators of clipper ships when doubling the Horn, and also the Government which became better informed about Oregon and California. But all this had little to do with the publication of scientific volumes which almost nobody saw, few appreciated, and which left congressmen cold.

An appropriation of $25,000 in 1853 carried the proviso that "this appropriation shall finish the publication," a mandate that Senator Pearce attempted to carry out. Wilkes argued that the expenditure of a few thousand dollars was unimportant compared to what the volumes already in print were doing "to elevate the character of our country," and refused to make any move to bring the work to an end. It was true that respect for the Expedition's achievements had been augmented in academic circles as a result of the high quality of Hale's and Dana's volumes and Gray's on *Botany*. Louis Agassiz, a recognized authority, agreed to write a volume on ichthyology and said that in his opinion these writings

surpass in scientific importance the publications of all the explor-

29 Autobiography 7: pp. 1473–1475.

ing expeditions issued by Europeans taken separately . . . Nothing
could be more timely, more desirable & productive of more immediate advantage to the cause of science than the publication of a
large edition of these works especially if it can be made accessible to
the universally limited means of scientific men.[30]

Efforts were made to find ways of reducing costs without
sacrificing quality but Wilkes told the Library Committee that
it was difficult to dictate to men of science regarding matters
involving their reputations. They could not be expected to
give their whole time to this kind of work unless the Government was prepared to pay them five times as much as they
were offering, for "in science as in law you must expect to pay
well for talent."[31]

In 1855 Congress agreed to another "final" appropriation,
this time for $29,320, and Senator Pearce insisted that costs be
whittled down to that amount, pointing out that Agassiz had
been paid almost four thousand dollars and had not, after six
years, sent a single page to the printer. Pickering, too, had
supposedly begun his "Geography of Botany" seven years before and had only completed an introduction. Wilkes answered
that to stop now would be to throw away money already spent
and quoted Agassiz's assertion that Drayton's drawings were
the most accurate ever made and that the Expedition had discovered forty-seven new genera of fish. Agassiz had been ill
and not paid while not working but the Library Committee
required him to send his manuscript to Washington to show
what he had done.[32] On top of these difficulties the printed
sheets at Gaskill's bindery in Philadelphia were destroyed by
fire in 1856.[33]

Pearce, losing patience, told the Commander to turn the
agency over to someone else if he could not reduce costs, and

30 Agassiz to Wilkes, Oct., 1854, Ex.Ex. Miscel. Letters.
31 Wilkes to Pearce, May 13, 1855, Ex.Ex. Letters and Papers, Library of Con-
    gress.
32 Autobiography 7: pp. 1466–1468.
33 Wilkes to Pearce, May 28, 1856, Ex.Ex. Letters and Papers. The building was
    considered safe since it had an all-night watchman and tanks holding three
    hogsheads of water, but a fire, started by a gas burner two floors above the
    bindery, caused its destruction.

Wilkes resigned in favor of Drayton.[34] However, Drayton was ill and died two months later, so that the Library Committee had to reappoint Wilkes in February, 1857. In October of that year, Congress turned the collections over to the newly established Smithsonian Institution.

The volume on *Herpetology* (XX) was published in 1858. Pickering was to have been its author, but Wilkes, despairing of its ever being done by him, contracted with Professor Baird to complete it and, when the latter became Assistant Secretary of the Smithsonian, the work was turned over to his assistant Dr. Charles Girard. Baird, however, persuaded Secretary Henry, head of the Smithsonian, to accept the Expedition's reptile collection, which he did reluctantly because he thought the National Museum should concern itself only with new undescribed specimens. Its acceptance signaled the adoption of a broader policy by that Institution.[35]

Agassiz's volumes on *Ichthyology* (XXI and XXII) were never published because of lack of appropriations and the onset of the Civil War. The Expedition's fishes (1,128 specimens representing over 500 species) which had been loaned to Agassiz were returned to the Museum in 1885 along with his manuscript and the drawings.[36]

Wilkes took no active part in the Mexican War, seeing no opportunity for a command that he considered adequate and being told by Secretary Bancroft that he was needed in Washington. His volume on *Meteorology* (XI), distributed in 1854, retraced the cruise, summarizing meteorological observations in each area, and contained a series of tables giving temperatures and barometric readings. His volume on *Hydrography* was the last official publication of the series. The Commander had begun work on it in 1844, intending to have it accompany the charts, but it took a long time to write, print, and distribute. Ten years after beginning work on it he wrote Jack that there was so much to be examined "that my head gets addled sometimes and the progress with the press is so slow in proofs of the *Hydrography* that I get out of all patience and yet I can not move much faster." The sheets but not the manuscript were

[34] Wilkes correspondence with Pearce from March, 1855, to December, 1856, Ex.Ex. Letters and Papers.
[35] A.P.S. Cent., pp. 683–687.
[36] Haskell, pp. 102–104.

destroyed in the bindery fire and it was reprinted in 1861 when the Civil War interfered with its distribution.[37]

In 1859 the Library Committee reported that the publications had cost $279,131 and that $56,000 was needed to complete the series, but it requested a mere $8,220, and that was voted only after prolonged and acrimonious debate. Two small appropriations in 1861-1862 were followed by one for $9,000 in 1872, and that was the really final one. It paid for the distribution of Wilkes' *Hydrography* (XXIII) and the second volume on *Botany* (XVII).[38]

---

[37] *Ibid.*, pp. 104–107; John Wilkes, Letter Book 5, July 3, 1854. Wilkes read his paper on the "Theory of the Winds" before the American Scientific Association at its meeting at Providence in August, 1855.

[38] Resolution of May 28, 1872, Ex.Ex. Miscel. Papers.

Bibliography

MANUSCRIPTS

ALDEN, JAMES. Lieutenant. Journal. The Mariners Museum (Newport News, Va.).

Anonymous. Three Journals one of which was probably kept by R. P. Robinson, Purser's Clerk. Navy Department, National Archives, Record Group 45 (Washington, D.C.).

BLAIR, JAMES L. Passed Midshipman. Journal. Western Americana, Yale University Library (New Haven, Conn.).

BRACKENRIDGE, WILLIAM D. Horticulturist. Journal 2 v. and Letters. Collection #88, Maryland Historical Society (Baltimore, Md.).

BRISCOE, WILLIAM. Armorer. Journal. Navy Dept., NA, RG 45 (Washington, D.C.).

CASE, AUGUSTUS L. Lieutenant. Journal. U.S. Naval Academy Museum (Annapolis, Md.).

CHAMBERLAIN, LEVI. Missionary. Journal 23. Honolulu Mission Society Library (Honolulu, Hawaii).

COAN, TITUS. Missionary. Letters. New-York Historical Society (New York, N. Y.).

CLAIBORNE, M. G. L. Lieutenant. Journal. Navy Dept., NA, RG 45 (Washington, D.C.).

CLARK, GEORGE W. Midshipman. Journal. Navy Dept., NA, RG 45 (Washington, D.C.).

CLARK, JOSEPH G. Seaman. Journal. Library of Congress (Washington, D.C.).

COLVOCORESSES, GEORGE M. Passed Midshipman. Journal. Western Americana, Yale University Library (New Haven, Conn.).

Consular Reports: Honolulu, Tahiti, and Sydney. State Department, NA, RG 59.

Courts-Martial 43, #823–826, 44, #827 and Court of Inquiry 51, #854, Records of Navy Department, NA, RG 45 (Washington, D.C.).

COUTHOUY, JOSEPH P. Conchologist. Journal. Science Museum Library (Boston, Mass.).

DALE, JOHN B. Lieutenant. Journal. New England Historic Genealogical Society (Boston, Mass.).

DANA, JAMES D. Geologist. Letters. Academy of Natural Sciences of Philadelphia (Philadelphia, Pa.) and Yale University Rare Book Library (New Haven, Conn.).

DANA, MARIE T. Typescript account of her father's experiences on the Expedition based upon his letters (New Haven, Conn.).

DE HAVEN, EDWIN J. Lieutenant. Journal. Navy Dept., NA, RG 45 (Washington, D.C.).

DICKERSON, MAHLON, Secretary of the Navy. Letters and Diary. Historical Society of New Jersey (Newark, N.J.).

—— Letters. American Philosophical Society (Philadelphia, Pa.) and Peabody Museum (Salem, Mass.).

DU PONT, SAMUEL F. Lieutenant. Letters. Eleutherian Mills Historical Library (Greenville, Del.).

DYES, JOHN W. W. Taxidermist. Journal. Navy Dept., NA, RG 45 (Washington, D.C.).

ELD, HENRY, JR. Passed Midshipman. Journal 2 v. New Haven Colony Historical Society (New Haven, Conn.).

421

___ Journal of Northwest excursion and Letters. Western Americana, Yale University Library (New Haven, Conn.).

___ Letters. Library of Congress (Washington, D.C.).

ELLIOTT, JARED L. Chaplain. Journal 2 v. Library of Congress (Washington, D.C.).

ELLIOTT, SAMUEL B. Midshipman. Journal. Navy Dept., NA, RG 45 (Washington, D.C.).

EMMONS, GEORGE F. Lieutenant. Journal 3 v., scrapbook, and sketchbooks. Western Americana, Yale University Library (New Haven, Conn.).

GILCHRIST, EDWARD. Assistant Surgeon. Journal. Navy Dept., NA, RG 45 (Washington, D.C.).

HARTSTENE, HENRY J. Lieutenant. Journal. Navy Dept., NA, RG 45 (Washington, D.C.).

___ Letters, Gratz Collection, Historical Society of Pennsylvania (Philadelphia, Pa.).

HOLMES, SILAS. Assistant Surgeon. Journal 3 v. Western Americana, Yale University Library (New Haven, Conn.).

HUDSON, WILLIAM H. Midshipman. Journal. Navy Dept., NA, RG 45. (Washington, D.C.).

HUDSON, WILLIAM L. Lieutenant, second in command of the Expedition. Journal. American Museum of Natural History (New York, N.Y.).

___ Journal #2. Microfilm. University of North Carolina Library (Chapel Hill, N.C.).

JOHNSON, ROBERT E. Lieutenant. Journal 2 v. Navy Dept., NA, RG 45 (Washington, D.C.).

___ Letters. Duke University Library (Durham, N.C.).

KNOX, SAMUEL R. Lieutenant. Journal. Peabody Museum (Salem, Mass.).

___ Letters. Western Americana, Yale University Library (New Haven, Conn.).

LONG, ANDREW K. Lieutenant. Journal. Navy Dept., NA, RG 45 (Washington, D.C.).

MAURY, MATTHEW F. Lieutenant. Papers. Library of Congress (Washington, D.C.).

PEALE, TITIAN R. Naturalist. Journal nos. 1,2,3,5,7. Library of Congress (Washington, D.C.).

___ Letters, American Philosophical Society (Philadelphia, Pa.).

PICKERING, CHARLES. Naturalist. Journal 2 v. The Academy of Natural Sciences of Philadelphia (Philadelphia, Pa.).

___ Letters. Massachusetts Historical Society (Boston, Mass.).

POINSETT, JOEL R. Secretary of the Army. Papers 10 v. Historical Society of Pennsylvania (Philadelphia, Pa.).

REYNOLDS, WILLIAM. Passed Midshipman. Journal 2 v., Letters, and Critique. Franklin and Marshall College Library (Lancaster, Pa.).

RICHARDS, REV. WILLIAM. Missionary. Letters. State Archives of Hawaii (Honolulu, Hawaii).

SANDFORD, JOSEPH P. Passed Midshipman. Journal. Navy Dept., NA, RG 45 (Washington, D.C.).

SANDWICH ISLANDS MISSION. The United Church Board for World Ministries Library. (Boston, Mass.).

___ Correspondence of Mission Members.

SICKLES, FREDERICK K. Surgeon. Journal. Navy Dept., NA, RG 45 (Washington, D.C.).

SINCLAIR, GEORGE T. Lieutenant. Journal 2 v. Navy Dept., NA, RG 45 (Washington, D.C.).

STRAUSS, WALTER P. Typescript Thesis entitled, "Early American Interest and Activity in Polynesia, 1783-1842." Columbia University (New York, N.Y.).

STUART, FREDERIC D. Captain's Clerk. Journal. Navy Dept., NA, RG 45 (Washington, D.C.).

TAPPAN, BENJAMIN. Judge and U.S. Senator. Papers. Library of Congress (Washington, D.C.).

THOMPSON, EGBERT. Midshipman. Journal. Navy Dept., NA, RG 45 (Washington, D.C.).

United States Exploring Expedition. Letters and Papers 4 v. Library of Congress (Washington, D.C.).

—— Letters relating to preparations 4 v., incoming letters relating to the Expedition 2 v., incoming miscellaneous, General Letter Book 22, Letters to Officers, Ships of War 25 NA, RG 45 (Washington, D.C.).

—— Miscellaneous letters, Mystic Seaport Library (Mystic, Conn.).

UNDERWOOD, JOSEPH A. Lieutenant. Journal. Western Americana, Yale University Library (New Haven, Conn.).

WHITTLE, JOHN S. Assistant Surgeon. University of Virginia Library (Charlottesville, Va.).

WILKES, CHARLES. Commander of the Expedition. Journal 3 v. Navy Dept., NA, RG 45 (Washington, D.C.).

—— Autobiography and Letters. Library of Congress (Washington, D.C.).

—— Letters. Kansas State Historical Society (Topeka, Kansas).

—— Letters. American Philosophical Society (Philadelphia, Pa.).

—— Letters. New York Public Library (New York, N.Y.).

—— Letters. Science Museum Library (Boston, Mass.).

—— Letters of Wilkes and other members of the Expedition. Franklin D. Roosevelt Library (Hyde Park, N.Y.).

—— Letters of Wilkes and other members of the Expedition U.S. National Museum (Washington, D.C.).

WILKES, JOHN. Son of Charles. Letter Books 7 v. Library of Congress (Washington, D.C.).

ARTICLES

ANDRIST, RALPH K. 1966. "Ice Ahead!" *Amer. Heritage* **17**: pp. 60–63, 92–103.

Anonymous. 1836. "Naval Education." *Naval Magazine* 1836: pp. 213–218.

BARTLETT, HARVEY H. 1940. "The Reports of the Wilkes Expedition, and the Work of the Specialists in Science." *Proc. Amer. Philos. Soc.* **82**: pp. 601–705.

BOGGS, S. WHITTEMORE. 1938. "American Contributions to Geographical Knowledge of the Central Pacific." *Geog. Rev.* **28**: pp. 177–192.

BRYAN, G.S. 1939. "The Wilkes Exploring Expedition." *Proc. U.S. Naval Inst.* **65**: pp. 1452–1464.

—— 1940. "The Purpose, Equipment and Personnel of the Wilkes Expedition." *Proc. Amer. Philos. Soc.* **82**: pp. 551–560.

CARROL, ANNE E. 1871. "The First American Exploring Expedition." *Harpers New Monthly Mag.* **44**: pp. 60–64.

COLLINS, FRANK S. 1912. "The Botanical and Other Papers of the Wilkes Expedition." *Rhodora* **14**: pp. 57–68.

CONKLIN, EDWIN G. 1940. "Connection of the American Philosophical Society with our First National Exploring Expedition." *Proc. Amer. Philos. Soc.* **82**: pp. 519–541.

COOLEY, MARY E. 1940. "The Exploring Expedition in the Pacific." *Proc. Amer. Philos. Soc.* **82**: pp. 707–719.

COUTHOUY, JOSEPH P. 1842. "Remarks upon Coral Formations in the Pacific." *Boston Jour. Natural History* **4**: pp. 66–105, 137–162.

—— 1842. "Reply to accusations of J. D. Dana." *Amer. Jour. Science and Arts.* **45**: pp. 378–389.

DALL, WILLIAM H. 1888. "Some American Conchologists." *Proc. Biological Society of Washington* **4**: pp. 95–134.

DANA, JAMES D. 1844. "Reply to Mr. Couthouy's Vindication Against the Charge of Plagiarism." *Amer. Jour. Science and Arts* **46**: pp. 129–136.

___ 1849. "Notes on Upper California." *Amer. Jour. Science and Arts,* ser. 2, **7**: pp. 247–264, 376–394.

DAVIS, CHARLES H. 1845. "The United States Exploring Expedition." *North Amer. Rev.* **61**: pp. 54–107.

EDEL, WILLIAM W. 1924. "The Golden Age of the Naval Chaplaincy, 1830–55." *Proc. U.S. Naval Institute* **50**: pp. 875–883.

FEIPEL, L. N. 1914. "The Wilkes Expedition." *Proc. U.S. Naval Institute* **40**: pp. 1323–1350.

FELTON, CORNELIUS C. 1846. Review of Dana's and Hale's scientific reports. *North American Review* **63**: pp. 211–236.

HALE, HORATIO. 1846. "Migrations in the Pacific." *Amer. Jour. Science and Arts,* ser. 2, **1**: pp. 317–332.

HOBBS, WILLIAM H. 1932. "Wilkes Land Rediscovered." *Geog. Rev.* **22**: pp. 632–655.

___ 1940. "The Discovery of Wilkes Land, Antarctica." *Proc. Amer. Philos. Soc.* **82**: pp. 561–582.

HOFFMEISTER, JOHN E. 1940. "James Dwight Dana's Studies of Volcanoes and of Coral Islands." *Proc. Amer. Philos. Soc.* **82**: pp. 721–732.

MACKENZIE, ALEXANDER S. 1836. Comments upon the Official Correspondence Connected with the Southern Exploring Expedition. *Army and Navy Chronicle* **3**: pp. 337–342.

MADDEN, E. F. 1882. "Symmes and his Theory." *Harpers New Monthly Magazine* **65**: pp. 740–749.

MAWSON, SIR DOUGLAS. 1934. "Wilkes' Antarctic Landfalls." *Proc. Royal Geog. Soc. of Australasia, South Australian Branch* **34**: pp. 70–113.

PAULLIN, CHARLES O. 1924. "Beginnings of the United States Naval Academy." *Proc. U.S. Naval Institute* **50**: pp. 173–194.

PEALE, TITIAN R. 1874. "The South Sea Surveying and Exploring Expedition." *Amer. Hist. Record* **3**: pp. 244–251, 305–311.

POINSETT, JOEL R. 1843. "The Exploring Expedition." *North Amer. Rev.* **56**: pp. 257–270.

REHN, JAMES A. G. 1940. "Connection of the Academy of Natural Sciences of Philadelphia with our First National Exploring Expedition." *Proc. Amer. Philos. Soc.* **82**: pp. 543–549.

REICHELDERFER, FRANCIS W. 1940. "The Contributions of Wilkes to Terrestrial Magnetism, Gravity, and Meteorology." *Proc. Amer. Philos. Soc.* **82**: pp. 583–600.

REYNOLDS, J. N. 1839. "Mocha Dick or the White Whale of the Pacific." *Knickerbocker Magazine* **13**: pp. 377–392.

ROSS, FRANK E. 1935. "The Antarctic Explorations of Lieutenant Charles Wilkes U.S.N." *Proc. Royal Geog. Soc. of Australasia, South Australian Branch* **35**: pp. 130–141.

STRAUSS, W. PATRICK. 1959. "Preparing the Wilkes Expedition: A Study in Disorganization." *Pacific Hist. Rev.* **28**: pp. 221–232.

BOOKS

ADAMS, CHARLES FRANCIS (ed.). 1875. *Memoirs of John Quincy Adams* (12 v., Philadelphia).

BAIRD, SPENCER F., and CHARLES GIRARD. 1858. *Herpetology* (U.S. EX. EX. **20**, Philadelphia).

BALLOU, H. M. (ed.). 1911. *Fragments II; The Letters of Dr. Gerritt P. Judd, 1827–1872* (Honolulu).

BARCLAY, WADE C. 1950. *History of Methodist Missions* (New York).

BASSETT, JOHN S. (ed.). 1926-35. *Correspondence of Andrew Jackson* (7 v. Washington) **4-5**.

BRACKENRIDGE, WILLIAM D. 1854. *Botany. Cryptogamia. Filices* (U.S. EX. EX. **16**, Philadelphia).

CASSIN, JOHN. 1858. *Mammalogy and Ornithology* (U.S. EX. EX. **8**, Philadelphia).

CHAPELLE, HOWARD J. 1949. *The History of the American Sailing Navy* (New York).

CLARK, JOSEPH G. 1848. *Lights and Shadows of Sailor Life* (Boston).

COLVOCORESSES, GEORGE M. 1852. *Four Years in a Government Exploring Expedition* (New York).

DANA, JAMES D. 1846. *Zoophytes* (U.S. EX. EX. **7**, Philadelphia).

___ 1849. *Geology* (U.S. EX. EX. **10**, Philadelphia).

___ 1852-1853. *Crustacea* (U.S. EX. EX. **13-14**, Philadelphia).

DELLENBAUGH, FREDERICK S. 1914. *Fremont and '49* (N.Y. and London).

DOWNEY, JOSEPH T. (Howard Lamar ed.). 1958. *The Cruise of the Portsmouth, 1845-1847* (New Haven).

DUMONT-D'URVILLE, M. J. 1842. *Voyage au Pol Sud et dans l'Océanie Sur les Corvettes l'Astrolabe et la Zelée*, (23 v., Paris) **8**.

ELLIOTT, JARED L. 1840. *A Sermon Occasioned by the Death of Lieutenant J. A. Underwood and Midshipman Wilkes Henry* (Honolulu).

ERSKINE, CHARLES. 1890. *Twenty Years before the Mast* (Boston).

FAIRBURN, WILLIAM A. 1945-55. *Merchant Sail* (6 v., Center Lovell, Maine) **2**: pp. 993–1045.

FANNING, EDMUND. 1838. *Voyages to the South Seas* (2nd ed., New York).

GALBRAITH, JOHN S. 1957. *The Hudson's Bay Company as an Imperial Factor, 1821-1869* (Berkeley and Los Angeles).

GILMAN, DANIEL C. 1899. *The Life of James Dwight Dana* (N.Y. and London).

GOULD, A. A. 1852. *Mollusca and Shells* (U.S. EX. EX. **12**, Philadelphia).

GRAEBNER, NORMAN A. 1955. *Empire on the Pacific* (New York).

GRAY, ASA. 1854. *Botany. Phanerogamia.* (U.S. EX. EX. **15**, Philadelphia).

GREENHOW, ROBERT. 1840. *Memoir Historical and Political on the Northwest Coast of America and the Adjacent Territories* (Washington).

___ 1844. *The History of Oregon and California.* (Boston).

HALE, HORATIO. 1846. *Ethnography and Philology* (Philadelphia).

HASKELL, DANIEL C. 1942. *The United States Exploring Expedition, 1838-1842, and its Publications 1844-1874—a Bibliography* (New York).

HAWTHORNE, HILDEGARDE. 1943. *Matthew Fontaine Maury* (New York).

HENDERSON, DANIEL. 1953. *The Hidden Coasts* (New York).

HEROLD, AMOS L. 1926. *James Kirke Paulding: Versatile American* (New York).

HORNE, C. SILVESTER. 1895. *The Story of the L.M.S., 1795-1895* (2nd ed., London).

JARVES, JAMES J. 1843. *History of the Hawaiian or Sandwich Islands* (Honolulu).

JENKINS, JOHN S. 1850. *United States Exploring Expedition* (Auburn).

LEE, DANIEL, and J. H. FROST. 1844. *Ten Years in Oregon* (New York).

LOVELL, RICHARD. 1899. *The History of the London Missionary Society 1795-1895* (2 v., London).

LYMAN, HENRY M. 1906. *Hawaiian Yesterdays* (Chicago).

LLOYD, CHRISTOPHER (ed.). 1949. *The Voyages of Captain James Cook Round the World* (London).

MERK, FREDERICK. 1963. *Manifest Destiny and Mission in American History, a Reinterpretation* (New York).

MORRIS, CHARLES. 1880. *The Autobiography of Commodore Charles Morris, U.S. Navy* (Boston).

PALMER, JAMES C. 1843. *Thulia: a Tale of the Antarctic* (New York).

PEALE, TITIAN R. 1848. *Mammalia and Ornithology* (U.S. Ex Ex. v. 8 — suppressed, Philadelphia).

POESCH, JESSIE. 1961. *Titian Ramsay Peale and his Journals of the Wilkes Expedition* (Philadelphia, Mem. Amer. Philos. Soc. 52).

REYNOLDS, JEREMIAH H. 1836. *Address on the Subject of a Surveying and Exploring Expedition to the Pacific Ocean and South Seas* (New York).

___ 1841. *Pacific and Indian Oceans* (New York).

RHEES, WILLIAM J. 1901. *The Smithsonian Institution; Documents Relative to its Origin and History* (2 v. Washington).

RICHARDSON, JAMES D. (ed.) 1903. *A Compilation of the Messages and Papers of the Presidents* (10 v. Washington) 2.

ROSS, SIR JAMES C. 1847. *A Voyage of Discovery and Research in the Southern and Antarctic Regions, During the Years 1839-1843* (2 v., London).

SIMPSON, SIR GEORGE. 1947. *An Overland Journey Round the World During the Years 1841 and 1842* (Philadelphia).

SOLEY, JAMES R. 1876. *Historical Sketch of the United States Naval Academy* (Washington).

SULLIVANT, WILLIAM S. *et al.* 1874. *Botany. Cryptogamia* (U.S. Ex. Ex. 17, Philadelphia).

TRUE, WEBSTER P. 1929. *The Smithsonian Institution* (Washington).

United States Naval Lyceum. 1835. *The First Annual Report of the Administrative Committee.*

United States. 1828. 20 Cong., 1 Sess., *House Report #209.* Committee on Naval Affairs regarding memorials requesting expedition to the South Seas.

___ 1835. 23 Cong., 2 Sess., *House Report #94.* D. J. Pearce from Committee on Commerce introducing H.R. #719 to aid exploration of Pacific Ocean.

___ 1836-1837. 24 Cong., 2 Sess., *House Report #2.* Secretary of the Navy Dickerson explains Captain Jones difficulties in recruiting for Exploring Expedition.

___ 1838. 25 Cong., 2 Sess., *House Report #147.* Documents explaining delay in starting the Expedition.

___ 1839. 25 Cong., 3 Sess., and 26 Cong., 1 Sess., *House Reports #194 and #83,* respectively. Secretary of the Navy Paulding on the subject of pay given to officers of the Exploring Expedition.

___ 1839. Navy Dept. *Court of Inquiry Record* 51, #884. Case of Dale (Valparaiso).

___ 1842. Navy Dept. *Courts Martial Records* 43, nos. 823–826, (Cases of May, Johnson, Guillou, and Pinkney; 44, #827, (Case of Wilkes).

WALKER, WILLIAM M., *et al.* 1847. *Memorial of Officers of the Exploring Expedition to the Congress of the United States* (Washington).

WAYLAND, JOHN W. 1930. *The Pathfinder of the Seas; the Life of Matthew Fontain Maury* (Richmond).

WEINBERG, ALBERT K. 1935. *Manifest Destiny; A Study of Nationalistic Expansionism in American history* (Baltimore).

WILKES, CHARLES. 1845. *The Narrative of the United States Exploring Expedition* (5 v. Philadelphia). On reverse of title page: Stereotyped by J. Fagan. Printed by C. Sherman.

___ 1849. *Western America, including California and Oregon, with Maps of those regions and of the "Sacramento Valley"* (Philadelphia).

___ 1858. *Hydrography* (U.S. Ex. Ex. 23, Philadelphia).

NEWSPAPERS

Army and Navy Chronicle (Washington), Dec. 15, 1836.

Daily National Intelligencer (Washington), May 16, 1836; July 26 and Aug. 18, 1838; Apr. 1, 1840; June 11, 1842.

The Friend (Honolulu), Feb. 1, 1847.

The Globe (Washington), Mar. 29 and Apr. 4, 1838; Apr. 1, 2, 1840.

The Long Island Star (Brooklyn), Jan. 25, July 2, and Aug. 6, 1838.

The Missionary Herald (Boston), Dec. 7, 1841.

The Morning Herald (New York), Mar. 30, 31, 1840; and June 11, 13, 1842.

New York Courier & Enquirer, Dec. 1837-Jan. 1838.

New York Sun, Aug. 18, 22, 1838; June 11, 13, 1842.

New York Times, July-Sept. 1837.

Niles Weekly Register (Philadelphia), Dec. 21, 1839; July 23, Aug. 27, Oct. 1, Dec. 10, 1842; May 20, 1843.

The Polynesian (Honolulu), Oct. 31, Nov. 28, 1840; June 6, 1846.

Index